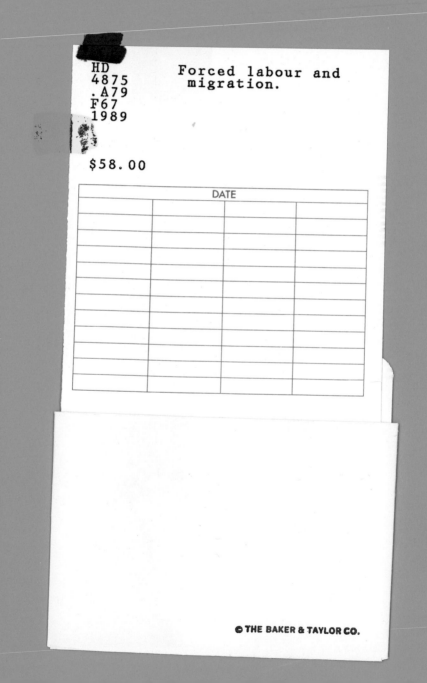

DATE			

Forced Labour and Migration:
Patterns of Movement within Africa

Oxford Centre for African Studies – African Discourse series

No. 1: Forced Labour and Migration: Patterns of Movement within Africa

Forced Labour and Migration
Patterns of Movement within Africa

Edited by
ABEBE ZEGEYE
and
SHUBI ISHEMO

HANS ZELL PUBLISHERS
London · Munich · New York · 1989

Hans Zell Publishers
An imprint of the Bowker-Saur division of Butterworths
Borough Green, Sevenoaks, Kent. England TN15 8PH

British Library Cataloguing in Publication Data

Forced labour and migration: patterns of movement within Africa. –
(African discourse series: no. 1)
1. Africa. Internal migration, 1850–1980
I. Zegeye, Abebe   II. Oxford Centre for African Studies
III. Studies
304.8'096

ISBN 0–905450–36–1

Library of Congress Cataloging-in-Publication Data

Forced labour and migration: patterns of movement within Africa /
edited by Abebe Zegeye.
    p. cm. – (African discourse; no. 1)
"Published for the Oxford Centre for African Studies."
ISBN 0–905450–36–1
1. Forced labor – Africa. 2. Forced migration – Africa.
I. Zegeye, Abebe.   II. Oxford Centre for African Studies.
III. Title: Forced labor and migration. IV. Series.
HD4875.A79F67   1989
331.11'73'096–dc19   89–30267
                                                CIP

Printed on acid-free paper.

Typeset by DMD, St. Clements, Oxford
Printed and bound in Great Britain
by Bookcraft Ltd.,
Midsomer Norton, nr. Bath

This volume is dedicated to J. Clyde Mitchell,
whose interest in labour and migration has
produced works which have stimulated the
imagination of so many scholars.

Contents

Contents

Introduction

Abebe Zegeye and Shubi L. Ishemo

The idea for this volume grew out of a Conference on Forced
Labour and Migration held at Nuffield College, Oxford, in
February 1987. Not all the papers and contributions presented
at the Conference appear in this volume, but sufficient interest
was generated for the editors to invite additional contributions
from scholars who had not been able to participate, in order to
broaden the range of issues discussed. The diversity of the
contributions demonstrates a continued need to examine the
processes of socio-economic and political change from a wider
viewpoint by incorporating new perspectives that are not
necessarily antagonistic to earlier approaches, but which
enrich our understanding of the causation and reproductive
mechanisms of social phenomena.

The authors of this volume do not claim to offer the last
word on forced labour and migration. Rather, they seek to
offer, in an individual and collective sense, a scope for further
research – both historical and contemporary – on the origins
and reproduction of this phenomenon. In an extended study,
we incorporate a paper by J. Clyde Mitchell which neatly
summarizes the level of the debate on the causes of migration.
Situated in a colonial context, most of these debates operated
within a colonial ideological framework and sought to explain
migration in a Durkheimian theoretical mould. Subsequent
theoretical developments, on the contrary, saw forced labour
and migration as main components of colonial capitalist
development and their reproduction in the post-colonial era as

a colonial legacy. This is indeed the perspective adopted by most of the contributors in this volume.

The precise form of the origin of forced labour and migration is not contested. What matters here is the timing. Thus in one contribution on Namibia, the origins are to be sought in the pre-colonial period, not as an African tradition as the earlier theorists outlined by Clyde Mitchell held, but as a consequence of the pre-capitalist states' response to the penetration of European merchant capital. With the development of colonial capitalism, the pre-capitalist aristocracy became transformed into agents of the colonial state and with the introduction of taxation, forced labour and migration proliferated. The precise role of the colonial state is investigated in a number of contributions. One by Zeleza warns of the tendency to absolutize the hegemony of the colonial state and prefers to see it as weak, unstable and virtually powerless to destroy the peasant economy. Thus according to this view, migrant labour was not a simple outcome of capitalist manipulation. It was an outcome of struggle and not structure.

We are reminded that the study of migrant labour solely in terms of men periodically entering wage labour is meaningless unless it takes on board the question of gender relations, not only in terms of a restructured division of labour in the peasant households, but also in the context of how women responded to male labour migration and the use of patriarchal and colonial state ideological apparatuses as mechanisms of social control directed at women. In some places, the disruption of peasant material production produced a situation in which entire families were involved in migration, with females and juveniles, in particular, representing the cheapest and most exploited form of labour. A variation of female responses is represented in a study of how Egyptian women migrants in Iraq adapted.

Notwithstanding the dangers of absolutizing the hegemony of the colonial state, the role of that state in the procurement of labour was crucial. The racist characteristics of the colonial justification of forced labour are well known, but they were of crucial importance in the reproduction of conditions for forced labour and the development of migrant labour as its highest manifestation. A very fascinating perspective on this is represented in a study on how the French colonial state in Senegal set up a penal settlement to supply labour to a company which had failed to obtain labour from voluntary sources.

The study of ecological change, and its social manifestations such as famine, disease and migration, is a growing subject. What some of the essays seek to do in this volume is to situate such change in a socio-economic context. Thus as a starting point, causation is situated in the way colonial capitalist development disrupted indigenous production processes. In an independent state like Ethiopia, ecological crises, the state's response of initiating a resettlement programme and the question of which sections of the population migrated, are well documented.

By situating the various essays in a wider perspective, we hope we can contribute modestly towards an understanding of why and how migrant labour became a structural feature of African economies. First let us examine individual contributions a bit further.

The first contribution in the book is a reprint of J. CLYDE MITCHELL's paper 'The Causes of Labour Migration', first published in 1959. It is a significant study because it represents a synthesis of the early debates on the causes of labour migration during the colonial phase of African history. He outlines the colonial motives for the study of the causes of migration. Functionaries of the colonial states, including missionaries and anthropologists, were stimulated to study such causes because of what were considered to be the consequences of male labour migration on African societies: 'a general state of disorganization involving sexual licence, divorce, crime and lack of respect for authority, children growing up in broken families, religious practices abandoned and above all poverty.'

Clyde Mitchell advances the following propositions: that the main feature of labour migration cannot be simply explained by the fact of men seeking wage labour, but in the recurrent nature of the phenomenon; that it is simplistic to view it solely as a matter of the mobility of labour because movement from one area to another does not guarantee work. To Mitchell, an analysis of labour migration must explain 'not only why the men leave their tribal homes – and the causes for this may be more complicated than merely economic reasons – but also why they should consistently circulate between their tribal homes and the labour centres.' To view labour migration as the principal cause of other social phenomena, he stresses, is false. 'It may deepen our understanding of labour migration,' he suggests, if we view it and many of its concomitant social manifestations, not as causes and effects, but rather as concomitant adjustments within a changed social system.

He questions the adequacy of 'common sense' single factor explanations. These include, firstly, innatist explanations which assume 'a genetic tendency on the part of the Bantu to migrate.' He criticizes this explanation for its emphasis on 'human behaviour as something immutable and fixed and not as a response to social pressures.' He similarly criticizes the 'bright lights' explanation. A satisfactory explanation of causal factors must involve two levels of enquiry: first, what he terms the *nexus of centrifugal tendencies*, which induces men to migrate and, secondly, the nexus of centripetal tendencies which explain why the migrants return to their homes – in short, the recurrence of labour migration.

Mitchell examines the works of Schapera on Botswana, Read on Malawi, Richards on the Hutu migration from Rwanda and Burundi to Buganda, Houghton and Walton on the Eastern Cape, Gulliver on Southern Tanzania, Prothero on Northern Nigeria, and Winter on the Amba of Uganda. Schapera categorized the causes of labour migration as social, psychological, economic necessity, and political pressure. Under these, migration would also constitute adventure, initiation into manhood, a mark of maturity. Political pressure on the part of the colonial state, labour recruiters and chiefs, he suggested, were of declining significance in propelling male migration.

In the case of Nyasaland (today Malawi), Read's work, while subscribing to Schapera's argument that men migrated because of a spirit of adventure, showed that there were more migrants (62%) in poor areas with no export crops, and less

(24%) from areas characterized by peasant commodity production. She suggests that in areas where there were fewer opportunities for cash revenue but where there was a correlation between 'education, a rising standard of living and emigration', the level of migration was very high. This economic motive is further advanced in a study by Richards on the migration of colonial Rwanda and Burundi peasantry to Buganda. But unlike Read's study, Richards stressed the need of the Hutu peasantry to avoid labour service and other feudal obligations to the Tutsi aristocracy. Other motives, she noted, included visiting relatives, seeking better wages in order to meet bride wealth payment, etc. In contrast to Schapera, however, she rules out the 'adventure' motive and stresses economic necessity, as well as political and kinship obligations. In a further survey, Mitchell outlines the work of Southall on the Alur of Uganda. Similar to Richards, Southall saw the motives for migration as being the need to pay tax, and escape from obligations imposed by chiefs and elders. Like Schapera, however, he saw migration as important in enhancing the status of young men. This, he suggested, was the principal reason why migration was recurrent among the Alur. Houghton and Walton repeated this factor in their work on the Kieskammahoek District of the Eastern Cape Province.

The outline of Gulliver's study on the Ngoni people of Southern Tanzania stands out in marked contrast to the other work which Mitchell examines. Gulliver ruled out the 'adventure' factor because he argues that migration did not offer prestige to anyone. In fact those who migrated were often pitied. The principal factor was economic necessity. Gulliver's other study on the Nyakyusa people of South Western Tanzania showed the economic motive being principal and that migration offered young males the opportunity to purchase their own cattle to pay brideprice and therefore extricate themselves from dependence on family cattle.

The studies which Mitchell outlines identify, in their respective perspectives, three major features. First, that there were exogenous factors like taxation which initially sparked off the process of labour migration, and which in the long term internalized the phenomenon in the labour exporting societies; second, that there was an economic basis for migration – the

exception here being the work of Winter on the Amba of
Uganda who, he argued, migrated because of psychological
reasons; and thirdly, that there was an army of personal
reasons.

Why was there, during the colonial period, recurrent
oscillation of labour between country and town? What
propelled migrant workers to return home are what Mitchell
termed centripetal tendencies and which he strongly argues,
were inherent in the migrants' social relationships in the rural
areas.

> A person in a social system, particularly in a well-
> integrated system . . . occupies a position which links
> him to many other people around him. These links serve
> to define for him exactly his rights and obligations
> towards those persons and it provides for him . . . a set of
> blue-prints by means of which he is able to predict their
> behaviour towards him. In other words, he lives in an
> ordered society where his behaviour towards others and
> others towards him is known and relatively predictable.
> A person enmeshed in such a system of social relationships
> therefore has that sense of security and confidence which
> springs from the familiarity of his role vis-à-vis his
> fellows around him. He does not lightly abandon this
> security for the uncertainty and caprice of the polyglot
> aggregations of the labour centres.

In this formulation, Mitchell suggests the operation of two
opposed influences: *Centrifugal* largely determined by economic
motivation and *centripetal* (the social system) operating through a
network of social relationships. Causes for labour migration,
he suggests, must be sought 'as much in the labour centres as
in the rural areas'. Thus where there is a negation of *centrifugal*
tendencies through cash cropping, *centripetal* tendencies, he
argues, dominate and labour migration is absent or infrequent.
Where there is a balance between economic necessity and
social obligations, labour migration is present. But where
there is a migrant's involvement in a system of social
relationships in towns and his long absence from the rural
area, there may evolve a negation of social obligations in the
rural area. If this happens, therefore, the oscillation of labour
between country and town ceases.

RICHARD MOORSOM examines the relation between the tributary states of Ovamboland and the government of those areas of Namibia – the Police Zone – subject to direct colonial control, particularly as regards attracting contract labourers to the south, an aim of importance to the Administration at all times, but of increasing urgency after the Uprising of 1904. In order to achieve this end, the social structures of Ovambo society are described as they developed from a period when trade in ivory and ostrich feathers were of paramount importance to a time when, these resources being exhausted, the Ovambo rulers relied on the supply of contract labour for access to prestige goods.

The study deals with a period extending to the 1920s and examines the ability of the migrant workers to take advantage of their joint access to subsistence economy in Ovamboland, wage labour in southern Namibia, and the conflict of interests this led to with the colonial administration which, under the rule of South Africa, retaliated by imposing harsh labour laws. Moorsom examines the degree of solidarity found among the Ovambo and considers to what degree it may be explained by indigenous social structures.

The Ovambo population was distributed in clusters mostly on *oshana*, shallow channels from which water could be obtained during the dry season. The dominant mode of production was effected through lineages, products mostly being appropriated communally, although herders possessed milk individually. By the middle of the nineteenth century heads of particular lineages possessed a monopoly of certain ritual powers, notably rain making, and asserted a hereditary right to govern and claim tribute. The tributary mode thus co-existed with the lineage mode. Absolutist tendencies on the part of rulers was restrained by rivalries within the royal clans and by the existence of a consultative council. Royal prerogatives were delegated to clan leaders. The society was patriarchal, lifelong rights to land use being assigned to male household heads to whom women were subordinated, working both within the house and as agricultural labourers.

Portuguese traders reached Ovamboland in the late 1840s and within a decade regular trade relations were established through Mossamedes and Walvis Bay and from the late 1870s

on through the central Kalahari. The principal raw materials
sought were ivory and ostrich feathers which, through over-
exploitation, became almost exhausted by the 1880s. There
was also a limited market in cattle and slaves, but owing to
difficulties in transportation no market in crops developed.
The kings were particularly interested in acquiring firearms
and luxury goods for prestige.

As cattle were a principal subsistence resource, the kings
could only appropriate them by means of antagonistic social
relations. Initially this was through raiding parties which
intensified during the 1880s and 1890s. The *okasuvu*, a ritual
seizing of cattle for the king's use (and originally voluntary)
became extended into a forcibly levied tax.

As the result of increased raiding a military class of war
leaders known as *lenga* developed, who received horses and
rifles from the king and lead raiding parties of approximately
one hundred men. The *lenga* were chosen for ability rather
than according to clan structure, and in time acquired
personal wealth and a following of retainers.

In 1897 Ovamboland was ravaged by rinderpest, from
which as much as 90 per cent of the cattle died, thus rendering
raiding parties unproductive. Colonial powers had also
fortified the northern and southern borders rendering such
expeditions more dangerous. As a result of this the activities of
the *lenga* turned inwards, towards collecting *okasavu*, an
increasing amount of which was retained for their own use.
Men who were deprived of their cattle had little choice but to
attach themselves to *lenga* as clients, or to engage in migrant
labour. Before 1907 the number of migrant labourers in the
Police Zone probably never exceeded 1,700 but by 1910 the
number had soared to 9,000. In 1908 the Ovambo kings
formalized their relations with the German Administration
through 'protection treaties' but maintained considerable
independence and exerted control over migrant labourers,
from whom in return they exacted taxes, also controlling the
duration of their stay, which was timed to coincide with the
period when no heavy agricultural labour was required.

The German Administration refrained from coercion in
attempting to secure labour supplies, working in cooperation
with the kings who, when possible, adapted the institution of

the raiding party to this new end. It is probable that direct royal control became weaker after the rate of migration increased steeply between 1907–10. After the defeat of the Germans in 1915 the South Africans established an administrative presence in Ovamboland, and applied the principles of indirect rule, working where possible through the kings and the *lenga*, winning over the latter by acknowledging their executive authority.

Under the South African regime the freedom of labour migrants to choose the place and duration of labour was gradually limited but it was only in 1926 that a recruiting monopoly was established that took away all freedom of choice from the migrants. From then on the only choice was whether to migrate or not. Once recruited, workers were arbitrarily assigned to employers and were contracted for a minimum of one year with severe penalties for defection. Thus the Ovambo were no longer able to participate both in their traditional modes of subsistence and in wage labour.

SHUBI L. ISHEMO studies taxation, forced labour, famine and migration in the Lower Zambezi region of Mozambique during the early colonial period. Ishemo seeks to examine the centrality of taxation (*mussoco*) in initiating and fuelling the process of colonial capital accumulation and its role in the reproduction of the conditions for the acquisition of labour by the colonial state, capital and *latifundio*. Like the Mozambican historian, Carlos Serra, Ishemo advances the thesis that *mussoco*, as the summation of colonial capitalist development, was the singular extra-economic mechanism which partly transformed the Zambézian 'petty-commodity producer into a forced-seller of labour power.' This transformation, he shows, was expressed through the payment of labour rent, rent in kind, and later money rent. It was through such mechanisms that the Zambézian peasants' agricultural calendar and the entire process of production were disrupted and social as well as ecological conditions for the outbreak of famine were set in motion and reproduced.

Ishemo takes issue with the thesis originally advanced by Leroy Vail and Landeg White in their 1980 study of capitalism and colonization in lower Zambézia. In it, Vail and

White had argued that between 1870 and 1890 the plank of the Portuguese colonial state's policy was not so much to encourage a colonial plantation economy as to encourage peasant petty-commodity production, and to promote free trade. They concluded that because of this assumed minimal state intervention, this period was characterized by peasant prosperity. In contrast to this, Ishemo argues that far from being a period of free trade and peasant prosperity, it was a period characterized by the development of monopolistic tendencies as manifested in the colonial plantations. And far from being free, Indian merchant capital which had hitherto operated autonomously became subordinated to European commercial houses. What appeared as competition between Indian merchants, he argues, was in fact competition between European commercial houses. What appeared to be a liberal tariff designed to benefit peasant petty-commodity producers, in fact benefited European commercial capital. The role of the colonial state in this was of crucial importance. From the late 1870s, the instrument for the disruption of peasant production processes was the mussoco regime. In spite of the initial failure of colonial plantations, the colonial state's policies were directed towards the creation of favourable conditions for the development of a plantation economy with guarantees of cheap and abundant labour supplies. Such labour supplies, he stresses, did not become available through the operation of 'free market' forces but through extra-economic mechanisms which were essentially ideological.

In both empirical and theoretical elaboration, he catalogues evidence of the disruption of peasant petty-commodity production, and a decline in the production of the means of existence. Conditions for famine, he notes, were evident from the late 1870s through the 1880s. Famine, 'as a child of the mussoco regime,' became with the more concerted development of the colonial plantation economy after 1892, instrumental in the further partial withdrawal of labour from peasant agricultural production, and the maintenance, in a restructured form, of family production units, and the reproduction of the phenomenon of migrant and seasonal labour. In that sense, he stresses, the preconditions for capital accumulation were also the preconditions for the outbreak of famine, disease and the pauperization of the Lower Zambezian peasantry.

The process of the disruption of peasant production processes was formally institutionalized in the period after 1890. With large-scale concessions awarded to European (largely non-Portuguese) capital, *mussoco* became legally linked to forced labour, and in effect all such concessions became *mussoco* farms. Linked to this, too, was the monopolization of trade by capital and latifundio, and the barring of intra-peasant commodity exchange. In some areas, especially in the coconut producing belt, land was seized thus producing a marginalized peasantry akin to peons with weak rights to the means of production and tied to capital and latifundio through debt bondage. Other methods of marginalizing the peasantry included the seizure of their instruments of production, canoes, and their alienation from forest resources. While wage levels remained static from the late 1870s through to the 1920s, *mussoco* levels increased rapidly. In a detailed elaboration, Ishemo sees an increasing burden on the peasantry, with male members of households expending more time in wage labour so as to pay *mussoco*. In consequence, the shift of food production from peasant households to plantations and the linking of food rations to wages represented what was to constitute the principal colonial characteristic of the Zambezian social formation: a worker-peasant continuum.

TIYAMBE ZELEZA takes as his starting point opposition to studies of labour coercion and migration in Kenya which reify the colonial state and deal with static models rather than using concepts of dynamism which see it as a continuous site of struggle. He also questions concentration on settler estates to the exclusion of the 'hidden' labour history of the peasant farm based on household labour.

He considers the institutional weaknesses of the colonial state embedded as it was in metropolitan practices, and shows how this led to economic interventionism and political authoritarianism. The state acted to favour accumulation of capital on the settlers' behalf through the establishment of a suitable infrastructure, but was unwilling to destroy the peasant economy whose importance was considerable for the generation of surplus, given the weakness of settler capital.

Zeleza argues that the impact of land alienation and taxation, the latter being widely avoided, had less influence on labour mobilization and recruitment than has often been thought. Land alienation was concentrated in the Central Province and parts of the Rift Valley and Coast provinces. Other regions were comparatively untouched. Settlers were to find that control of labour did not automatically follow control of land, particularly as peasant commodity production had increased in just those regions – Central and Nyanza Provinces – from where settlers hoped to draw labour. This led to forced labour being particularly predominant in these provinces. Men worked far from home, whereas women and children contributed 'communal labour' for public works programmes, a practice sanctioned by the 1912 Native Authority Ordinance.

Forced labour for government purposes was legalized in 1908, whereas recruitment for settlers was merely 'encouraged'. This distinction was effectively removed in 1919 making forced labour available to any employer.

From 1920 the *kipande* registration system was put into practice, which restricted workers' freedom of movement, and applied penal sanctions to those who deserted their employers. Desertion, however, was widespread, and often successful, as the chiefs who were supposed to trace deserters and provide forced labour wère often willing to accept bribes.

As a result of resistance against forced labour, squatter and migrant labour systems developed. These, Zeleza argues, cannot be reduced to the reproductive imperatives of capitalism. They may represent as much African resistance to capitalist work rhythms as a cost-minimizing strategy of employers. Zeleza takes issue with Kitching's account of the labour process in colonial Kenya, denying that a large 'spare capacity' of under-utilized male labour was available and could be withdrawn from peasant households without ill consequences.

It is next argued that different regions and sectors of the colonial economy gave rise to different patterns of labour migration. Estates and plantations relied on squatter labour, the Mombasa Port on casual labour, while the railway attempted labour stabilization. In the coastal region, colonial capitalism was superimposed on a declining plantation economy. When slavery was abolished in 1907 the plantocracy found it difficult to control labour. Neither landlords nor squatters could accumulate capital, and the making of a backward region began. The government would not allow indentured Indian labourers and labourers from Nyasaland who were accustomed to relatively high wages.

Mombasa attracted migrant labourers mainly from Nyanza and Kikuyuland, who generally left their families behind. In 1925 there were 7,555 registered workers. These different patterns of migration resulted in the establishment of different types of household. A squatter household was co-residential, while the household of the urban worker was structured by its income-pooling functions.

In the White Highlands settlers could neither control forced labour nor secure fully waged labour, and relied on the squatter system, some even offering prospective squatters livestock. By 1930 squatters here numbered 120,000, and far from running capitalist enterprises, the settlers were transformed into semi-feudal barons, threatened by the independent commodity productions of the squatters.

Squatter conditions worsened from the mid 1920s and deteriorated further from the 30s. In 1918 the Resident Native Ordinance had insisted that future squatter payments should be made in labour and not in cash or kind. Having adult children, established squatters needed more settler land, and the reserves also became overcrowded.

These factors led to the reduction in size of squatter plots and an increase in labour demanded (3 months in 1918, 6 months in 1925). Thus began the struggle between settlers and squatters which was later to erupt into the 'Mau Mau' anti-colonial war.

C. M. F. LWOGA traces the origin of patterns of labour migration to the demands of colonial plantations, originally German and later British, which led to the establishment of labour reserves: those in the Iringa Region are specifically discussed.

The major plantation crop was sisal and labour flow from distant regions was coerced, partly because peasants in the vicinity of the plantations were encouraged to produce and sell food crops to colonial plantations in order to feed the plantation workers. As conditions of workers and wages were poor in the plantations, conscript labour was important when the voluntary work force fell short of requirements and was particularly important during the Second World War when sisal was declared necessary for the war effort.

Professional recruitment agencies worked in adjacent areas such as Njombe. In 1945 some 2,880 labourers were recruited. The principal labour reserves were in regions where there was little or no peasant commodity production. Njombe District was an example of such an area; for although there was some settler production of coffee and pyrethrum, peasant commodity production was subject to severe legal restrictions.

Migration of able-bodied male labour from labour reserves led to an increased dependence on female and child labour for the meagre cash crop production. A total of three pyrethrum farms in Njombe District employed an aggregate of 238 men, 27 women and 342 children in 1946. Colonial regulations restricting the use of child labour were widely flouted.

During the 1950s conflict arose between the local District Commissioners, who were interested in improving the local economy by encouraging cash crop production, and the Department of Labour whose interests lay with the recruitment of labour for plantations. In fact, the local peasants experienced difficulty in breaking into such potentially lucrative cash crop production as that of coffee, because of the initial costs involved, and the lack of credit facilities. In Njombe, pyrethrum production by smallholders, however, increased from 2 tons in 1955, to 350 tons in 1961, whereas settler production stagnated at 175 tons.

Although the pattern of migrant labour established in colonial times persisted after independence in 1961, its destination and duration were gradually to alter. Reorganization of the sisal plantations led to a decreasing demand for labour and the post colonial state decided to concentrate on cash crop production in rural areas. Three years after independence, the post-independence government decided to stop labour recruiting from both outside and within the country.

This policy came up against patterns already experienced by the colonial regimes: firstly, until cash crop production was fully established in labour reserves, the only way to gain cash income was by becoming a migrant labourer for part of the year; and, secondly, plantations were unable to attract an adequate labour supply without some measure of implicit or overt coercion. Once again the conflicting interests of local leaders and the Department of Labour came into play. A serious decline in the production of tobacco in Iringa District led the government to intervene on the behalf of the growers, thus ending official opposition to recruitment in Njombe District. Lack of labour, however, led to some land under tobacco cultivation being surrendered to that of maize, as plantation labour was seen by migrants as less attractive than ever, now that a mere two months cash employment might suffice. Thus, despite the government's *volte-face* concerning labour recruitment, plantations still experienced difficulties, in part because propaganda against labour migration had made some impression on those involved, but also because 'The labour market was being regulated by so-called market forces, and the state-owned plantations had become a less attractive sector of the market.' Indeed, in order to maximize profits the plantations could only intensify the labour process or extend land uses, neither of which were practicable in the circumstances.

Labour migration from the labour reserves is now short term and involves working for smallholders rather than on plantations, and represents one side of an economic pattern consisting of subsistence food production at home and wage earning elsewhere. Despite the disapproval of local authorities, some of whom fine returning migrants, the necessity deriving from the economic structure itself ensures the continuation of migrant labour. Peasants on the labour reserves have only two ways to escape from it: 1) produce surplus or cash crops sufficient to meet the monetary requirement, which needs high government investment, or 2), enter the bureaucracy, which requires more education than is usually available.

MARJORIE MBILINYI questions the studies which have
emphasized male labour migration in the colonial period.
Such studies have situated women in the restructured sexual
division of labour in which they became sole family producers
or 'heads' of households in the absence of men. Mbilinyi's
work is concerned with gender relations and the intervention
of the British colonial state in the labour reservoir of Rungwe
District in colonial Tanganyika (today mainland Tanzania).

Rungwe District had in 1954 a quarter of the men as
migrant workers, eighty-five per cent of all young males had
been migrants and a quarter of all male migrants had travelled
with their wives. This level of migration is interesting because
the area was productive in both cash and subsistence crops.

The main part of the paper examines the intervention of the
colonial state in supporting customary marriage practices
which operated to the advantage of the elders in a strongly
patriarchal society, where social bonds were formed by the
exchange of women for cattle. The societal forces operated
strongly to keep women in a position of subjugation to their
husbands, as a break-up of marriage required the direct
repayment of the bride price, or an equivalent, by a man with
whom a woman had left to live.

This traditional pattern and models proposed by missionaries
tended to conflict. In theory both were recognized by the
colonial administration. Such marriages tended to be monog-
amous and the bride was not inherited by her husband's
brother as was customary. Mbilinyi examines court records to
show that some Nyakyusa women did not hesitate to use the
legal system to attempt to break free from male domination.

The colonial state's use of the concept of 'customary
marriage' was aimed at social control as regards women.
Mbilinyi uses the concept of 'marriage politics' to characterize
this social control associated with 'indirect rule'. In this
connection, the migration ('running away') of women was
seen as a challenge to the colonial state, colonial chiefs, and
male elders. She forcefully argues that 'running away' was not
stimulated by the 'male agency' working on 'female passivity'.
Rather she sees it as constituting resistance against 'forced
marriage, child betrothals, physical violence, failure to remit
wages home, impotence, wife beating . . .' etc.

The colonial state's response was to institute a 'pan-territorial' policing – a system of social control specific to women – extending to Northern Rhodesia and aimed at upholding parental authority over women. State intervention, Mbilinyi argues, led to change in the definition of 'marriage politics' *from* adultery, runaways and therefore compensation *to* divorce with husbands demanding return of bridewealth not wives. In this connection she examines the contradictions that emerged between the colonial state, the collaborationist aristocracy, and male elders on the one hand, and mission educated Christian women on the other. Educated Christian women, she suggests, were a threat to indirect rule. The colonial state therefore responded by reinforcing the authority of chiefs and elders over young males and women. Women's defiance of this resulted in jail sentences. Such sentences were significant in that they were, as Mbilinyi notes, a women's choice. They 'challenged the legitimacy of the colonial ideology' and served as an example to other women that 'resistance without accommodation was possible and potentially successful.'

BABACAR FALL and MOHAMED MBODJ contribute two papers on the nature of forced labour in Senegal. The first paper written by these scholars jointly describes the existence of forced labour in the form of corvée exactions, and analyses its significance in a colonial country where the free labour market is usually considered to have been of greater importance than in most. The second paper (written by Fall) considers the anomolous case of the Société des Salines du Sine-Saloum, which drew upon convict labour to ensure its operation.

Fall studies the history of the Société des Salines du Sine-Saloum, established to extract salt from the left bank of the Saloum in Senegal, concentrating particularly on problems of labour recruitment, and government efforts to overcome them dating from the war years, when salt was officially declared a strategic product.

In the early years, between 1914 and 1924, production was less than 5,000 tonnes annually, considerably less than that of indigenous production which varied between 9,000 and 12,000 tonnes p.a. Only after 1940 did it exceed 10,000 tonnes, helped by the growth of the port of Kaolack and its connection to the Dakar–Niger railway. As work extracting salt was very unpleasant, the company found it difficult to attract labour to take advantage of the opportunity for increased markets offered by the war situation. In 1942 more than 20,000 tonnes of salt were abandoned to the rain through labour shortages.

In December 1943 notice was given of the decision of the Federal Authorities that production must be increased to supply other colonies of the Federation. From 1943, prison labour and conscripts were made available to the company, although this was viewed initially as a provisional measure, the company being expected to recruit labour from the market place during the agricultural slack season. This was theoretically possible, as the agricultural season extended from June to November, whereas the active season for salt working was November to May. But the director of the salt works was well aware that given conditions of labour and wages he would not be able to attract the necessary work-force.

Forced labour had played a smaller part in the labour market of Senegal than in other markets of the Federation of French West Africa. In 1933 the Governor General noted 'Senegal is living under a system of free labour, and salaries vary according to the law of supply and demand.' This was a result of the long French occupation of the territory, the politically active life of the communes and above all of the role played by the groundnut economy in promoting trade. The existence of conscript labour of the deuxième portion excited public protest and the last recruits were liberated from 15 February 1949. Public attention, however, ignored the convict labour employed by the Kaolack salt works, having little sympathy with those in a state of rupture with the rules of society.

In order to provide a permanent work-force of convict labour to the salt mines a penal camp was established at Kaolack in 1944, with approximately 200 prisoners. The director of the company thought it essential to have a permanent work-force of 250 men from December to be augmented by an additional 400 temporary workers from mid-April. The Kaolack camp failed to meet this requirement as within a month of its opening only 40% of the prisoners were available for labour. A further 100 civilian prisoners were made available by the local governor but this was still considered inadequate, particularly because of the high rate of defection among voluntary workers. Of 800 engaged at the beginning of May only 200 remained by the 17th.

Appalling working conditions took a high toll of the workers and nutrition was inadequate, falling far below statutory requirements. A report on the prison camp also showed inadequate clothing and prevalent ill health although a doctor should have visited the camp once a week; inspectors in late 1945 showed the last recorded visit as happening 6 months earlier. A report drawn up by the commission advocated the abolition of the system, claiming that as large supplies of salt were no longer required for the war effort the company should rely on voluntary labour. This suggestion was rejected by the Governor General, who thought the salt mines could not be operated on this basis. And so despite France's advocacy of free labour in West Africa the camp at Kaolack continued until 1956 when the salt work required a smaller labour force as a result of mechanization.

In conclusion, state intervention on behalf of the Salines du Kaolack, triggered by the status of salt as a strategic product during the war, may be considered instrumental in delaying the mechanization of sea-salt extraction operations. It also protected the company from facing competition in the labour market which would have forced improved working conditions and wages upon it.

The social marginalization of prisoners condemned to hard labour allowed the system to continue without exciting public protest.

COLIN MURRAY's study is about the forceable eviction of eighteen black families from the small farm of Ngoanyana in the Eastern Orange Free State in 1979. These were relocated at Botshabelo, the largest relocation rural slum in South Africa which in 1980 had over 500,000 people. Murray's study is aimed at reconstructing the socio-economic changes that have taken place in this part of the South African countryside through a micro-study of one farm over a period of 100 years. The title to this farm in the Thaba'Nchu District dates from

1886 and was a result of the speculative capital in the area
after the discovery of gold. The farm belonged, for 80 years, to
an Irish family who acquired it in 1902. Bankruptcy in 1979
was the factor that precipitated the eviction of the eighteen
black families.

He takes the transmission of the title to the farm as a tool for
understanding the processes of socio-economic change. Three
themes emerge in this enquiry: first, there was a predominance
of share-cropping involving white landowners and African
peasant cultivators. Secondly, after the Boer War there was
rapid capital accumulation aided by the state in favour of
white farmers. This was to destroy the possibility of independent
African agricultural production. Thirdly, there was the
intensification of white agriculture through rapid mechanization
in the 1960s and early 1970s. This last phase had two
consequences: first, the white farmers became increasingly
indebted to the Land Bank and insurance companies; secondly,
mechanization resulted in black structural unemployment
which became manifest in the relocation of the African
population from 'white' farms to the Bantustans.

Murray charts how the Barolong Territory of Thaba'Nchu
came to be annexed by the Orange Free State in 1884. A
succession dispute among the Barolong aristocracy resulted in
annexation by the Boer Orange Free State in 1884. Freehold
titles to ninety farms (including) Ngoanyana farm were
granted to the aristocracy. But by the early 1890s about three-
quarters of the land granted to individual Barolong had been
sold to white farmers. Why such a rapid alienation of land?
Murray suggests three reasons: that there was a black
demoralization by Free State rule; that the Barolong had no
capital to farm successfully and, lastly, that the millers who
handled grain were awash with capital after the discovery of
gold. This, he suggests, lay at the bottom of the Barolong
aristocracy's decision to sell and buy land more cheaply
elsewhere.

The transfer of land to English settlers ruled out a secure
access to the means of production by black residents who had
been betrayed by the Barolong aristocracy. Those who
remained were joined by the Barolong and Basotho who had
been displaced elsewhere by the state. Most of the landowners

being absentee landlords, facilitated black residents to become
squatters with share-cropping constituting the dominant
contractual relationship. But in the post-Boer War period,
this relative security of tenure changed with new conditions
involving the removal of white and black residents to
concentration camps. The bulk of the land was sold to the
colonial state in 1901. With the colonial state seeking to break
the Boer dominance of the countryside, the Thaba'Nchu
District became a concentration of new white settlers. Some of
these had no capital and therefore depended on black
sharecroppers.

The role of the Union government was crucial. In the 1912
Act it virtually accorded settlers freehold with the proviso that
they enter mortgage bonds in favour of the government to
cover the repayment of the balance of the purchase price of
their farms. In 1932–3 the government extended the redemption dates of settlers' mortgages. The 1913 Land Act
prohibited share-cropping. Consequently, over half the black
residents in the Thaba'Nchu District were evicted. By 1920,
wage labour on many farms had completely replaced share-
cropping. On one owned by Lurie, farm labour was believed
to have been mostly women from Basutoland. Significantly,
these women were stereotyped as 'loose' and therefore thought
to be easy prey to men seeking marital partners. On a potato
(later wheat, maize and cattle) farm owned by McPherson,
seasonal labour with harsh working conditions and low pay
were common. Increasingly labour came to be drawn from
seasonal migrants from Basutoland.

Despite the strict influx control measures of the apartheid
state in the 1950s and 1960s, many Africans moved to live on
the farms. Some escaped temporarily to evade the Bantu
Administration and Development functionaries. There emerged
a link between the mines, with some residents dependent on
wage remittances from the mines/towns. This unofficial
'squatting' produced over-crowding and deteriorating living
conditions. Bankruptcy in 1979 resulted in the state and white
farmers evicting the black families. Over the region, this
resulted in large numbers of the African population seeking
refuge in the rural slums of Onverewacht and Botshabelo.

ALULA PANKHURST examines the development of the
resettlement programmes in Ethiopia since the Revolution in
the period 1979–84. The main determinant of a massive
resettlement programme was famine; and the reason for
resettlement was to ensure the material well-being of families
from regions worst affected by famine. In this, the role of the
state was crucial. It established structures which were
allocated resources to implement resettlement. Indeed, in the
ten years following the Revolution, state expenditure on
resettlement increased six-fold, or US$14.3 million annually.
Pankhurst outlines the problems involved in the resettlement
programme. First, the programme was too slow to meet the
projected target. Secondly, the programme incurred high
costs and low productivity in the settlements; and thirdly, the
policy proved unpopular because of coercion – especially
among the unemployed urban youths. In other cases, individual
isolation from families and wives encouraged desertion. In all,
family reunions were considered essential. In January 1986,
the Ethiopian government temporarily suspended the resettlement programme, not because of external pressure, but
because the famine threat was considered to be under control.

Pankhurst argues that with the worsening of the famine
crisis, indicated by peasants selling their plough-oxen and
therefore losing their stake in the land, the state sought long-
term solutions rather than adopting panic measures. 'It is not
surprising,' he notes, 'that resettlement was resumed at what
to foreign eyes seemed the worst possible time, when resources
were most stretched, as the new famine was predicted.'

Pankhurst conceptualizes resettlement by taking into account
three factors which he considers as components of organized
schemes: settler backgrounds and motivations, settlement
environments, and external inputs. Settlers included peasants,
nomads and urban dwellers. In 1976, he notes, 43% of the
settlers were urban, 23% peasants with little or no land, 18%
nomads, 9% agricultural labourers and 7% charcoal producers
or retired soldiers. By 1981 he sees a reverse of the origins of
settlers. Increasingly, over 50% came from famine-prone and
overcrowded highlands, and 39% were victims of drought etc.
The reasons for resettlement were drought, famine, overpopulation, land degradation and war.

Resettlement was an extreme choice by those whose material situation was desperate. As Pankhurst argues:

> Willingness to resettle did not mean that settlers were not reluctant to leave their homes, nor that the decision was an easy one; but peasants were faced with a desperate situation: as the famine worsened, the longer they tried to keep their oxen, in the hope of being able to last out until the next ploughing season, the more the price of oxen decreased, and the terms of trade between livestock and grain became unfavourable. However, once peasants were forced to sell, or let their animals die for lack of fodder, they no longer had a stake in the land.

Oxen were therefore crucial to the peasants' ability to hold out for the next season. Without oxen, families were left with no choice but to migrate.

If famine was the principal motive for migration, Pankhurst identifies groups who migrated but who were not famine victims. These included large numbers of young men who led a marginal existence. He classifies these as ones who were 'dissatisfied with the old world and seeking a new world on the frontier', and who hoped for self-improvement through education or joining the armed forces. But there were those who migrated to seek waged labour or relief food. Women who left home often faced material hardship and unilaterally joined the resettlement. In extreme cases, material hardship caused marriages to break down.

Pankhurst identifies two types of settlement: *conventional* and *integrated*. The former involved mechanized agriculture. Such settlements were favoured for the development of producers' cooperatives and therefore enjoyed state and party support. It was here, too, that mass organizations such as Peasants', Women's and Youth Associations were formed. Integrated settlements, on the other hand, were assisted by Peasants' Associations. They had horizontal links with these associations, while conventional settlements had vertical links with the state.

In a study on migration and gender relations, CAMILLIA FAWZI EL-SOLH examines the migration of Egyptian peasant families to Iraq. Starting in 1975, this migration was stimulated by a high population density and land shortage in Egypt, and an oil rich economy but one which required labour resources to develop its agriculture. Migration was facilitated by an Egyptian-Iraqi accord. Those who migrated were mostly poor peasants who, in rural Egypt, had owned or rented insufficient land to supplement wage labour. Two thirds of the men and ninety per cent of the wives were illiterate.

Central to Fawzi El-Solh's study is the readaptation of Egyptian women in the Khalisah settlement near Baghdad. She sees a shift in the socialization process from the 'traditional' form which places emphasis on hospitality to 'an incipient individualism' which accords priority to economic expediency. This shift is not absolute. There is, she continues, a 'pattern of reflective accommodation between what is economically necessary and what is socially desirable'.

The families at the Khalisah settlement arrived from two main regions in Egypt. The mode of socio-economic organization in each of the regions varied. In Lower Egypt, the predominance of agricultural commodity production aided by perennial irrigation – started in the nineteenth century – resulted in larger villages and social differentiation. With population pressures and land scarcity, the nuclear family is dominant. In Middle and Upper Egypt, the commoditization of peasant agricultural production did not become dominant until the 1960s. Here, too, there was a decreasing dominance of the extended family. The role of women in agricultural production is varied. In Middle and Upper Egypt, women do not work on land except for specific tasks during the harvest season. In Lower Egypt, there are no such constraints, except that female seclusion is more of a 'cultural ideal' reflecting the husband's success. In all three regions, female circumcision is a form of social control.

These regional variations were not reflected in the Khalisah community, where individual family economic self-interest and success became dominant. Indeed, regional consciousness was spatially minimized by the unfamiliar environment. But she argues that although regional consciousness was minimized, it nevertheless surfaced in inter-household conflicts, elections and in struggles over water resources and agricultural equipment. Secondly, she sees a decline of regional conscious-ness in the rise of individualism; a 'novelty of economic success, measured in terms of the standard of living prior to migration, which in turn has increased its sense of security'. She equates such individualism to a self-reliance which, in the social milieu of Khalisah, has done away with the historic system of patronage that had characterized social relations in the Egyptian village. This shift was therefore determined by post-migration socio-economic circumstances.

Fawzi El-Solh then applied the above framework to gender relations. Each family constituted a production and consump-tion unit. It produced for exchange, so hiring of labour was uncommon because the aim was to maximize income. While there was no change in household labour, it was in production that there was a noted change. Women from Middle Egypt, for example, worked on land and sold produce in markets. Importantly, Fawzi El-Solh explains female economic activities outside the home as having been determined by social distance from the village of origin. On subsequent return, such change would not be replicated in Egypt. Returned female migrants would revert to secluded life 'in accordance with the higher social status that successful migrants aspire to upon their return'.

While women entered production areas which they were excluded from in Egypt, this did not constitute a fundamental restructuring of gender relations. Rather, they continued unchanged with males remaining dominant. Male children were preferred, while girls were circumcised to control their sexuality and socialized for seclusion. Notwithstanding the unchanged male dominance, Fawzi El-Solh suggests that the position of women in the household strengthened because of the absence of a female hierarchy based on age. In relations with outsiders, however, the village community in Egypt continued to function as a social frame of reference. The strictly guarded alley-ways of Khalisah became an exclusive socialization zone between women. But this did not result in long-term cooperation as in Egyptian villages. They only enabled women to avoid social isolation.

Whether the future of the Khalisah families lies in Iraq or

Egypt is uncertain. The ideal of returning to marry their daughters to non-peasant Egyptians is rendered more difficult by inflation at home. Good possibilities, however, exist for the sons' futures in Iraq. What Fawzi El-Solh demonstrates is the complexity of cultural and economic relations. Peasant women are not resistant to change. The experience of Khalisah belies cultural determinism.

Conclusion

The contributions in this volume do not claim to represent the study of forced and migrant labour on a continent-wide basis. They are, however, representative of the specific forms of this phenomenon on an historical thematic or regional basis. Through historical explanation, they seek to provide a basis for the understanding of why some post-colonial African states have been unable to autocentrize their economies, that is, to provide alternative material bases to stem the reproduction of migrant labour. With a few variations, the origins of forced and migrant labour are sought in the development of colonial capitalism. The reproduction of such social phenomena is a consequence of the reproduction of the capitalist economic structure and its manifestations in gender relations, regional imbalances, environmental factors, etc. To effect an historical break with this structure has been problematic. Even where migrant labour was opposed through 'socialist' rhetoric, there was no real change in the material conditions of the labour reserves that were reproduced from the colonial period.

Ideological factors, too, continue in such circumstances to play a part in the reproduction of migrant labour. Attempts to stop migrant labour through political and ideological means have proved meaningless. As Ruth First and her colleagues at the Centro de Estudos Africanos in Maputo argued in their seminal work on the export of Mozambican labour to South Africa:

> if an economic process as old, as deeply laid and as
> widespread as mining labour export is to be dismantled,
> all its implications must be analysed. It cannot be

combated on an ideological level alone, by an appeal to the political commitment of the migrant. This would be to dismiss the system of migrant labour as an act of will by a host of migrant workers, to miss the essence of a deep-seated economic system that has permeated the political economy of the countryside . . .

[Ruth First, *Black Gold*, Brighton, Harvester Press, 1983, p. 3]

In the current economic crisis in Africa, the effect of the structural adjustment programmes imposed by the International Monetary Fund and the Western 'aid donors', as well as the various forms of destabilization, in the Africa South of the Sahara in particular, calls for the need to examine the possibility that migrant labour and certain forms of unfree labour are in the process of being reproduced. This lies outside the scope of this book, but it is hoped that the authors of this volume will have contributed towards that much-needed study.

Acknowledgements

The Oxford Centre for African Studies wishes to thank Nuffield College, Oxford, for kindly making available the facilities for the conference which generated this volume. We also wish to thank Julia Maxted and Connie Sansom for their tireless efforts in preparing the manuscript.

The Causes of Labour Migration

J. Clyde Mitchell

The circulation of workers between their traditional rural areas and commercial and industrial enterprises is a familiar phenomenon all over the world where Western civilization has come into contact with traditional societies. It is true not only of Africa but also of Polynesia, Melanesia, South-East Asia and many other regions. In Africa it has been growing in volume since about the middle of the last century and has now become firmly rooted in the traditions of many communities stretching from the Cape to the Sahara. Houghton quoted in 1958 an estimate of five million immigrant labourers in Africa, but he warned that accurate estimates were not known.[1] Certainly reports from individual areas in different parts of Africa have the same general story to tell: that something of

This is a slightly edited version of a paper which originally appeared in the *Bulletin of the Inter-African Labour Institute* 6 (1), 1959, pp. 12–46; it is reproduced with permission of the author – who has added a Postscript – and of the Organization of African Unity, Scientific Technical and Research Commission. The paper was also printed in *Migrant Labour in Africa South of the Sahara*, proceedings under Item II of the Agenda of the Sixth Inter-African Labour Conference, Abidjan 1961 (Commission for Technical Co-operation in Africa South of the Sahara), publication No.79, pp. 259–80. Part of this material was presented to the Eleventh Conference at the Rhodes-Livingstone Institute in January 1958 and it was subsequently published in Apthorpe 1958. The paper was also published in John Middleton's *Black Africa: Its Peoples and Cultures Today* (New York, Macmillan, 1970).

the order of half of the able-bodied adult men are absent from rural homes at any one moment and that almost all have been away at some time or another.

These reports also tell of widespread changes going on in the rural areas. They frequently refer to a general state of disorganization involving sexual licence, divorce, crime and lack of respect for authority, children growing up in broken families, religious practices abandoned and, above all, poverty. Usually these undesirable features of modern rural life are traced back to the disproportion in population following the absence of a large proportion of able-bodied men. It is for this reason that the attention of missionaries, administrators and anthropologists has been directed to the study of labour migration and its causes. From the administrative point of view, it is clear that once it is accepted that the undesirable social changes which have been reported can be traced to the absence of men from their tribal homes, and if the root causes of the migration can in turn be uncovered, then clearly one way in which to ameliorate these conditions is to attack the phenomenon at its source.

On the surface of it, it may appear that the search for the causes of migration is a search for the obvious. The descriptive phrase used to identify it tells us from the beginning that it is a form of population movement concerned with seeking work. But behind this simplicity lies a complexity which has not yet yielded easily to analysis. The distinctive feature of labour migration in Africa is not so much the seeking for work but the recurrent nature of the phenomenon: that men leave their tribal area for a while and then return to it and possibly go out and return again. It is not simply a matter of the mobility of labour: they do not simply move from one area where there are no labour opportunities to another where there are. Instead they often undertake long and frequently hazardous journeys, sometimes a thousand miles or more, to some labour centre, spend several years there, and then face the same journey back home. In some areas the men have been doing this for a century or more. An analysis of labour migration, therefore, must set out to explain not only why the men leave their homes – and the causes for this may be more complicated than merely economic reasons – but also why they should consistently circulate between their tribal homes and the labour centres.

The Concept of Causality

An attempt to achieve a satisfactory explanation, therefore, must involve us in a consideration of the nature of causality. This abstruse problem lies at the heart of science and its philosophy and has been the subject of much philosophical discussion. In the social sciences, the idea of causality is particularly complicated because of the degree to which human beings are free-acting units. I do not intend to follow this interesting problem further than to provide a brief outline of what appears to be one of the more fruitful ways of looking at causality.

Perhaps we can understand the scientist's concept of causality by examining the way in which he thinks about his material. Scientists are forever trying to construct simplified models of reality. These models are intellectual constructs in which the scientist assumes certain constant relations between different parts of his machine. He then tries to fit the parts of his machine together in a way that reproduces reality. Usually, the scientist's model is only a partial representation of reality and the results the scientist predicts through his understanding of how his theoretical model works sometimes are not borne out by his observations in real life. Scientists, for example, set up a model of how the universe worked. This placed the earth in the centre and made the sun circulate round it. The model explained certain regularities they had observed in the movement of heavenly bodies but left other regularities unexplained. When Copernicus rearranged the model and placed the sun at the centre of the planetary system, the new model explained both the regularities that had been explained by the old model and the regularities it had not explained. The new model was, thus, more satisfactory since its heuristic or explanatory value was greater.

Social scientists are trying to do exactly the same sort of thing. They examine some aspect of reality and try to isolate what appear to them to be the relevant enduring relationships between its different components. These relationships are then expressed in a logically consistent paradigm. This paradigm is tested against reality, and the degree to which it can be used to predict reality gives some measure of its utility as a heuristic device. The social scientist prefers to work with an imperfect paradigm, the logical construction of which he understands, rather than with one which may in fact reproduce reality more accurately but of whose composition he is uncertain.

It should emerge from this that the social scientist's concept of causality differs considerably from the common-sense view. He does not see an effect B arising from some known cause A but rather phenomena A, B, C, D, E, and so on, back to A, all related to each other in particular ways, these relationships being such that a change in, say, E will modify the relationships of E to F and to D, hence F to G, and D to C, G to H, and C to B, and so on.

The Complex Causality of Labour Migration

Labour migration is a social phenomenon which may be fitted into an abstract series of this sort and if viewed in this light it is to be seen that it is dynamically related to a variety of other phenomena in the same social field. There are several implications which arise from taking this viewpoint.

One is that the falsity of viewing labour migration as itself a cause of various types of social phenomena is immediately apparent. Labour migration and any other phenomena such as, for example, an increased divorce rate, may vary concomitantly but this variation itself may be a reflection of a change in a third phenomena such as, for example, the declining unity of corporately acting kinship groups. It may deepen our understanding of labour migration if we view it and many of its concomitant social manifestations, not as causes and effects but, rather, as concomitant adjustments within a changed social system. In other words it is virtually impossible to separate out in terms of causes and effects the relationships of labour migration to marital fidelity, crime, the growth of separatist sects, and the hundred and one other changes going

on in rural areas in Africa. To see an increase in the instability
of marriage as a result of labour migration is analogous to
looking upon the increased rate of sparking in the cylinders of
an internal combustion engine as the cause of the increase in
the rate of operation of the exhaust valves. The rate of
sparking and the rate of operation of the valves of the motor
are, of course, related, since the crankshaft drives both the
distributor arm and the valves, but a change in the speed of
rotation of the crankshaft must in turn be traced to the
increase of the supply of fuel, the greater intake of oxygen, and
so on. In the same way, labour migration and marriage
instability may well be concomitant reactions to a change in
some sector of the social system such as the kinship
relationships and we should treat with caution over-zealous
accounts that relate all the social disabilities in rural areas to
the evil effects of labour migration.

Another implication of viewing labour migration as a
component change in a changing social system is that single-
factor explanations are seen to be patently inadequate.
Common-sense explanations of labour migration consistently
tend to be of the single-factor sort. One of the most extreme of
this type of explanation is that which assumes a genetic
tendency on the part of Bantu-speaking Africans to migrate.
The argument runs that the Bantu have been migrating across
the face of Africa for several millenia past and there is no
reason why they should cease doing this now. This explanation
looks upon human behaviour as something immutable and
fixed, and not as a response to social pressures: that
behavioural patterns in the past persist into the present in
spite of radically different social and cultural environments.
Another popular common-sense explanation is that which
looks upon labour migration as a response to curiosity.
Gulliver has given this type of explanation the appropriate
name of 'the bright lights theory'.[2] Briefly, the argument is
that, as against the exciting attractions of city life, with its
brightly lit shop windows, the hustle and bustle, the cinemas,
the entertainment, the sporting and welfare facilities, the rural
areas are dull places. Young men in particular, therefore,
hanker after the 'bright lights' of the city and sooner or later
succumb to their allure.

Both of these explanations see some single causal factor A, whether it is some deeply ingrained wanderlust in the Bantu people or the unresistable lure of 'bright lights', impelling labourers out of their rural homes into distant labour centres. Yet to react against this causal monism by asserting a plurality of causes and in so doing presenting a supposed exhaustive list of causes, hardly deepens our understanding of the processes involved.

In order to appreciate the process of causality, we must be able to link together these multiple causes and relate them to one another within some logical framework. If we fail to do this we end up with a series of partial explanations of the sort: poverty plays a part in labour migration, family difficulties play a part in labour migration and so may fear of witchcraft, desire to escape traditional tribal obligations, and so on. But we are left with no yardstick against which to assess the importance of any one of these factors against the others, nor of the way in which the various factors interact with each other. This is the weakness of otherwise clear and cogent analyses of the causes of labour migration.

We must therefore attempt to arrange this variety of causal factors in a scheme whereby they are set in some logical relationship to each other. To do this we may separate two different networks of labour migration. The first, or the nexus of centrifugal tendencies, organizes factors that induce a man to leave his tribal home. The second, or the nexus of centripetal tendencies, seeks to explain why the migrant comes back again, i.e. why labour migration is a recurrent phenomenon.

The Nexus of Centrifugal Tendencies

We may approach the analysis of the factors that operate to ease a man out of his tribal area by considering the point of view taken by several writers on labour migration.

Fieldwork reports on labour migration usually contain a section entitled 'Causes of Migration'. Let us begin by considering some of these. Schapera, in his study of conditions in the Bechuanaland Protectorate,[3] presents the causes of migration under three main headings: social and psychological factors, economic necessity, and political pressure. At the beginning of his analysis, Schapera mentions that 80 per cent of the people he studied had some experience of labour migration. It had come to be accepted almost as a matter of course that a man should go to the mines or other industries in South Africa at least once during his lifetime. But as migration is not an inevitable part of tribal life itself, the question arises, Why do particular people go abroad and why do they go at a particular time?

Factors to be taken into consideration, urges Schapera, include adventurousness, escape from the dull and lonely life of cattle posts, and the fact that migration has come to be widely regarded as a form of initiation into manhood. Labour migration has almost entirely replaced traditional initiation as a mark of maturity. As a recruited boy is immediately registered as a taxpayer, he can no longer be regarded as a boy. Moreover, girls prefer men who have faced the risks of town life, and have shown that they are willing to work for the support of a family. Escape from domestic control is another important factor. A son who resents paternal interference and dictation now that he is an adult, or who is denied the girl he wishes to marry, will seldom hesitate to seek freedom by migrating to South Africa. The case might also be one of domestic disputes, or the assumption of domestic control on the death of a father by an unsympathetic kinsman. Also, serfs can escape in this way from their serfdom at cattle posts, and men who wish to escape their communal (unpaid) labour obligations under tribal custom. Occasionally also, a man may be punished for some misdeed by being dismissed from his home area, and migration to the town might then offer the only possible means of livelihood for him.

The above considerations, however, do not in themselves account for the perennial exodus from Bechuanaland of so many thousands of people. A far more universal and important cause is economic necessity. In replying to Schapera's questioning, only 1.8 per cent gave non-economic reasons (and 35 per cent said they went in order to be able to pay their taxes). But let us leave this aspect for later discussion. It may, lastly, be noted here of Schapera's account that propaganda and political pressure is of declining importance nowadays. Initially, pressure had to be brought to bear by the labour recruiters, government and chiefs, to persuade migration. Today, there is very little need for this.

In Nyasaland a Commission set up in 1935 also examined the reasons for labour migration.[4] In the opinion of the Commission these were overwhelmingly economic. While the Commission was prepared to admit that some young tribesmen may become labour migrants to prove that they are men, or out of a spirit of adventure, it argued nevertheless that this would not account for the second, third and subsequent trips. The basic cause clearly lay in the economic field. Later Read made a detailed study of labour migration in six different areas in Nyasaland. On the basis of her experience she argues that: 'Even if the economic situation is favourable for growing export crops, sociological factors arise partly from the tribal organisation of the people and partly from the degree of western contact, which has changed their outlook and activities.'[5] The evidence that Read presents, however, shows clearly that the most impoverished areas, with poor land and no export crops, have the largest proportion of men away, 62 per cent of them classified as permanently away. The wealthiest part, in a tobacco growing area and not far from European settlements, has only 24 per cent of its men away, and only 33 per cent of these away permanently. Read does bring out clearly, however, that in order that migration should occur there should be not only the lack of opportunities of acquiring a cash income, but also the stimulus that creates a demand for a higher standard of living for which the cash is required. In remote areas where villages are little affected by the Western cash economy, not many men are away. In areas where there is closer contact, however, and where there are no local means of finding cash, they have become aware of higher standards of living, and the proportions of men away are higher. Because more men are away, more cash is sent back into these areas and this is spent on consumer goods. At the same time, the experiences of the labour migrants abroad have introduced them to higher standards of living and these new ideas are brought back with them to their rural homes. Hence, labour migration and a higher standard of living tend to reinforce each other so that the correlation Read notes between 'education, a rising standard of living and emigration' is not a simple causal one but a functional type of the kind that I have described, where cause and effect are interchangeable.[6]

Of 200 men investigated in a survey made by Richards on a migration route into Buganda, only one said he was avoiding labour obligations, 9 said they were visiting relatives, 31 were coming to settle, and the rest (75 per cent) said they were coming for a variety of reasons, for example, better pay, bridewealth, and money needed for domestic uses. Richards discredits explanations of this migration in terms of either habit or adventure.

> The Ruanda and Urundi peasants are not reckoned as adventurous peoples as distinct from their warlike overlords, and they usually figure in their reports as shy, timid and easily scared. They certainly give that impression in the camps and villages and most spoke of the sheer economic necessity or of particularly unpleasant political or kinship obligations they wanted to avoid, rather than of desires to see European life, get a reputation for sophistication or similar motives given to Schapera. . . . Evidence from other parts of Africa tends also to show that Africans rarely travel long distances if they can make money under satisfactory conditions at home.[7]

The picture gained from Richards' survey is that of a people continually in need of money to satisfy their social obligations and aspirations. Tutsi chiefs had the reputation of demanding much work from their subjects until many of them reached a point when migration to Uganda seemed the only escape. The picture is simply one of a movement from a poor, over-populated area to a wealthy one, from an area of mainly subsistence economy, to one where the population was largely engaged in the production of cash crops, from a traditional system where feudal dues had only recently been prohibited to an area in which they had been limited for 30 years by an administration that had been in control for a much longer period.

To move now to the Alur of East Africa, an account of their labour migration has been provided by Southall.[8] Degrees of migration of these people, he says, are related directly to economic development. A regular cash income is not needed: only sporadic needs for marriage, tax and clothes, for example, must be met by cash. The Alur of Buganda have all left Alurland partly in order to escape from those obligations which tend to disperse wealth as soon as it is accumulated, imposed by chiefs or elder kinsmen. Also, young men are able to achieve leadership positions in Buganda which they could not at home due to age and status restrictions. Their behaviour of extreme swagger before the girls at home, when migrants return home, must be noted here as an important evidence of a consciously formulated factor in Alur migration. Particularly important is the fact that the habit of migration is now formed, and has acquired a kind of prestige, at least for the young. Thus any government or other measures to restrict this migration would probably encounter many resistances in addition to those now consciously formulated by the people themselves, that have unobtrusively developed in consistency with this habit.

Houghton and Walton, on the basis of a thorough-going study of Kieskammahoek District in the eastern part of the Cape Province, argue that:

> Poverty and economic necessity drive people out of the district to sell their labour in the urban centres where remuneration is higher and opportunities of employment greater than in the Reserve. There may be subsidiary reasons, such as the desire of young men to prove their manhood, or of the lure of the city life for young people of both sexes, but the principal reason is to be found in the failure of the Reserve to provide an adequate living for its population.[9]

Gulliver's account of labour migration among the Ngoni of southern Tanganyika also puts great stress of economic necessity as the overwhelming reason why Ngoni leave their homes to seek work.[10] Men cannot, or feel they cannot, earn sufficient money at home to satisfy their basic cash needs and a minimum standard of living; alternatively, they suppose that it is easier to earn sufficient abroad than at home. Gulliver's analysis of more than 2,500 journeys shows that 90 per cent were for economic reasons. Furthermore, almost every man stated that he would have preferred to stay at home but was compelled to migrate by force of what appeared to him to be economic necessity.

Gulliver's analysis, however, reveals more than economic factors in migration. He also describes how, for the particular individual concerned, the immediate or 'last straw' cause of migration may well lie in another direction. All or almost all Ngoni feel the pinch of current economic conditions at home; some are immediately induced to go away to where money is most readily obtainable, but others continue to manage until some final constraint on top of economic necessity sends them off. In practice, the latter category is the smaller of the two, and of course the existence of additional and 'last straw' causes does not in any way diminish the real importance of the basic motivation.

Other causes additional to economic circumstances that induce Ngoni migration are quarrels that can be settled by either a permanent or temporary moving to another area and, sometimes, government resettlement policy. On the negative side, we must note that the factor of desire to see the world and boredom at home is not important among the Ngoni. The majority of these people have no desire to go outside their own country or, indeed, very far from their everyday community. Nearly all Ngoni, whilst agreeing on the economic causes of migration, also say readily and voluntarily that were it not for such necessity they would prefer to stay at home. Were there, they say, reasonable and reliable opportunities to earn sufficient money at home, they would definitely not go away to work. No special prestige is gained from migrating to seek work. The few who have migrated a large number of times are often pitied.

Gulliver has also studied Nyakyusa labour migration from south western Tanganyika.[11] He concludes that the basic and overwhelmingly important cause of Nyakyusa labour migration is an economic one – the search for money and goods that cannot be obtained at home in a sufficient quantity or which men feel they can obtain more easily, quickly and readily abroad. Without exception, all Gulliver's informants gave economic advantage or necessity, as the chief cause of their migration.

The Nyakyusa commonly are unimpressed by what appear to the European or urbanized African as the amenities and satisfactions of the towns. On the other hand, it has become a well-established custom for the young Nyakyusa to go away to work, though nevertheless there is very little inherent in their traditional life that compels this custom, and those who live in the coffee-producing areas appear to manage satisfactorily without economic disadvantage or social difficulty. A returned migrant gains a certain prestige from his new wealth, colourful clothing and foreign experience – girls prefer young men who have a bright shirt and shiny shoes – but this is a short-lived prestige and does not count for much in tribal cultures. An important incentive we must not overlook here is the incentive to earn money to buy one's own cattle for bridewealth, to avoid waiting for one's father's and elder brother's permission to use the family cattle.

Two more areas may be briefly described before I turn to an analysis of the chief features of labour migration that emerge from the various accounts. Firstly, let us look at R. M. Prothero's account of migration from north-western Nigeria, 92 per cent of which is on account of economic causes – 53 per cent seeking money, 16 per cent seeking food, and 24 per cent trade.[12] Only a low percentage say they migrate for customary reasons, but Prothero argues that this should not lead the analyst to minimize traditional influences on migration. He points out that opportunities for cash earning are available in other parts of the region, although people prefer to migrate seasonally to satisfy other economic wants and not to settle in the more productive areas.

Let us, lastly, refer to the Amba of Uganda of whom Winter writes that

> among the Amba of his acquaintance, who left the country to seek employment elsewhere, very few had monetary gain uppermost in their minds. Most of them

left because of trouble at home or because they wanted to
see places beyond the bounds of their restricted world.
Although non-economic reasons may be more prominent,
however, it is possible that people could not leave
Bwamba unless opportunities to earn existed elsewhere.[13]

But if we compare Winter's estimate of the cash value of
income per family in Bwamba, i.e. sh.512 per annum, and the
estimated income for an unskilled labourer at Kampala, i.e.
sh.527, it is difficult not to conclude that psychological rather
than economic motives cause Amba migration. Of the number
of people involved there is, unfortunately, no estimate
available.

In these accounts, although economic factors predominate,
it is clear that they are not the only ones. We are then left with
the task of separating out the different types of factors
involved and relating them to each other. From the material
we have examined it appears that motivations behind labour
migration operate at three different levels or along different
axes.

1 *Through the normative system of the society.* Schapera and
   Gulliver both state that labour migration has become a
   habit and Schapera, Southall and the Lacey Commission
   all say that migration is considered almost a *rite de passage*,
   marking the attainment of adulthood. The implication of
   this is that migration has become, in some of the societies,
   the expected type of behaviour for young men. The
   motivation for the migration is incorporated, therefore, in
   the normative social system concerned and presumably
   operates through the normal social controls of that society.
   The definition of the appropriate role for a young man of a
   certain age therefore is to leave the tribal area and to make
   his way in the outer industrial world.

2 *Through the economic system.* All writers on the movement of
   peoples have emphasized its economic basis. Winter's
   material on first sight seemed to refute the universality of
   the economic basis to migration but on further analysis
   this does not seem to be upheld.

3 *Through the personalities of individuals.* A hundred and one

different personal reasons may be adduced from the statements of informants – to escape quarrels, to escape witchcraft, to avoid arduous duties, etc.

In so far as the social controls operate to induce a man to leave the tribal area because it is the 'done' thing, it is clear that this pattern of behaviour has arisen in the past in response to specific social needs and that these needs still persist. We would not expect that a custom would persist for long when the basic need out of which it arose has disappeared. We assume, therefore, that the basic cause of migration rests with either or both of the other two categories.

Some of the difficulties of disentangling the significance of personal factors as against non-personal factors appear to lie in the way in which studies have been conducted. Several writers have pointed out that we should be cautious of the technique which asks the direct question to the migrant. Schapera warns against it though he quotes statistics he derived in this way. Richards writes on the subject:

> It is probable that a concrete objective or a dramatic event stands out in some immigrants' narrative rather than the cumulative effects of hopes and fears which are probably the real cause of pushing a man to leave his home. He may be quite unable to describe the whole process of the gradual deterioration of local conditions which finally resulted in the situation that became unbearable to him. Again a particularly angry scene with his local chief may have become dramatised in his mind for all time and quite obliterate consciousness of a long series of economic frustrations and hardships which were equally 'motives for travel'.[14]

Gulliver puts the proposition in terms of 'last straw' causes.

> For particular individuals . . . the causes of migration, and especially the reasons for a particular journey to work, may well show a different range of factors. This is so especially when an individual Nyakyusa, who is questioned, thinks primarily of the immediate reason for his leaving home at a certain time. That reason may be a

specific crisis in his financial affairs, a pressed demand by his father-in-law for another contribution of bride-wealth cattle, a quarrel with his brother or neighbour, a current resentment against his chief, an unsuccessful love affair, or even the immediate attraction of a newly returned acquaintance resplendent in fine clothes and with a new bicycle. These are indeed true causes of labour migration for individuals at certain times; but they are not the root causes for the people, as a whole, nor even for those individuals. They are merely factors which go to tip the balance at those times and which determine the actual occasion of departure.[15]

Gulliver's argument appears to contain the essence of the relationship between the 'personal' and 'economic' factors involved in the nexus of centrifugal tendencies. In logical terms, economic factors appear to be a necessary condition, but they may not in themselves be a sufficient condition. In other words if the economic drives to labour migration are not present it is unlikely that it will occur, but if the economic conditions are present the actual migration may not occur until some event in the personal life of the individual precipitates things and triggers off his decision to go.

One of the advantages of separating out economic and personal factors in this way is that it enables us to distinguish between the *incidence* and the *rate* of labour migration.[16] When we talk about the incidence of labour migration, we refer to the set of unique circumstances that induces a particular emigrant to leave his rural area. It implies, therefore, a complete appreciation of the conditions underlying the migration, both economic and personal.

The personal factors of the type that have been mentioned as 'causes' of labour migration are of the type that operate independently of the underlying economic conditions. Tensions arise between kinsmen, regardless of changes in economic condition: the desire to experience town life and to savour the adventures of travelling, are probably constantly present. Therefore, as Durkheim cogently argued concerning the operation of similar factors in causing suicide, these factors cannot explain the size and trends of the *rate* of labour migration.[17] The rate of labour migration, it appears, is determined mainly by economic factors. As Schapera puts it: 'The [personal] factors described above have been directly responsible for migration in many individual instances. But they do not account in themselves for the perennial exodus of so many thousands. A far more universal cause, and certainly the most important of all, is economic necessity.'[18]

There is a good deal of evidence to support this contention. Economic factors appear to affect the rate of labour migration through two different but related conditions. The first relates to the degree to which subsistence is possible within the rural area. Prothero, for example, found that 16 per cent of the migrants from north-western Nigeria he studied attributed their migration to a search for food.[19] And Schapera points out that the annual reports of the mine recruiting organizations in South Africa show greater recruitment in times of drought and famine, and other occasions of economic depression.[20] This is also strikingly confirmed by material presented by Houghton and Walton who show that in five different years in which there were poor crops the proportion of migrants who left in the succeeding January and February was on average 30.3 per cent of the annual figure, while after good crops in five other years the corresponding figure was 18.2 per cent.[21]

The second set of basic economic conditions refers to the standard of living and the vastly increased new wants created by contacts with Western civilization. The need for cash in the modern rural situation is important here. The earliest incentives for labour migration were undoubtedly taxes, but contact with industrial and other centres soon widened the range of wants immensely. Some of these are translated back into the traditional idiom, for example, the purchase of cattle for bridewealth among the Nyakyusa to avoid delay of marriage by fathers who want to take second wives, and the first marriages of older brothers who have prior claim on the family cattle over younger brothers. Other wants are valued in the new idiom of bicycles, gramophones, and so on, new tastes for tea and sugar, and capital goods such as ploughs.

Where alternative cash sources are available it seems, in general, that the rate of labour migration drops. The Lacey

Report observed that:

> The further south one comes as opportunities increase for
> earning cash either by working for wages or by growing
> cash crops, the proportion of emigration diminishes. If
> employment is available, and if the price of crops is fair,
> emigration decreases: bad seasons, low prices and
> unemployment send up emigration. We have found that
> among people who are accustomed to emigration the
> balance between the advantage of staying at home and
> growing a crop for sale, on the one side, and the lure of
> employment for wages out of the Protectorate, on the
> other, is a very delicate one. If, for example, the tobacco
> crop is good, the price satisfactory and market facilities
> available there is practically no emigration from the
> producing district: if the crop fails or the price drops, or
> market facilities are lessened, emigration commences
> almost automatically.[22]

Schapera shows variation also with reference to the ownership
of land among the Malete and Tlokwa.[23] Of the percentages
of these people away, approximately twice as many did not
have fields, as those who did. Gulliver's material shows this
even more clearly. From the northern uplands of the area he
studied, with their valuable coffee lands and enough land
available for young people to come and settle, only 20–22 per
cent of his sample were absentees; but for the central region,
too high for rice and too low for coffee, the figure was 25 per
cent. He records 33 per cent on the figure of absentees from
the alluvial plains – where there is insufficient land for
cultivation.[24] Southall's material from Alurland also supports
this conclusion: 15 per cent were absent from Okoro district,
where no cotton will grow; 6 per cent from Jonam where the
cultivation of cotton is not developed; and only 2 per cent from
the Padyere area, which is highly productive of cotton.[25]
Watson has been able to demonstrate this in connection with
the Mambwe of Northern Rhodesia where he has been able to
show that as soon as a large government agency started
operations at the nearby district headquarters, additional
wage-earning opportunities existed locally and the proportion
of men going to the distant labour centres such as the
Copperbelt decreased.[26]

The administrative implication of identifying the necessary conditions of labour migration is that any attempt to control the rate of migration is probably best approached through manipulating the economic factors involved. We sometimes hear of schemes to build cinemas and football fields to provide counter-attractions to young men in rural areas who might otherwise migrate to town. Such schemes, on the basis of our analysis, are bound to be stillborn since they affect the incidental and not the necessary economic conditions underlying labour migration.

The Nexus of Centripetal Tendencies

The essential feature of labour migration is that it is a recurrent phenomenon: the flow from country to town and back from town to country goes on from generation to generation. Sometimes, an African may circulate between labour centres and his rural home for the whole of his working life. Some of the material presented by Houghton and Walton shows this very clearly.[27] One case history shows a man who over 40 years had made no less than 56 separate trips to labour centres. As Houghton observes, there are millions of such Africans who spend their lives alternating between the tribal and the modern industrial worlds.[28]

On what does this instability of residence rest? We may seek a clue to the possible explanation in Prothero's study to which I have already referred. Prothero pointed out that although the opportunities to earn cash in other parts of the region were present, the people he was studying preferred to migrate seasonally to satisfy their economic wants rather than settle in the more productive parts.[29] Prothero suggests an explanation of this preference for migration in terms of the desire of young men to go out into the world to prove themselves in the eyes of their community. It may be more profitable, however, to approach the problem by examining, rather, the resistance to movement. From the point of view of the development of my argument, the significant point appears to be that if a family were to migrate to an area where there are better economic opportunities, they automatically move out of the system of social relationships in which they were formerly immersed. The Nigerians in Prothero's study are apparently able to satisfy their economic needs and at the same time retain their social relationships within the tribal system by engaging in seasonal immigration. The set of social relationships a person builds up in a rural area, therefore, possesses a certain centripetal influence; once the social relationships are built up they are difficult to break. This centripetal influence is connected with the nature of the social system. A person in a social system, particularly in a well-integrated system such as a tribe, occupies a position which links him to many other people around him. These links serve to define for him exactly his rights and obligations towards those persons and it provides for him, as it were, a set of blue-prints by means of which he is able to predict their behaviour towards him. In other words, he lives in an ordered society where his behaviour towards others and others towards him is known and relatively predictable. A person enmeshed in such a system of social relationships, therefore, has that sense of security and confidence that springs from the familiarity of his role *vis-à-vis* his fellows around him. He does not lightly abandon this security for the uncertainty and caprice of the polyglot aggregations of the labour centres.

Watson has been impressed by the significance of land holding as a factor in the security Africans feel in their tribal areas.[30] I would argue that the security the African tribesman feels in his rural environment or alternatively the insecurity he feels in an urban environment is, therefore, not entirely a matter of economic security. It arises also from the psychological security that derives from the network of social relationships in which he is enmeshed. This is the point which the Dow Report makes when it states:

> We think it important to recognise, however, that the removal of the obstacles to the creation of settled labour does not lie solely on the side of urban industry. The creation of new forms of urban security, whether by the provision of pensions for long service, or in other ways, may not be sufficient in themselves to persuade the African to abandon whatever traditional interests he

may possess in tribal areas. Even if we could equate the alternative securities in actuarial terms, which is of course impossible, the comparison would not necessarily exercise its proper influence on the African mind, for the one security appears to him a certainty whereas the other is both novel and conditional.[31]

We may, therefore, look upon labour migration as the resultant of the operation of two opposed influences. From the point of view of the rural areas, the economic drives as a rule operate centrifugally to force men, and sometimes women, outwards to distant labour centres where they are able to earn cash wages to use in order to satisfy their various wants. The social system, operating particularly through the network of social relationships, tends to act centripetally to hold a man within its grip and to resist the influences pulling him away.

It follows from this argument that if a person is able to meet his economic wants while at the same time retaining the network of social relations in which he has become enmeshed, he will do so. Hence, if alternatives to migration exist, as for example by growing cash crops or by finding a wage-earning occupation within the tribal areas, these will be seized upon. The opposition of the centripetal and centrifugal tendencies is, thus, avoided. Once centrifugal have overcome the centripetal tendencies and a man migrates to a labour centre, he is, however, subject to the opposing pulls of these influences. The dilemma in which he finds himself may be resolved either when his economic wants are satisfied and he is drawn back into the social system out of which he recently moved, or when, with continued absence, he starts to build up a new network of social relationships where he happens to be working and these tend to replace and weaken those left behind him.

Labour migration, therefore, looked at in this light is a compromise solution to the opposing pulls to which a tribesman is subjected. As Houghton and Walton point out: 'The reaction to the economic pressure in the Reserve by migrating alone or with his family is an attempt to maintain his family unit and to fulfil his social obligations'.[32]

It follows from this that a man's obligations to his fellows deriving from the system of social relationships in which he is involved may conflict with his obligations to his employer. The migrant's solution to this is to vacillate between the two sets of obligations with the result that the labour turnover is very high. The Lacey Report describes this in vivid terms:

> It seems to be the universal experience that the African labourer, regarded purely as a machine to get work done in the shortest time, works far better away from his own home and country than in it. Family obligations, the necessity for attending every village function, visiting funerals, weddings or the like, have still a strong hold on the worker who is working in the vicinity of his home. He will continually be taking 'off days': he is too much interested in his family and village life. When he goes afield to work – he goes to *work*. He wants to earn as much as he can as soon as he can. There are no family hindrances.[33]

The Plowman Report drew attention to the same point when it observed that: 'Indeed there is reason to believe that the relative ease with which men can see their wives when the rural area is near at hand gives rise to a more regular and disruptive type of absenteeism than occurs when the distances are much greater'.[34] Houghton and Walton draw attention to the high rate of turnover at the Good Hope Textile Factory at Zwelisha. This factory was erected close to a reserve, therefore close to a source of labour, and the conditions of work and the remuneration compared favourably with those in the city. Yet the labour was far from stable.

Houghton and Walton explain this by arguing that in cities the young men are out of reach of parental and tribal sanctions and 'they need send home only as much or as little as they feel inclined'.[35] At Zwelisha, the boys were required by their parents to hand over the bulk of their earnings for the support of the family. This does not immediately explain the high turnover unless we assume that the boys sought work initially at Zwelisha and then went on to the cities to escape these obligations. An alternative explanation is that their obligations to their kin, of which financial support is only one aspect, also involved their presence, as for example at weddings, funerals, ancestor ritual and so on. The pull of the social system in which, by their very proximity, they were still involved took them away from their work at frequent intervals.

By an extension of this reasoning, we are driven to the conclusion that we must seek the 'causes' of continued labour migration as much in the labour centres as in the rural areas, with the labourer newly arrived in a town from the reserve participating in social relationships in two different and possibly unrelated fields. In the first, he is still a member, albeit an absent one, of the rural community he has just left. This is shown by the remittances he sends home, the letters he writes, the visitors he receives, the messages and gifts he sends back with his returning tribesmen. At the same time, he is a member of an urban community building up social relationships with fellow workmen, with his compatriots living in the same town, with co-religionists, with other members of political and social associations. The longer he stays in town and the more tightly the social structure in the town is organized, the more likely it is to form a centripetal influence counteracting similar influences of the tribal social system. Hence, at a certain point of time, he ceases to be a labour migrant and becomes a permanent town-dweller.

The information we now need is that which will enable us to determine the sort of social system in towns which successfully holds persons in opposition to the similar pulls of social systems in the rural areas. About this we know little as yet. Clearly, the whole political setting is of the utmost significance here. If legislation exists, as it does in some parts of Africa, which prevents a man from marrying and settling down in urban areas, then clearly a social system in which he is deeply implicated cannot easily develop. But detailed studies are also needed of urban systems of prestige, of neighborhood cliques, of marriage and kinship and many other similar topics which will enable us to assess their importance in maintaining or reducing the recurrent flow of people between town and country.

On this basis, therefore, we are able to isolate three situations, depending on the relationship of the centrifugal and centripetal influences as I have outlined. We assume that

everywhere the need for money has become important.
Therefore we find:

1   The negation of the centrifugal (economic) influence by
    cash cropping or local employment so that the centripetal
    influences arising from the involvement in a social
    structure prevail. In this situation labour migration is
    absent or infrequent.
2   An oscillating balance between the two influences so that
    economic needs cannot be satisfied in the rural areas and
    people migrate to satisfy their needs. Social obligations in
    the rural areas, however, sooner or later force them back
    again where they once again feel the necessity to seek
    wage-earning occupations. Here, labour migration is
    present.
3   An involvement in a system of social relationships in town
    negating the social obligations in the rural areas so that
    the need to return is reduced. At the same time, the ever-
    expanding economic wants linked with the prestige
    systems in towns implies that the economic pulls remain
    unaltered. Here, labour migration and the circulation
    between town and country ceases.

It will become immediately clear that the rate of labour
migration from any particular area is determined by the
complex interrelationship of all these factors. In empirical
reality, all three of these analytical abstract situations may
exist simultaneously in one area in that some, but insufficient,
local labour or cash cropping may exist and the pattern of
social relationship in the labour centres to which the migrants
go may be as yet unformed. We can only appreciate the causal
factors in labour migration by trying to see town and country
or reserve and labour centre as one social field and to analyse
the forces operating within it.

Postscript, 1988

Any academic paper is always written at a particular juncture
of time and is always conditioned by theoretical and political
issues which are alive at the time. When I was asked to write

something on 'labour migration' in 1956 it was, of course, in
the context of the writing and thinking of which I was aware
at the time. I remember that I was concerned at the time that
there did not seem to be a plausible way of relating the vast
complex of factors which had been mooted as determining the
phenomenon of labour circulation in the colonial Africa in
which I was then working. In particular, there were a number
of explanations of labour circulation, usually of lay origin,
which seemed to me deliberately to ignore the basic economic
underpinnings of the phenomenon. I gave as examples of
these explanations those which attributed the migration of
men away from the rural areas in which they were then living
to such considerations as the wish to experience the exciting
environment of city living, the fear of witchcraft at home and
even a genetically determined drive to move around! The
feature of all of these interpretations was that the basic
economic circumstances underlying the migrations, which
were under a good deal of political control, were totally
ignored. They were essentially monocausal explanations
which ignored unpalatable political facts.

My purpose then was simply to try to point to the
essentially complex nature of the phenomenon by separating
out fundamental structural factors – economic factors – which
on the evidence I had available to me varied concomitantly
with the *rate* of migration and which, therefore, could be
looked upon as factors which possibly could be manipulated
to effect a change in labour circulation if that was required.
The other factors, I argued, referred to a rather different
calculus which required reference to the reaction of particular
kinds of social actors within the context established by the
wider political and economic circumstances over which they
had little control.

That essay, published originally in a rather obscure journal
run by The Commission for Technical Cooperation – an
organization supported by the main colonial powers in Africa
at the time – was subsequently republished in a general reader
edited by John Middleton.[36] It has apparently been fairly
widely referred to in the 30-odd years since then and has
naturally drawn some criticism. The most cogent of these that
I know of was by Colin Murray in what appears to be an

unpublished paper.[37] In this paper Murray seems to have two main objections to the ideas that I put forward. First, because I drew from Durkheim's work on suicide the importance of emphasizing structural as against personal factors for understanding the underlying factors influencing changes in labour circulation over time and between different regions, and because I used Talcott Parsons for the distinction between *rate* and *incidence* (which Durkheim did not use and which seemed to me to capture the distinction I wanted to make), Murray seems to assume that my orientation was essentially a 'functionalist' one. I would maintain, however, that the tone of my analysis was structural.

Rather more important was his criticism that I was treating the personal or 'social factors' as 'motivations' and, therefore, less important than economic factors. He argues, in effect, that the social factors that I emphasized cannot be separated from economic ones. With this I would, of course, agree. In any analysis of reality, a myriad of circumstances are operating to induce people to behave in the way they do. I argue only that the fieldworker engaged in studying the complex set of activities surrounding a phenomenon such as labour migration must of necessity treat various elements which clearly have a bearing on the phenomenon under consideration in different degrees of detail. My own training and interests led me to treat the wider political and economic circumstances which indubitably underlay processes of labour circulation as relatively given and to concentrate, not on motivations as Murray seems to assume, but on the nexus of social relationships which bound people together in both rural and urban circumstances, and which provided pressures persuading people to seek wage employment in the towns or, alternatively, to stay in their rural villages. The original purpose of my essay was to plead for a more detailed assembly of empirical evidence relating to labour circulation instructed by more rigorous analytical frameworks. If in the years my essay has had this effect, then it has not all been in vain.

Notes and References

1 D. H. Houghton, 'Migrant Labour', in: P. Smith (ed.), *Africa in Transition* (London, Reinhardt, 1958) p. 42.

2 P. H. Gulliver, 'Nyakyusa labour migration' *Rhodes-Livingstone Journal*, 2139–68, 1957 p. 58.

3 I. Schapera, *Migrant Labour and Tribal Life* (London, Oxford University Press, 1947).

4 Nyasaland Government, *Report of the Committee appointed by H. E. the Governor to Enquire into Emigrant Labour* (Nyasaland, Zomba, Government Printer, 1935), pp. 20ff. Known as the Lacey Report.

5 M. Read, 'Migrant Labour in Africa and its Effects on Tribal Life', *International Labour Review* 14(6) 1942, p. 617.

6 *Ibid.*, p. 626.

7 A. I. Richards (ed.), *Economic Development and Tribal Change* (Cambridge, Heffer, 1954), pp. 64–72.

8 A. Southall, 'Alur Immigrants' in Richards, *Development and Tribal Change*, pp. 141–60.

9 R. D. H. Houghton and E. H. Walton, *The Economy of Native Reserve, Kieskammahoek Rural Survey* (Pietermaritzburg, Shuter and Shooter, 1952). Vol. II.

10 P. H. Gulliver, Labour Migration in a Rural Economy, *East African Studies 6* (Kampala, East African Institute for Social Research, 1955).

11 Gulliver, 'Nyakyusa labour migration'.

12 R. M. Prothero, 'Migratory Labour from North-Western Nigeria', *Africa*, 27 (3) (1934), pp. 251–61.

13 E. H. Winter, 'Bwamba Economy' *East Africa Studies 5* (Kampala, East African Institute for Social Research, 1955).

14 Richards, *Development and Tribal Change*, p. 66.

15 Gulliver, 'Nyakyusa labour migration', p. 59.

16 T. Parsons, *The Structure of Social Action* (London, Allen and Unwin, 1937).

17 E. Durkheim, *Suicide: A Study in Sociology* (London, Routledge and Kegan Paul, 1952), pp. 145–51.

18 Schapera, *Migrant Labour and Tribal Life*, p. 121.

19 Prothero, 'Migratory Labour from Nigeria'.

20 Schapera, *Migrant Labour and Tribal Life*, p. 144.

21 Houghton and Walton, *Native Reserve Kieskammahoek*, p. 87.

22 Lacey Report, para 42.22.

23 Schapera, *Migrant Labour and Tribal Life*.

24 Gulliver, 'Nyakyusa labour migration'.

25 Southall, 'Alur Immigrants'.

26 W. Watson, *Tribal Cohesion in a Money Economy* (Manchester, Manchester University Press, 1958).

27 Houghton and Walton, *Native Reserve Kieskammahoek*, pp. 120–4.

28 Houghton, 'Migrant Labour', p. 42.

29 Prothero, 'Migratory Labour from Nigeria', p. 258.

30 Watson, 'Tribal Cohesion'.
31 British Government, *Report of the East Africa Royal Commission 1953–55* (London, HMSO, 1955). Known as the Dow Report.
32 Houghton and Walton, *Native Reserve Kieskammahoek*, p. 119.
33 Lacey Report, p. 20.
34 Plowman Report, Southern Rhodesia Government, 1958, p. 18.
35 Houghton and Walton, *Native Reserve Kieskammahoek*, p. 119.
36 J. Middleton (ed.), *Black Africa: Its Peoples and Cultures Today* (New York, Macmillan, 1970).
37 C. Murray, 'Explaining Migration: The Tradition in Eastern and Southern Africa', Paper given at the Institute of Commonwealth Studies, London, 1979.

The Formation of the Contract Labour System in Namibia, 1900–1926

Richard J. B. Moorsom

Introduction

This paper is presented as a contribution towards the analysis of the political economy of Namibia. More particularly, it investigates the origins of an institutionalized structure of labour exploitation central to colonial power and profit – the contract labour system.[1] It is exploratory in character. Not being based primarily on archival research, it attempts to synthesize a broad interpretation of one of the major historical processes in the colonization of the region.

The origins of the paper lie in the pioneering phase of modern Namibian historiography, during which the extraordinarily brutal system of labour coercion imposed by the German colonial regime was a principal focus of research.[2] On the region now divided between northern Namibia and south-western Angola, the more protracted process of economic incorporation and political colonization and the origins of labour migration were the principal themes.[3] More recently, the pace of research on the transitional period (c. 1870–1930) has intensified: the coordinated Finnish history project is yielding its first results; and theses are in preparation on mission ideology and early labour migration.[4] For the first time, the extensive mission, administrative and private archival resources are being professionally researched and the results will modify and deepen our understanding of a key period and region in the history of south-western Africa, both largely neglected hitherto.

In Namibia, colonization proper was telescoped into a 20-year period under German rule. Not until the 1890s was over half a century of 'informal colonialism' whose chief agents were itinerant traders and missionaries, reinforced by German military intervention. Yet by the outbreak of the First World War, most of the land in southern and central Namibia had been expropriated, some of it already settled with immigrant farmers; internal resistance had been crushed in genocidal war; and the Namib diamond deposits and Tsumeb copper, still among the territory's main mineral resources, had been put into full production by international mining capital.

None of the sectors of capital that developed during this period had more than a marginal interest in the human resources of the country except as labour-power, whose recruitment, distribution and control were from the start among the principal functions of the colonial administration. However, the terrible cost exacted by the initial phase of military conquest was sufficient to deter the German colonizers from completing the physical separation of subsistence agriculturalists from their means of production. From 1904, the year of the great uprising against colonial rule, the level of resentment from the ranks of the dispossessed consistently failed to meet the aggregate labour demand of colonial capital and the state. It became the central motive of both German and South African colonial regimes, in conserving the remaining areas of subsistence production, to close this gap with migrant labour and to secure the latter's long-term reproduction.

On the Class Analysis of Labour Migration

I do not intend to enter here into the complex debate on the articulation of non-capitalist with capitalist modes of production. However, since my analysis is informed by both the problematic and the debate, it is necessary to touch on a few conceptual issues. Labour migration implies the articulation of two modes of production within a single social formation, the dominant mode in this case being capitalist. At an advanced stage, as in parts of the South African reserves, such articulation may entail the complete dissolution of non-capitalist relations of production. At its formation, the system may follow the extension of the political hegemony of a capitalist state over a previously politically autonomous non-capitalist formation. Even at the outset, however, as will be seen in this study, the articulation may operate more strongly at the economic than at the political level. A proportion of the direct producers in the non-capitalist formation may be compelled, for temporary or permanent want of their subsistence by other means, to sell their labour-power before separation from their means of production at the hands of capitalists or, more forcibly, the capitalist state.

The particular configuration of capitalist interest within the state – perhaps even independently of it – will have a strong bearing on the form and scale of recurrent labour migration it attempts to institute. However, the system that finally emerges under capitalist control is forged in a complex process of struggle and collaboration with non-migrant workers, with the exploiters, the exploited and the marginalized in the non-capitalist social order, as well as with the migrant labourers themselves. For the non-capitalist society, into which the capitalist state intervenes politically to subordinate it to its production needs, is often not – as it was not in Namibia – in a pristine state of 'primitive communism', whether differentiation was generated by indigenous or external forces. Where antagonistic social relations are incipient or developed, the politics of alliance and conflict between classes from different modes of production within a common social formation is integral to the analysis. Under such circumstances, labour migrants face struggle on two fronts. This double dimension of class conflict, once placed in the centre ground of the historical process, allows space to the underclasses as well as to the rulers as historical subjects.

The analytical framework is still incomplete, for there is a further and equally fundamental dimension of exploitation and conflict – the exploitation of women or, as some would define it, the sphere of patriarchy. This theme can receive only limited treatment here, a product both of the silences in many of the published and archival sources, of many of the already scanty written sources, and of the formative state of much feminist theory, particularly as applied to social analysis in the Southern African context. It is, nevertheless, a central plank of the argument presented here, for one of the most striking features of the contract labour system that was constructed in Namibia was its attempts to exclude all rural women from the north from wage labour. This exclusion cannot be fully explained by deploying 'patriarchy' simply as a description of male privilege or the subordination of women, for, as with other social hierarchies, the social interest and the source of power of the advantaged and the oppressors remain untouched. Nor is it sufficient to define it in terms solely of other particular modes of production, in other words, a concept with only relative (and hence subordinate) autonomy. To do so is to reduce the different forms it takes to a set of arbitrary particularisms, related not by their common content but by their location in other varieties of class oppression.

The standpoint taken here is, rather, that patriarchy is amenable to materialist analysis as a species of exploitation in an absolute sense: it may be specified in the absence of other forms of class 'exploitation and, although this may be anathema to a strong current in the socialist feminist critique of capitalist society, it may equally be absent in their presence. As such it refers to an appropriation of surplus labour, both productive and non-productive, within or by means of the domestic or household economy. Why gender should become the criterion of class identity and men rather than women the exploiters requires, like racialism, particular historical explanations, for there are exceptions as well as an infinite variety of forms.

That explanation, in turn, however, requires the prior concept of patriarchal exploitation. It also entails acceptance of the plurality of class exploitation and the complex, almost contradictory, nature of the notion of objective class position. Historically, patriarchy has usually coexisted with, and its classes have participated in, other modes of production. Male household heads or female housewives may at the same time be landlords, capitalists or petty commodity producers, wage labourers, or perhaps none of these. A similar plurality in the relations of production governing the productive labour of migrating workers is an essential concept in understanding the strategies of struggle and survival under the migrant labour system.

This interpretation has an important bearing on the analysis of labour migration in the Namibian context. First, it directs attention to social relations between men and women in non-capitalist as well as capitalist society, especially where other forms of class exploitation are non-existent or incipient. The demand for male rather than female labourers may not be solely the product of the ideological expectations of the executives of the intruding capitalist class. Second, it brings household labour, servicing as well as productive, into the foreground of the analysis of the relations of production and the restructuring of the labour process, urban as well as rural. Third, it brings women into the foreground in analysing the complex class conflicts which created the contract labour system not merely as a residual peasantry, or the passive and shadowy appendages of a stratum of the new Namibian working class, but as a specific class with its own interests, consciousness and sphere of struggle.

Capital Formation and Labour Demand

The Ovambo–Nkhumbi population zone forms an island of dense settlement near the northern edge of the vast Kalahari basin. Largely waterless during the dry winter, in the mid-nineteenth century the Kalahari sandveld was occupied, except along the few perennial rivers, by dispersed bands of nomadic hunter-gatherers and cattle-pastoralists. During the 1840s and 1850s, itinerant traders rapidly established a network of routes and exchange relations throughout the interior. Ovamboland became the interface between three such routes, based on Walvis Bay, Mossamedes, and Lake Ngami and the 'missionary road' through Botswana.

The agrarian societies of the interior were thus articulated by means of commercial ties to the metropoles of world capitalism in an epoch of industrialization. Yet, for over half a century thereafter, attempts to start up local production in capitalist enterprises were spasmodic, small-scale and mostly short-lived. Such attempts included intermittent copper mining

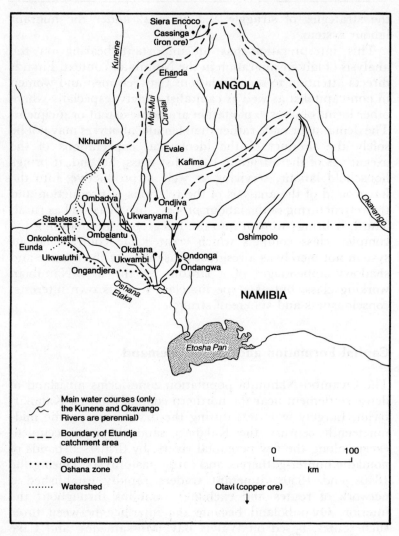

Map 1 Ovamboland

in central Namibia; guano (bird-dung) recovery and sealing along the southern Namib coast; fishing and oasis plantation agriculture in the northern Namib (southern Angola); settler farming around the southern Angolan escarpment; and caravan and later ox-wagon transport. Nowhere before the late 1890s was potential labour demand substantial or regular. Nor, when it did exist, were either the relations of production those of wage labour – slavery predominated in coastal Angola and quasi-feudal bonds in settler agriculture – or the preferred sources of supply wholly or partially internal to local social formations.[5] Thus, at the same time that the penetration of commodity exchange was catalysing incipient class antagonisms within the Ovambo social formation which, as will be shown, was generating a stratum of marginalized men, the local demand for wage labourers remained insignificant.

From the late 1880s, European and South African based corporate capital dominated local investment, if at first only negatively. Before the national uprising of 1904, its primary interest was to speculate and to exclude competitors by securing exclusive concessions to land and mineral rights. Only where major mineral reserves were proven – copper at Tsumeb (1906) and diamonds in the southern Namib (1908) – did corporate capital move decisively into local extractive production.

German colonization policy, however, for political reasons outside the scope of this analysis, was not exclusively or at times even predominantly tied to the interests of German *Grosskapital*. From the mid-1890s, the point at which the German imperial state assumed decisive control of the colonization process, a principal objective was the establishment by state- and privately-sponsored schemes of capitalist settler agriculture on expropriated tribal lands in central and southern Namibia. Colonization itself necessitated fluctuating but often large-scale expenditure both on infrastructural projects, notably railways, and on administration and the forces of repression. After the South African military conquest in 1915, military and infrastructural expenditure was substantially reduced. On the other hand, the pace of land settlement

was stepped up, with greater tolerance of peasant as opposed
to capitalist farming by the incoming settlers.
The formation of the colonial economy thus falls into two
broad stages. Between 1894 and 1904 – the years of piecemeal
conquest – agricultural settlement was sparse, unstable and
barely capitalist. An inflated bureaucracy and military
establishment sustained large- and small-scale transport and
construction contractors, and a mainly urban petty-bourgeoisie.
After the uprising, a minority of capitalist farmers were
augmented by increasing numbers of marginally subsistent
peasant settlers; capital expenditure by the state continued at
a high level for over a decade more; and the territory's two
large mines began full production.

The level of wage employment in the colonial economy is
hard to gauge from the few available published sources,
though it is likely that it continued to fluctuate markedly after
the national uprising (1904–7). More significant for colonial
recruitment policy was the gap between the aggregate
demand for local labour and the potentially available supply
from that part of the indigenous population subject to the
coercive activity of the colonial state locally – broadly
speaking those living in the aptly named 'Police Zone' which
comprised the whole of the centre and south of Namibia
brought under direct German rule. Prior to the uprising, the
demand was largely fulfilled except for brief periods on large-
scale production projects. The methods of recruitment ranged
from free wage labour to the forced labour of prisoners of war.
During the 1904–7 war, absolute demand expanded rapidly,
and for a decade thereafter remained at a high though
fluctuating level. The national uprising marked the total
collapse of the gradualist policy of piecemeal exploitation and
accelerated underdevelopment that had been officially in force
since 1894.[6] The disaster was compounded by the military
intervention of the imperial power, whose deliberate strategy
of genocide destroyed an estimated 60 per cent of the black
population in the Police Zone.

The result was a major and chronic aggregate labour
shortage which conscripted labour and the forced labour code
of 1907 could do little to resolve, even if they had been
completely successful. The prolonged passive resistance by

the expropriated peoples, which took the forms of emigration, desertion, illegal mobility and collective celibacy,[7] ensured that this optimum was not attained and deepened the crisis of labour supply, a crisis that equally confronted the South African regime after it took over in 1915.

The crisis was, at least after 1904, in no way open to resolution by varying wage rates or working conditions. The major employers were, therefore, compelled to seek to recruit outside the political domain of the colonial state. Neither companies nor administration were well placed economically or politically to compete on the world market for indentured labour. Most attempts failed, except within Southern Africa, which was in any case an uncertain source of supply owing to the overriding sub-continental power of Rand mining capital. At the height of railway building in 1913, the number of 'Cape Boys' (mainly Transkei Africans) employed in Namibia reached a temporary peak of 11,000, about 25 per cent of the entire wage labour force. In 1923–4, Consolidated Diamonds Mines (CDM) could manage only with difficulty to recruit labourers elsewhere in Southern Africa to break an Ovambo boycott. It had, however, been recognized as early as 1904 that Ovamboland was to be the principal external source of labour-power, whose form, both at its inception and throughout its institution, was to remain that of recurrent labour migration on fixed-term contracts.

The migration of Ovambo men as wage labourers, however, did not simply 'happen'. It is the task of the remainder of this paper to propose explanations for several of the principal outstanding questions:

1 Why did the initial demand for labourers between 1905 and 1909 meet with so massive a response when even the rudiments of a recruiting organization and of means of direct inducement and coercion were lacking? Explanation must be rooted in the specific trajectories of social transformation in the Ovambo social formation, particularly in incipient class antagonism.
2 When the supply of labourers continued to fail to meet its aggregate requirements, why did the German colonial state not move to complete the forcible dispossession of the

peoples within its allotted domain? Why, too, did the post-
1915 South African regime, which did bring Ovamboland
under its direct administration, perpetuate the policy?

3 What were the concrete conditions of struggle for labour
migrants within both modes of production, and how
successfully did they exploit them? In particular, why was
it necessary for the South African administration, ten
years after the conquest, to bring the recruitment and
distribution of all Ovambo labour migrants under the
control of a monopoly labour organization?

Ecology and the Ovambo Social Formation

Precise specification of the Ovambo mode of production prior
to its penetration by commodity exchange relations is not
possible here, for lack of detailed contemporary descriptive
accounts, anthropological studies, or oral evidence.[8] It is
apparent, however, that the local ecology established particular limiting conditions given a low level of development of the
productive forces.[9] Average rainfall allows adequate pasturage
for cattle pastoralism over much of the subcontinental
Kalahari basin and suffices over the northern half for dryland
cereal cropping which becomes marginal below about 450 mm
per annum. But the deep Kalahari sands restrict the potential
of each, in the case of the former by phosphorous deficiency, of
the latter by low organic content, and of both, crucially, by the
lack of surface water, which is almost totally absent throughout
the rainless winter.

Ovamboland forms the level flood-plain of one major and
several minor wet-season rivers rising to the north, whose
flood-waters combine with local run-off to percolate through a
maze of shallow channels (*oshana*) towards the Etosha Pan. It
therefore benefits in two respects: alluvial sediment, although
poor, slightly increases the potential crop yield; and a leached
impervious sub-soil layer improves the retention of fresh water
above the deeper saline groundwater. Water is thus generally
accessible for approximately half the year on the surface and
for the remainder of the year underground at shallow depths.
These advantages are qualified by the general unreliability of

Table 1 Climatic and harvest data, 1868–1937

Year	Regional rainfall %	Floodplain		NE		Central		SW	
		R	H	R	H	R	H	R	H
1868–9			Fam						
1872–5		D							
1878–9		D							
1879		D	H–						
1880			Fam						
1881									
1882									
1883									
1884	113								
1885	132								
1886									
1887	129						Fl		
1888	58						Dx		
1889	61						Dx		
1890	84						N		
1891									
1892	143						F		
1893	174						F		
1894	83								
1895	65								
1896	50								
1897		125P (rinderpest)							
1898	129								
1899	126								
1900	87	D							
1901	68	D							
1902	82	D							
1903	61	D					N		
1904	111						N		
1905	101						H–		
1906	92						N		
1907	103	P (locusts)			Fl		N		
1908	68				Fam	D	Dx		D
1909	160	Fl	H		Fl		Fl		
1910	122				N		N		
1911	42				Fam	Dx	Dx		
1912	122						N		D
1913	54			H–	N	D	H–		Dx
1914	82	P (caterpillars)				D	H–/Hx		

Table 1 Continued

Year	Regional rainfall %	Floodplain R	Floodplain H	NE R	NE H	Central R	Central H	SW R	SW H
1915	81		Fam	Fam		Dx	Hx		Fam
1916	51	Dx	Fam						
1917	139								
1918	106	D	H–						
1919	56	D	H–						
1920	91	D				D			H–
1921	123								
1922	43	Dx							
1923	133	N	H+						
1924	71	D	H–	H–	N			Dx	
1925	164	Fl	H+	H	Fl				
1926	74		H/H–						
1927	93	D	H						
1928	88	D	H–	H					
1929	55	Dx	Fam	H–			Hx		Hx
1930	56	Dx	Fam	H–			Hx		Hx
1931	87		H/H+						
1932	56	Dx	H–/Hx	Hx					
1933	50	Dx	H–/Hx	H–			H–/Hx		H–/Hx
1934	211	Fl	H/H+						
1935	84			N	H	Dx		Dx	
1936	93	N	H						
1937	96	N	H+						

Note: 'Regional rainfall' is Wellington's table of annual mean rainfall for Namibia north of Windhoek. For Ovamboland, the figures are here related to a long-term mean of 450 mm. However, in many years rainfall figures are lacking or incomplete and descriptive information has been used where available.

Symbols:

Rainfall (R):
Fl – Floods (over 150%)
N – Normal (85–150%)
D – Drought (under 85%)
Dx – Severe drought (under 70%)

Harvest (H):
H+ – In surplus
H – Adequate
H– – Poor
Hx – Crop failure
Fam – Famine

General:
P – Pestilence (rinderpest, locusts, caterpillars etc.)
Blank – no available data

Source: J. H. Wellington, *SWA and its human issues* (Oxford, Clarendon Press, 1967), p. 43; published station records; contemporary descriptive accounts, mainly from missionary sources.

annual rainfall; by drought being usually worsened by the simultaneous failure of the seasonal flood-waters (*efundja*); by the unpredictable incidence of rainfall across the growing season; and by its uneven regional and local distribution. (See table 1.) Furthermore, those indices of unreliability increase from north-east to south-west as the average rainfall decreases and the external floodwater catchment area shrinks. The southern margin of the floodplain coincides roughly with an annual rainfall of 400 mm, sub-marginal for cropping.

The precise linkage between these ecological constraints and the overall settlement pattern is, at present, obscure. In the mid-nineteenth century, as at colonization in 1915, the Ovambo population was clustered into continuously and densely settled pockets, separated by uninhabited swathes of virgin woodland and pasture. The territory of each cluster was defined, as we shall see, by a unitary political system, though its precise form varied. Few significant ties of reciprocity existed between clusters at either the ideological or the economic level. The major exception was trade in three principal manufactures (copper and iron artifacts, and salt), the production of which was dominated by single or associated clusters,[10] and more irregularly, in foodstuffs, handicrafts and war captives.

Most of the clusters lay astride a major *oshana*, emphasizing the critical importance of dry-season water supplies. Furthermore, cluster size decreased dramatically from north-east to south-west. The source of this systematic variation is not to be sought in the nature or the level of the productive forces, which appear to have been similar across the whole social formation. Instruments manufactured by handicraft were the principal means in all branches of production, both direct (hunting, fishing) and processing (crops, animal products), except one (gathering of wild plants); as well as in household production. Given an iron-age technology, the principal instruments of production (spear, bow, knife, hoe) and storage (stockade, pottery, basketry) were probably near full development and were widely distributed through the social formation. The reasons for the variation in scale and for the clustering itself, which the ecological conditions made possible, must therefore be sought in the social relations of production within each cluster.

At first sight, the dominant mode of production in Ovamboland appears straightforwardly enough to be a lineage mode. The social product was appropriated to a limited extent individually, notably cow's milk by herders while on seasonal migration, but for the most part communally, through a variety of overlapping mechanisms generally coinciding with the major sources of subsistence. Surplus labour fell largely into the second category; and the whole was anyway determined at the ideological level by hierarchies of kinship ties that constituted the relations of production. The primary unit of production was the extended family, settled in a single stockaded homestead situated in the midst of its own fields. Distribution of the main food staples (millet meal and sorghum beer, and domestic animal products, especially from cattle) as well as subsidiary and seasonal supplements (game, fish, wild herbs and fruit) was organized according to complex rules within this social unit under the overriding authority of the usually male homestead head.

Wider networks of circulation also operated, however. Locality-based working parties would be called upon in exchange for standard rewards of food and drink at points of peak labour input in the cropping cycle (field-clearing, harvesting) and for the frequent resiting of the homestead necessitated by termite attrition of the stockades. Social and ritual celebrations, as well as hospitality, also redistributed surplus labour within a wider social network, framed by both neighbourhood and kinship ties. Kinship relations were organized into matriclans, which for the purposes of redistribution served three main functions: first, the allocation of cattle on a share-cropping basis; second, the inheritance of non-personal moveable property, notably cattle; and third, by the rule of clan exogamy, the exchange of wives. The combination of matrilineality with patrilocal residence entailed the broad territorial dispersal of means of production and subsistence, principally cattle, and a framework of social relations defined at the level of the population cluster.

The advantages of extended and complex reciprocity, given a high incidence of both local and regional climatic fluctuation and the devastating coincidence of deficiencies in natural resources induced by drought, do not require elaboration. Food storage precautions within the primary production unit, notably the basket granary capable of holding up to five years of grain supplies, bear additional testimony. The survival of small clusters on the marginal south-western edge of the flood-plain suggests that lineage social relations were a sufficient condition for the long-term reproduction of the social formation. However, occasional sequences of severe drought, on average once in about 30 years, could kill an appreciable proportion of the population by both famine and drought.[11]

There are, nevertheless, aspects of the social formation for which lineage relations of production cannot fully account. In the small and even the medium-sized clusters, for instance Ombalantu and Ombadya, it is probable that such relations could structure real appropriation in its variety of forms to the limits of its general ecological potential. Although it is not possible on the available evidence to posit an optimum cluster size, however, the proposition becomes increasingly untenable for the largest clusters. This conclusion presumes a generally uniform instrument technology and the universality of the dispersed settlement pattern, which did in fact continue to hold until at least the late 1950s.

The tenacity of the resistance to village formation cannot be fully explained on available data, but may well be associated with: (i) field manuring by rotation of the homestead site and (ii) in view of the concentration of sites in *oshana* margins, optimal articulation between the principal sites of labour. Any substantial increase in the size of a population cluster, therefore, entailed a lateral expansion in its settlement area. Beyond a certain point, such expansion would begin to impede access for those near the centre to important directly appropriated natural resources and to cattle pasture, to an extent beyond the capacity of lineage reciprocity to compensate.

By-passing the theoretical controversy on this point,[12] we may specify the social relations that integrated these larger communities as a tributary mode of production. In the two large (Ondonga and Ukwanyama) and some of the medium-sized clusters (Ongandjera, Ukwambi, Ukwanyama), the heads of particular matriclans had, by the mid-nineteenth

century, inserted themselves at the ideological level by
claiming religious and ritual powers, most critically to make
rain and, at the political level, by asserting the hereditary
transmission of the rights to govern, to make war, to exert
judicial and limited legislative authority, to exact customarily
defined tributes, and to apportion land. The tributary mode
did make possible a limited development of the productive
forces, though more by increasing labour productivity and
insurance against climatic uncertainty, than by instituting
new methods of production. It was distinguished by the
conservation of natural resources (wood, certain fruit trees,
dry-season cattle pasture) and especially of the wells which
guaranteed dry-season water supplies; and by the central
regulation of the timing and articulation of the seasonal
production cycle.[13] It was precisely in Ukwanyama, the
largest cluster, in which the regulatory and military powers of
the state were highly developed, that systematic exploitation
of wet-season pastures outside the flood-plain through large-
scale seasonal cattle migration was the most advanced.

It is uncertain to what extent surplus labour was expanded
under the incipient tributary mode. It was, however, under
centralized kingships, and again to the fullest extent in
Ukwanyama, that strata of specialist trader-artisans formed.
Tightly controlled by the kings – a control later exercised over
European traders – these strata remained part-time specialists
despite establishing long-distance networks of exchange.
Nowhere in the Ovambo social formation was class formation
more than incipient, and hesitantly so.

The postulation of a tributary mode implies its coexistence
with the lineage mode. Despite the obvious political dominance
of its hereditary governing stratum, it is not possible for
reasons of scarce evidence cited earlier, to specify either the
precise balance in relations between the two, or the main
historical trend in the transformation of that balance, except
that it was slow and irregular. Appropriation of surplus
labour through the exaction of tribute was irregular, ill-
defined and small-scale. The bulk of the product at the king's
disposal was produced directly by his own household, which
differed from others only in scale and its elaborate functional
social organization. Indeed, the king's right to communal

labour for field work and for resiting the royal kraal can be interpreted as the exploitation of standard lineage reciprocity.

Kinship tensions within the royal clan and the continuing *de facto* authority of leading members of other clans severely inhibited despotic tendencies. This was expressed at the level of the state by, in particular, customary restrictions on the king's marriage policy and by commoner representation through a consultative council. In executive functions, it limited the king's role as war leader and allowed clan leaders to assume formally delegated royal prerogatives such as land allocation. That contradictions in the coexistence of the two modes did exist occasionally found dramatic evidence in moments of crisis in a medium-sized cluster, when the failure of a major function of the tributary political leadership, often rain-making, could lead to its overthrow.

Patriarchy formed the third mode of production to be found in precolonial Ovambo society, and its social relations were more pervasive than those of the tributary mode. It was founded on the monopoly of male household heads over the lifetime use-right to the family homestead and fields. Women could survive only as wives or as subordinate kin in the households of male relatives, and only in rare cases had direct access to land, whether household or commonage. Men appropriated women's labour mainly in the form of services within the household (house maintenance, food preparation, fetching water, care of young children), but also from productive agricultural labour. This was divided according to sex, men controlling hunting and cattle, the principal source of animal protein and store of wealth, leaving women to undertake the cultivation and gathering of grain and vegetables.[14]

A fair measure of reciprocity, nevertheless, remained in the consumption of the products of men's and women's labour, as also in the training of children to their adult gender skills and social identity. Furthermore, women were able as of right to appropriate much of their field and handicraft labour and to engage in trading. In particular, women worked their own fields as well as their husbands', and appropriated the product directly for the consumption of their immediate families and for exchange when in surplus. Furthermore, since there was no bridewealth, although marriage was inescapable, women retained the possibility of mobility for themselves and their children, and thereby real bargaining power. In both household and agricultural labour, and in the field of matrilineal kinship relations, women also retained a substantial degree of autonomy, probably more so than in the Nguni societies of south-eastern Africa. Nevertheless, men's managerial authority and control over accumulated wealth remained dominant. The acquisition of women as field-workers, housewives and mothers was the chief mechanism by which male household heads expanded household production and their own personal consumption, and polygamous marriage was the usual method of exchange of women's labour.

Little attention has, thus far, been devoted either to the technical division of labour or to forms of cooperation in the labour process. Where the labour processes of two modes of production are articulated, it is the dominant mode which, although modified by class struggle, will be able in the main to structure the subordinate process to its requirements and to exploit its internal weaknesses when the two are dissonant. Of concern here is not the long-term disruptive impact of articulation with capitalism on the non-capitalist mode as such, but the space for struggle by migrant workers subject to the structural determination of such articulation. Capital and the colonial state called forth, specifically, young to middle-aged men as wage labourers. As we will see, it was precisely this category whose role in the labour processes of both modes of production of Ovambo society was the most drastically modified by the catalytic intrusion of commodity exchange relations.

The forms of cooperation bear a different significance. No peasants, suddenly proletarianized, whether temporarily or long-term, enter the new relations of production with a blank consciousness. Their past socialization will modify their ability to develop new tactics of struggle under new antagonistic social relations. In particular, experience of cooperative labour, whether or not productive, may provide models for building collective methods of resistance where of necessity a proletarian tradition is still embryonic.

External Trade and Class Polarization

The first Portuguese traders reached Ovamboland from the north in the late 1840s. Within a decade, regular trade relations through Mossamedes and Walvis Bay, and from the late 1870s through the central Kalahari, had brought Ovamboland into the global sphere of commodity exchange. Although control of trading and of trade credit was soon highly centralized, throughout the precolonial period its scope was restricted by fluctuations in the pattern of industrial capitalist demand, by the distance and difficulty of the trade routes and by the carrying capacity of ox-wagon transport. Thus, traders sought raw materials in commercial demand with a high price-to-weight ratio, such as ivory, and a market for field crops never developed. Limited and unstable local markets also developed for cattle and slaves, whose particular advantage was that they could transport themselves to the market.

It is impossible, because of the lack of data, to make any precise calculation of the scale of the trade.[15] Nevertheless, its general course is reasonably clear. Between the 1850s and early 1880s, the principal export commodity was ivory and, to a lesser extent, ostrich feathers. In return, the Ovambo kings, victims between 1859 and 1863 of armed incursions from the west by a Portuguese military expedition and from the south by the Oorlam ruler, Jonker Afrikaner, demanded arms. The power of the tributary states was sufficient to enable them to regulate ivory hunting by foreign traders and impose a substantial levy on its proceeds. Firearms, initially sought for defence against external aggression, were turned also to productive use as the kings themselves accumulated ivory for sale. Since elephants were not an existing subsistence resource and the local labour diverted into hunting them was minimal, the relations of production were barely affected.

However, the kings' ability to extend the control they exerted over their own specialized artisan-traders to the commercial agents of capitalism strengthened their political and economic power in crucial respects. Besides extracting a substantial levy in kind in desired commodities, they were able to regulate both the scale and, to a certain extent, the content of direct exchange between traders and peasants. Thus, in the first phase, firearms were reserved as a royal monopoly, and barter trade was restricted principally to luxury manufactures in return for ivory and cattle. Firearms greatly increased the potential productivity of royal hunting and were directly appropriated. The king's monopoly over the principal trade commodity tied the content of capitalist manufactures for which they were willing to exchange it to their own luxury consumption. Together with the large subsistence resources at their disposal, it enabled them to expand their political power through mechanisms of patronage.

The Ovambo kings, however, permitted hunting on a scale far beyond the animals' natural reproductive capacity and, by the early 1880s, the elephant and ostrich population had been all but wiped out. By now, although evidence is sparse, the kings were already substantially dependent on imported arms and luxury goods, the former for general defence against external aggression and for the competitive local petty raiding that had long been traditional, the latter principally as means of political patronage, and both for prestige. Lacking alternative raw materials in demand on industrial capitalist markets, they were compelled to resort to the only commodity saleable on local markets – cattle and slaves. Cattle were used as feedstock in the trading and missionary network. More particularly, flourishing export markets had opened up by the early 1890s among the emigrant Boers on the Humpata plateau, in the Atlantic plantation islands via Mossamedes, and along Rhodes's Bechuanaland railway.[16] Slaves could be sold to the Ovimbundu in central Angola, although the trade in people was never large-scale.

Cattle were a principal subsistence resource, and the appropriation of both them and slaves as trade commodities could only proceed by means of antagonistic social relations. To achieve their ends, the kings transformed or redirected several pre-existing methods of surplus appropriation. Probably anxious to minimize the risk of internal resistance, they channelled their newly acquired military technology into external raiding. Small-scale inter-tribal raiding, seizing cattle and people, who were ransomed or incorporated into lineages as debt slaves, appears to have generally intensified during the

1880s and 1890s. Simultaneously, long-distance raiding, of which Ukwanyama was the leading exponent, developed to the north for cattle and slaves, who were either absorbed or sold to traders. Increasingly, however, the kings resorted to internal expropriation, mostly in the form of cattle. The frequency of witchcraft accusations and 'judicial raids', traditionally sanctioned instruments of political policy, and taxation on wealth, exceeded their ideological legitimacy to become arbitrary exactions. Above all, the *okasavu*, formerly 'the traditional ritual seizure of cattle for the king's court, became a harsh and arbitrary tax',[17] its voluntary nature superseded by military force.

It is important to note that intensified surplus appropriation by the tributary state was firmly established before the rinderpest disaster struck Ovamboland in 1897. The diary of the Swedish traveller Möller, who crossed the area in 1895–6, mentions Ovambo refugees settled in the middle Kunene, mainly from Ukwanyama and Ukwambi. Most 'have left their tribe to escape the oppression and system of plunder that the despotic chiefs exercise towards their people. It is particularly the cattle that the chiefs extort for themselves.' An accurate reporter, Möller's assessment of Ukwanyama,[18] less than two years before the rinderpest catastrophe, is suggestive. Weyulu, the king, himself owned 'about 20 excellent modern guns', and 'about as many horses', the latter bought for about 60 oxen each. He was able to offer £25 in gold coins for Möller's repeating rifle. Weyulu hinted in conversation that long-distance raiding was the principal means of supporting such an investment, but still found it necessary, according to Möller, to 'tax his people very heavily in their cattle'. Despite the constant circulation of functionaries between court and country, he did not possess sufficient 'iron discipline' to prevent a constant trickle of emigration.

Initially, the embryonic tributary state lacked even a rudimentary apparatus of coercion outside the royal entourage. However, the escalation of raiding, especially of regular long-distance expeditions, 'led to the formation at court of a permanent group of war leaders, the *lenga*, each of whom received a horse and a number of rifles from the king and led a body of about 100 men on raiding expeditions'.[19] This new

stratum of military leaders, normally recruited on grounds of
ability rather than lineage authority,[20] built up personal
wealth and a body of retainers proportionate to their success
in royal service, to counterbalance which the state possessed
neither an administrative bureaucracy nor ideological legitimation for its oppressive role. To a limited extent the *lenga*
could, therefore, exploit the contradiction between the king's
needs to increase the rate of appropriation and his delegating
the power essential to achieve it in order to consolidate their
relative autonomy. One instance of the ideological expression
of this tension is given by Möller, who noted the use in
Ukwanyama of insignia of rank and rewards for bravery.[21]

The 1897 rinderpest epidemic, from which drought and
pestilence hindered recovery, devastated raider and victim alike,
and destroyed the Bechuanaland market. In Ovamboland,
the cattle mortality rate reached as high as 90 per cent. Long-
distance raiding was already subject to diminishing returns as
the tribes under attack developed defensive techniques, broke
up or moved north. After 1904, and more particularly after
1907, when the Portuguese established a ring of forts around
the northern perimeter of Ovamboland, raiding became
militarily more hazardous as well. At the same time, the
growing military power of colonial regimes on both flanks,
especially after 1904, enhanced the need for defensive rearma-
ment. It is thus not surprising that the *lenga* were progressively redirected into collecting the *okasavu*, and were able
(possibly because the kings' means of patronage were reduced)
to appropriate an increasing proportion of the proceeds of this
and other forms of arbitrary exaction to their own use. By
these means, and through external and inter-tribal raiding,
they built independent clientage networks.

Although the evidence is fragmentary,[22] it is likely that the
level of peasant consumption declined in the 30 years before
colonization (mid-1880s to 1915). Not only were cattle stocks
decimated by natural catastrophe, but the rate and generality
of taxation began to exceed the capacity of lineage reciprocity
to compensate. It is possible that limited forms of peasant
resistance – holding back crop and stock production, even
emigration – reinforced the tendency.[23]

The mediation of patriarchal social relations made the

impact of impoverishment, in fact, more specific. A minority of households, the survivors of inter-tribal raiding or of 'judicial raids', had no option but to flee and/or attach themselves as clients to powerful *lenga* lineages. For the rest, the material and cultural shock at the sudden seizure of cattle lay particularly heavily on the men. Furthermore, game-hunting became an aristocratic monopoly.[24] Younger men were recruited as retainers and for military expeditions. Even so, a substantial number faced either social dislocation or, in the sudden appropriation of their cattle, the loss not only of means of subsistence but also of social wealth.

The particular forms of surplus appropriation under tributary relations of production thus affected women rather less, since taxation in cattle did not seriously damage either social reproduction or crop output. Although the more violent methods of appropriation – judicial raids and inter-tribal raiding – often did entail the complete dispossession, capture or death of whole households, their victims were a minority of the social formation, and their intensification was a product of the post-rinderpest crisis in the tributary mode itself.

The impact of embryonic class formation on and through patriarchal social relations led to modifications in the forms of cooperation in the labour process whose ideological spin-off influenced the tactics of organized struggle developed by labour migrants. In the long term, they also strengthened the managerial autonomy of women in rural production. The annual cattle migration, restricted to men and boys, and undertaken in a difficult environment, had long ingrained techniques of cooperation and improvization at the level of groups comprising lineages or a number of homesteads. The deployment of tribute labour into raiding parties, as many as 100–150 strong, assisted in welding a strong, all-male tradition of group solidarity.

It is suggested, therefore, that in the years following the rinderpest epidemic the tributary state was already approaching a crisis; that peasant consumption was being depressed to the margins of subsistence on too wide a scale for the compensatory mechanisms of lineage social relations fully to counterbalance; and that the specific form of tributary state surplus appropriation and labour conscription had a particularly adverse impact on younger men in the divided labour process.

Migration statistics from the last five years of German rule point to the scale on which Ovambo households were turning to migrant labour out of necessity.[25] Over the four years 1910–13, outgoing migrants exceeded those returning by as many as 8,145 out of 36,480, or 22 per cent, and even after the shutdown of most businesses in late 1914 a net surplus of over 5,000 (11 per cent) remained. It is during those years that permanent urban Ovambo settlements were first noted. The fact that peasants could opt to settle under a savagely labour-repressive colonial regime is further evidence of the deterioration of economic and political conditions in Ovamboland.[26]

Figures for individual clusters in the year ended June 1911 tend to confirm the differential development of internal class-formation.[27] Although population estimates at this time were no more than informed speculations, it appears that labour migrants formed about 10 per cent of the Ndonga population – or about 30 per cent of active men, a remarkably high proportion even for a famine year – as against 7, 5 and 2.5 per cent for Ukwambi, Ukwanyama and Ongandjera respectively, with very few from further north and west.[28] In general, the great majority of migrant workers came from the larger clusters, ruled by kings and subject to more definite social differentiation. The evidence is incomplete, but it can reasonably be concluded that, exacerbated by prolonged drought and by increasing internal social dislocation and surplus appropriation, appreciable numbers of peasants had been pushed to the margins of subsistence; and that the massive wave of labour migration after 1908 was a direct response.

Colonization, Collaborators and Labour Migration

The year 1904 marked the beginning of both the national insurrection in the Namibian 'Police Zone' and a more deter-mined Portuguese attempt to conquer northern Ovamboland. Simultaneously, the rate of labour migration began to rise. Yet the greater part of Ovamboland was not subjected to colonial rule before 1915, and then only fortuitously as a result of a change in colonial regime. Furthermore, it was another decade before the new colonial power established total control over labour migration through a monopoly recruiting system. Although the outcome of this transitional period was predictable, its form and timing were strongly modified by the conflicting interests and strategies of Ovambo political leaders, the three colonial governments, and the labour migrants themselves.

The growth of labour migration can be charted with reasonable accuracy. Small numbers of Ovambo worked in the interstices of the trading network in both Namibia and Angola during the 1880s and 1890s,[29] and on the smaller mines and guano workings in Namibia after 1892.[30] Hundreds were recruited for the Swakopmund harbour works (November 1893 to 1903) and the railways to Windhoek (September 1897 to June 1902) and Otavi (October 1903 to December 1906).[31] Up to 1907, however, there were probably never more than about 1,700 in the Police Zone at any one time.[32] Yet by 1910 the annual total of incoming migrants had shot up to over 9,000 or, assuming an average migrancy cycle of 8–9 months each, a labour force of over 6,000; and this high level was maintained until 1914.[33] After the temporary shutdown in 1914–15, as the South African military force fought and defeated German colonial troops and assumed control, the rate of recruitment probably continued at this level for the first five years (statistics are scarce), and settled back to an annual 3,500–4,500 for the second.[34] There are no precise statistics for Angola, but recruitment for the Mossamedes and Benguela railways from 1904, mostly from conquered areas subject after 1907 to hut tax, probably never exceeded an annual 2,000.[35]

The broad outlines of Portuguese and German colonial strategies are fairly clear.[36] The former, intent on imposing 'direct rule' and taxation, embarked on the military conquest of the southern interior, occupying Ombadya (1907) after a crushing initial defeat (1904), three small northern Ovambo clusters (1908–10), and the Okavango River.[37] But fear of Kwanyama military power and their need for railway labour deterred the Portuguese from completing the process of subjugation. Ukwanyama, straddling the disputed border and well within the German 'sphere of interest' under the secret Anglo–German participation treaty of 1898 for the partition of Angola if Portuguese rule were to collapse, now became the centre of rivalry between German and Portuguese diplomats, labour recruiters and traders.[38]

The newly established German regime (1894–5), on the other hand, remained preoccupied with the colonization of the Police Zone until the collapse in 1904 of its treaties with local chiefs and leaders. The imperial government baulked at the anticipated military and, after 1904, political cost of conquest. It steadfastly rejected any local initiative, both before and after the uprising, to intervene militarily and establish a direct administration in the north, to the extent that even retaliatory raids were banned. Nevertheless, Ovamboland, now that it was a major supplier of essential labour, was the object of close political attention as the Germans tried to maximize the supply through diplomatic ties with the political leaderships.[39]

After 1904, the scope for strategic manoeuvre by the Ovambo kings narrowed. The Portuguese occupation of their perimeter made long-distance raiding hazardous for the Kwanyama. The incidence of internal inter-tribal raiding was probably increasing, with smaller clusters the chief victims; yet none was able to secure any significant military ascendancy, and the mode of warfare changed little, despite the increased efficiency of imported arms technology.[40] The tributary states were, therefore, increasingly forced back upon internal methods of surplus appropriation. Realization through trade of its proceeds, however, was becoming more difficult and less reliable as colonial occupation of trade routes placed controls on access to markets and to essential commodities. By the mid-1890s, both the Germans and the Portuguese had banned trade in firearms; when rinderpest reached Namibia the Germans stopped the entry of all cattle from Ovamboland; from 1906 they allowed traders access only by licence; and at about this time the Portuguese banned trade altogether.[41] Although smuggling was possible through Hereroland before 1904 and through Angola up to and beyond 1915,[42] it was subject to considerable risk during the last decade of independence.

Given the tightening constraints of their strategic situation, the Ovambo kings were relatively successful in exploiting colonial rivalries and the misperceptions of colonial agents. In 1908, after more than a decade of almost open hostility before and during the genocidal suppression of the 1904–1907 insurrection, the Ovambo kings allowed their political relations with the Germans to be formalized in 'protection treaties'. In practice, most succeeded in keeping their distance. At least one maintained an efficient intelligence network;[43] and visitors, missionaries and migrant workers were used as ongoing sources of information. Though good relations with traders were indispensable, very few were either allowed to settle permanently in tribal territory or given the freedom to operate outside royal control. As late as 1911, when Portuguese traders tried to exploit famine conditions by overcharging, the Kwanyama king Mandume expelled them from his territory.[44]

Notwithstanding this, the kings could not escape the contradiction which bound them: that internal taxation on cattle was yielding diminishing returns from a static subsistence productive base. Not only was the power of the state threatened for lack of adequate means of exchange for the instruments of appropriation, which indigenous metal technology could not reproduce, but also the stability of the kings' alliance with the new stratum of functionaries (the *lenga*), which its methods of surplus extraction had called into being. Increasingly, the kings were losing exclusive control over the possession of guns and horses, and the *lenga* were channelling appropriated cattle and people into their own retinues. In general, the price of royal supremacy over the *lenga* seems to have been regular dispossession, judicious marriage and patronage strategies, and an authoritarian personal rule dependent in varying degrees on a court-based military contingent.[45] Inevitably, the efficiency and articulation of the tributary state were impaired.

In this context, the suddenly urgent colonial demand for labour after 1904 held advantages for the rulers of the tributary states. It was the only substantial bargaining counter they possessed against colonial encroachment, particularly from the German side, as the degree of official involvement in recruiting efforts must have made plain. It was certainly a means of obtaining regular trade and political information, and possibly of smuggling in arms.[46] It provided an outlet for the victims of their more arbitrary methods of surplus appropriation and alleviated the burden of providing relief after bad harvests. It was an alternative to raiding, which the *lenga* would not oppose and would possibly assist in supervising, a politically valuable point since the *lenga* seem generally to have been hostile to diplomatic relations with the colonial powers,[47] understandably in view of their stake in raiding. Above all the export of labour under official direction offered the kings a new opportunity for taxation through levies on the goods with which the workers returned.

Despite the scale of their requirements, the German authorities went little further than setting up border control posts on the two main migration routes and, from 1906, restricting entry to approved recruiters. They resisted pressure from recruiters for open access and from the diamond companies for a recruiting station inside Ovamboland. The colonial government, having adopted a policy of co-option, was anxious to maintain harmonious relations with the kings (thus serving political as well as economic ends) which competition between recruiters and unscrupulous practices on the latters' part might jeopardize. Instead, officials toured the country with increasing frequency to persuade the kings to encourage labour migration. In 1911, private recruiters were barred altogether and a 'Native Commissioner', symbolically the veteran Ovamboland missionary Tönjes, was appointed at Lüderitz.

To a considerable extent, the disadvantages to the Germans of not having permanent representatives or administrators at the royal capitals was offset by the network of mission stations, which were generally located, both geographically and politically, near the centres of state power. Missionaries of the Finnish Missionary Society, established in the area since 1870, and the Rhenish Missionary Society, strategically located in Ukwanyama since the early 1890s, proved willing and reliable sources of intelligence and, on balance, influential surrogates for colonial political advisers.[48]

Within these limits, the Germans exploited their opportunities to the full. The years 1907–16 witnessed an unparalleled sequence of bad harvests (1910 and 1912 were the only exceptions), culminating in the devastating famines of 1911 and 1915. In 1908, the year in which Hauptmann Franke was sent north to secure protection treaties and encourage labour migration, the Germans sent 80 tons of relief supplies via the Finnish Mission for 'free distribution', a practice which became regular in succeeding years and a powerful inducement to royal goodwill.[49] Government representatives distributed gifts judiciously and, sensing the structure of power in matrilineal succession, cultivated the more powerful of the king's female relatives.[50] Ondonga, with its troubled royal succession which left the kingdom divided between two rulers for several decades, and provided an unfavourable situation for raiding, came in for special attention. The government intervened directly in its succession dispute, and plied the half-blind and alcoholic Kambonde II (1884–1909) with liquor and a sizeable bribe.[51] In the last year of their regime, the Germans took the first rudimentary steps to improve the conditions of travel for migrants on the hazardous, waterless route to the Otavi railhead by drilling boreholes and starting a railway from Otjiwarongo to Ondonga. Whether in the latter venture military or economic motives were the foremost consideration, the First World War brought the project to an abrupt and permanent halt.[52]

Although the Germans held back from both indirect and direct coercion in seeking to secure large-scale labour supplies, the Ovambo kings never seriously opposed the growth of labour migration after 1907. By the turn of the century, an increasing number of Ovambo men were being reduced to the margins of subsistence and deprived of status and employment by the appropriation of their cattle. Wage labour was one among several alternative forms of subsistence, whether as a temporary means of recovery or a permanent change in class position. Its explosive growth might be interpreted as an independent response by the more impoverished peasant households to their material and political circumstances, a response which their rulers were powerless or uninterested in opposing. The extent to which the tributary states exceeded a merely passive role in either promoting labour migration or regulating its form is important in determining the margins and context of struggle available to labour migrants.

Hauptmann Streitwolf, who visited Ovamboland several times on recruiting missions, concluded in 1913 that verbal commitments by the Ovambo kings to itinerant German officials made little impact on the trend of recruitment.[53] Whatever negotiating tactics the kings may have employed, there is evidence that they did in fact take an active part in both promoting and regulating the flow. Schlettwein gave an explicit description of the mechanics of state control in 1907:

> The chief chooses the men and sends them out under a foreman to acquire clothes and other useful articles. The final date by which such a party has to be back is precisely stipulated, and woe betide anyone who doesn't return at the correct time . . . With their earnings the men must buy goods, all of which they are required to set down before their chief. The chief then takes for himself whatever he likes, and disposes of the rest quite arbitrarily.[54]

That the king was able to levy a tax in kind on returning workers was confirmed by a second observer 20 years later: 'Every black who returns from the mines must report immediately to the chief and give a detailed account of everything that happened and hand over the gifts expected of him.'[55]

Fragmentary evidence from the early years of labour migration tends to confirm Schlettwein's view that the king also controlled the call-up and dispatch of workers, though the criterion of selection is not clear. In 1896, Möller reported of the Kwambi king: 'Nezumbo rules his people with an iron hand but also with wisdom. He wants absolute obedience from everybody; before they marry the young men must work with the white people on the other side of the Kunene and from there bring back a cow as payment.'[56] Clearly, the dividing line between the redeployment or extension of tribute labour by the state and the dispatch of sub-marginal peasants as labour migrants was delicate and by no means absolute. Similarly, the extent to which forcible methods of appropriation of cattle and people were specifically translated into conscription for labour migration cannot be determined on the available evidence.

It is probable that the stronger kings adapted the institutions of the raiding party to labour migration. Several times between 1900 and 1925 it was reported that Ovambo migrants travelled in groups and refused to be broken up.[57] Indeed, one Omaruru farmer on the route put the average number of each group at 100–150, a size equivalent to the raiding party. Migration statistics for the period 1910–14 tend to confirm that the six-month maximum period of absence usually stipulated by the king[58] was being observed by many workers. In 1904–5 one Ovambo king, Nehale, was strong enough to enforce a ban on migration after German provocation.[59] In Ukwanyama, the continuing ability of the king to bargain with rival Portuguese and German recruiters indicates a degree of regulation over outgoing workers. It may be tentatively concluded that the Ovambo kings attempted to retain some control over this new source of revenue by putting migrants under their own representatives, by limiting the period of absence, and by sanctions against those who disobeyed royal injunctions.

It is not likely, however, that after the four-fold increase in the annual rate of migration between 1907 and 1910, the kings could continue to exercise detailed personal supervision over the recruitment, dispatch and return of the labourers. Schlettwein's description was written before this escalation; nor is it known whether most or all migrants travelled in groups, or whether those who did were always led by tribal officials. As early as 1902, a drought year, the northern recruiting station reported a surplus of new arrivals over demand, and according to Stals, 'many Ovambos' at this time were coming 'on their own initiative'.[60] Later, while the five to seven months lag between emigration and return may have indicated observance of the royal injunction, it also conformed roughly to the rhythm of peasant production, the men returning in time either for field preparation in spring or for cattle pasturing and the harvest in late summer.[61]

Interpretation of the migration statistics for the period 1910–14 (see table 2) is not easy, since at least three out of the

Table 2 Labour migration to and from the Police Zone 1910–15

Year	Jan.	Feb.	Mar.	Apr.	May	Jun.	Jul.	Aug.	Sep.	Oct.	Nov.	Dec.	Total
1910													
to	1,436	2,501	702	537	432	573	1,351	674	425	215	241	268	9,355
from	443	727	695	589	235	134	505	991	726	692	440	628	6,805
1911													
to	1,144	615	591	1,532	1,581	626	393	383	553	623	603	649	9,284
from	438	225	197	560	432	100	588	1,164	593	680	667	935	6,579
1912													
to	646	160	135	540	625	798	550	547	623	611	498	343	6,076
from	491	229	341	413	504	197	570	340	108	424	569	587	4,773
1913													
to	1,049	1,364	1,558	1,404	1,271	860	745	1,115	719	630	538	511	11,764
from	730	436	572	721	737	986	589	1,121	824	1,275	1,015	1,171	10,177
1914													
to	1,167	1,064	1,246	977	400	1,531	1,430	403	46	31	39	508	8,824
from	560	735	910	508	875	460	664	4,543	300	749	292	447	11,023
1915													
to	776	49											
from	453	1,108											

Note: The figures indicate the number of migrant workers passing the two northernmost border posts.
Source: E. L. P. Stals, 'Die aanraking tussen Blankes en Owambo's in Suidwes-Afrika 1850–1915', *Archives Yearbook for South African History*, 31 (2) (1968), p. 333.

five years saw bad harvests, and short-term variations were at times strongly influenced by local hostilities and anti-colonial resistance.[62] In general, however, they support the view that periods of labour migration were integrated with the seasonal cycle of subsistence production. Peaks of emigration tended to follow closely periods of heavy demand upon male labour-time, or to coincide with crop or pasture failures. Comparison of the out-migration figures for 1912, a year of good rainfall, with those for 1911 and 1913 shows, predictably, that the seasonal peaks were much reduced in expectation of good crops and pastures. It also reveals that the total for 1912 was still 60 per cent of the average for 1911 and 1913, indicating the scale on which labour migration was by this time structurally necessary.

In general, the statistical evidence remains ambiguous on this question. For the purpose of preventing permanent emigration and the loss of both labour-power and revenue, a short maximum period of migration was as much in the king's interest as was continuous supervision of the migrants. Since both maximizing the output in cattle and securing tribute labour and military service remained principal state concerns, it is likely that the king's policy would have reinforced the tendency to articulate migration with the seasonal production cycle. Nevertheless, the steady flow underlying the seasonal climatic peaks indicates that such articulation was of lesser importance to a substantial number. When taken together with the gaps between the kings' promises to recruiters and their actual fulfilment, it also suggests that tributary states could do little more than organize peasants acting in their own interest.

The outbreak of the First World War in 1914 intruded abruptly upon relations between the colonial and the tributary states. After a brief skirmish with a German force, the Portuguese abandoned the whole of southern Angola in panic. The Germans, however, soon had to confront an invading force from South Africa. In the brief hiatus that followed, the Kwanyama king Mandume, who had since his accession in 1911 substantially reasserted royal ascendancy over his *lenga* by combining autocracy with populist measures, attempted to establish Ukwanyama as the leading military power in

Ovamboland. This embryonic paramountcy can be seen as a new stage in the uneven evolution of the tributary states.

The tendency lasted barely long enough to reveal its form, however. In mid-1915, the Portuguese returned in force to inflict a total and bloody defeat upon Ukwanyama, and the leadership and sections of the surviving population fled across the border. Representatives of the South African invading force, arriving at the same time from the south, found Ovamboland in the grip of severe famine and were able to establish an administrative presence without opposition. From this point the character of colonial rule north and south of the border diverges, and I will be concerned for the most part only with the latter.

From the outset, the new colonial power applied to its northern reserves the standard principles of indirect rule: a skeleton administration, relying on the personal and paternalist influence of white officials, and backed where necessary by overwhelming military force; minimal interference in tribal affairs; and the least possible state expenditure. Politically, the government attempted, with some success, to secure the collaboration of the *lenga* by recognizing their executive authority and by setting up councils of headmen as the subordinate judicial and political authority where kings were non-existent or deposed. Relations with the kings, still potential symbols of resistance within their communities, and occasionally on a broader front, were often uneasy and two, Mandume and Ipumbu, were deliberately deposed by force.[63] Aside from the obvious advantages of collaboration, the *lenga* had little option but to cooperate: raiding and violent methods of extortion, their principal revenue earners, were suppressed and trading was reduced to an illegal trickle.[64] There were no permanent stores before 1925 and very few itinerant traders, while barter exchange across the Angolan border remained on a small scale.

Collaboration, on the other hand, formalized their delegated local powers of land allocation, their rights, sometimes usurped from deposed kings, to taxation on grain and cattle and to tribute labour, and their control over migrant labour. The price of confirmation in their executive and taxation rights was subordination as administrative 'headmen' to the overlordship of colonial officials, whose chief priority now lay in the labour requirements of the colonial economy.

The form of colonial intervention struck at the core of the tributary states by either removing or emasculating their central political and ideological institution – the kingship. The power of the co-opted *lenga* was confined to more-or-less fixed districts within each cluster. The social formation was now articulated at the level of the reserve administration in the overriding interest of colonial capital.

Under the pragmatism implied by the policy of co-option, particular variations between clusters were occasionally considerable. In general, however, lineage relations of production, with which the patronage mechanisms of headmen tended to mesh, strengthened at the expense of antagonistic methods of surplus appropriation, which were in any case limited and standardized by the colonial administration. Cattle levies were substantially reduced and their principal trading purpose, the acquisition of arms, was banned, as were most of the arbitrary methods of expropriation such as 'judicial raids'. Colonial taxation was not introduced until 1929, and even then could be paid in kind. The trend in the use of tribute labour was unclear but demands by the colonial administration were small and periodic, while one major activity employing younger men (raiding) was now ended.

The sudden ending of inter-tribal raiding removed one major disincentive from colonizing the forest belts or from exploiting them more freely for raw materials. Ukwanyama is likely to have been an exception to this general conclusion, however. Refugees from the Portuguese military conquest in 1915, from the redrawing of the precolonial boundary further south in 1926, and from Portuguese repression and taxation, continued to settle on a narrow strip of territory adjoining the border in substantial numbers. The incidence of labour migration, in contrast to the pre-conquest years, was if anything slightly above the regional average in the mid-1920s, when Kwanyama men accounted for 60 per cent of all contract workers from Ovamboland.[65]

For lack of direct evidence, any assessment of the impact of these changes in social relations on either the level of production or the labour process must remain speculative.

With traders barred before 1925 and the export of cattle banned, the only means of access to capitalist-produced commodities was through wage labour by migration. For the kings and headmen, the taxation in kind of returning migrants, whether formal or informal, was thus their only means other than government subsidies of acquiring items of luxury consumption or prestige. For peasants, on the other hand, direct dependence on external commodities was still small, except where ideologically induced as amongst the growing number of Christians. Indigenous smiths continued to produce the bulk of the instruments of production well into the 1920s, although their long-term fate was sealed by the loss of their ore sites at Otavi and Kassinga to capitalist concerns.

Stock levels were, however, undoubtedly lower in general following the devastating drought of 1915–16. They were also more unevenly distributed in the aftermath of heavy taxation and raiding. Trade goods bought with wages were one ready means of acquiring cattle by exchange. An assessment in the late 1920s of the average expenditure pattern of Ovambo migrants points to such a tendency: out of an annual wage of £30, fully one-third was spent on 'purchases', and a further £4–5 at the mine store by then established in Ovamboland – (see table 3). Aside from taxation ('gifts' to tribal functionaries), much of the remainder went on the worker's own reproduction costs. The lower and fairly stable rate of migration throughout the 1920s suggests that, subject to the determining framework of long-term or periodic impoverishment and of pressures by headmen, the principal objectives of migration were two-fold: (i) to acquire items of exchange for means of production, particularly the case with younger men establishing a homestead; and (ii) ideologically determined consumption, fulfilling household, prestige or religious needs. In view of the scanty evidence, however, this must remain a tentative hypothesis.

Finally, the question, although often taken for granted, must be asked, Why was labour migration an exclusively male preserve? Much of the answer has already been implied. Men monopolized the long-distance seasonal migrations to the cattle posts, an annual experience for many from boyhood onwards. The cooperation and shared solidarity of men in

Table 3   Usual expenditure of an Ovambo contract worker, late 1920s

At work	'Gifts'	Clothes	Purchases in Ovamboland	Total wage^a
£ 5	4	4	10	4–5 30

a For 10 'months', the earning is approximately 300 shifts, or nearly one
calendar year. This figure suggests a rate of 2/– per shift, rather high
when compared with the minimum rates then prevailing.
Source: V. Lebzelter, *Die Eingeborenenkulturen in Südwest und Südafrika* (Leipzig,
Vlg. Karl W. Hirsemann, 1934), vol. 2, p. 219.

groups drawn from a number of homesteads was reproduced
in a more intense form in the long-distance raiding parties of
the 30–40 years before colonization in 1915. Correspondingly,
the increasing loss of cattle through taxation, judicial raids
and inter-tribal warfare hit at the foundation of male
economic power and social prestige. On the other hand,
although a minority were severely victimized by raiding,
women's labour and its products were less generally affected
by the increased surplus appropriation, the absolute decline in
cattle production, and the heavier demand for tribute labour.
The first phase of labour migration can be interpreted in part
as a period of uneasy cooperation between younger men and
the rulers of the tributary states, transferring the ideological
prestige, the tradition of male solidarity, and the organizational
experience of the raiding party and the cattle trek to the long-
distance work-gang.

By the time the South Africans took over, the pattern was
entrenched. For women, land for fields became more accessible.
For men, although surplus appropriation and tribute labour
were reduced, they were not ended. Labour contracts remained
a principal means whereby younger men paid tribute and
accumulated the savings in cattle needed to marry and
establish a homestead. Women, who had in any case been
excluded from the start from the colonial regimes' recruiting
mechanisms, continued to reach the towns in small numbers
after 1915 as before, despite the extreme hardships and
illegalities of travel. But they were totally barred from the
large-scale employment on the mines, public works, and
railways to which at that time contract workers were
exclusively directed.

The intrusion of the wage relation strengthened the articulation of productive and reproductive roles. Male labour-power was now removed from the agrarian production cycle for long, continuous periods. Despite attempts by both peasants and the tributary states to render the articulation non-antagonistic, the reduction in available labour time, as opposed to means of subsistence, decreased both the forms of output for which men were alone responsible (cattle, hunting) and also heavy labour inputs at points of peak seasonal demand, as well as small kinds of craft and repair work. Since wages were calculated at little above the worker's immediate subsistence, this loss could only be compensated, and even then only partially, by an intensification of women's labour and an extension of their role in the labour process.

Worker Consciousness and Labour Action

Up to this point I have considered tendencies towards class formation within the Ovambo social formation, forms of surplus appropriation, their impact on the direct producers and the technical division of labour, and the space for tactical manoeuvre remaining to peasants to cope with the resulting pressures. The structural constraints left migrant workers little scope (though probably rather more in the 1920s) for tactically exploiting the duality of their class position, although the evidence suggests that the kings reinforced for their own ends attempts by peasants to integrate wage labour with the agricultural production cycle. To what extent labour migrants exploited that scope as wage labourers, and the forms of consciousness and collective action they developed in struggle within capitalist relations of production, will be examined below.

A number of general factors operated to condition the manner in which labour migrants came to experience wage labour. The length and difficulty of the migration routes was not the least of these. The tracks to Okaukuejo and Namutoni were almost waterless during the dry winter months, as were long stretches of the roads in central Namibia, where water-holes had become private property. Food for the trip had to be carried. In the early years, mortality was high.[66] Although railway travel and official measures in 1911 improved conditions in the Police Zone somewhat, contemporary accounts make it plain that the journey was an ordeal not lightly to be undertaken. The Lüderitzbucht Chamber of Mines complained both before and after 1915 of the number of migrant workers who had to be hospitalized on arrival. In the late 1940s, workers were still cooped up for days *en route* in cattle trucks without food or water.[67]

Whether or not parties set out under the discipline of the kings' delegates, such conditions were conducive to group solidarity, notably for protection against robbers on the return leg of the journey.[68] Since most workers came on fixed-period contracts with large employers, the travel party is likely to have held together through the employment period and the return journey.[69] In an environment both unfamiliar and hostile, the traditions of male group solidarity reinforced the cohesion of the travelling and working party.

Conditions at the rough construction and mining camps were generally, though not uniformly, harsh.[70] The sharp temperature variations inland and, particularly, the cold and damp climate of the coastal desert, rendered workers from sub-tropical Ovamboland vulnerable to disease. Accommodation was often primitive, sometimes non-existent; company rations were commonly insufficient for basic survival in good health and alternative shop supplies were rarely available. On the isolated diamond fields and railway construction sites, labour supervision, necessarily self-reliant, was frequently violent. In addition workers had little protection from swindling.[71]

In such circumstances, avoidance of the worst locations and the most notorious employers, as well as tactics for self-defence on the work-sites, were at times a matter of life and death. The work itself was heavy and dangerous in construction and underground mining, lighter but tedious in diamond recovery. In all cases, large bodies of workers were concentrated in the production process and in their residence, an environment that facilitated communication and collective forms of action. Wages on the diamond fields were relatively high by the standards of a forced labour economy, but the fact that thousands of contract workers from the Cape earned two-and-a-half times as much as Namibian workers on the railways must have been well-known.[72] Taken overall, the contrasts between the work environments and routines of agrarian production and wage labour could hardly have been more extreme. On the other hand, workers could draw on a number of organizational and ideological resources to strengthen their tenuous bargaining position.

At the most general level, labour consciousness in a work-force finds expression in patterns of communication and common response. In Namibia, the constant circulation of labour migrants between isolated centres of peasant and capitalist production fostered communication networks that could be put to effective tactical use. A particularly clear instance of such a network in operation occurred in 1924–5 on the diamond fields.[73] Conditions on the fields at this time were so bad that in 1924 there were no fewer than 296 cases of scurvy, an incidence of 50 per 1,000. As many as 52 men actually died. Overall mortality was an astronomical 437, or 74 per 1,000. Very few of these deaths can have resulted from accidents at work. At the same time, the average monthly Ovambo work-force dropped from 3,565 in May 1924 to a low of 1,513 exactly a year later. New arrivals totalled a mere 214 in the last half of 1924, compared with 1,901 for the same period in 1923. Furthermore, assuming the one-year contracts which were then standard,[74] departures in July 1924 exceeded arrivals in July 1923 by the abnormally large figure of 224.

Since the respective harvests can have played little part in this – they were good in 1922/3 and below normal in 1923/4 – the figures suggest a concerted boycott as migrants returning in the first part of the year warned their comrades of this death-trap. Indeed in the following year, while overall recruitment from northern Namibia remained the same, the number of workers actually on the mines fell by 22 per cent over the 1924 average, and on the diamond fields themselves by 38 per cent. Conditions were so extreme that a group of 163 Xhosa contract workers, who, the South West African administrators complained, 'had a mania for making complaints', made a suicidal bid to escape to South Africa across the Namib desert, in which at least 14 died.[75]

The evidence is too fragmentary to permit close analysis of types of worker action during these early years. Nevertheless, migrants appear to have discriminated actively over terms of employment in a way that presumes a degree of consensus over tactics. Conditions on farms were notorious and they were effectively boycotted from an early stage.[76] Workers resisted contracting for periods that would interfere with the next season's agrarian production in Ovamboland, and when deceived in this, they insisted on terminating before completion.[77]

As early as 1909–10, workers were sufficiently alive to tactical openings to use the Tsumeb copper mine as a temporary staging-post *en route* to the diamond fields. At a time when migration to the south had reached full flood, the Tsumeb mine was so undermanned, 'because a pronounced emigration of Ovambos to the Lüderitzbucht diamond fields became disturbingly noticeable',[78] that it had to import 250 expensive 'Cape Boys' to maintain production. At this time, the fields were offering better wages and hours, and the work was lighter and above ground.[79] Tsumeb was soon notorious amongst Cape workers as well, although a German official later reported a considerable improvement in conditions.[80] At the end of 1917, it is interesting to note that the positions were reversed: with wage-rates now equal, Tsumeb had a full labour complement at the same time that the diamond fields were over 1,000 men short.[81]

In general, choice of employer could often be a matter of life or death. It is perhaps significant that at the same time that the mortality on the diamond fields rose to an incredible 149.6 per 1,000 (in the year to March 1911), both the total number of incoming migrants and the average diamond fields work-force changed little between 1910 and 1911, respectively years of good rainfall and dire famine. Similarly, the year to March 1913, with the new labour regulations in force and a mortality rate down to 41, saw the diamond fields work-force increase by 38 per cent over 1911/12 and by 6 per cent of the total recruited over the same months.[82]

At the point of production there is some evidence of considerable resistance to intolerable conditions by workers acting individually or in small groups, mainly by desertion and by complaints to officialdom.[83] The penalty for desertion, if not recapture, was frequently hardship or death on the road, and for 'false complaint', arbitrary imprisonment or flogging.[84] Neither option was to be lightly taken. Nevertheless, a minority of workers could, and did, take advantage of the willingness of some employers and recruiters in conditions of chronic labour shortage to take on workers illegally, by re-engaging or signing on outside state supervision.[85]

Individual action – 'beating the system' – and passive resistance in a variety of forms are likely to have been the dominant modes of self-defence, particularly before 1912, in a work and social environment that was dehumanizing and disorientating. Little is known of the extent or forms of collective action amongst Ovambo migrants before 1915. Ovambo workers were, however, involved as early as December 1893 in a strike for higher wages by the ethnically mixed work-force at the Gross Otavi mine of the South West Africa Company (SWACO), against a background of passive resistance which reveals, Gordon considers, a sharp appreciation of labour tactics.[86]

The reports of the government mining inspector between 1915 and 1925, on the other hand, provide ample evidence of the militancy and flexibility of workers' tactics, particularly on the diamond fields, where, as we saw earlier, conditions remained primitive and dangerous to life before the mid-1920s, with frequent outbreaks of epidemic disease. Workers exploited the demoralization of the largely German fields supervision after conquest, the reduced police cover, and the restrictions on arbitrary and corporal punishment,[87] to protest about specific grievances and, more generally, to break up the discipline of capitalist production.[88] Their principal tactics were the flash strike and the go-slow;[89] both were widely used in a protracted struggle against the deferred pay system, which the South Africans imposed in late 1915.[90]

Even at this early stage, workers were able to generate a grass-roots leadership and a tradition of solidarity on which they could rely for effective support.[91] By 1917, workers were operating 'a kind of mutual benefit society' to indemnify those victimized in labour action.[92] It is probable, to judge from official concern, that the politically conscious Cape workers, who were employed in large numbers on railway building and, in the early 1920s, on the diamond fields, materially aided by example and contact the raising of Ovambo worker consciousness.[93] The South West Africa Administrator could describe Lüderitz in the early 1920s as being 'the centre of the Native political movement in this country. Several Unions were in existence there, the chief of which were the Universal Negro Improvement Association and . . . the International [sic] and Commercial Workers' Union.'[94]

Nor was militancy confined to the fields. At Tsumeb, a strike by black workers in 1920 followed one by their white counterparts, who were unionized and militant until broken by the management in 1925.[95] A description in 1925 of Tsumeb, where workers, mostly Ovambo, were taken on at the mine rather than recruited through the contract labour administration, highlights the degree of relative autonomy workers had secured: 'From the 1st to the 8th of every month the underground complement is depleted, the natives absenting themselves from work; some stay in the compound or do a round of the 30-odd stores in the village, others go away into the bush for a bit, and others even, without word or sign return to their homes.'[96] During the six months from September 1924 to February 1925, the last week's complement was an average of 36 per cent greater than the first week's in any one month; and the management admitted that it had little option but to acquiesce. Most workers also preferred to build their own houses rather than live in the compound, so as to bring their families with them.[97] Even the few Ovambos on farms were asserting their interests by deserting after six to eight months.[98]

It will be apparent that the conventional image of migrant workers as 'docile' and helpless labour units is a poor parody of the reality; that isolation did not prevent them developing a labour consciousness and tactics of struggle appropriate to their circumstances; and that this consciousness did not grow in simple linear proportion to length of industrial experience. These points do not, however, shed light on the general trend in the formation of class consciousness as peasants or workers

Table 4 Monthly totals of workers recruited in Ovamboland

From	Jan.	Feb.	Mar.	Apr.	May	Jun.	Jul.	Aug.	Sep.	Oct.	Nov.	Dec.	Total
1926													
Ovam.	250	344	603	541	316	290	454	382	395	144	173	141	4,033
Ang.	70	97	170	152	90	81	140	60	109	44	72	49	1,134
1927													
Ovam.	408	554	1,062	361	325	335	356	308	159	101	97	145	4,211
Ang.	56	82	222	101	204	117	150	137	66	106	57	105	1,403
1928													
both	319	604	648	690	621	432	469	300	179	209	184	246	4,091
1929													
Ovam.	383	301	390	588	475	218	240	230	117	106	65	158	3,271
Ang.	106	54	121	252	321	224	218	216	115	79	117	82	1,905
1930													
Ovam.	242	428	355	154	491	287	307	107	19	9	16	92	2,507
Ang.	125	150	153	97	182	247	316	191	33	29	42	84	1,649

Note: The distinction is between workers arriving from south and north of the border with Angola.
Source: SWA Administrator, *Annual Reports of the Administrator for SWA to the League of Nations, 1926–30.*

amongst labour migrants. That a constant trickle of migrants continued to settle permanently in Police Zone towns; that women as well as men fled to the south from the 1915 famine;[99] and that a semi-permanent settled community formed at Tsumeb, which long remained largely outside the contract labour system, suggests a commitment to their proletarian status by a minority. But it is unlikely to have been an attractive option, even in the towns, except for those whose returns from subsistence production were becoming regularly sub-marginal.

In the early 1920s, the impact of evangelical Christianity, reflected in the inculcation of the work ethic, the costs of church maintenance and new cash essentials (such as clothes, compulsory under the Finnish Mission), was still slight, albeit increasing. In 1913–14, the Finnish Mission (mainly Ondonga) had 2,873 members and the Rhenish Mission (Ukwanyama), 729. By 1930, the former had increased its members to 23,126.[100] Some migrants were still trying to buy cattle and horses;[101] and migration statistics for 1927 suggest that although the minimum contract period permitted was now usually a year, migrants were, nevertheless, timing their departure to follow the planting and harvest seasons. (see table 4). The evidence, although of course inconclusive, does suggest that most migrants exploited what limited scope their class duality allowed them to assert the primacy of their peasant interests but that, within the capitalist production process, they rapidly developed effective tactics of common or collective struggle and a tradition of solidarity.

The Formation of the Contract Labour System

Whichever of their class interests was dominant, the ability of labour migrants to exploit their opportunities as workers presented colonial capital with a considerable challenge. Both the German and the South African colonial administrations were pre-occupied with the task of subordinating worker bargaining power to the exigencies of large-scale capitalist production. Above all, with labour chronically short and its quantity rather than terms more important in the first instance, they were concerned to ensure its distribution proportionate to requirements by preventing a bidding up of wages in which not all concerns could compete equally.

Comprehensive labour-repressive legislation enforced by a strong works supervision and police force would partially have achieved the first objective. Neither colonial regime was slow to take legal powers. Indeed, almost the first major South African enactment applied its domestic mining labour law to Namibia.[102] As we have seen, however, German controls were not fully effective, and the local officials compensated with arbitrary violence; nor, before the mid-1920s, was South African legislation effective either. Crucial to the South African system, both to eliminate the mobility of labour and to establish round-the-clock social control, was compulsory residence in a bachelor compound. It is likely that full implementation of this policy could only have followed the completion of major new blocks by Consolidated Diamond Mines (CDM) in 1925 and by Tsumeb in 1926.[103]

The key to effective control, however, lay in regulating the circulation of labour. Both regimes legislated for a compulsory contract system with criminal penalties for evasion, and for official supervision of re-hiring. These laws were reinforced by a thicket of labour-repressive proclamations, particularly pass and vagrancy enactments, applied to the black Police Zone population.[104] The Germans never stamped out illegal recruiting, however, and, despite tight restrictions on licensed recruiters, never entirely eliminated the workers' ability to choose between them.

The Ovamboland administration, on taking responsibility for recruiting, channelled supplies of Ovambo labour to the mines and railways.[105] But whether or not it tried to cut out worker choice, it was not successful in this in the early years.[106] However, in order to dampen down the often extreme clashes between the cycle of peasant and capital production, it soon imposed a standard length of contract – one year for the mines – thereby robbing the labour migrant of the opportunity to articulate wage labour with subsistence production.

The prolonged labour crisis in the diamond industry between 1923 and 1925 prompted the colonial administration to act decisively to remove the workers' ability to discriminate between employers. After previous attempts had failed, conferences of the large employers in 1925 (government, railways and mines) established early in 1926 a semi-official recruiting monopoly in the form of the Northern and the Southern Labour Organizations, precursors of the South West African Native Labour Organization (SWANLO).[107] Henceforth, the only option allowed to labour migrants was whether or not to migrate; once recruited, workers were graded for job categories according to a rough scale of physical fitness, and assigned arbitrarily to employers. A more complete mechanism for the reduction of workers to atomized units of labour power could hardly have been devised. It was to last unaltered until the great contract workers' strike in 1971–2 for the abolition of the contract labour system itself.

Notes and References

1 The research for this paper, undertaken during 1975-6, was limited largely to the contemporary non-Portuguese literature and published documents and to selected file groups in the Central South African Archives, as well as the records of the Anglican Mission. Many of its conclusions are, therefore, tentative. It forms the second paper in a trilogy on the origins and evolution of the migrant labour system in Namibia. The others are W. G. Clarence-Smith and R. J. B. Moorsom, 'Underdevelopment and class-formation in Ovamboland, 1844-1917', in R. Palmer and N. Parsons (eds), *The Roots of Rural Poverty in Central and Southern Africa* (London, Heinemann, 1977), pp. 96–112; also in *Journal of African History*, 16 (3) (1975), pp. 365–81; and R. J. B. Moorsom, 'Underdevelopment, contract labour and worker consciousness in Namibia, 1915–72', *Journal of Southern African Studies*, 4 (1) (1977), pp. 52–87. An edited version of this paper appeared in the University of York, Centre for Southern African Studies, *Collected Seminar Papers*, 5 (1978/79), pp. 17–44.

2 In particular: H. Bley, *SWA under German Rule* (London, Heinemann, 1971); H. Drechsler, *Südwestafrika unter Deutscher Kolonialherrschaft* (Berlin, Akademie-Verlag, 1966), translated as *Let Us Die Fighting* (London, Zed Press, 1980).

3 Substantial work on the precolonial social formations of south-western Angola and northern Namibia includes W. G. Clarence-Smith, *Slaves, Peasants and Capitalists in Southern Angola, 1840–1926* (Cambridge, Cambridge University Press, 1979); L. Berger, 'Der Einfluss der Grenzziehung auf die Ovambo' (University of Mainz, MA thesis, 1980); and C. Borkowsky, 'Zu einigen Aspekten des Ovambolebens', (Free University of Berlin, MA thesis, 1975).

4 Under the Finnish project, a three-year research programme (1984–7)
   described in M. Eirola et al., *The cultural and social change in Ovamboland,
   1870–1915)*, Joensuu, University of Joensuu, Faculty of Arts, 1983, two
   licentiate theses on political resistance to colonization and long-
   distance trade, are being extended to doctorates: M. Eirola, 'Ondangan
   kuningaskunnan vastaus saksan siitomaavallen lähestymiseen, 1884–
   1910', (University of Oulu, Licentiate thesis, 1987) and H. Siiskonen,
   'Kunikaiden kauppa eurooppalaisten ehdoilla . . . 1850–1898'
   (University of Joensuu, Licentiate thesis, 1987); and a third, of political
   anthropology, is in preparation (M. Salokoski at Helsinki). Two
   further theses have recently been completed on mission ideology (T.
   Varis at Tampere, Finland), and on migrant labour in the diamond
   fields to 1914 (R. Strassegger at Graz, Austria). A third in progress on
   the rural origins of labour migration to c. 1930 (P. Hayes at
   Cambridge).
5 W. G. Clarence-Smith, 'Slavery in coastal southern Angola, 1875–
   1913', *Journal of Southern African Studies*, 2 (2) (1978); 'The thirstland
   trekkers in Angola: some reflections on a frontier society', (Institute of
   Commonwealth Studies, London, Seminar Series 'Societies of Southern
   Africa', hereafter ICS SSA, November 1974).
6 Bley, *SWA*, parts 1 and 2.
7 H. Bley, 'German SWA', in R. First and R. Segal, *SWA: A Travesty of
   Trust* (London, Deutsch, 1967); also Drechsler, *Let Us Die Fighting*.
8 For a preliminary analysis, see Clarence-Smith and Moorsom,
   'Underdevelopment 1844–1917'. A later paper by Clarence-Smith on
   the Nyaneka points to the possibility of a more rigorous interpretation
   of contemporary sources: 'Capitalist penetration among the Nyaneka of
   Southern Angola, 1840–1918' (Lusaka, University of Zambia, History
   Seminar, August 1976).
9 Clarence-Smith and Moorsom, 'Underdevelopment 1844–1917',
   pp. 365–7 and sources listed in note 2. For a more detailed analysis of
   climatic factors, Moorsom, 'Underdevelopment 1915–72'; J. H.
   Wellington, *SWA and its Human Issues* (Oxford, Clarendon Press, 1967);
   Clarence-Smith, *Notes on Drought in SW Angola/N Namibia* (London,
   SOAS African History Seminar, 1974).
10 Iron smithing Ukwanyama; copper smithing Ondonga; salt processing
   Ukwambi and Ongandjera.
11 For a harrowing description of such a famine, see South Africa, *Report
   on the Tour to Ovamboland by Major Pritchard*, (Pretoria, Government
   Printer, 1915, UG 38–15).
12 See P. L. Bonner, 'Classes, the mode of production and the state in precolonial Swaziland' (ICA SSA, 10 February 1977).
13 Notably the first planting, which with the often premature onset of the
   first rains depended on experienced judgement, in which the king had
   greater resources, sometimes in the form of professional rainmakers.
   See Clarence-Smith and Moorsom, 'Underdevelopment 1844–1917',
   p. 369; and M. Salokoski, 'Rain making and power in pre-colonial

Ovamboland', paper delivered to the 20th Nordic Congress of Historians (Reykjavik, 9–15 August 1987).

14 The principal exception was fishing, an important source of protein during the summer floods, although men and women cooperated separately and used different techniques.

15 For a detailed empirical treatment, see Siiskonen, 'Kunikaiden kauppa'.

16 In addition to references in Clarence-Smith and Moorsom, 'Underdevelopment 1844–1917', note 19, see P. A. Möller, *Journey into Africa through Angola, Ovamboland and Damaraland* (Cape Town, Struik, 1974, translated from the Swedish edition of 1899), pp. 7, 32; entries in E. C. Tabler, *Pioneers of SWA and Ngamiland* (Cape Town, Balkema, 1973); Q. N. Parsons, 'The Economic History of Khama's Country in Southern Africa', *African Social Research*, 18 (1974).

17 Clarence-Smith and Moorsom, 'Underdevelopment 1844–1917', p. 376.

18 Möller, *Journey*, pp. 110–13. He may be partially reflecting the views of the veteran trader Eriksson, with whom he was travelling. See also the account from oral tradition in E. M Loeb, *In Feudal Africa*, Supplement to *International Journal of American Linguistics.*, part 2, XXVIII (3) (July 1962), chapter 1.

19 Cf. Schinz's description of a returning Kwambi war-party in 1885 (H. Schinz, *Deutsch-Südwest-Afrika, 1884–7* (Oldenburg/Leipzig, Schulz, 1891), p. 236). Owing to scarcity and disease, the horse was an extremely expensive and short-lived animal.

20 Möller, *Journey*, p. 126; W. G. Clarence-Smith, 'Mossamedes and its hinterland, 1875–1915' (SOAS African History Seminar, 1 May 1974), p. 3.

21 Möller, *Journey*, p. 126; H. E. Schoch, diary 20/6/20 (Witwatersrand University Archives, hereafter WU Arch, A839/Ja2); South Africa, *Report by Pritchard*, para. 85.

22 Schinz, *Deutsch Südwest-Afrika*, pp. 298–9, 311; H. Tönjes, *Ovamboland* (Berlin, 1911), p. 69; G. Nitsche, 'Ovamboland' (University of Kiel, dissertation, 1913), p. 130.

23 Schinz, *Deutsch Südwest-Afrika*, p. 298; Dr Gelber (1902), reported in T. Leutwein, *Elf Jahre Gouverneur in Deutsch Südwestafrika* (Berlin, Mittler, 1906), p. 201; Loeb, *In Feudal Africa*, pp. 31–2; A. W. Urquhart, *Patterns of Settlement and Subsistence in South West Angola* (Washington, 1963), p. 111.

24 Tönjes, *Ovamboland*, p. 69; Möller, *Journey*, p. 115; V. Lebzelter, *Die Eingeborenenkulturen in Südwest und Südafrika* (Leipzig, Vlg. Karl W. Hirsemann, 1934), vol. 2, p. 190.

25 Cf. E. L. P. Stals, 'Die aanraking tussen Blankes en Owambo's in Suidwes-Afrika, 1850–1915', *Archives Yearbook for South African History*, 31 (2) (1968), pp. 333–4.

26 O. Köhler, *District of Karibib* (South Africa, Department of Bantu

Administration and Development, Ethnological Publications Series, 1958–9); Pretoria Central Archives, Department of Native Affairs (hereafter NA) 4349/639; Imperial Native Commissioner, Windhoek, report for year ended March 1913.

27 Nitsche, *Ovamboland*, p. 134. Note this was a famine year.

28 Possible reasons why the Ondonga rate was double that of Ukwanyama are the former's proximity to the migration routes, its more advanced penetration by missionaries, and the greater marginality of both its water supply and its adjacent grazing areas.

29 Tönjes, *Ovamboland*, p. 88; Tabler, entry Björklund; Möller, *Journey*, pp. 15, 46.

30 E. Stals, 'Die aanraking', pp. 323–4; R. Gordon, 'A note on the history of labour action in Namibia', *South African Labour Bulletin* (April 1975), p. 9; K. Dove, *Deutsch-Südwest-Afrika* (Berlin, 1903), p. 186.

31 H. E. Lenssen, *Chronik von Deutsch-Südwestafrika, 1883–1915* (Pretoria, 1953), pp. 7, 171; J. Irle, *Die Hereros* (Gütersloh, Bertelsmann, 1906), p. 219; Stals, 'Die aanraking', p. 323.

32 Nitsche, *Ovamboland*, pp. 130–9.

33 Stals, 'Die aanraking', p. 333. A nine-month average per worker allows for longer-term contracts and re-hiring, but it is a very rough estimate. Assuming that very few workers would migrate more than once a year, the annual recruitment statistics are the better guide to the actual number involved.

34 South Africa, Department of Foreign Affairs, *Owambo* (Pretoria, 1971), p. 20; SWA Administrator, *Annual Reports of the Administrator for SWA to the League of Nations*.

35 Clarence-Smith and Moorsom, 'Underdevelopment 1844–1917', p. 377.

36 On the Portuguese, Clarence-Smith, *Slaves*. On the Germans, Stals, 'Die aanraking'; F. R. Lehmann, 'Die politische und soziale Stellung der Häuptlings in Ovamboland', *Tribus*, 4–5 (1954–5).

37 Clarence-Smith and Moorsom, 'Underdevelopment 1844–1917', p. 375.

38 *Ibid.*, p. 379.

39 Lehmann, 'Die politische', for details from German records; also Leutwein, *Elf Jahre*, pp. 175–6, 92; Stals, 'Die aanraking', p. 290.

40 Lehmann, 'Die politische', pp. 282–3, 93, 95; *Südwest*, 4/2/13: Mbadya v Ukwanyama (in NA 1161/179). For effective resistance by 'kingless' tribes, NA 4994/1227, Res. Comm. – SWA Sec. 173/16; Schoch, diary 24/6/20. For earlier descriptions of border cattle-raiding, e.g. Schinz, *Deutsch Südwest-Afrika*, p. 320; *Narrative and Journal of Gerald McKiernan in SWA* (Cape Town, Van Riebeeck Society, 1954), p. 109.

41 Stals, 'Die aanraking', p. 291; Möller, *Journey*, p. 33; Landeshpt. Enactment 29/3/97 para. 4 and regulations under Proclamation 9/10/07; Ovamboland Proc. 25/1/06; Lehmann, 'Die politische', p. 289.

42 Between the turn of the century and 1915, the quantity of arms in Ovamboland appears to have increased considerably: compare Möller,

Journey, pp. 102, 23 and Nitsche, *Ovamboland*, p. 147, with South Africa, *Report by Pritchard*, para. 39, and NA 4994/1227 Res. Comm. – NA Windhoek 10/1/16 (report), Res. Comm. – Dep. Sec. Windhoek 6/8/16. On arms smuggling after 1915, Lebzelter, *Die Eingeborenenkulturen*, p. 208.

43 E.g. Lehmann, 'Die politische', p. 274 (Nehale, 1902).

44 E.g. Lehmann, 'Die politische', p. 289.

45 Mandume was perhaps the clearest example of a strong reforming ruler, who nevertheless lacked the means to transcend his dependence (see Lehmann, 'Die politische', pp. 288–91; NA 4994/1227, H.M. Consul, Lüderitzbucht, Memo, January 1912, also NA 1161/179, Consul – Sec. NA 16/7/12.

46 Lehmann, 'Die politische', p. 270 (1905), p. 298 (1912).

47 Lehmann, 'Die politische', p. 286 (Ukwanyama 1901), p. 283 (Ukwambi 1911/12).

48 Lehmann, 'Die politische', p. 272, esp. p. 278; Stals, 'Die aanraking', p. 334; South Africa, *Report by Pritchard*, para. 23; NA 4994/1227, Res. Comm. – SWA Sec. 1/3/16, memos by Rautanen and Wulfhorst; Consul, Memo. ? January, 1912.

49 On 'gifts' e.g. NA 4994/1227, Consul – Sec. NA (Personal) 6/6/12, citing 'lecture' by Tönjes; on relatives, Lehmann, 'Die politische', *passim*.

50 Clarence-Smith and Moorsom, 'Underdevelopment 1844–1917', p. 378; Lehmann, 'Die politische', *passim*, esp. on Ondonga; Stals, 'Die aanraking', p. 299.

51 Lehmann, 'Die politische', pp. 269–73.

52 NA 4994/1227, Consul – Sec. Int, 14/2/13 and 19/11/13 (enclosure); South Africa, *Report by Pritchard*, para. 13; South Africa, *Memorandum on the Country known as German SWA* (Pretoria, 1915), p. 86.

53 Lehmann, 'Die politische', p. 284; Stals, 'Die aanraking', p. 333, a view which Stals endorses.

54 C. Schlettwein, *Der Farmer in Deutsch-Südwest-Afrika* (Wismar, 1907), p. 255, translated.

55 Lebzelter, *Die Eingeborenekulturen*, p. 219, also 209.

56 Möller, *Journey*, p. 117.

57 Lenssen, *Chronik*, p. 171 (1904/5); Nitsche, *Ovamboland*, p. 135 (c. 1910/11); Stals, 'Die aanraking', p. 325 (1910), also p. 331 for possible government reinforcement of tribal authority; SWA Administrator, *Annual Report 1921*, p. 12.

58 Nitsche, *Ovamboland*, p. 136; Lüderitzbucht Chamber of Mines, (hereafter LCoM) *Annual Report*, 4/3/11 (in NA 4994/1227 Consul – Sec. NA 29/8/11), p. 3.

59 Cf. Lennsen, *Chronik*, p. 171; Leutwein, *Elf Jahre*, pp. 195–6.

60 Stals, 'Die aanraking', p. 326.

61 Many migrants not possessing cattle could expect subsequently to build a herd through kinship mechanisms or through barter exchange using purchased goods.

62 These remarks apply particularly to Ukwanyama (Stals, 'Die aanraking',

pp. 334–5; see NA 4994/1227, Consul, Memo. January 1912; Memo 14/2/13, press extracts).

63 Mandume of Ukwanyama (1917) and Ipumbu of Ukwambi (1932); on the former, see NA 4994/1227, correspondence March–September, 1916.

64 NA 4994/1227, Res. Comm. – SWA Sec. 1/3/16, Report; Schoch, diary 24/6/20 (Ombalantu).

65 South Africa, *Report by Pritchard*; Loeb, *In Feudal Africa*, pp. 37, 43; SWA Administrator, *Annual Report 1926*, pp. 34–5.

66 Schoch, diary 17/6/20; Stals, 'Die aanraking', pp. 324–5.

67 Cf. e.g. NA 4994/1227 Sec. State FA – Consul 5/6/12 (enclosure); LCoM, *Annual Report 1910/11*; LCoM – IM 16/10/16, and Inspector of Mines' comments (Pretoria Central Archives, Department of Mines and Industries, Inspector of Mines, Windhoek, *Monthly* and *Annual Reports*, hereafter IM, 10/16); V. Ndadi, *Breaking Contract* (Oakland, California, LSM Press, 1974), pp. 20–1.

68 Stals, 'Die aanraking', p. 324; A. Graham, 'The response of African societies in Namibia to white administration, 1915–39' (London, SOAS, MA thesis, 1971), p. 11.

69 Cf. Nitsche, *Ovamboland*, p. 135.

70 For details, Stals, 'Die aanraking', pp. 334–43; NA 2410/1227 (c. 1910–12); after 1915, IM reports. After new regulations came into force in March 1911 and January 1912, conditions of employment and travel improved somewhat, but were still bleak (see IM, Military Magistrate, hereafter MM, 2070/17, Herbst, Memo 17/5/17).

71 NA 4994/1227, Consul, Memo. 30/6/10; MM 2070/17, NA Officer, Lüderitz – SWA Sec. 8/5/17. On the forced labour regime generally, Bley, *SWA*, part 3.

72 A. F. Calvert, *SWA During the German Occupation, 1884–1914* (London, T. W. Laurie, 1915), p. 23.

73 Statistics from IM reports and SWA Administrator, *Annual Reports*.

74 Arrivals and departures correlate fairly closely at a lag of one year during 1923–5.

75 SWA Administrator, *Annual Report 1924*, pp. 22–3, which also describes the desperate recruiting drive of Consolidated Diamond Mines (CDM) throughout southern Africa for alternative labour supplies.

76 Foreign Office Handbook no. 112, *SWA* (London, 1920), p. 43; SWA Administrator, *Annual Report 1921*, p. 12.

77 Lüderitzbucht Chamber of Mines, Annual Report 1910/11; Stals, 'Die aanraking', p. 330.

78 Nitsche, *Ovamboland*, pp. 135–6, translated. His figures for the black complement at Tsumeb, which established large short-term variations, suggest that the tactic was established practice.

79 Calvert, *SWA*, p. 23; Stals, 'Die aanraking', pp. 348, 343; NA 4994/1227, Consul, Memo. 30/6/10.

80 Stals, 'Die aanraking', p. 341; NA 4349/639, Consul – Gov. Gen. 9/10/11.

81 IM, *Annual Report 1917*. Other factors also probably influenced the workers' preference, see below.
82 Stals, 'Die aanraking', p. 337.
83 *Ibid.*, pp. 334–43, *passim*; cases are also scattered through the IM reports.
84 For the treatment of 'privileged' Cape workers who complained, see NA 2410/1227. For a detailed historical analysis, W. Beinart, ' "Jamani": Cape workers in German SWA, 1904–12', in W. Beinart and C. Bundy, *Hidden Struggles in Rural South Africa* (London, James Currey, 1987), pp. 166–90.
85 Cf. Stals, 'Die aanraking', pp. 327, 329.
86 Gordon, 'A note on labour action', pp. 8–11.
87 Many IM reports, esp. MM 2070/17 Herbst, Memo, 17/5/17, pp. 2, 5, and MM Report 22/17; Inspector of Mines, Lüderitz Office (hereafter IM LO), 8/17, *Annual Report 1917*; IM 9/24.
88 IM 5/16, IM LO 10/24.
89 On strikes, IM 10/16, LCoM–IM 16/10/16 IM 10/16; IM LO 6/17, 8/17, 12/24, 2/25, 9/25. On go-slows, MM 2070/17, MM., report 2/2/17, NA Officer, Lüd. – SWA Sec. 8/5/17; IM LO, *Annual Report 1917*, 10/24, 2/25; IM 9/24, 2/25.
90 IM reports and memos, 1916–17. The system had been abolished by October 1917 to 'humour' the workers (IM 10/17).
91 IM 8/16; IM LO 8/17, 12/24; IM 8/16, 10/16; MM, Report 2/2/17; IM LO 8/17. For a synopsis of her research based on the Windhoek Archives, see E. Thompson, 'Organised labor activities among Namibian workers, 1910–1950', paper presented to the International Conference in Solidarity with the Struggle of the People of Namibia, Paris, 1980.
92 IM LO, *Annual Report 1917*.
93 E.g. NA 4349/639, Native Affairs Department, Memo. 8/15, enclosure: Minutes of Landesrat 14/5/12.
94 SWA Administrator, *Annual Report 1924*, pp. 27–8. As a fishing port, Lüderitz had already attracted Cape fishermen, who were politically active. The results of extensive research on the UNIA/ICU movement in the early 1920s is to be found in G. Pirio, 'The role of Garveyism in the making of the southern African working class and Namibian nationalism' (University of California, unpublished paper, 1982), and A. B. Emmett, 'The Rise of African Nationalism in Namibia (1915–1966)' (University of the Witwatersrand, PhD thesis, 1987).
95 Schoch, diary 12/7/20; IM 10/24, 8/25.
96 IM 3/25, cf. also 10/24.
97 IM LO, *Annual Report 1917*; SWA, *Report of the Drought Investigation Commission* (Windhoek, 1924), para. 299.
98 *SWA Drought Investigation Commission*, para. 295, evidence of K. Altman (from central Namibia), 3.
99 NA 4994/1227, Res. Comm. – SWA Sec. 1/3/16, report, part IV p. 4.
100 Stals, 'Die aanraking, p. 285; G. K. H. Tötemeyer, 'Die rol van die

Wambo-elites in die politieke ontwikkeling van Owambo' (University of Stellenbosch, PhD thesis, 1974), p. 82.

101 WU Arch, AB. 851. *Damaraland Diocesan Records*, Rev. Tobias, letter 14/12/24.

102 Mines and Works Proc. 3–17, specifically modelled on the gold mines (SWA Administrator, *Annual Report 1922*, p. 16).

103 IM 1924–5, esp. 11/25; SWA Administrator, *Annual Report 1926*, p. 91.

104 Bley, *SWA*, pp. 170–3; Stals, 'Die aanraking', p. 323ff; R. J. B. Moorsom, 'Colonisation and proletarianisation: an exploratory investigation of the formation of the working class in Namibia under German and South African colonial rule to 1945' (University of Sussex, MA thesis, 1973), chapters 4 and 5.

105 SWA Administrator, *Annual Report 1919*, p. 5, also pp. 24 and 21.

106 E.g. MM 2070/17, Herbst, Memo. 17/5/17, p. 5; and discussion of Tsumeb above.

107 IM 5–6/23, 9/23, 3–6/24; SWA Administrator, *Annual Report 1922*, p. 14; *1925*, p. 28; *1926*, p. 36.

Forced Labour, *Mussoco* (Taxation), Famine and Migration in Lower Zambézia, Mozambique, 1870–1914

Shubi L. Ishemo

> The arrendatários are the senhores of the life and death of the natives . . . [They] all live through the exploitation of the mussoco tree.[1]

In an introduction to a special issue of *Estudos Moçambicanos* on forced labour, Professors Aquino de Bragança and Ruth First argued that,

> Colonial capitalism . . . (not only) prospered on cheap and forced labour, but it also prospered on the production of cheap commodities, and it instituted rigorous forms of exploitation of peasant production in order to guarantee these . . . Unlike the process of the installation of capitalism in Europe, this was not a peasantry expropriated from the land and converted into 'free' workers, 'free' to sell their labour power to capital. Rather colonial capitalism ensured a certain reproduction of peasant production for two reasons: firstly to transfer part of the capital's costs of the reproduction of the migrant, or *chibalo* worker and his family to the peasant household, and secondly, to coerce the peasantry into the production of cheap food and raw materials.[2]

Research for this paper was carried out in Mozambique. I am most grateful to the late Professors Aquino de Bragança and Ruth First, then Director and Director of Research respectively of the Centro de Estudos Africanos, to Dr Maria Ines Nogueira da Costa, Director of the Arquivo Histórico de Moçambique, to Drs Carlos Serra and Armando Jorge Lopes for their constant encouragement, and to Professor Terence O. Ranger who supervised this research at the University of Manchester.

Similarly, Carlos Serra has underlined this by identifying five principal characteristics of capitalist exploitation in Mozambique:

> the imposition of taxes (*mussoco*) in labour, in kind, and in money;
> the utilization of seasonal labour;
> the export of labour;
> the production of agricultural primary materials in the plantations with a later development of industrial processing; and
> the preservation of family (household) production units.[3]

The preservation of family production units was one of the key components in the process of capital accumulation. It meant that the obligation to pay *mussoco* propelled labour (mainly male) from household production to centres of capitalist production. But the wages paid were totally inadequate for the maintenance and reproduction of family production units. This task was off-loaded by capital, the colonial state and large estates (*latifundios*), on to the rest of the family unit whose labour was not withdrawn.[4]

In this study, I examine the centrality of *mussoco* (head-tax) in initiating and fuelling the process of colonial capital accumulation and its role in the reproduction of conditions for the acquisition of labour by the colonial state, capital and *latifundios*. *Mussoco*, as the summation of colonial capitalist development, was the singular extra-economic mechanism which, as Carlos Serra has correctly argued, partly transformed the Zambézian 'peasant petty-commodity producer into a forced seller of labour power'.[5] This transformation was expressed through the payment of labour rent, rent in kind and, later, money rent. During this transition, the peasants' agricultural calendar and the entire process of production were disrupted and social conditions for the outbreak of famine were set in motion and reproduced.

L. Vail and L. White have argued that during the period between 1870 and 1890, the Portuguese state set out to encourage peasant petty-commodity production and that this period was characterized by peasant prosperity.[6] But as I have argued elsewhere, this argument cannot be wholly sustained because the colonial state simultaneously created conditions for the development of a colonial capitalist plantation agriculture, and the *mussoco* regime, the constraints of trade, alienation of land and requisition of labour, etc. undermined the process of the commoditization of peasant agricultural production.[7]

Famine was a consequence of the disruption of peasant production processes. As a child of the *mussoco* regime, it also became, with the development of a plantation economy in the period after 1892, instrumental in the further partial withdrawal of labour from peasant agricultural production, and the maintenance, in a restructured form of family production units, of the reproduction of the phenomenon of migrant and seasonal labour. In this sense, the preconditions for capital accumulation were also preconditions for the outbreak of famine.

Colonial Views on African Peasant Agricultural Production and Famine

The views of colonial theorists like those of António Enez on Mozambique are too well known to repeat here.[8] But their significance can neither be minimized nor ignored because they provide an ideological framework for the creation of conditions favourable for the exploitation of labour, for capital accumulation and, consequently, for the disruption of peasant production processes.[9]

At a local level, these views were used to explain the causes of famine. For instance, the *latifundiarios* of Prazo Boror, Farinha e Lopes, saw the famines of the 1890s as a consequence of the so-called 'indolence of the natives'[10] which, in the words of the *latifundiarios* of Prazos Marral and Mirrambone, was indicative of 'the negligence of the native who never reserves food to meet his basic needs beyond a period of three months. It is this laxness which causes famine in all the years.' The material needs of the peasantry, so the argument continued, were few: '[the] land they cultivate is so small that the production only satisfies their meagre ambitions, like the purchase of bracelets, cotton cloth, and beads while

the rest goes to meet their sustenance and mussoco requirements.'[11]

Such views situated in Social Darwinism, were the manifestation of Portuguese and other European colonial racist
ideology.[12] To such an approach, the roots of famine were
situated in the 'nature' or 'innate' inability of the African
peasantry to produce sufficient to avoid food shortages during
periods of drought, floods, locust invasions, etc. These views,
it will be shown below, cannot be sustained at all.[13]

In recent years, a number of significant works on Eastern
Africa have highlighted the historical relationship between
colonial capitalist development, on the one hand, and famine
and ecological crises, on the other. A proper understanding of
the roots of famine, drought and ecological crises, Mamdani
strongly argues, must not involve the separation of society
from nature:

> nature is not a fixed, a historical category which
> regularly and ceaselessly produces droughts [etc.] in
> certain environments . . . [B]etween nature and society,
> between geography and history, there exists no Chinese
> Wall. Nature is itself a historical product. It is continu-
> ously being reproduced. Human beings are not animals
> who simply adapt to their environment. Human relation-
> ship to their environment is far more acute; it involves
> both adaptation/transformation. Through their pro-
> ductive activity, humans transform themselves and their
> natural environment – for good or bad. No analysis of
> any famine is possible without a firm grasp of these
> elementary tenets of historical materialism.[14]

In a similar manner, Meredeth Turshen advances our
understanding further by linking colonial capitalist relations
to ecological crisis and disease. She adopts a political ecology
approach which 'gives central importance to human energy in
the transformation of the complex interacting web that
characterises the environment.'[15] She argues that colonial
capitalist relations 'transformed the African ecology, which
also affected productivity, created malnutrition and produced
a new disease environment.'[16]

Such insights are central to our argument that the famines,

droughts and epidemics of the last quarter of the nineteenth century and early twentieth century in Zambézia cannot be regarded either as coincidental with colonial capitalist development, or as a consequence of the mythical 'innate' inability of the peasantry to produce sufficient material needs to avoid such crises. They were the manifestation of the general crisis set into motion by colonial capitalist development. I examine below the development of the *mussoco* regime: the principal mechanism of colonial capital accumulation, the principal agent of the retardation of the peasants' productive forces, the principal cause of countless deaths among the peasants of the Zambezi Basin, and the principal determinant of labour migration.

The Growth of the '*Mussoco* Tree', 1870–1923

In the Zambézian pre-capitalist societies, *mussoco* (or *mutsonko*) had been a customary tribute (rent in kind) paid by peasant producers to the pre-capitalist aristocracy or lineage chiefs. Isaacman has noted that 'The tax [*mutsonko*] seems to have been quite small, usually a bushel or two of sorghum or a comparable number of goats, sheep or chickens. The *mambos*, the indigenous pre-capitalist aristocracy, also received a series of symbolic gifts.'[17] Such produce was distributed to other members of the aristocracy or dominant lineages while commodities like ivory were exported to external markets in exchange for commodities of use-value. The appropriation of surpluses from peasant family production units was reproduced through the ideological, religious and political hegemony of the aristocracy.[18] The old *prazo* *(latifundio)*-holders (the *prazeros*) adopted the *mutsonko* and significantly reduced the political and economic power of the *mambos*. The *prazeros* maintained slave armies (the *Achicunda*) which reinforced mussoco collection. As is well known, the *Achicunda* were a parasitic, non-producing organ of *prazero* power. Their presence substantially increased the amount of *mussoco* collected from the peasant producers. Apart from ivory, most of the proceeds of the *mussoco* were use-values consumed by the *prazeros* and their retinues.

The *mussoco* was extracted in the context of the operation of merchant capital and did not lead to the development of the productive forces in the region. In fact, the decline of the *prazos* was a consequence of the intensive operation of merchant capital in the form of a resurgence of the slave trade to Brazil, Cuba and the Indian Ocean islands. Peasant agricultural production declined, and the export of agricultural produce like sugar from Tete, which in 1806 had been 115 arrobas of fine sugar and 589 arrobas of muscovado sugar, had, by 1885, completely declined.[19]

In a series of unsuccessful measures, the Portuguese state attempted to reverse this trend by attempting to initiate a process of colonial capitalist development. In 1832, it passed a decree abolishing the Crown *prazos*, which was followed in 1838 by a measure which withheld further land grants. A more fundamental, but unsuccessful, measure that set up the basis for the future *prazo/mussoco* regulations, was the 1854 decree which, like that of 1832, abolished the *prazos* and ordered that they revert to the state. Unlike earlier decrees, however, it sought to grant land to African peasant producers on condition that they carried out agricultural production and paid to the state an annual hut tax (*imposto de palhota*) of 1,600 reis in kind or in money.[20] Linked to the abolition of slavery and the creation of a new social category of *libertos*, the 1854 decree was significant in two ways. First, it implied, in theory, the setting into motion of a process towards the transformation of former slaves into free peasants producing an agricultural surplus for export. Second, the surplus product would be appropriated by the colonial state in the form of hut tax in place of the old head tax. This would then place the responsibility for the production of export crops and hence the payment of tax or rent on the peasant family production units rather than the old *prazeros*. In this way, the Portuguese state sought to accumulate without itself entering the sphere of production. These measures were theoretical and they failed because of the increased export of slaves and because the extent of Portuguese colonial occupation was restricted to the vicinity of Quelimane while throughout the rest of Lower Zambézia, the old *mussoco* continued.

As I have shown elsewhere,[21] the liberalization of trade in

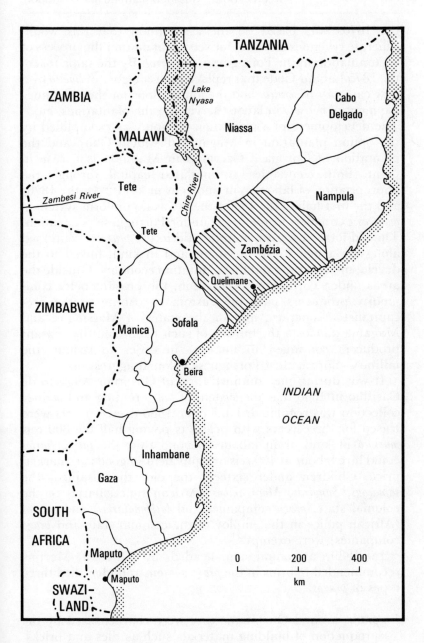

Map 1 People's Republic of Mozambique

the 1870s was based on the assumption that this would generate revenues essential for setting in motion the process of accumulation in the Portuguese economy. By the same token, the 1875 Labour Code that replaced the category of *liberto* by a new category of *serviçal* laid the foundations for the obligatory payment of *mussoco* in labour service on the plantations, etc.[22] The development of a plantation economy as exemplified by the opium plantation in Maganja d'Aquem Chire and the plantation of Correia e Carvalho in Mahindo is a case in point. Both companies accumulated capital through the appropriation of labour rent and rent in kind.[23] In the 1870s and the first half of the 1880s, there was no uniform system of *mussoco* extraction in the areas under Portuguese occupation. The old form of *mussoco* in kind paid to the *prazeros* continued alongside a new form, in labour and in kind, linked to the development of the capitalist plantation economy. Outside the areas under Portuguese occupation, the peasant petty commodity producers paid the customary tribute to the pre-capitalist aristocracy, and in the states of Massingire and Maganja da Costa the burden of such tribute on the peasant producers continued to increase in order to sustain the military effort against Portuguese colonial aggression.

It was during the administration of Governor Augusto de Castilho in 1886 that the system of *prazo* renting and *mussoco* collection was regulated. Under the 1886 decree, *prazos* were leased for three years with peasants paying half the 800 reis *mussoco* in kind or in labour. Beyond this, the *latifundiarios* could hire labour at 400 reis or equivalent in goods at 'market' price. Children under sixteen, the old, the disabled, the *samaçoas, Sangiras, Moçazambos* (African functionaries of the colonial state, *prazo* companies and *latifundiarios*) and *sipaios* (African police in the employ of the colonial state and *prazo* companies) were exempt.[24]

In 1889, a commission headed by Oliveira Martins recommended reforms in the *prazo* system and identified three types of *prazos*:

1 *prazos* around Quelimane that were characterized by the production of building materials such as tiles and bricks, the distillation of alcoholic beverages, etc.

2 fiscal *prazos* around Sena for the purpose of *mussoco* extraction; and

3 'feudal' *prazos* in the interior of Tete, which the colonial state deemed hostile and therefore leased to the old *prazeros*.

The Commission saw Mozambique not as a colony of settlement, a commercial colony, but potentially a plantation colony. It recommended the maintenance of the *prazo* system as a basis for the development of a plantation economy and that part of *mussoco* be paid in labour.[25]

The Commission's recommendations were adopted in the decree of 18 November 1890 issued by António Enes. This translated the Castilho formula of the *optional* payment of *mussoco* in labour into the *obligatory* payment of half of the 800 reis in labour. As the decree put it, this was 'to promote the development of agriculture, converting the *mussoco* into an indirect means of compelling those who pay it, and those who collect it, to apply themselves to the exploitation of the soil.'[26] There was to be a census every five years and rent paid by the *prazo*-holders to the colonial state would be adjusted in proportion to increases in the population. Significantly, *feiras* (fairs) would be established in every *prazo* with the peasants prohibited from selling to any party other than those operating at such *feiras* under the supervision of the *latifundiario*. Like the 1886 measures, the pre-capitalist aristocracy in the service of the colonial state and *latifundio*, children under fourteen, old people over sixty, the disabled and *sipaios* were exempt.[27] The 1890 measures were reinforced by the 1892 regulations, under which peasants were obliged to pay half the *mussoco* in money rent or in kind (export crops such as sesame, groundnuts, etc.).[28] In effect, money rent was to be computed from labour rent. In 1899, the level of *mussoco* was increased by 50 per cent to 1,200 reis, of which one-third was to be paid as labour rent amounting to one week's wages of 400 reis. It declared peasants with 'no fixed address' to be 'vagrants'. This was aided by the limitation of the powers of the Inspectorate-General of the *prazos* in the decree of 1896.[29] The plantation companies, the *latifundiarios*, were thus accorded unlimited powers to appropriate labour on an increasing

scale. The 1909 regulation setting up what were in effect
'reserves' in which peasants were legally not owners of the
means of production (land) 'tied the producer to the land in
order to facilitate the collection of mussoco'.[30]

Subsequent measures included first the 1913 increase in the
level of *mussoco* to 1,600 reis for peasants resident in the *prazos*
and 1,400 reis for those resident elsewhere. This was aimed at
raising funds to finance the construction of the Quelimane
railway.[31] Then in 1916 a ministerial order set up a
commission to recommend the reform of *prazos*. Its recommendations were adopted in the decree No. 5: 713 of 10 May
1919, under which labour rent was fixed at half the *mussoco*
level and the period of work by peasants on the plantations,
etc. was fixed at a maximum of 180 days not to exceed 60 days
at a time. This could, however, be varied. All labour beyond
this was to be 'voluntary'. Agents of Authority (Agentes
d'Autoridades) were forbidden from interfering with this kind
of labour. The payment of *mussoco* in labour service was not to
exceed half the *mussoco* level, although total payment of *mussoco*
in labour service could be made only under 'agreement'
between labour and capital/*latifundio*. Children under fourteen
could only perform domestic labour. The lessees were
forbidden to collect *mussoco* in kind. This decree repealed the
restrictions in the regulations of 7 July 1892 which had
accorded commercial monopoly to the lessees. The weekly
wages were retained at the 1886 and 1892 level of 40 centavos
(400 reis) for men and 20 centavos (200 reis) for women and
children aged between fourteen and eighteen. Wages were to
be paid in cash and not in tokens as before, although children
could be paid in clothing.[32] The 1921 decree by the High
Commissioner of Mozambique increased the 1913 *mussoco*
level to 2.5 escudos.[33] Two years later, the *mussoco* level
increased to 10 escudos for single men and 20 escudos for
married men.[34] In order to enforce these changes, Zambézia
was divided into four circumscriptions under the direct
administration of the colonial state.[35]

The increases in the level of *mussoco* were very steep indeed
and they do suggest a higher rate of accumulation. Now I will
briefly consider the relationship between the colonial state
and the capital/*latifundio* with regard to their respective share

of the *mussoco* revenues. In the 1892 regulations, the colonial state fixed the amount of rent payable to it by the lessee at 50 per cent of the potential *mussoco* revenue, calculated by means of a population census held every five years. The lessee would collect *mussoco*, half of which he was permitted to retain.[36] The colonial state made provisions for adjusting the *mussoco* and rent levels. It could alter the rent paid by the lessees in some proportion to the increase or reduction in the level of *mussoco*: a reduction of 25 per cent of the increase would be retained by the lessee as compensation for what was assumed to constitute the added costs of administering the collection. In the 1913 increase, however, this provision was dropped.[37] The 1892 regulations had allowed the lessees to appeal for a moratorium in rent payment but never a decrease in rent, especially when it was fixed by the Portuguese state as was the case with Prazos Maganja d'Alem Chire and Massingire. In this case, if *mussoco* was not extracted from peasant producers in full, the rent to the colonial state had still to be paid in full.[38] That may explain why, between 1907 and 1909, 77 per cent of the *mussoco* collected in 17 out of 20 *prazos* in Zambézia (except Milange, Lugela and Lómuè) reverted to the colonial state.[39] The grave implications of this on peasant agricultural production, on their food reserves, simple commodity exchange, etc. will be examined later. The 1919 decree fixed rent at 70 per cent of the produce of *mussoco* and provided for a 5 per cent increase in rent levels every five years.[40] Out of a total of 2.5 esc. reis *mussoco* in 1921, 1.2 esc. was considered to be the *mussoco* out of which the lessee had to pay 50 per cent while the remaining 1.3 esc. was considered additional, to be collected and remitted in full to the colonial state. In the 1923 legislation, 8.5 esc. out of the 10 esc. *mussoco* was to be remitted to the colonial state, while the remaining 1.2 esc. was considered as *mussoco* subject to a 50 per cent rent.[41] From this it is clear that a greater percentage of the *mussoco* increasingly reverted to the colonial state.

The colonial state retained the direct administration of Alto Molócuè and Maganja da Costa, from 1892 and 1898 respectively, extracting *mussoco*, selling labour to the plantation companies in lower Zambézia and, up to 1913, exporting labour to the Transvaal and, thereafter, to São Tomé. In this way, it could accumulate without entering into production. In effect, its relationship to peasant producers in these areas was parasitic and similar to that of the *latifundiario*. It is probably not difficult to imagine the magnitude of the burden that the peasantry of the Zambezi Basin faced. For the *latifundiarios* and capital, increases in rent to the colonial state meant greater extraction of peasants' labour time and surplus product as *mussoco* payment far above the official level and, all too often, labour without payment. In real terms, the value of the wages paid since 1886 declined while *mussoco* levels rose dramatically. The rate of the withdrawal of male labour time from peasant family production units increased so as to enable the producers to pay *mussoco*. The burden for the maintenance and reproduction of peasant family units, therefore, fell increasingly onto the backs of female producers. *Mussoco* became the principal mechanism for the reproduction of such a sexual division of labour and above all, for the provision of labour to the colonial state and capital. The mechanisms for this and the effect on peasant agricultural production will be elaborated on later. As a product of the 'mussoco tree', *ekwethe*[42] or forced labour was the principal source of capital accumulation in Zambézia.

Mussoco as Rent

From the above, we can identify two distinct historical periods in the function of *mussoco*. Up to about 1850, the *prazos* were characterized by the operation of merchant capital. Paid in kind and in labour, the product of *mussoco* was directed towards use-values. The second epoch – after 1870 – was one of colonial capitalist development, characterized by specific forms of capitalist relations. Also paid in kind, in labour, and, later, in money, *mussoco* was directed towards the process of capital accumulation. Although in both epochs the *prazeros* – the indigenous pre-capitalist aristocracy of the colonial state – capital and *latifundiarios* were the normal landowners, and appropriated the peasant producers' surplus product, the producers were not separated from the means of production – land. The surplus product thus appropriated as tax (or tribute) also constituted rent, and could in both epochs be extracted through extra-economic mechanisms – politico-military, ideological and juridical.

The process of colonial capitalist development in the Zambezi Basin was characterized by forms of pre-capitalist rent and after 1919, as we have seen above, by money rent. Colonial capitalist development did not dissolve the old forms in total. Rather, they were subordinated to it and served as the basis for its accumulation. This explains why the colonial *latifundio* and the *prazo* companies of the last quarter of the nineteenth and early twentieth centuries retained a seemingly feudal or semi-feudal superstructure. Indeed Marx underlined this when he wrote about rent in kind: 'In the first place, it is a mere tradition carried over from an obsolete mode of production and managing to prolong its existence as a survival . . . Secondly, however, where rent in kind persisted on the basis of capitalist production, it was no more, and could be no more, than an expression of money rent in medieval garb.'[43] *Mussoco*, as labour rent, withdrew labour from peasant agricultural production. *Mussoco*, as rent in kind, deprived the peasant producers of their food resources and, in years of poor harvest or drought, even of the means of subsistence. The price of the surplus product so extracted and the social conditions within which such surpluses were produced, were never the concern of the *latifundiarios*. To have been so concerned would have prejudiced the rate of accumulation. Consequently, *mussoco* did separate the producers from working their means of production at crucial moments in the agricultural calendar when there were no alternative sources of sustenance. In many ways, therefore, *mussoco* was the principal mechanism for the transformation of the Zambézian peasants into forced sellers of labour power.

The Administration of *Mussoco*

As is well known, the colonial state's role was to prepare favourable conditions for capitalist penetration and to establish the framework for the exploitation of labour and land. Between 1870 and 1890, the administration of *mussoco* was carried out by the *prazo* administrators, some of whom were simultaneously *latifundiarios* or merchants.[44] With the decree of 18 November 1890, the colonial state was represented by a so-called Agent of Authority (Agente d'Autoridade). Far from serving the colonial state, the Agentes d'Autoridades were, in effect, functionaries of the *latifundiarios* who appointed and paid them. Their function, aided by a force of *sipaios*, was to enforce the collection of *mussoco* on behalf of the colonial state and *latifundiarios*.[45]

The peasant pre-capitalist political structures were utilized for *mussoco* collection and labour procurement. This involved either the cooperation or overthrow of the pre-capitalist aristocracy as tools of the colonial state and *latifundios*. In areas where the pre-capitalist aristocracy was overthrown, the old *Achicunda* military elite – the *Moçazambos*, *samaçoas* and *Sangiras* – were promoted to the status of a village aristocracy.[46] Some of the aristocratic allies of the Portuguese were even promoted to military ranks and received a monthly pay of 4,500 reis.[47]

In Maganja da Costa, Alto Molócuè, Baixo Molócuè and Moebaze, the colonial state paid 10 reis to the pre-capitalist aristocracy for every worker recruited for the Transvaal, Southern Rhodesia and the Lower Zambézian plantations.[48]

The decree of 18 November 1890 and the subsequent regulations of 7 July 1892 permitted the *latifundiarios* to exercise wide powers and raise a force of *sipaios*. These were to be organized on similar lines to the old *Achicunda ensacas* (regiments) to assist the *Moçazambos*, *Sangiras* and *samaçoas* to enforce the *mussoco* and hut tax collection, organize the *mussoco* census, and procure labour for public works.[49] In cases where peasants refused to pay *mussoco*, *sipaios* were sent in to either seize food reserves or men for public works. In other cases, *samaçoas* arrested peasants and handed them over to the *sipaios*.[50] Most of the *sipaios* were not local and did not know local languages. In Prazos Anguaze e Andone, for instance, there were Angolan conscripts.[51] As the demand for labour increased – for example at the brick-making plant at Chipaca – so did the number of *sipaios*. In 1893, there was a total of 60 *sipaios* in the two *prazos*.[52] By February 1895, there was a total of 100 *sipaios* organized in four *ensacas*.[53] An increase in such a parasitic and non-productive organ of the colonial state and *latifundiario* power exerted pressure on peasant food resources, particularly when they arbitrarily seized food reserves. Such a practice was known as *sesura mafundo*. Early examples of this were in Prazo Melambe, south of the Zambezi, where peasants' food reserves, instruments of production, such as hoes, and prestige goods, such as brass bracelets, were seized by *sipaios*.[54] In 1881, the *sipaios* ransacked peasant food reserves in Maganja and Mugovo.[55] Other instances were in Prazo Guengue in 1888,[56] and in Prazos Luabo and Melambe during 1892.[57] In the vicinity of Quelimane, peasants were driven by such practices to work in Quelimane so as to sustain their families.[58] These are but a few of the various incidences of *sesura mafundo* covering the last quarter of the nineteenth century. They demonstrate the virtual absence of conditions of peace to facilitate peasant agricultural production.

Mussoco as the Negation of Peasant Petty-Commodity Production

The view advanced by Vail and White that the period between 1870 and 1890 witnessed an 'agricultural revolution'[59] presents us with unanswered questions. It does not tell us whether there was a change in the relations of production. Flowing from this, to characterize the Zambézian pre-capitalist economy undergoing transformation as one 'exclusively based on slaving and hunting and gathering ivory and beeswax' is totally to overlook agricultural production which was central to the Zambézian economy, and grossly to underrate the level of social development. To assume that the imported iron hoes, axes, etc. revolutionized production is to ignore the disruption of handicraft production. Finally, to dwell exclusively on trade[60] is to ignore the social relations of production and hence the effect of colonial capitalist development on pre-capitalist internal structures. In short, we are not given an analysis of the effect of capitalist development on peasant production processes, the extent of the disruption of these processes, and the development of famine.

It is because of the above omissions that the period 1870–90

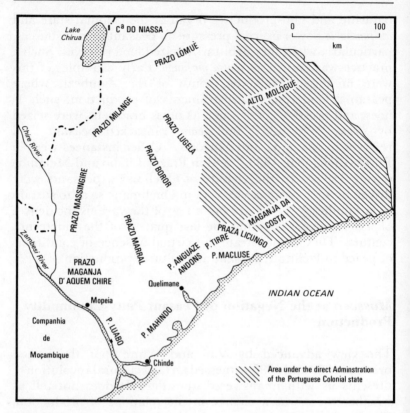

Map 2 Zambézia in 1914

is misleadingly taken to be one of uniform prosperity for peasant producers. No evidence is given as to whether the peasantry devoted more labour time to producing commodities for export rather than domestic food production and no indications are given as to what effects the *mussoco* regime had on the production of commodities and means of existence.[61]

While the availability of more historical data would greatly assist us in answering the above questions in a more meaningful way, we may, nevertheless, argue that within the contradictions unleashed by colonial capitalist development, were conditions for famine which were evident from the late 1870s through the 1880s. The serious famines and droughts of

Table 1   Recorded periods of famine 1862–1907

Year	Area
1862–3	Lower Chire, Lower Zambézia
1869, 1872, 1874	Lower Zambézia
1881–2	Lower Zambézia (Prazo Tirre)
1885–7	Lower Zambézia
1893–5	Lower Zambézia (Mirrambone e Marral, Nameduro e Tirre, Boror, Ancuaze e Andone, Quelimane do Sal e Carrungo)
1896–7	Tete
1900–3	Lower Zambézia
1905	Lower Zambézia
1906	Lower Zambézia
1907	Lower Zambézia

Source: Shubi L. Ishemo, 'Economy and Society of the Lower Zambezi Basin in Mozambique ca. 1850–1914' (University of Manchester, unpublished PhD thesis, 1986), pp. 216–17.

the 1890s and early twentieth century (see table 1) were but a manifestation of the process that emerged and developed during the late 1870s and 1880s. *Mussoco,* as the principal mechanism for capital accumulation, was the principal factor in initiating this process and reproducing it. The conditions of famine, therefore, were conceived in the womb of colonial capitalism. As a child of the *mussoco* regime, famine had long-term implications on social formation in the Lower Zambézian region.

Table 2 shows the value of exports through the port of Quelimane between 1881 and 1910. It illustrates three distinct periods. First, as I have already shown elsewhere,[62] there was a general increase in peasant petty-commodity production from the late 1870s to 1890. But, simultaneously, the *mussoco* regime was undermining such production. Unfortunately the sources consulted do not provide a breakdown of the figures into commodities. It is possible, however, to do that for the figure of 1886, as shown in table 3. The decline in the value of exports for that year could be accounted for by the introduction of new *mussoco* measures by Governor Augusto Castilho and famine.

Table 2 Trends of export trade through Quelimane, 1881–1910

Year	Exports (value in Reis)
1881	204 187 549
1882	291 394 024
1883	440 954 598
1884	360 941 164
1885	415 830 324
1886	298 478 787
1887	478 895 626
1888	380 697 326
1889	418 335 083
1890	356 346 804
1891	502 555 753
1892	507 675 065
1893	349 776 125
1894	338 173 515
1895	280 581 945
1896	252 127 478
1897	354 266 022
1898	321 896 808
1899	222 022 460
1900	158 216 525
1901	125 538 476
1902	170 375 836
1903	149 314 975
1904	176 830 446
1905	186 629 327
1906	246 971 345
1907	176 290 159
1908	195 333 560
1909	320 704 085
1910	290 066 325

Source: F. Carvalho, *Relatório do Governador, 1911–12* (Lourenço Marques, 1912), pp. 102–3, quoted in Carlos Serra, *A Introdução do Capitalismo na Baixa Zambézia e emergência do sistema de plantações (1870/1915)* (Departamento de História, Universidade Eduardo Mondlane, mimeo, March 1979), pp. 11, 14, 16.

Table 3   Decline in exports: comparative figures for February and
October 1886 (value in Reis)

Commodity	February 1886	October 1886
Groundnuts	64 179 260	⎫
Sesame	54 880 395	⎬ 29 844 600
Copra	27 287 360	⎭
Rubber	10 600 800	266 825
Ivory	167 935 576	2 000

Source: Boletim Oficial, 34 (1888), quoted in Serra, *A Introdução do Capitalismo*,
p. 11.

The figures in table 3 show a dramatic decline in the export of
seeds, rubber, and ivory. The decline in the export of oil seeds
reflected a decline in peasant petty-commodity production
while the low figure for rubber demonstrated a decrease in
gathering. The sharp fall in ivory exports was the result of re-
routing the ivory traffic by the Yao pre-capitalist aristocracy
to the northern Mozambican and southern Tanzanian ports.
This was prompted by the disruption, as a result of the
introduction of the *mussoco* regime, of the production of food
surpluses which had hitherto sustained the ivory caravans to
Ingode and Bajone in Maganja da Costa. Such a decline in
the ivory traffic from the Chire Highlands, Lake Nyasa and
Milange is dated from 1885 and took a sharp fall with the ban
on the import and sale of firearms and gunpowder to the pre-
capitalist aristocracy in Lower Zambézia.[63] From 1890
onwards, ivory hardly featured in the exports through
Quelimane.[64]

The second period, 1891 to 1892, recorded the peak exports
for the entire period. The data available leave a lot of
questions unanswered as to why there was a record increase in
the value of exports. But we do know that during 1891 there
was a concerted campaign in the areas already under colonial
occupation to collect the *mussoco* that had not been collected
throughout 1890. For 1892, British consular reports attribute
the record figure not to an unprecedented increase in peasant
petty-commodity production, but rather to old stocks of
produce being held over from 1891 by the *latifundiarios* and the

European and Indian commercial houses in anticipation of better prices than those obtaining at the end of 1891.[65] From 1893 to 1910, there was a steady decline in exports through Quelimane. It is not possible, because of the nature of the data, to provide a breakdown commodity by commodity. But, during this period, the expansion of the plantation economy, the monopolization of commerce by the plantation companies and *latifundiarios*, and the increase in the level of *mussoco* led to the decline in peasant petty-commodity production. Peasants virtually ceased to produce for exchange.[66] Before 1900, the *latifundiario* of Prazo Marral, Romão de Jesus Maria, obtained through *mussoco* extraction an average of 55 tons of groundnuts per annum. In 1911, the new leaseholders of the *prazo*, the Sena Sugar Factory, obtained only 5 tons.[67] Increasingly during the years after 1900, the majority of the exports were drawn from such commodities as sugar and coconuts produced on the plantations. The decline in the peasant production of oilseeds for exchange corresponded with the expansion of a plantation economy whose dependence on forced labour was to turn the pre-1892 petty-commodity producing peasant household units into labour reserves. This process was manifest in the periodic outbreaks of famine, drought, disease, etc. In the rest of this paper, I examine the process as it developed from the late 1870s.

It is probable that during the late 1870s, the introduction of *mussoco* and the subsequent uprisings spreading through the 1880s greatly disrupted peasant agricultural production.[68] Referring to Prazos Marrongane, Nameduro and Tirre during this period, the *latifundiario*, Thomas d'Aquino Lobo, reported that the local population was 'famine-stricken'.[69] Famine was exacerbated, first, by the *sipaios'* raids to seize food reserves for their own use and, secondly, by the tribute-collecting raids of the *ensacas* of the state of Maganja da Costa.[70]

The decline in the export figures for 1886 corresponded to the introduction of the new *mussoco* measures by the administration of Governor Augusto de Castilho. The serious famine of 1886 was a consequence of the earlier *mussoco* measures which had precipitated peasant uprisings and hence insecure conditions for agricultural production. This was particularly the case in Prazos Marral, Mahindo, Maganja d'Aquem

Chire, Luabo, Anguaze and Andone. Between 1886 and 1892, there was a decline in rice production in the *prazos* which had hitherto been the principal sources of grain for Quelimane, namely Inhassunge, Cheringane, Tangalane, Luabo, Andone and São Paulo.[71]

The crisis in peasant agricultural production was reflected in the decline of *mussoco* collection during this period. In Prazo Inhassunge, the Administrator claimed that the colonial state was 'owed' 44 contos worth of rice.[72] Notwithstanding the famine conditions, the colonial state and *latifundiarios* violently seized the peasants' food reserves. In 1887, they attempted to collect *mussoco* 'arrears' for 1885 and 1886 from peasants in Prazo Luabo. Near Quelimane, in Prazos Cheringoma and Tangalane, they seized almost the entire peasants' reserves of rice and beans.[73]

Throughout the region, the amount of *mussoco* extracted was always greater than the official level. Between 1887 and 1892 in Prazo Guengue, the *latifundiario*, António Francisco Dulio Ribeiro, extracted *mussoco* in beans and grains. The magnitude of the disruption of the peasants' production processes in Guengue can be extrapolated from a report on Dulio Ribeiro.

> He practised high irregularities and indignities against the colonos (peasants) as well as exacting from them exorbitant amounts of mussoco higher than the official figure; he forced women to work for him and the disabled whose health did not permit them to work in the fields; he destroyed the colonos' huts and violently acquired porters and machilleiros hammock bearers.[74]

Ribeiro's *mussoco* regime was aimed at an accelerated process of capital accumulation. Between 1887 and 1890, he had not paid rent to the colonial state; yet, during the period of acute food shortages in 1890, he collected *mussoco* in kind valued at 6 contos of reis and earned more than 1,000 Indian rupees from selling grain to the military command post in Guengue.[75] Other observers noted that the extraction of *mussoco* above the official level was common throughout the region. 'The natives pay their tax in their own produce; the lessee fixes the value of such produce, and also measures it with his own measure, so that 27 litres nominal is often really 40 or 45 to the lessee.'[76] Another observer added, 'When paying their taxes in oil seeds or in grain, [they] had to pay beyond the real value of the tax.'[77]

To the functionaries of the colonial state, the inability of peasants to pay *mussoco* had nothing to do with the disruption of the peasants' production processes by the very *mussoco* that they were enforcing. To them, the peasants were simply looking for 'excuses' not to pay: 'If they do not refuse to pay, they excuse themselves on the grounds that they do not have much. In the past year they did the same and to date many have not paid.'[78] That 'past year' was 1886, a year of famine. Famine was, however, immaterial to the *latifundiarios* and the colonial state. Whatever the conditions, *mussoco* had to be paid. This was the case during the period of food shortages in 1891. Campaigns to collect *mussoco* 'arrears' for 1890 were launched.[79] It was common practice for the *sipaios* to raid villages before the harvest season began. In such cases, *mussoco* could only be extracted from the peasants' food reserves. This was the case in the district of Mutonganhita in Prazo Anguaze in 1892, where peasant households were forced to pay *mussoco* from their food reserves despite pleas for deferment until after the rice harvest in May.[80] In February and March 1893, the *samaçoas* of Marrongane in Prazo Anguaze were ordered to collect *mussoco*. While expressing their willingness to cooperate, the two local *muenes* declared that their people did not have the agricultural produce with which to pay *mussoco* as the district was experiencing an acute famine. Despite these pleas, the *sipaios* seized food reserves consisting mainly of beans.[81] The consequences of such food seizures are easy to imagine, as many were left in a state of acute malnutrition and therefore vulnerable to disease. The resultant debilitation of peasant producers may account for the decline in agricultural production and the devastating periods of famine and epidemics in the years after 1893. *Mussoco* and the subsequent increases in its levels reproduced this process – the absolute pauperization of the peasant household production units, and the creation of a reserve army of labour.

The roots of the decline in peasant production of agricultural surpluses and the crisis in the production of the means of existence lie, therefore, not in the post-1890 period, but in the period that preceded it. While not denying the development of peasant petty-commodity production in the period before 1890, it would be absurd not to recognize that this development was in contradiction to the needs of the Portuguese colonial state, capital and *latifundios* to accumulate. It would be naive to imagine that such accumulation could take place in conditions characterized by an autonomous petty-commodity producing peasantry. All or part of the pre-capitalist social formation characteristic of the Zambézian petty-commodity production had to be subordinated to the needs of colonial capitalist development. I consider below the decline of *akaporo* (slave labour) in peasant petty-commodity production.

The Decline of the *Akaporo* and the Resurgence of the 'Free Emigration Scheme'

The decline in the external slave trade and the development of peasant petty-commodity production had significantly led to the internal absorption of slave labour (*akaporo*). In Prazo Marral, Cundine had been the principal terminus for the slave traffic, from Matapwire's state of Milange, destined for sale to peasant family production units in Marral, Mahindo, Luabo, and Maganja d'Aquem Chire.[82] In Boror, Nameduro, Tirre, Anguaze, Andone and Macuze, the *akaporo* had become integral to the Lower Zambézian structure of social production. First, it had become important in the production of surpluses to sustain the trade caravans from Milange and beyond to Ingode, Quelimane, Maganja da Costa and Macuze. Secondly, it was increasingly used in the production of oilseeds for export. Colonial occupation and the *mussoco* regime neutralized the power of the local aristocracy who had been intermediaries in the slave and ivory trade between the Yao pre-capitalist aristocracy of Milange and beyond, on the one hand, and the military aristocracy (Cazembes) of Maganja da Costa, on the other. The extraction of peasant agricultural surpluses as *mussoco* payment similarly deprived the trade caravans of sufficient provisions. In short, the insecurity created by *mussoco* campaigns was not conducive to the production of agricultural surpluses by the local peasant family units. Consequently, the Yao aristocracy switched their ivory traffic to the northern Mozambican and southern Tanzanian ports.[83] As an example, the value of ivory through the port of Quelimane declined from 167,935,576 reis in February 1887 to 2,000 reis in October 1887.[84] Between 1885 and 1887, the export of ivory to Bombay, which had been the principal destination of Mozambican ivory, declined dramatically.[85] By 1890, ivory exports through Quelimane had almost disappeared,[86] and trade caravans from Milange and the Lake Nyasa region no longer operated through Lower Zambézia to Quelimane.[87]

The decline of exports through Quelimane, therefore, provides us with indicators as to the decline not only of the production of agricultural surpluses for sustaining the transiting trade caravans, but also for export and, above all, for sustaining the producers themselves. Consequently, the demand for slaves fell. Under conditions characterized by a decline in the production of surpluses, and a general food shortage, the pre-capitalist aristocracy and other peasant household production units started, during the early 1890s, to dispense with the *akaporo*.

In Boror and Nameduro, the *muenes* were offering what was derogatorily termed *moleques* (young male slaves) to the *latifundiarios* as payment for *mussoco*.[88] As these were periods of famine and food shortages, the *latifundiarios* accepted the *akaporo* as *mussoco* payment in addition to seizing food reserves.[89]

How were the *akaporo* used? In June 1881, a colonial decree legalized the so-called *Esquema Livres Engajados* or 'Free Emigration Scheme' which had been nominally abolished in 1864 and was a euphemism for the French slave trade to the Comoros (Mayotte and Nossi Be).[90] After 1890, the Portuguese colonial state was directly involved in the export of labour to the French Indian Ocean island colony of Réunion. It encouraged the French to open 'recruiting' offices at Quelimane and Macuze.[91] Indeed, one of those agencies of free trade, of 'prosperity', in the period of peasant petty-commodity production, the French commercial house of

Mante Freres et Borelli de Regis Aine under its Quelimane manager, M. G. Eigermann, became the chief 'recruiting' agency of the so-called *engajados livres* in Zambézia.[92] Under this scheme, the pre-capitalist aristocracy were invited to 'deliver' men at Quelimane and Macuze for transportation to Réunion. Yet this 'recruitment' filled the local peasants with fear. Many working in the public works programme fled for fear of being transported into slavery.[93]

For the Portuguese colonial state, the resurgence of the 'Free Emigration Scheme' provided it with the opportunity to extract *mussoco* from would-be 'emigrants', their family production units, and their pre-capitalist aristocracy. It required that registers of 'emigrants' specified the names of their villages, and those of their respective pre-capitalist aristocracy. The *prazos* particularly affected by this scheme were Anguaze and Andone where the 'emigrants' registers were used to extract *mussoco* in kind even from households which had already paid. Thus the linking of transportation to Réunion with the payment of *mussoco* in kind had the effect of withdrawing young male productive labour from the household production units, and of depleting the peasants' food reserves. Those unable to pay *mussoco* were forcibly marched to Quelimane or Macuze where the 'emigration' agents paid *mussoco* 'on their behalf' in exchange for transportation to Réunion.[94] Anguaze and Andone suffered about one-third of the total deaths caused by the famine of 1906 in Zambézia.

Rupture of Simple Commodity Exchange

The *prazo* regulations of 7 July 1892 accorded commercial monopoly to the *latifundiarios*, and prohibited the itinerant Indian traders from operating freely in the *prazos*.[95] They could trade only through the *prazo feiras* subject to paying licence fees to the colonial state. These regulations did not restrict the exchange of agricultural produce between peasant producers, but such exchange was only permitted within the confines of each *prazo*.[96] Some *latifundiarios* extended the restrictions to include inter-peasant exchange of use-values. These use-values comprised surplus agricultural produce essential for supplementing the means of existence of peasant households. For example, the peasants of Nameduro exchanged fruit such as mangoes, oranges, etc. for tobacco, *magagada* (cassava), rice and maize from the peasants of Macuze and Licungo.[97] For some *latifundiarios* like Pedro Valdez of Macuze, such exchange of use-values between peasants of different *prazos* constituted an infringement of their commercial monopoly. In many instances, peasants travelling from Macuze to trade in Nameduro and Licungo, and vice versa, were intercepted by *prazo sipaios* and had their goods confiscated without compensation. They were taken to Segune, the principal *feira* in Macuze, where Valdez employed Indian store attendants. Here they were warned not to use Prazo Macuze as a transit area to other *prazos* in the inter-peasant simple commodity exchange. As an Indian attendant put it, 'The people of each prazo could only do business, be it selling or buying, in their respective prazos.'[98]

In many *prazos*, *latifundiarios* sought to prevent inter-peasant simple commodity exchange by seizing what they considered to be in excess of the household's needs. In this respect, the British Vice-Consul reported that 'Any native produce found therein [in the huts] beyond what is necessary for the needs of the little household is seized and forfeited, and the person found to have secreted it is severely punished without respect to either age or sex.'[99] Peasants were barred from entering into direct commodity exchange with Indian merchants at the *feiras*. The British Consul, Maugham, noted that the Companhia do Boror, Empresa Agrícola do Lugela often 'inflicted punishment upon natives for the offence of dealing with persons other than their prazo lessee which are of a terrible kind.'[100] In a petition to the British Vice-Consul, Indian merchants at Quelimane complained that 'the prazo-holders prevent the native from bringing his produce to the open market by forcing him through the prazo-police to bring up the whole of his crop, which the native has to dispose of to the prazo-holder not at a proper market value but at a price arbitrarily fixed by the purchaser.'[101]

Lower Zambézia was endowed with navigable rivers for small craft. Peasants in the region had navigated these waterways, transporting commodities such as oilseeds for export and facilitating inter-peasant exchange of commodities of use-value. In addition to using porterage, Portuguese, Indian and British traders frequently hired canoes and canoe-men for both passenger and goods traffic. With the 1892 *prazo* regulations, the ownership and operation of canoes by peasants was considered illegal. Consequently, the *latifundiarios* and some Portuguese traders appropriated the canoes they had hired and punished the owners for attempting to reclaim them. The excuse given was that 'blacks cannot own canoes'. An example of this was the case involving two peasants Arrufinado and Jussare, on the one hand, and a Portuguese trader, Manoel, resident at Inhamacata in Prazo Anguaze, on the other.[102] Similarly affected were peasant canoe owners in Macuze who used to ferry peasants and their produce across the River Mahali to Mucorrine in Prazo Nameduro. After 1892, Pedro Valdez prohibited this traffic and confiscated many canoes. He, however, had no objections to peasants from Nameduro selling their produce at his *feiras* in Macuze.[103]

While all the *latifundiarios*' aim in monopolizing commodity exchange was to fuel the process of capital accumulation, their tactics, although not contradictory to this aim, varied, especially with regard to inter-peasant simple commodity exchange. Raphael de Mello Amaral of Prazos Nameduro and Tirre considered the restrictions on inter-peasant simple commodity exchange across *prazo* boundaries to be counter productive. He disapproved of Pedro Valdez's methods in the neighbouring Prazo Macuze and considered inter-peasant commodity exchange as advantageous to merchants and *latifundiarios*. He argued that 'the little business of the blacks would result in greater and larger transactions' for the *latifundiarios*. He therefore doubted the usefulness of the 1892 *prazo* regulations:

> The blacks who go to the interior to buy one *cangarra* of *magagada* [cassava] or other produce which they lack, cannot be equated with the itinerant trader . . . I see the spirit of the law being to prevent the activities of traders; and the exploitation of the peasant who goes to buy one *cangarra* of *magagada* is contrary to the individual liberty to which they are all entitled.[104]

It should be emphasized that Raphael de Mello Amaral fully endorsed the restrictions on Indian traders. His defence of the 'individual liberty' of the peasants to exchange their produce with other peasants was meant to attract peasant petty-commodity producers from the surrounding *prazos* to his *feiras*; for as he tersely put it, at his *feiras* peasants 'bought dear and sold cheap'. Consequently the level of trade in Nameduro had increased despite the presence of Valdez's *sipaios* patrols along the Macuze–Nameduro border.[105]

Appropriation of the Peasants' Land

In 1913, a former Director of Agriculture in Mozambique estimated that the total area of Zambézia was 9 million hectares, of which 5,400,000 hectares were under the *latifundiarios* and 3,600,000 hectares under the direct administration of the Portuguese colonial state. But out of this only 0.5 per cent of 45,000 hectares were under plantation agriculture.[106] Prazo regulations granted all natural and labour resources to the leaseholders. Although this did not mean the separation of the peasant producers from land, the leaseholder could, in effect, appropriate such land with little or no compensation. The 1909 Land Law reserved areas for peasants but deprived them of the right of ownership, and occupation was conditional on production.[107] The significance of this, as Carlos Serra has correctly argued, was 'to tie the producer to the land in order to facilitate *mussoco* collection'.[108] Notwithstanding the 1909 law, this practice had been in operation from the 1890s.

In the coastal *prazos*, peasant coconut holdings were seized by the *latifundiarios* and traders. For instance in Prazo Anguaze, a Portuguese trader Dulio Ribeiro who was also *latifundiario* of Prazo Guengue, forced the local peasants to sell him their coconut plots. Furthermore, he encroached on their land by removing the demarcation lines of the plot that he had leased from the colonial state for trading purposes, and forbade the peasants from harvesting coconuts and clearing the bush for cultivation.[109] This deprived many peasant households of land for cultivation during November and December 1894. As the *prazo* administrator admitted, 'they desperately need the land to cultivate because they feared hunger for their children.'[110] In Prazo Carungo, the *latifundiario* confiscated 80 hectares of peasant coconut palm holdings. Peasant protests were dismissed on grounds that the land so appropriated was *baldio* (unused).[111]

It was through the seizure of the peasants' coconut holdings that some *latifundiarios* claimed to have initiated plantations. These plantations did not involve any initial investment of capital. Rather, seizures of such peasant holdings constituted the sole precondition for capital accumulation. Extra-economic factors, *mussoco*, further land seizures and commercial monopolization ensured the reproduction of this process. The result of this was to restructure the fundamental relationship between the peasantry and *latifundiarios*. For example, when famine broke out in 1895 in Prazos Carungo, Pepino and Quelimane do Sal, the *latifundiarios* lent food provisions to the famine victims.[112] Similarly, during the famine of 1893, the Companhia do Assucar de Moçambique initiated a 20-hectare cassava plantation so as to tie the local-peasantry to long-term labour service on the sugar plantation.[113] At M'landi, 10 kilometres from Mopeia, it seized fertile land on high ground which was less vulnerable to periodic floods and which the local peasantry had used to produce grain.[114]

The implication of the examples outlined here was the emergence of a marginalized peasantry – akin to *peons* – which was constituted through debt bondage as an unfree labour reserve possessing weak rights to the means of production. As Marx argued, in this type of social relations, 'slavery is hidden under the form of *peonage*. By means of advances, repayable in labour, which are handed down from generation to generation, not only the individual labourer, but his family, become, *de facto*, the property of other persons and their families.'[115] Related to this was the seizure of peasants' instruments of labour such as hoes, knives, axes, etc.[116] Thus 'working without payment', 'working much more than the law obliges'[117] became a manifestation of the increasingly insecure relationship of the peasantry to their means of production. This reproduced conditions for the extraction of labour rent, a mechanism for accumulation. Famine was a manifestation of this process.

Alienation of Forest Resources

Before 1892, the forest resources of Lower Zambézia were deemed to belong to the Portuguese colonial state. The *latifundiarios* could cultivate 'unoccupied' land but they were not permitted to exploit and export timber without a special concession.[118] In practice, however, *latifundiarios* exploited such resources without applying for this concession. Some 'claimed exclusive rights to the *butaca* (land) even though [their] property was insignificant'. Such 'exclusive rights' referred to their relationship with the local peasantry and all the resources including forest land.[119] The regulations of 7 October 1892 banned the destruction of bush and forests without the authority of the Governor through the advice of the Inspector General of the *prazos*. This ban, however, was aimed at peasant producers. The *latifundiarios* were given a free hand to exploit forest resources.[120]

The effect of these regulations was to deprive peasant communities of their rights to forest resources for household uses relating to fuel, the construction of houses and canoes, and for making instruments for the processing of grains such as wooden mortars. Furthermore, the *latifundiarios*' monopoly of forest land lessened the availability of land for peasant agricultural production to meet their necessary needs and surpluses for exchange.[121] Conversely, the *latifundiarios* were beneficiaries of these measures through the exploitation and sale of timber to the colonial state for the construction of administrative and military command posts, as well as to Indian traders for the construction of stores at the *prazo feiras* and to individuals in Quelimane.

During the 1890s and early twentieth century, the commercialization of timber was accentuated. The Companhia do Assucar de Moçambique, for instance, set up saw mills and sold timber to Quelimane. It had a total labour force of 4,110 adults and 466 children engaged in timber production, and in place of importing building material, it used local timber.[122] With greater sugar production, it increasingly used wood as fuel for its boilers. Indeed, for the Companhia, timber production 'constituted a great economy'.[123] In the first decade of the twentieth century, hundreds of thousands of trees were felled, without replanting, to provide fuel for steamships navigating the Lower Zambezi and the Lower Chire.[124]

The frequent periods of famine and drought from the late 1880s through to the end of the first decade of the twentieth century were a consequence of ecological despoliation by colonial capitalist development. For instance deputations by the pre-capitalist aristocracy of Malinguine linked famine to the monopolization and exploitation of forest resources by the *latifundiarios*.[125] This goes some way to highlight the local peasants' concern not only about the *mussoco* regime and about the resources from which they were increasingly being separated, but also perhaps the quality of their environment.

During the 1860s, Lower Zambézia experienced a very serious famine. But never had there been such a persistent frequency of drought as there was in the late nineteenth and early twentieth centuries. That this happened during the time of colonial occupation and of the establishment of specific capitalist relations of production, was no coincidence at all. Certainly Mahmood Mamdani's argument about the causes of drought in the Karamoja District of Uganda has great relevance to our argument concerning drought and famine in Lower Zambézia. He writes

> Colonial rule produced a new type of drought, new in its intensity and frequency, because its basic consequence was a transformation for the worse of the very natural context of productive activity of the Karamojong people. The 'roots' of the resulting famine lie in the very disruption of the process of production, and not simply of 'ways of coping' with an already produced drought.[126]

Crisis in Peasant Agricultural Production, 1890–1914

In 1909, the colonial governor of Quelimane District (Zambézia) noted that 'the intensive development of plantations has fatally turned the native away from his own crop'.[127] Before him in 1898, a British consular official reported that peasants objected 'to work when deriving no benefit from the crop he produces' and that 'no further effort is

made beyond what is necessary to furnish his family with the
common necessities of life'.[128] This process of a growing crisis
in peasant agricultural production was already in motion at
the beginning of the 1890s. A British consular report noted
with alarm the gravity of food supplies in the *prazos* in the
immediate vicinity of Quelimane. 'The rice and grain crops,'
he reported, 'have been rather less than average, and at the
present time native food is somewhat scarce and dear.'[129] By
the end of the first decade of the twentieth century, the
Governor General reported that rice production was 'disappearing little by little' and the dehusking plant of the
Companhia da Zambézia was inoperative because of the lack
or shortage of rice.[130] Let us examine the factors underlying
this crisis.

The relationship between the rent payable to the colonial
state on the one hand, and the rate of accumulation by the
latifundiarios and capital, on the other, had a bearing on
peasant agricultural production. The case of the Companhia
d'Assucar de Moçambique is relevant. When it acquired its
concession in Maganja d'Aquem Chire in 1890, it was
required to pay rent, retroactively, for three semestres.[131]
Although it protested, it agreed to pay the rent by instalments,
because it was confident that this would be easily offset by
mussoco extraction and labour service. 'It is only from the point
of view of getting labour that the possession of a Prazo is useful
and convenient to us. Apart from ground produce, a good
source of revenue is available to us in the 'mussoco' which can
grow in size as the population increases.'[132] The acquisition of
labour for opening up its establishment was a necessary
precondition for accumulation and for paying rent to the
Portuguese colonial state. In their report, the company's
Managing Director, J. Greenfield de Mello, and its Manager
in Africa, John P. Hornung, were clear as to how this would
be achieved.

> It is easy for those who know the organisation of the
> Crown Prazos . . . and for those who know what goes on
> there, to understand that if we are to attempt clearing
> and cultivation on a big scale without having sufficient
> labour at our disposal the difficulties would be insuper-

able. In such conditions, the Company would have to go
on bended knee to the concessionaires or administrators
for the labour it needed, and pay whatever price they
asked, acceding without question to their demands and
whims. The situation, apart from its servility, would
have been embarassing.

Indeed to avoid such 'embarassing servility', 16,645 peasants
were rounded up from 14 areas in Maganja d'Aquem Chire
during March 1891. Such was the extent of withdrawal of labour
from agricultural and other related spheres of production in
the peasant household units.[133]
    I have shown elsewhere that the *mussoco* regime provoked wars
of resistance which in turn exacerbated famine conditions.[134]
The war of 1891 against the state of Maganja da Costa clearly
demonstrates this point. In an attempt to sustain its forces,
the Portuguese colonial state resorted to a wholesale expropriation of peasant food reserves. In this context, the subsequent
low yields of grain could be explained by the insecure
conditions for agricultural production created by the *mussoco*
regime and the colonial state's military operations to quell
peasant uprisings.[135] Furthermore, the drought of 1893 and the
locust plague of 1894–5 exacerbated the crisis in agricultural
production.[136] The Companhia do Assucar argued that with
the exception of sweet potatoes and *mapira* (sorghum), the
decline in the production of groundnuts, sesame, millet and
rice occurred 'because the native is already convinced that by
working for the Company he can gain the means with which
to pay mussoco and satisfy his needs'.[137]
    This, however, is grotesque. In the period 1894–6, the
whole of Zambézia was gripped by a serious famine which was
compounded by a locust plague. Almost the entire grain crop
was lost.[138] And far from swarming to work for the company,
in fact many of those peasants working for it fled. By June
1894, the company was already requesting the colonial state
to reduce the rent level. It complained that out of 4,911,000
reis it received from *mussoco* collection, it had to pay 4,390,000
reis to the colonial state. The colonial state dismissed the
request and attributed the flight of peasants and hence the fall
in *mussoco* collection to the abuses practised by John Hornung.[139]

While the crisis in peasant agricultural production was generalized throughout Lower Zambézia, nowhere was it as grave as in Prazos Anguaze and Andone. We can gauge this from the decline in the *mussoco* collected in kind between 1893 and 1897. During the first half of 1893 the *mussoco* collected was 9 per cent of that collected in the first half of 1897.[140] In the years 1896 and 1897, the Companhia da Zambézia estimated that the peasantry of Anguaze and Andone 'owed' it a total of 29,900,000 reis.[141] This colossal figure demonstrates the increased pressure which the *mussoco* regime exerted on the peasants' labour time for agricultural production, and the appropriation of entire food reserves to pay the *mussoco* 'arrears'. The consequence of this was absolute pauperization and it explains why out of an estimated 30,000 deaths during the famine of 1906, 8,534 were peasants in Anguaze and Andone.[142]

It is well known that poor diet causes malnutrition and lowers the general resistance to disease. Recent work on disease causation in colonial Tanzania has greatly enhanced our understanding of the link between malnutrition and disease on the one hand, and colonial capitalist development on the other. Meredith Turshen, for example, has argued that 'malnutrition and tropical diseases are the products of specific historical stages of colonialism and underdevelopment,'[143] and that 'disease causation is located in modes of production (that is, the social system by which work is organised to provide the means of subsistence) or more specifically, in the forces of production (the level of development) and the social relations of production (the rapport between producers and owners).'[144] There is no doubt that a detailed study of the political economy of disease causation in Lower Zambézia during this period is important. This task, however, lies beyond the scope of the present study. From the analysis advanced so far it is, however, possible to make some tentative observations on the link between disease and colonial capitalist accumulation.

For Mozambique, as for the rest of Eastern Africa, the 1890s and the early twentieth century were periods of famine, drought, locust plagues, and outbreaks of epidemic diseases such as smallpox.[145] During the famine of 1895, peasants consumed the entire groundnut crop before it matured and 'resorted to eating roots containg few nutrients and often prejudicial to health'.[146] The drought and famine of the period 1900–3 were the worst since the 1860s. 'For many years', a British consular official reported, 'the district of Zambezia has not been in such a deplorable condition as it is at present.'[147] In the last months of 1899 and continuing through 1900, the region was swept by a smallpox epidemic: 'many families became extinct, and thousands of natives starved by this terrible disease.'[148] This was compounded by the drought which destroyed the entire food crop that had been planted. 'All that had been sown,' the British Vice-Consul wrote, 'burnt in the earth, and at harvest-time the more than fertile Zambezia had turned into dry fields. Rice and seeds were nearly all spoiled and groundnuts rotten away in the ground. Mangoes and fruit were very scarce and hundreds and hundreds of natives died for want of food and of misery.'[149]

The conditions caused by the disruption of the peasants' process of production rendered people vulnerable to disease. The system of migrant labour to the plantations and the living and working conditions contained therein, the migration of people escaping from *mussoco*, forced labour and famine, may have contributed to the spread of diseases.

We do not have data on the incidence of other diseases during this period. However, in a study of health conditions between 1920 and 1960 on the plantations run by the Sena Sugar Estates, Judith Head has noted the prevalence of over-crowding in labour compounds, poor hygiene and inadequate diet, and incidences of smallpox, tick fever, pneumonia and dysentery.[150] Although the annual reports of the Companhia do Assucar (the predecessor of the Sena Sugar Estates) during this period do not contain accounts of conditions on the plantations, the plantation system was well-enough established in the period between the early 1890s and 1915 for such diseases to be endemic among plantation workers and, by extension, household units.

Since malnutrition had become endemic, the spread of plantation-related diseases to the countryside reproduced conditions of pauperization which could not be resolved by increased production because of the 'rapacity with which their produce is and has been seized by the prazo-holders at prices which are next to no price at all.'[151] Neither could they be resolved by the purchase of food because the wages earned were inadequate and their value had considerably declined over the years. Furthermore, peasant households were being compelled to pay *mussoco* in far greater quantities of agricultural produce than they could possibly reserve for their own sustenance. The result was to compel peasant producers to do more wage labour in order to pay *mussoco*. In this way, as Carlos Serra has pointed out, 'the surplus labour extracted in the plantations was no longer just a direct and strict "feudal" rent. The extraction of that surplus labour was done increasingly through the appropriation of the surplus product contained in the commodities produced.'[152] With this, household production became increasingly subordinated to wage labour and was in many respects unable to provide adequate nutrition for ensuring good health.

By 1900, peasant household units hardly produced agricultural surpluses for exchange and the decline continued throughout the period of my study. In 1907, this decline became so critical that the colonial state was obliged to relax the import restrictions which, in 1892, it had imposed on grain and pulses from India.[153] During the first two decades of the twentieth century, exports principally consisted of commodities like sugar and copra that were produced on the plantations. This was a manifestation of the increasing concentration of forced labour on the plantations and of the crisis in peasant agricultural production. Consequently, Indian and European commercial houses which had, since the 1870s, dealt in commodities produced by peasant household units, terminated their operations in Zambézia.[154]

Mussoco, Famine and Migrations

The *mussoco* regime and famine – in short the disruption of the peasant productive and reproductive processes – gave rise to internal and external migrations. These migrations started during the 1880s and continued through the 1890s and early twentieth century. Internal migrations took place regardless of the level of *mussoco* in the receiving area. In 1899, for instance, peasants from the concession of the Companhia do Luabo fled to Prazo Madal.[155] Between 1894 and 1900, the population of Goma and Mugovo trebled as a result of peasants fleeing from famine-stricken areas.[156] Between 1892 and 1905, many peasants fled from the concession of the Companhia do Assucar de Moçambique to the territory administered by the Companhia de Moçambique on the south bank of the Zambezi.[157]

The massive migration of Lower Zambézian peasants to Nyasaland (present day Malawi) during the period 1900–20 was a consequence of the *mussoco* regime and the crisis in peasant agricultural production that it had caused. It has been estimated that between 1900 and 1903, about 3,000 people entered Blantyre district.[158]

During the famine of 1906, more than 20,000 people migrated to Nyasaland,[159] and many were recruited for the construction of the Transvaal–Swaziland railway.[160] By 1920, an estimated 100,000 people had migrated to Nyasaland. The consequence of such migrations on peasant material production in the regions neighbouring Nyasaland can be extrapolated from a report by the British Consul, R. C. F. Maugham. In an overland journey from Nyasaland to Quelimane in 1911, he noted that a large and fertile area to the west of the Lugela River which had been densely populated was abandoned:

> One noticed that the path frequently led through abandoned native gardens and past deserted houses, but the people were no longer there. I was informed that in many cases they had quit the country since recruiting [to São Tomé] had commenced, some of them to the northern prazos of the Anguru [sic] country, some south to Boror and many into Nyasaland Protectorate.[161]

This region had been leased to the Empresa Agrícola do Lugela which, during the first two decades of the twentieth century, exclusively farmed *mussoco* and exported labour to the cocoa plantations of São Tomé e Principe.[162] Such dependence on the '*mussoco* tree' produced rivalries first between the *prazo* companies and secondly between the *prazo* companies and the colonial state.

The Companhias, the Colonial State and the Struggle for the '*Mussoco* Tree'

It has already been noted that, after 1900, the bulk of exports from Lower Zambézia represented less the commodities produced by peasant family units than commodities such as sugar and copra produced by peasant labour on the plantations. In the decree of 1890, the colonial state warned that 'The lease of *mussoco* has, nevertheless, one concealed danger: the danger that the arrendatario will pocket more of what he receives than what he pays, and live as a parasite without working or making the "natives" work'.[163] Laying too much emphasis on harvesting from the '*mussoco* tree', various *prazo* companies made simultaneous claims and clashed over the control of territory.

Between 1892 and 1897, the Companhia do Assucar which was the *prazo*-holder of Maganja d'Aquem Chire, launched *mussoco* raids across the River Longose into Prazo Massingire.[164] In 1894 and 1895, the Companhia de Moçambique repeatedly clashed with Wiese and Dulio, the *prazo*-holders of Prazo Massingire, over the ownership of the islands of Ducuta and Sapembeza next to Prazo Maganja d'Alem Chire.[165] In 1900, there were similar clashes between the Companhia de Moçambique and the Companhia da Zambézia over the ownership of islands on which they both carried out census and collected *mussoco*.[166]

In 1910, Governor Ernesto Vilhena called for a thorough revision of the 1892 *prazo* regulations and in particular those relating to the operation of *feiras*. They were, he argued, 'now absolutely unsuitable and inoperable'. Belatedly, however, he noted that these regulations were not only 'fatally leading to monopoly', but also to an uncontrollable situation in which the *prazo* companies would be above the existing legislation. He proposed the abolition of all guarantees relating to commercial monopoly because, he argued, the original regulations had been, in part, directed against the importation and circulation of firearms in Zambézia. He proposed the adoption of the system that was in operation in Maganja da Costa where buying and selling was permitted without restrictions.[167] As we have seen, this alarm was caused, first, by the decline of peasant petty-commodity production and the general decline of exports through the port of Quelimane. Second, the colonial state became increasingly aware of the *prazo* companies' dependence on *mussoco* extraction as the principal mechanism for accumulation. Since 1892, the *prazo* companies evaded remitting to the colonial state the legally required percentage of the *mussoco* they collected. Throughout this period, the colonial state increasingly raised the percentage of the *mussoco* and rent payable to it by the *prazo* companies. However, the higher the rent the *prazos* paid, the more they transferred this burden onto the peasant producers. As I have already argued, this underlay the frequent occurrence of famine.

In 1893, the Portuguese state sent an exploratory mission led by Arturo Marinha de Campos to Zambézia to investigate the workings of the *prazos*. It was to

> ascertain the relations between the real working of the system and the law on the subject . . . with a view to arriving at a conclusion whether the protection and welfare of the native population, the local economic development, and the financial and political interests of the Colony and Mother Country require the mainten-ance, alteration, or complete suppression of the system, without prejudice in the latter case to whatever rights have been legally acquired.[168]

As we have already seen, the Commission of 1916 recom-mended revisions in the *prazo* regulations. These were enacted in the decree of 1919 which fixed the rent payable to the colonial state by the *prazo* companies at 70 per cent of the product of *mussoco*. The subsequent legislation of 1921 and 1923 increased this further. In 1923, the *prazo* companies consisting of the Companhia da Zambézia, the Empresa Agrícola do Lugela, Société du Madal, Sena Sugar Estate Limited, and their pressure groups – the Gremio de Proprietários e Agricultores da Zambézia and the Associação de Classe dos interessados nos Prazos da Zambézia – appealed to the colonial state to revise the new measures in their favour. This was rejected.[169]

The increases in rent payable by the *prazo* companies,

however, did not reduce the *mussoco* burden on the peasantry. While the *mussoco* levels rose steeply, the wages paid remained at the level of 400 reis that had been in operation since the 1880s.[170] Increasingly, the male productive members of peasant households expended more labour-time in wage labour on the plantations in order to meet the *mussoco* demands. As Carlos Serra has argued, this significantly shifted the production of food crops from peasant households to the plantations. This development 'signified', he writes

> that the peasant produced on the insistence of the lease-holder the means of reproduction of his own labour power. In other words part of the family production was 'transported' from the village to the plantation. A part of the pre-capitalist peasant economy thus reproduced itself in the pores of capitalist production, which allowed it to keep wages low.[171]

Notwithstanding the higher rent that they had to pay to the colonial state, the *prazo* companies derived great benefits from this situation. The higher *mussoco* levels compelled the peasantry towards wage labour on the plantations. On the other hand, the production of food crops like cassava on the plantations enabled the *prazo* companies to link food rations to wages.[172] This kept the wages low and with the *mussoco* regime a worker–peasant continuum was reproduced. Herein lay the secret of capital accumulation. From 1870, the colonial state had created favourable conditions for this and was to play an even greater role after the abolition of the *prazos* in 1930.

Notes and References

1 João António da Silva, *Os Simples*, 30 April 1912.
2 Aquino de Bragança and Ruth First, 'Do Chibalo à Libertação da Africa Austral', *Estudos Moçambicanos*, 2 (1981) p. 5.
3 Carlos Serra, 'Da economia de trafico ao imperialismo: Introdução um itinerário (1886/1930)', *Tempo*, 572, 27 September 1981, p. 42. See also Departamento de História, Universidade Eduardo Mondlane (hereafter DH/UEM), *História de Moçambique* (Maputo, 1983), vol. 2, p. 30.

4 Carlos Serra, 'O Capitalismo Colonial na Zambézia 1850–1930', *Estudos Moçambicanos*, 1 (1980), pp. 49, 50.

5 *Ibid.*, p. 35; see also his 'A Introdução do Capitalismo na Baixa Zambézia, e emergência do sistema de plantações (1870/1915)', (DH/UEM, Maputo, mimeo, March 1979), p. 17.

6 L. Vail and L. White, *Capitalism and Colonialism in Mozambique* (London, Heinemann, 1980), chapter 2.

7 For a detailed critique of the Vail and White thesis see S. L. Ishemo, 'Economy and Society of the Lower Zambezi Basin in Mozambique ca. 1850–1914' (University of Manchester, unpublished PhD thesis, 1986), chapters 5 and 6.

8 See António Enes, *Moçambique, Relatório apresentado ao governo* (Lisbon, 1946).

9 For an excellent critique of these views see DH/UEM, *História de Moçambique*, vol. 2, pp. 88–95; Valentim Alexandre, *Origens do Colonialismo Português Moderno* (Lisbon, 1979), pp. 209–10.

10 Arquivo Histórico de Moçambique (hereafter, AHM) Cx 8–43 m 5 (1) Farinha e Lopes to Governador, Zambézia, 28 April 1895.

11 AHM Cx 8–44 m 3 Arrendatário, Marral e Mirrambone to Governador, Zambézia, 24 April 1895.

12 Such ideas were propounded by Oliveira Martins and translated into official colonial policy by António Enes and other subsequent colonial theorists. The colonial view of the African as 'indolent', as an adult child who could be 'educated' only through force was put into effect in the labour code of 1890:

    all natives of the Portuguese overseas provinces are subject to the legal and moral obligation to acquire through work the means that they lack to overcome and improve their present social situation. They have every right to choose the manner in which they will fulfil this obligation but if they fail to fulfil it the authorities will ensure that they do so.

    J. M. da Silva Cunha, *Questões Ultramarinas* (Lisbon, 1960). vol. 1, p. 100, quoted in Carlos Serra, 'O Capitalismo Colonial na Zambézia', p. 37. See also DH/UEM, *História de Moçambique*, vol. 2, p. 91. In the light of the above, Vail and White's assumption that Oliveira Martins had an 'interest in socialism' (*Capitalism and Colonialism*, p. 88) is a gross error indeed.

13 See Karl Marx, *Capital* (London, 1977), vol. 1, pp. 667–8.

14 Mahmood Mamdani, 'Colonial Roots of Famine in Karamoja: a Rejoinder', *Review of African Political Economy*, 36 (1986). See also his 'Karamoja: Colonial Roots of Famine in North-East Uganda', *Review of African Political Economy*, 25. Other works on Eastern Africa include: Helge Kjekshus, *Ecology Control and Economic Development in East African History* (London, Heinemann, 1977); Meredith Turshen, *The Political Ecology of Disease in Tanzania* (New Brunswick, Rutgers University Press, 1984).

15 Turshen, *Political Ecology of Disease in Tanzania*, p. 17.
16 *Ibid.*, p. 65.
17 Allen F. Isaacman, *Mozambique. The Africanisation of a European Institution. The Zambezi Prazos, 1750–1902* (Madison, 1972), p. 26; see also José Capela, *O Imposto de palhota e a introdução do modo de produção capitalista nas colónias* (Porto, 1977), pp. 36–7; S. L. Ishemo, 'Some Aspects of the Economy and Society of the Zambezi Basin in the Nineteenth and Early Twentieth Centuries', in H. Dickinson (ed.), *Mozambique* (Edinburgh, Centre of African Studies, 1979), pp. 27–8.
18 See Isaacman, *Mozambique*, pp. 26–7; Ishemo, 'Some Aspects of Zambezi Basin', p. 20.
19 See S. J. Xavier Botelho, *Memória estatistica sobre as dominios portuguezes na África Oriental* (Lisbon, 1835), pp. 263, 271–2.
20 A. de Sousa Ribeiro, *Regimen dos Prazos da Corôa* (Lourenço Marques, 1907), pp. 11–17; DH/UEM, *História da Moçambique*, vol. 2, pp. 142–30 Capela, *O Imposto de palhota*, pp. 41–2.
21 See Ishemo, 'Economy and Society', chapter 5.
22 See *Diario do Governo*, 11 May 1875; PRO FO 84/1411: *State Papers* (GB) 66 (1874–5), pp. 212–17, 519–36.
23 For further dimensions and consequences of *mussoco* extraction by the two companies see Ishemo, 'Economy and Society', chapters 5 and 7.
24 DH/UEM, *História de Moçambique*, vol. 2, p. 148; Carlos Serra, 'A Introdução do Capitalismo', p. 12; M. D. D. Newitt, *Portuguese Settlement on the Zambezi* (London, 1973), pp. 342, 356; Lionel Decle, *Three Years in Africa* (London, 1900), pp. 241–2.
25 Sousa Ribeiro, *Regimen dos Prazos da Corôa*, pp. 211–24; DH/UEM, *História de Moçambique*, vol. 2, p. 149; Serra, 'A Introdução do Capitalismo', p. 12; Newitt, *Portuguese Settlement*, pp. 353–4.
26 Quoted in *Lourenço Marques Guardian* (n.d.), cutting enclosed in PRO FO/237 No. 50153.
27 *Boletim Oficial* (hereafter, *BO*), 33, II Série, 16 August 1924, pp. 267–8; Manoel António Moreira Jr., *Relatório referente ás Provincias Ultramarinas* (Lisbon, 1905), p. 217; Serra, 'O Capitalismo Colonial na Zambézia', pp. 36–7.
28 *Ibid.*; see also PRO FO 367/282 No. 13814, Report by Alfredo de Freitas Leal (Advocate), 1912; PRO FO 367/327 No. 40394 Maugham-Grey, 23 September 1911.
29 See Serra, 'O Capitalismo Colonial na Zambézia', pp. 37, 38; Sousa Ribeiro, *Regimen dos Prazos*, pp. 143–7.
30 Serra, 'O Capitalismo Colonial na Zambézia', pp. 37–38. For the full text of the 1909 Land Law see *BO*, 2 September 1909, reproduced in R. N. Lyne, *Mozambique: Its Agricultural Development* (London, 1913), pp. 235–54.
31 Serra, 'O Capitalismo Colonial na Zambézia', p. 38; *BO* 33, II Série, 16 August 1924; Distrito de Quelimane, *Relatório do Governador, 1907–1909* (Lourenço Marques, 1909), p. 73.
32 *BO* 35, I Série, 30 August 1919.

33 *BO* 52, I Série, 24 December 1921; *BO* 33, II Série, 16 August 1924.
34 *Ibid.*
35 *BO* 35, I Série, 30 August 1919.
36 *BO* 33, II Série, 16 August 1924; see also PRO FO 367/282 No. 13814, Report by Alfredo de Freitas Leal (Advocate), 1912; PRO FO 367/327 No. 40394 Maugham-Grey, 23 September 1911.
37 *BO* 33, II Série, 16 August 1924.
38 AHM Codices do Século XIX 11 – 1661 B d 3 Inspector-Geral dos Prazos Secretario Geral do Governo Geral, 19 September 1894.
39 See Distrito de Quelimane, *Relatório do Governador, 1907–1909.*
40 *BO* 33, II Série, 16 August 1924.
41 *BO* 33, II Série, 16 August 1924; Serra, 'O Capitalismo Colonial na Zambézia', p. 38.
42 Meaning being 'carried off bound with one's arms behind one's back'. See Serra, 'O Capitalismo Colonial na Zambézia', p. 48. Originating from Zambézia Province, this term had a wider meaning. It 'described the slavery and humiliation to which our people were subjected in the past'. This included transportation to the Americas and São Tomé. See *Domingo* (Maputo), 30 June 1985.
43 Karl Marx, *Capital* (London, 1977), vol. III, p. 788. See also Marc Wuyts, *Peasants and Rural Economy in Mozambique* (Universidade Eduardo Mondlane/Centro de Estudos Africanos, Maputo, August 1978), p. 4; Manuel Moreno Fraginals, *The Sugarmill. The Socio-economic Complex of Sugar in Cuba, 1760–1860* (New York, Monthly Review, 1976), p. 21.
44 For example Thomas d'Aquino Lobo of Prazo Tirre. See AHM Cx 8–45 m 1 Thomas d'Aquino Lobo to Secretario do Governo, Distrito de Quelimane, 17 February 1877.
45 Public Record Office (hereafter, PRO) FO 367/237 No. 45446, FO Minute, 19 November 1911; PRO FO 367/282 No. 13814 Report by Advocate Alfredo de Freitas Leal, 1912.
46 See DH/UEM, *História de Moçambique*, vol. 2, pp. 148, 324. AHM Cx 8–24 m 1 Thomas d'Aquino Lobo to Presidente da Delegação da Junta da Fazenda em Quelimane, 12 March 1877. AHM Cx 8–24 m 2 Leandro António do Rego to Governador, Distrito da Zambézia, 19 January 1897.
47 DH/UEM, *História de Moçambique*, vol. 2, p. 144.
48 Serra, 'O Capitalismo Colonial na Zambézia', p. 41; The Companhia do Assucar de Moçambique, for example, co-opted the *inhacuauas* as *mussoco* collectors and labour recruiting agents. Each *inhacuaua* retained a register of work gangs (*registos das ensacas*) 'recruited' in their respective areas. Such *ensacas* were accompanied by *sangiras* (who were, in this case, confidantes of the *inhacuauas*) to the plantations and escorted back to the villages after the 'contract' period. See Companhia do Assucar de Moçambique, *Relatórios e Contas, 1895–96* (Lisbon, 1897), p. 49.
49 A. Enes, *Moçambique*, p. 127; PRO FO 367/237 No. 40394 Maugham-

Grey, 23 September 1911; PRO FO 367/282 No. 13814, Report by Advocate Alfredo de Freitas Leal, 1912.

50 AHM Cx 8–45 m 2 Ambrosio Cypriano de Miranda to Governador, Distrito de Quelimane, 2 June 1881; AHM Cx 8–45 m 2 Joaquim Xavier da Silva Cunha to Governador, Distrito de Quelimane, 20 April 1887; AHM Cx 8–45 m 2 José da Silva Pimenta to Inspector-Geral dos Prazos, 13 May 1893, 24 May 1893; AHM Cx 8–45 m 2 José Silvestre Carreira to Governador, Distrito de Quelimane, 26 September 1893.

51 AHM Cx 8–45 m 2 Leandro Antonio do Rego to Governador, Zambézia, 29 January 1897.

52 AHM Cx 8–45 m 2 José da Silva Pimenta to Inspector-Geral dos Prazos, 14 July 1893.

53 AHM Cx 8–45 m 2 Jose Silvestre Carreira to Governador, Distrito de Quelimane, 18 February 1895.

54 AHM Cx 8–46 m 1 (5) Domingos d'Azevedo to Governador, Distrito de Quelimane, 4 January 1878.

55 AHM Fundo do Século XIX Governo Geral. Cx 8–88 m 1 Governador, Distrito de Quelimane to Governador Geral, 22 May 1881.

56 AHM Fundo do Sec. XIX Governo Geral. Cx 8–90 m 2 Secretario do Governo, Quelimane to Secretario Geral, 27 January 1888.

57 AHM Cx 8–46 m 1 (5) Augusto Cesar d'Andrade to Governador, Distrito de Quelimane, 1 June 1892.

58 AHM Cx 8–45 m 2 José Bernardo d'Albuquerque (Administrador) to Governador, Distrito de Quelimane, 6 June 1878.

59 L. Vail and L. White, *Prazos, Peasants and International Capitalism: A Reassessment of Lower Zambezian History, 1870–1900* (University of Zambia, History Seminar Series, mimeo, 1976–77), p. 10; see also their *Capitalism and Colonialism*, p. 65.

60 Vail and White, *Prazos, Peasants and International Capitalism*, p. 10; see also their 'The Struggle for Mozambique: Capitalist Rivalries, 1900–40', *Review*, III, 2 (1979), p. 249.

61 On this question, Marx noted the relationship between the labour time expended in the payment of rent and that spent in the production of means of existence, and surpluses for exchange.

> Take it, for instance, that the enforced labour for the landlord originally amounted to two days per week. These two days of enforced labour per week are thereby fixed, are a constant magnitude, legally regulated by prescriptive or written law. But the productivity of the remaining days of the week, which are at the disposal of the direct producer himself, is a variable magnitude which must develop in the course of his experience, just as the new wants he acquires, and just as the expansion of the market for his product and the increasing assurance with which he disposes of this portion of his labour-power, whereby it should not be forgotten that the employment of his labour-power is by no means confined to agriculture, but includes rural home industry.

> Marx, *Capital*, vol. III, chapter XLVII, p. 794.

62 Ishemo, 'Economy and Society', chapter 5.

63 *Diario do Governo*, 7 December 1888; *British Parliamentary Papers* (hereafter, *BPP*), LXXIV, 1888. Barros Gomes (Portuguese Foreign Minister) to G. Petre (British Ambassador Lisbon), 18 November 1888.

64 Serra, 'A Introdução do Capitalismo', p. 11; *BPP*, LXXXVII, 1892, Report for the Year 1891 on the Trade of Quelimane, FO Annual Series No. 1009; see also *Board of Trade Journal*, XIX, 2 (1895), p. 138.

65 *BPP*, XCV (1893–4). Report by Vice-Consul Ross on the Trade of Quelimane for the Year 1892, FO Annual Series No. 1316.

66 F. Carvalho, *Relatório do Governador, 1911–1912* (Lourenço Marques, 1912), p. 29.

67 *Ibid*.

68 See Ishemo, 'Economy and Society', chapter 7.

69 AHM Cx 8–46 m 2 (1) Thomas d'Aquino Lobo to Governador, Distrito de Quelimane, 13 December 1881.

70 *Ibid*.; see also Ishemo, 'Economy and Society', chapter 7.

71 AHM Cx 8–21 m 2 Comandante Militar de Inhamissengo to Governador, Distrito de Quelimane, 30 June 1887, 30 September 1887; AHM Cx 8–46 m 1 (4) Jose Bernardo d'Albuquerque (Tangalane) to Governador, Distrito de Quelimane, 9 July 1887; AHM Cx 8–46 m 2 (5) Jose Bernardo d'Albuquerque to Governador, Quelimane, 1 August 1887; AHM Cx 8–90 m 2 Administrador (Prazos Nameduro, Tirre e Andone) to Secretario do Governo, Quelimane, 20 April 1888; AHM Cx 8–44 m 2 Caetano Piedade de Sousa to Governador, Quelimane, 14 August 1892, 16 January 1894, 3 July 1894; AHM Cx 8–44 m 2 C. Piedade de Sousa to Inspector Geral dos Prazos, 28 September 1893.

72 AHM Cx 8–44 m 2 Caetano Piedade de Sousa to Inspector Geral dos Prazos, 28 September 18930 AHM Cx 8–44 m 2 C. Piedade de Sousa to Governador, Distrito de Quelimane, 14 April 1892.

73 AHM Cx 8–21 m 2 Comandante Militar, Inhamissengo to Governador, Distrito de Quelimane, 30 June 1887, 30 September 1887; AHM Cx 8–46 m 1 (4) Jose Bernardo d'Albuquerque to Governador, Distrito de Quelimane, 9 July 1887.

74 AHM Cx 8–22 m 1 Comandante Militar do Guengue to Governador, Distrito de Quelimane, 13 September 1892; AHM Fundo do Seculo XIX Governo Geral. Cx 8–90 m 2 Secretario do Governo, Quelimane to Secretario Geral, Moçambique, 27 January 1888.

75 AHM Cx 8–22 m 1 Comandante Militar do Guengue to Governador, Distrito de Quelimane, 15 March 1891.

76 Decle, *Three Years in Africa*, p. 243.

77 John Buchanan, *The Shire Highlands* (London and Edinburgh, 1885), p. 31.

78 AHM Cx 8–46 m 2 (5) Jose Bernardo d'Albuquerque to Governador, Distrito de Quelimane, 1 August 1887.

79 *BPP*, LXXXIII, 1892. Report for the Year 1891 on the Trade of Quelimane by Vice-Consul Ross, FO Annual Series No. 1009.

80 AHM Cx 8–45 m 2 José Maria Gameiro to Governador, Distrito de Quelimane, 22 February 1892.

81 AHM Cx 8–45 m 2 José da Silva Pimenta to Inspector Geral dos Prazos, 18 April 1893.

82 AHM Fundo do Século XIX. Governador Geral. Cx 8–88 m 3 Governador, Distrito de Quelimane to Governador Geral, Moçambique, 17 September 1883.

83 AHM Cx 8–44 m 5 Raphael de Mello Amaral to Secretario do Governo, Distrito de Quelimane, 28 December 1887. See also Ishemo, 'Economy and Society', chapters 2 and 3.

84 Serra, 'A Introdução do Capitalismo', p. 11.

85 Government of Bombay, *Trade for the Year 1885–1886* (Bombay, Central Government Printer, 1886), p. 60; *ibid., Trade for the Year 1886–1887*, p. 6.

86 Serra, 'A Introdução do Capitalismo', p. 11; Ishemo, 'Economy and Society, chapter 3.

87 *BPP*, LXXXIII, 1892. Report for the Year 1891 on the Trade of Quelimane by Vice-Consul Ross, FO Annual Series No. 1009; see also *Board of Trade Journal* (UK), XIX, 2 (1895), p. 138.

88 AHM Cx 8–43 m 5 (1) Farinha e Lopes to Governador, Distrito da Zambézia, 12 December 1893.

89 AHM Cx 8–45 m 2 Adrião M. Xavier to Governador e Inspector Geral dos Prazos da Corôa, Quelimane, 1 January 1892; AHM Cx 8–45 m 2 Jose Silvestre Carreira to Governador, Distrito da Zambézia, 1 August 1893, 1 January 1894.

90 AHM Cx 8–8 m 1 Secretario Geral to Governador, Distrito da Zambézia, 24 November 1900; *State Papers* (GB), 72 (1881–2), p. 663.

91 AHM Cx 8–44 m 5 Raphael de Mello Amaral to Secretario do Governo, Quelimane, 15 July 1890.

92 AHM Cx 8–5 m 2 Governador, Distrito de Quelimane to Secretario Geral, 17 March 1893. It must be noted that Vail and White have not failed to point out that the same company had participated in the shipping of slaves under the same scheme before 1864 (*Capitalism and Colonialism*, pp. 34, 64).

93 AHM Cx 8–44 m 5 Raphael de Mello Amaral to Secretario do Governo, Distrito de Quelimane, 15 July 1890.

94 AHM Cx 8–45 m 2 Thadeu Jose da Silva (Administrador, Prazos Ancuaze e Andone) to Governador, Distrito de Quelimane, 11 July 1890.

95 *BO* 35, I Série, 30 August 1919.

96 See Newitt, *Portuguese Settlement*, pp. 358–9; Ishemo, 'Economy and Society', chapter 8.

97 AHM Cx 8–44 m 5 Raphael de Mello Amaral to Inspector Geral dos Prazos, 20 August 1892, AHM Cx 8–44 m 5 Raphael de Mello Amaral to Governador, Distrito da Zambézia, 5 December 1895.

98 AHM Cx 8–44 m 5 Amaral to Inspector Geral dos Prazos, 20 August 1895.

99 *BPP*, CI, 1899. Report on the Trade of Quelimane for the Year 1898 by

Vice-Consul Greville, FO Annual Series, No. 2221; *Board of Trade Journal*, XIX, 2 (1895), p. 138.
100 PRO FO 367/237 No. 40394, Confidential Print, 23 September 1911.
101 Peasants attempting to sell their produce directly to urban centres risked having their produce confiscated. 'Even in the nearest neighbourhood of a town a native found to have secreted some of his produce, or being caught on his way to town in order to sell it, is severely punished and his produce is seized.' PRO FO 2/230 No.1 (Commercial) Petition Indian Merchants to Vice-Consul, Quelimane, 28 November 1899.
102 AHM Cx 8–44 m 5 Raphael de Mello Amaral to Governador, Distrito de Quelimane, 3 July 1893.
103 *Ibid.*, 14 August 1894, 5 December 1895.
104 AHM Cx 8–44 m 5 Raphael de Mello Amaral to Inspector Geral dos Prazos de Corôa, 20 August 1892.
105 *Ibid.*
106 R. N. Lyne, *Mozambique: Its Agricultural Development* (London, 1913), p. 200. See also Carlos Serra, 'Prazos e companhias na Zambézia', 2ª Parte, *Tempo*, 581, 29 November 1981, p. 35; see also his 'O Capitalismo Colonial na Zambézia', p. 37.
107 *BO*, 2 September 1909, reproduced in Lyne, *Mozambique*, pp. 235–70; see also Serra, 'O Capitalismo Colonial na Zambézia', p. 37.
108 *Ibid.*
109 AHM Cx 8–45 m 2 José Silvestre Carreira to Governador, Distrito de Quelimane, 18 February 1895.
110 *Ibid.*
111 AHM Cx 8–43 m 6 António Maria Pinto to Inspector dos Prazos, Quelimane, 17 July 1893.
112 AHM Cx 8–43 m 6 António Maria Pinto to Governador, Distrito da Zambézia, 20 April 1895; AHM Cx 8–44 m 1 Mariano Henrique de Nazareth to Governador, Distrito da Zambézia, 19 April 1895.
113 AHM Cx 8–44 m 4 Paiva Raposo to Governador, Distrito da Zambézia, 24 August 1893. This is comparable to other contemporary colonial situations. Writing about German-occupied Tanzania, Kjekshus has noted: 'famine was made into a useful occasion for the administration to gain labour' (*Ecology Control and Economic Development*, p. 140).
114 Companhia do Assucar de Moçambique, *Report and Accounts of Management, 1890–1891*, p. 18.
115 Marx, *Capital*, vol. I, chapter VI, p. 165.
116 AHM Cx 8–44 m 3 António Sebastião Nascimento da Costa to Inspector Geral dos Prazos, 10 November 1893.
117 AHM Cx 8–46 m 1 (4) Manuel António de Lima to Governador, Distrito de Quelimane, 11 December 1893.
118 Decle, *Three Years in Africa*, p. 242.
119 AHM Cx 8–44 m 5 António Augusto Carreira to Secretario do Governo, Distrito de Quelimane, 18 June 1887.

120 AHM Cx 8–44 m 5 Raphael de Mello Amaral to Governador, Distrito de Quelimane, 27 May 1895.
121 AHM Cx 8–44 m 5 Raphael de Mello Amaral to Secretario do Governo, Quelimane, 16 November 1887.
122 *Ibid.*, 16 November 1887, 14 December 1887.
123 AHM Cx 8–44 m 5 Raphael de Mello Amaral to Governador, Distrito de Quelimane, 27 May 1895. Letter, J. Hornung, Enclosure in Companhia do Assucar de Moçambique, *Report and Accounts of Management, 1890–1891*, p. 18.
124 See Carlos Serra, *A Zambézia entre 1890 e 1924: Introdução a via colonial do capitalismo*, p. 40.
125 AHM Cx 8–44 m 5 Raphael de Mello Amaral to Secretario do Governo, Quelimane, 14 February 1887.
126 Mamdani, 'The Colonial Roots of the Famine in Karamoja'.
127 Quoted in Serra, 'O Capitalismo Colonial na Zambézia', p. 44; see also his 'Prazos e Companhias na Zambézia', *Tempo*, 582, 6 December 1981, p. 34.
128 *BPP*, CI, 1899. Report of the Trade of Quelimane for the Year 1898 by Vice-Consul Greville, FO Annual Series, No. 2221.
129 *BPP*, LXXXIII, 1892. Report for the Year 1891 on the Trade of Quelimane by Vice-Consul Ross, FO Annual Series, No. 1009.
130 A. Freire d'Andrade, *Relatórios sobre Moçambique* (Lourenço Marques, 1907), vol. 1, p. 49.
131 Companhia d'Assucar de Moçambique, *Report and Accounts of Management, 1890–1891*, p. 16.
132 *Ibid.*
133 *Ibid.*, p. 15.
134 Ishemo, 'Economy and Society', chapter 6.
135 *BPP*, XCV, 1893–94. Report for the Year 1892 on the Trade of Mozambique by Consul W. A. Churchill, FO Annual Series, No. 7312.
136 *BPP*, XCIX, 1895. Report for the Year 1893 on the Trade of Mozambique by Consul W. A. Churchill, FO Annual Series, No. 1463; Companhia do Assucar de Moçambique, *Relatórios e Contas das Gerencias de 1895 e 1896* (Lisbon, 1897), pp. 45–6.
137 *Ibid.*, p. 62.
138 AHM Cx 8–46 m 1 (4) Nascimento da Costa to Governador, Distrito de Quelimane, 20 April 1895.
139 AHM Codices Século XIX. 11–1661 B d 3 Inspector Geral dos Prazos to Governador, Distrito de Quelimane, 11 June 1894.
140 AHM Cx 8–45 m 2 José Silvestre Carreira to Governador, Distrito de Zambézia, 1 January 1894; AHM Cx 8–45 m 2 Thadeu José da Silva to Governador, Distrito de Quelimane, 19 April 1890.
141 AHM Cx 8–45 m 2 Leandro A. do Rego to Governador, Distrito da Zambézia, 22 March 1897.
142 Serra, *A Zambézia entre 1890 e 1924*, p. 40; see also his 'O Capitalismo Colonial na Zambézia', p. 44; 'Prazos e Companhias na Zambézia', *Tempo*, 582, 6 December 1981, p. 34.
143 Turshen, *Political Ecology of Disease in Tanzania*, p. 14.

144 *Ibid.*, p. 15. See also D. E Ferguson, 'The Political Economy of Health and Medicine in Colonial Tanganyika', in M. H. Y Kaniki (ed.), *Tanzania under Colonial Rule* (London, Longman, 1980), pp. 307–43.

145 See Kjekshus, *Ecology Control and Economic Development*, chapter 7; Ferguson, 'Health and Medicine in Colonial Tanganyika'.

146 AHM Cx 8–44 m 5 Raphael de Mello Amaral to Governador, Distrito da Zambézia, 5 December 1895.

147 PRO FO 63/1368 Report for the Year 1900 on the Trade of Quelimane and the District of Zambezia by Vice-Consul H. R. Wallis, 31 December 1900 (original copy).

148 *Ibid.*

149 PRO FO 63/1368, 8 May 1901. Report on the Trade of Quelimane, FO Annual Series, No. 2654. See also enclosure in PRO FO 2/508.

150 Judith F. Head, 'State, Capital and Migrant Labour in Zambézia, Mozambique: A Study of the Labour Force of Sena Sugar Estates Limited' (University of Durham, PhD thesis, 1980), chapter VIII. Relevant to this study, Meredeth Turshen has noted the experience of workers on the sugar plantations of Kilosa in early colonial Tanzania: 'Plantations expose workers to parasitic and infectious diseases: where irrigation is used, for example, as on the sugar estates of Kilosa District, the incidence of schistosomiasis (a snail-borne parasitic condition) increases, and where housing conditions are crowded or unsanitary, diarrheal diseases are common.' (*Political Ecology of Disease in Tanzania*, p. 100).

151 PRO FO 367/237 No. 40394 Confidential Print. Report by Consul Maugham on the appearance and general characteristics of the District of Zambézia lying betwen the Mlanje mountains and Quelimane, 1911.

152 Serra, 'O Capitalismo Colonial na Zambézia', p. 51.

153 A. A. Freire d'Andrade, *Relatórios sobre Moçambique*, 1907, vol. 1, p. 49. See also *BPP*, XCIX (1912–13), Report on the Trade of Quelimane 1911, FO Annual Series, No. 4908.

154 *BPP*, CI, 1899 Report on the Trade of Quelimane for the Year 1898, FO Annual Series, No. 2221; *Board of Trade Journal*, XIX, 2 (1895), p. 138; *BPP*, CIX, 1902 report on the Trade of the Port of Chinde, FO Annual Series No. 2861. PRO FO 63/1386 8 May 1901. Report for the Year 1900 on the Trade of Quelimane, FO Annual Series, No. 2654. See also FO 2/508.

155 Manoel António Moreira, Jr., *Relatório referente as Provincias Ultramarinas* (Lisbon, 1905), p. 217.

156 AHM Codices do Século XIX 11–1661 Bd 3 19 September 1894; AHM Cx 8–46 m 1 (7) Raphael Bivar Pinto Lopes to Secretario do Governo, Quelimane, 6 January 1900.

157 AHM Codices do Século XIX 11–1661 Bd 3 Inspector Geral dos Prazos to Governador, Distrito de Quelimane, 11 June 1894; Freire d'Andrade, *Relatório sobre Moçambique* (Lourenço Marques, 1907), vol. 1, p. 156.

158 C. Baker, 'A Note on Nguru (sic) Immigration to Nyasaland', *Nyasaland Journal*, XIV (1961), p. 40.

159 Freire d'Andrade, *Relatório sobre Moçambique*, p. 171.
160 *BPP*, 1907. Report on the Trade and Commerce for the Year 1906 by Consular Agent G. Bovay, FO Annual Series, No. 3790. It is important to emphasize that famine elsewhere in Mozambique had served to reproduce migrant labour. During the famine of 1912 in Inhambane there was a record recruitment of labour for the Transvaal gold mines. PRO FO 367/341 No. 1523, 11 January 1913, Enclosure in McDonnell–Grey, 21 December 1912; *Lourenço Marques Guardian*, 9 December 1912.
161 PRO FO 367/234 No. 37288 Maugham–Grey, 23 September 1911.
162 See Ishemo, 'Some Aspects of the Zambezi Basin', pp. 27–8.
163 Cited in Freire d'Andrade, *Relatório sobre Moçambique* (Lourenço Marques, 1909), vol. IV, p. 231. See also Lyne, *Mozambique: Its Agricultural Development*, p. 201.
164 Companhia do Assucar de Moçambique, *Report and Accounts of Management 1890–1891*, p. 16. AHM Cx 8–46 m 1 (1) Carl Wiese to Governador, Distrito de Quelimane, 26 September 1892.
165 AM Cx 8–46 m 1 (2) Carl Weise to Anselmo Ferrão (Arrendatário, Prazo Magagade), 1 April 1894; AHM Cx 8–46 m 1 (2) Pereira e Dulio to Governador, Quelimane, 16 September 1895.
166 AHM Codices Séc. XIX 11–1478 Bb 8 Secretaria Civil do Governo da Zambéza to Chefe de Circunscrição do Sena, 23 May 1900.
167 Ernesto Vilhena to Secretario Geral, in Provincia de Moçambique, *Relatórios do Secretario Geral* (Lourenço Marques, 1910). See also *BPP*, CI, 1910. Report on the Trade and Commerce of the Portuguese Province of Mozambique for the Year 1909 by Consul Maugham, FO Annual Series, No. 4430.
168 Colonial Minister (Lisbon) to Governor General, Mozambique, 28 November 1913, *Official Gazette*, 2 December 1913. Enclosure at PRO FO 367/341 No. 1524, Minute, 10 December 1913.
169 *BO* 33, II Série, 16 August 1924, pp. 267–8; see also Serra, 'O Capitalismo Colonial na Zambézia', pp. 36–7.
170 See Ishemo, 'Economy and Society', chapter 6.
171 Serra, 'O Capitalismo Colonial na Zambézia', p. 46.
172 PRO FO 371/15768 No. W8241 Labour Conditions on the Sena Sugar Estates. Letter, Anti-Slavery and Aborigines Protection Society to FO, 14 July 1931.

Labour, Coercion and Migration in Early Colonial Kenya

Tiyambe Zeleza

Introduction

Some writers on Kenyan labour history concentrate excessively on the role of the colonial state in the labour process, thus reducing its complexities to the intricacies of state labour policy formulation.[1] Their accounts tend to ignore or slight the impact on the labour process of varying forms of worker resistance and manipulation. This tendency to reify the colonial state and absolutize its hegemony must be resisted. Not only was the colonial state a continual site of struggle, the coercive labour control system itself was neither stable nor unchallenged. Our approach must be premised on the notion of struggle, not structure. In this way, the particular forms that forced labour and migration took will no longer appear merely to be the outcomes of simple capitalist manipulation but of a complex series of struggles.

Another equally misleading tendency in Kenyan labour historiography is to assume that the labour process was synonymous with labour for the settler estates.[2] For example, Stichter contends that 'the basic unit of production in colonial Kenya was the estate based on migratory labour.'[3] Here Stichter evokes that salient half-truth in Kenyan historiography that settler estate production was predominant.[4] It was not, despite the immense and overgenerous support it received from the colonial state.[5] The basic unit of production in colonial Kenya was the peasant farm based on household labour. This 'hidden' labour history has yet to be fully researched and written about.

This paper traverses that over-trodden, if poorly understood, research route on forced labour and migration in colonial Kenya. It seeks, however, to map out some new directions. In the background is an awareness that the peasant household was the primary site of production and reproduction for the vast majority of Kenya's people. Grasping this elemental fact will help us to see more clearly the specificity, dynamics and contradictions of the migrant labour system. In this paper, an attempt will be made to show the extent and limits of forced labour and migration. The colonial labour process was not only complex but also contradictory. It was continually changing, sometimes in quite dramatic ways and sometimes in a manner that was almost imperceptible. These changes were based upon results of struggles between opposing and contradictory social forces and classes, which were rooted in material reality, and intermittently reached temporary resolution, from which further contradictory and opposing social forces and classes were generated.

The Growth and Limits of Forced Labour

The colonial state was both authoritarian and fragile. This arose in part from the imperatives and contradictions of capitalist state construction over conquered non-capitalist societies. The territorial personality of the colonial state was not only ambiguous, but also devoid of nationality, and its sovereignty ultimately resided in the imperial metropole. Its institutions of rule, legal order, and ideological representation were all extraverted and embedded in metropolitan practices and traditions.[6] Its hegemony was contested from the beginning, its security uncertain, its autonomy narrow, its legitimation limited and its revenue base weak. In short, the weaknesses of its institutional reflexes conditioned the colonial state towards highly pronounced authoritarian tendencies. Its complicated double task of incorporating the colonized people into the world capitalist system and reproducing capitalist relations of production within the colony led the colonial state towards extreme economic interventionism and political authoritarianism.

Within Kenya, the colonial state straddled rather uneasily the conflicting demands of European settler farmers and African peasants. It acted as an instrument of primitive accumulation of capital on the settlers' behalf by appropriating some African land, confiscating livestock, introducing inequitable taxation, building rail and road transport networks and creating marketing and financial structures highly favourable to settlers and, finally, through the imposition and institutionalization of forced labour. But the state neither had the power nor the will to 'destroy' the peasant economy. Indeed, because settler capital was so weak, the state needed the continued existence of a peasant sector that was productive enough to generate surplus, some of which could be appropriated by the state itself to be used for the running of the administration, to subsidize settler production, and for the rest to provide for such conditions that the maintenance and reproduction of the working class would be ensured. In any case, the initial contact with the expanding local and external markets at the beginning of colonial rule led to increased peasant commodity production. The conflict and uneasy coexistence between the settler and peasant sectors provided the warp from which the fabric of primitive accumulation in Kenya was woven. It defined the dilemmas of the colonial state and the nature of the labour process in the country.

At the beginning of colonial rule, massive supplies of labour were needed to lay the very foundations of the colonial economy: railway lines and roads had to be built, dams and bridges constructed, administrative centres erected, and forests cleared and settler farms established. Undercapitalized as the colonial state and the settlers were during this period, they could not provide wages and conditions that could attract and retain labour. Also, the need for Africans to sell their labour power was not yet compelling. Consequently, by the turn of the 1920s, neither taxation nor land alienation had as yet broken the backs of peasant households sufficiently for many of them to seek their reproduction through wage employment. This is to say that the impact of taxation and land alienation on labour mobilization and recruitment during the early colonial period has tended to be exaggerated. Taxation was, of course, a double-edged sword: it encouraged wage employment as much as commodity production. In any case, tax evasion was quite endemic. African resistance against taxation eventually contributed to the eruption of the Nairobi riots of March 1922. After the bloody massacre that accompanied the riots the government agreed to reduce the basic rate to sh.12, where it remained unchanged for most of the inter-war period.[7]

The impact of land alienation on labour recruitment during these years was also not as widespread as it is generally asserted. Except for the Central Province and parts of the Rift Valley and Coast provinces, there was relatively little land alienation in the other parts of Kenya.[8] Moreover, the settlers used little of the land alienated to them. Of the nearly 3,157,440 acres occupied by settlers in 1920, only 176,290 acres, or 5.6 per cent of the total, was under cultivation.[9] By 1939, only about 10 per cent of the settler lands were ever used for arable farming at any given time. In any case, transforming control of land to control of labour was not automatic as the settlers in the so-called White Highlands and the coastal landowners came to realize.

The supply of voluntary labour was also held back by the fact that peasant commodity production increased precisely in those regions where settlers hoped to draw labour, namely, the Central and Nyanza provinces. Colonial preference for the Central Province rested on its close proximity to settler areas while, in the case of the Nyanza Province, one of its main attributes was its relatively dense population. Also, both provinces were occupied by peoples with long sedentary agricultural traditions. The colonial authorities held deep doubts about the economic and labour potential of pastoral peoples like the Maasai or the Somali, who in any case were not fully subjugated until the 1930s.[10]

Forced labour, thus, developed in a context of uneven capitalist penetration and development. The methods used were direct and often brutal. Ultimately, however, forced labour was unreliable as a system of labour supply and control. Its spread and impact was uneven in spatial and social terms. It was prevalent mainly in the Central and

Nyanza provinces, and mostly affected poorer households. Traditional authorities, colonial chiefs and functionaries, merchants and the new salaried elite were normally exempt from forced labour. In fact, chiefs were expected to recruit labour on behalf of the settlers and government and provide communal labour for public works programmes. In so far as men were more likely to be commandeered to work far away from their homes on settler farms and for the government, women and children tended to dominate in the supply of 'communal labour'.

The practice of involving women and children in communal labour was enshrined in the 1912 Native Authority Ordinance which, in effect, amounted to forced labour for government purposes within the reserves. In spite of the constant attacks upon the use of forced female and child labour, the practice became more widespread in the 1920s and early 1930s, especially whenever the spectre of labour shortage reared its dreaded head. It was not until 1933 that legislation was passed which was, for the first time, specifically designed to curb the worst effects of forced female and child labour.[11] This was not simply a victory for the humanitarian lobby. The state had come to realize the ineffectiveness of forced labour. This realization was fostered by widespread African resistance and struggle against forced labour, in general, and forced female and child labour, in particular.

It is, of course, difficult to arrive at any accurate assessment of the numbers of people recruited as forced labourers. According to official estimates, about 15,000 people were called upon each year in the 1920s under the forced labour programme.[12] The official figures, however, grossly under-estimate the real numbers involved. For one thing, those conscripted for railway construction were excluded from the count. So were those engaged in communal labour.

Forced labour recruiters included chiefs, district commissioners and their deputies, and private European and Asian recruiting agents. Their recruiting methods ranged from armed raids to devious ploys, like holding women hostage in recruiting camps until they were substituted by their male relatives. Private recruiters also often misrepresented themselves as government agents.[13]

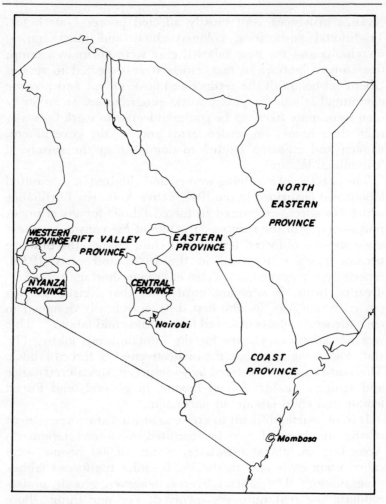

Map 1 Kenya

The ideological justification of forced labour underwent some changes. In the 1890s and early 1900s, forced labour was disguised as tribute labour. In 1908, while forced labour for government purposes was legalized on the basis that the state was the agent of the civilizing mission, labour recruitment for settlers was to be made in the name of 'encouragement'. In 1919, Governor Northey issued his notorious labour circulars in which the blurred distinction between forced labour for public purposes and 'encouragement' for private employers disappeared. The purposes and services for which forced labour was legal were so liberally defined as to include virtually any employer. In the warped rationalization of colonialism, forced labour was seen as a necessary evil to wake up a people long sunk in idleness and indolence. Even the celebrated humanitarian critics of forced labour like Leys and Ross did not question the need to inculcate a steady and disciplined capitalist work ethic among Africans as a precondition for their advancement.[14]

Northey's labour circulars were issued in the aftermath of the First World War when the demand for labour was at a record high and labour shortages were more acute than ever. Settlers had, of course, emerged from the war more assertive than before, and their confidence was buoyed by the arrival of many new European immigrants. Before long, however, post-war euphoria was dissipated by the financial crisis that rocked the colony. The crisis was provoked by the depression in international commodity prices and the change in local currency from rupees to shillings.[15] As a result, wages were reduced by a third. For its part, the government wanted large supplies of labour, as cheaply as possible, for its post-war infrastructural and public works programmes. All these factors reinforced old pressures for forced labour. Also, the war, following hard on the heels of a violent colonization process, had led to many deaths, especially of the forcibly recruited carrier corps, thus accentuating the demographic haemorrhage of able-bodied males. The hen of primitive accumulation was coming home to roost.

Attempts to regulate the flow and rationalize the use of forced labour reached their peak with the development of the *kipande* registration system. *Kipande* was first legislated in 1915, but was implemented from 1920 onwards. *Kipande*, of course, meant different things to the Africans, the state and the settlers. For Africans, the *kipande*, worn around their necks like a dog collar, was a 'badge of slavery'. Like land alienation, grievances against the *kipande* were to galvanize Africans into a nationalist crusade. In the eyes of the settlers and the state, the value of *kipande* was never in doubt. Since once registered a worker could not be deregistered, *kipande* was designed to be used as an instrument with which to keep track of the labour force. It restricted workers' freedom to leave their work and change employers. Also, the *kipande* system helped standardize low wages because it made it difficult for any worker to earn a wage that was higher and unrelated to his former wage, as recorded on his *kipande*. It is significant to note that the emerging African petty bourgeoisie were granted exemption from *kipande*, and compulsory labour, for a fee of £4.[16]

The *kipande* was also intended to facilitate the enforcement of labour contracts in that it enabled penal sanctions to be applied to 'deserters' and for the latter to be returned to their erstwhile employers. The concern by the state and employers with worker desertion shows how widespread desertions were. In fact, desertions represented the chief form of resistance against forced labour. In the early 1900s, people sometimes ran away from their villages and went into hiding to avoid forced labour recruitment. During the First World War, some went as far as Uganda to escape enlistment into the notorious carrier corps.[17] In this sense, desertion represented an attempt to avoid incorporation into the coercive colonial labour system. Desertions were also a means of protest against labour conditions by people already recruited. It was not unusual for people to desert from communal labour tasks, and 'bad employers', including the public works department and other government departments, the railway, Mombasa port, private contractors and others.

From time to time, deserters were caught and brought to book. More often than not, however, deserters easily slid back undetected into the anonymity of rural life. Desertions were effective during these early decades of colonial rule precisely because the peasant sector was able to absorb the deserters. Also, chiefs and other local colonial administrative function-aries represented a weak link in the chain of labour control. Chiefs were expected to trace deserters in their communities. While it paid for them to be 'colonial bully boys', it paid more to circumvent, indeed subvert, the law, in pursuit of private accumulation: remuneration from the state was too meagre to satisfy their growing appetites for material wealth. Thus, while chiefs derived their power from the colonial leviathan, their accumulative interests were served not by a 'proper' use of power, but by its abuse. They were among the first indigenous accumulators, who pirated access to state power for wealth. Among a host of self-serving 'abuses' chiefs committed, was the exaction of bribes from people who wanted to avoid conscription into forced labour. 'Corruption' then enriched chiefs, but it also freed some potential forced labourers or deserters from the constricting tentacles of state control.

It was not only the high incidence of desertions and the corrupt tendencies of chiefs that undermined the effectiveness of forced labour. Controlling labour at the point of production through force was neither practicable nor expedient. To be sure, the use of corporal punishment and other such coercive practices to control Africans while at work was widespread. It was very hard, however, to maintain such forms of control on a permanent basis. In fact, they provoked deep resentment and resistance, including desertions. It was certainly beyond the capacity of most settler farmers and other plantation owners to take direct control over all aspects of farming and assign workers to perform specific tasks under their supervision. To supervise and control workers in the process of production, therefore, was to enter a terrain of protracted struggle, waged and reproduced on a daily basis, whose trajectory was as unpredictable for labour as it was uncontrollable by capital. Thus, underneath the daunting exterior of labour coercion lay the production site where the control of the state and capital was uncertain and often compromised. It is in this sense that labour control through force was limited. It was in response to the struggles against, and limitations of, forced labour that the squatter and migrant labour systems developed.

This is to suggest that the practice of forced labour was neither stable nor omnipresent. It was regularly contested and struggled against and periodically reconstituted. Often, the concept of coercion is used only with reference to labour recruitment strategies. What the state and employers faced was, however, not simply the problem of mobilizing labour power, but the control of people who were members of societies with a strong sense of their cultural identity. The politics of this control had to be reproduced on a continual basis and at different sites, from the domestic sphere to the work place.[18] More work needs to be done in African labour history to unravel the content of coercion at the level of what Burawoy calls relations *in* production,[19] if we are to understand better the complexities and contradictions of colonial labour processes. For the colonial state and capital, mobilizing and controlling African workers was not easy. It involved multi-faceted struggles with the workers who of course tried, as far as was possible, to shape the pattern and define the conditions of their own lives.

The Contradictions of Labour Migration

All too often, the process of migrant labour is encapsulated within structuralist and functionalist notions of production and reproduction. It is argued that under the migrant labour system men were drawn, or forced, off the land leaving behind their women to maintain production. The costs of reproducing, maintaining and sustaining the cheap labour force were, therefore, borne by these 'precapitalist' areas. All this served to lower the costs of production and enhance the rate of profit.[20]

This approach attempts to explain the prevalence of low wages and the persistence of migration between the so-called capitalist and precapitalist sectors. It can degenerate into the dualist models of modernization theory, only that this time the 'rural' or 'traditional' sector is not seen as a drag on development but as the one that subsidizes the 'urban' or 'modern' sector. The articulation of the 'precapitalist' and 'capitalist' modes of production is interpreted mechanically, its trajectory is seen as given, predetermined by capital 'logic'.[21] But the process of articulation of modes of production involves struggles between social groups and classes as defined by these modes in their interaction, and the trajectory and resolution of these struggles is not predetermined by capital logic. Nor is any resolution permanent.[22]

By reducing migrant labour to the reproductive imperatives of capitalism, this approach fails to deal with how workers themselves acted, and how their actions redefined the conditions under which they operated and generated new contradictions in the labour process. 'Patterns of immigration', Cooper suggests, 'may have reflected as much African resistance to capitalist work rhythms as a cost-minimising strategy of employers.'[23] Also, the dichotomy between capitalist production and precapitalist reproduction is too neat, the geographical locus of each too contrived.[24]

It was certainly the case among many squatter households in Kenya that subsistence reproduction and capitalist production were combined on the same settler estate. This shows that labour migrancy, seen in terms of regular movement between geographically separate capitalist and precapitalist spheres, was not as pervasive as is so often assumed. Also, labour migrancy did not merely involve men. Even in cases where it did, however, the functionalist and structuralist approach does not explain why it was men and not women who left. It is simply assumed that female oppression was 'functional' to capital. The exploitation of women in the rural reserves was, however, made possible by the conjunction of the patriarchal practices and ideologies of precolonial societies and those of the British colonizers.[25]

One good illustration of the spurious generalizations that dominate so much Kenyan and African labour history can be found in Kitching's account of the labour process in colonial Kenya. He alleges, without much substantiation, that 'up to about 1930 the majority of those in the wage labour force at any one time were unmarried men'.[26] He concludes from this that the impact of migrant labour on peasant production was minimal. Indeed, he asserts that 'before 1930 the demands of the colonial economy for a redistribution of African labour time had hardly begun to utilise the "spare capacity" inherent in the pre-colonial division of labour. Such demands as were made could be met simply by redistributing a small part of the quantitatively underutilised male labour time toward wage and farm employment.'[27]

Even if it were true that the majority of wage seekers were unmarried men, however, that does not mean their withdrawal of labour from the peasant household was inconsequential. Husbands were not, after all, the only males whose work was important. It is certainly inadequate theoretically and empirically to talk of underutilized male labour time in precolonial times, especially as Kitching's discussion of the precolonial work pattern, on which these assertions are based, is too brief and schematic to be useful. Like accounts inspired by vent-for-surplus theory, this account ignores the actual nature of the colonial labour process and the fact that it did force very real sacrifices and important changes upon peasant household labour allocation. It is revealing that Kitching has almost nothing to say about forced labour and worker resistance. They do not fit into his 'structure'.

In examining the development of migrant labour in Kenya, we must eschew generalizations and note that different regions and sectors of the colonial economy gave rise to different patterns of labour migration. Also, distinctive types of households emerged, depending upon the political reorganization of each region, the nature of its resources, production practices and its level of commoditization. Each household type required a specific set of practices to assure both household production and reproduction.[28]

Broadly speaking, the colonial labour market was divided between government departments, private estates and plantations, domestic service and an assortment of public and private utility and transport services, principally the railway and the Mombasa port. There was, as yet, hardly any manufacturing industry. Labour relations in each of these sectors were distinctive. For instance, private estates and plantations relied considerably on squatter labour, the Mombasa port on casual labour, while the railway was among the first to attempt labour stabilization. Nor were labour relations within each sector homogeneous. Working as a clerk in a government department was not the same as working as a labourer within the public works department. The former was more likely to be able to live together with his family than the latter. Similarly, the household structure of farm contract workers was different from that of squatters, and the demands put on squatters by poor settlers were not the same as those put on them by rich settlers.

It would, of course, not be possible in such a short paper to examine in detail all these sectors and the types of labour practices that developed in each. I will only sketch the growth of migrant labour at the coast and in the so-called White Highlands in order to show the dynamics that led to, and were in turn affected by, migrant labour.

In the coastal region, colonial capitalism was superimposed on a declining plantation economy.[29] Slavery, on which the plantation system had been based in the nineteenth century, was abolished in 1907. Some ex-slaves moved further into the interior, others sought employment in Mombasa. A few settled in a small reserve for ex-slaves. The majority stayed with their old masters, now as squatters. With slavery gone, the old Arab–Swahili plantocracy found it difficult to control labour, and production began to decline. For their part, the new Indian and European landowners also failed to attract sufficient labour or to control it. Both groups saw the Mijikenda as their possible salvation. The Mijikenda were in the meantime spreading from the hinterland. Many became squatters on the coastal plantations and estates. They preferred, however, to be independent producers and would not submit to the demands and controls of coastal landowners. The memories of coastal slavery were too fresh in their minds, and the Mijikenda would not acquiesce to anything remotely resembling it.

The colonial state tried to smash squatter agriculture by the ex-slaves and the Mijikenda in an attempt to turn them into a pool of cheap labour for the coastal estates and Mombasa port. It tried to frustrate peasant production by creating marketing, licensing, taxation and transport conditions which presented obstacles to peasant accumulation. These pressures directly provoked the Giriama Rebellion in 1914, in which many Giriama were killed and a lot of their property lost.[30] Although militarily victorious, after the rebellion the government abandoned its dream of turning the Mijikenda into a cheap migrant labour force. In the ensuing stalemate, neither the landowners nor the squatters could accumulate capital. The former lacked control over labour, the latter lacked control over the land. Thus, an economic structure emerged which stifled increased productivity, investment, innovation and capital formation. The making of a backward region, to use Cooper's phrase, had begun.

In the aftermath of the First World War, some coastal

planters suggested allowing the immigration of indentured Indians and labourers from Nyasaland to alleviate the acute labour shortages they were experiencing. Indentured Indian labour had, after all, once been used to build the Uganda railway. The Colonial Secretary, however, decided against such immigration because settlers in the White Highlands were opposed to it: the Indians who were already in the country had proved that they could be formidable economic competitors. Settlers also objected to Nyasaland labour because it was accustomed to relatively high wages and, the settlers feared, it would 'tend to raise the price of other native labour'.[31]

The alternative was to recruit labour from other parts of Kenya. This labour was, however, already in high demand in the White Highlands. Moreover, the coastal plantations were poorly placed to compete with Mombasa for migrant labour from outside the province. To begin with, opportunities for squatting were already taken up by the ex-slaves and the Mijikenda. So the upcountry migrants flocked to Mombasa, where the main employer was the port. By 1925, there were 7,555 registered workers in Mombasa, of whom only 17 per cent were from the coast. The rest came mostly from Nyanza and Kikuyuland.[32]

These migrants tended to come alone, leaving their families behind. This was partly because of high transport costs, and partly because of their apprehension about the unfamiliar coastal environment. It was an environment that was not only different in terms of weather and types of diseases, which decimated many upcountry migrants,[33] but it was also an area that was steeped in Islam, a religion and way of life that was unfamiliar to the new immigrants. More importantly, perhaps, the casual nature of port labour made it risky to bring one's family. But it also maximized choices open to the migrant, so that sometimes he could secure several sources of income which could enable him to return home earlier than would otherwise have been possible.

It can be seen that migrant labour at the coast generated two different patterns of migration. The Mijikenda migrated to the plantations where they became squatters, while men from Nyanza and Kikuyuland migrated to Mombasa where they became urban workers. Each migration pattern led to a particular type of household structure. The squatter household was a co-residential unit under which production and reproduction were combined. Given the legacies of the Mijikenda rebellion, squatter production was less geared to the reproductive imperatives of capitalism, and more to those of the squatter household itself. The cohesiveness of the household of the urban migrant, on the other hand, was increasingly predicated on its income-pooling functions, not its co-residentiality.[34]

Squatter labour on settler estates in the White Highlands emerged partly because the grossly under-capitalized settlers could not effectively control forced labour or secure fully waged labour, and partly because some peasant households needed the alienated settler lands for their own production and reproduction. In this conjunction lay the genesis of the squatter system and the basis of its recurrent crises and eventual dissolution.

From as early as 1911, settler farmers came to rely on the squatter system as a means of keeping a 'free' cheap labour force. So desperate were some settlers for labour that they even offered prospective squatters livestock.[35] The trend towards the squatter labour system was intensified by the First World War, as shown in the passage of the Resident Native Bill in 1916, the first in a series of such bills. Increased post-war demands for labour only served to reinforce pressures to extend and legalize the system. By 1930, squatter labour had become the main source of labour on settler farms and estates, and the total number of squatters was in the neighbourhood of 120,000 people. They occupied at least 20 per cent of settler land.[36]

The early squatters were in many cases the original inhabitants of the alienated settler lands. Others migrated from reserves to become squatters when they lost access to land in the reserves, for example, the *ahoi* among the Kikuyu. Some people left the reserves for squatter life in order to escape the restrictions of reserve life, especially conscription during the war, and the rigours and abuses of communal and forced labour after the war. Food shortages in the reserves also pushed many to settler farms. So did the desire to escape the creeping Western cultural influences, such as education and missionary activities, which, paradoxically were becoming more pervasive in the reserves than on the settler farms.[37]

At first, both squatters and settlers benefited from the system. For the pioneer squatters, land was plentiful and the labour demands imposed on them minimal. For their part, the settlers paid little wages, but got labour services and sometimes produce as rent from the squatters. In fact, poor settlers, who were in the majority, actually depended on share-cropping or 'kaffir farming', as some called it. The settler estate was far from a capitalist enterprise. The settlers may have come from capitalist societies, and may have wished to operate like capitalists, but in the harsh and unpredictable world of colonialism, they were transformed into semi-feudal barons. This is what the celebrated 'civilizing mission' of colonial ideologues, and the 'capitalist mode of production' of radical theoreticians amounted to in reality – very little 'civilization' and very little 'capitalism'.

The central contradiction of the squatter system was that the more the system developed, the more squatters emerged as independent commodity producers and threatened to rob the settlers of their much desired economic hegemony. Attempts to control squatters and turn them into proletarians always met with resistance, occasionally fierce, and often subtle. Sometimes squatters would withdraw their labour by moving to other farms or returning to the reserves. Alternatively, they would resort to illegal cultivation and grazing, maiming of squatter stock and strike action. Or squatter households would pool together and carefully deploy their members' labour for their own needs and those of the settler. It was also not uncommon for a squatter household to employ casual labour.[38]

Given that so much capital and political stock had been, and continued to be, invested in settler enterprise, the colonial state dreaded this creeping eclipse of settlerdom. Consequently, in 1918, the Resident Native Ordinance was passed. It required future squatter payments to be made in labour services and not in kind or cash. Conditions for squatters began deteriorating from the mid-1920s, at first imperceptibly, then dramatically from the 1930s. Not only were the established squatters beginning to have adult children who needed, or actually occupied more settler land, but the reserves were also becoming more overcrowded as a result of both natural population increase and increasing land concentration due to growing commodity production. Thus, more people flocked from the reserves to become squatters, and the option of return to the reserves as a means of squatter resistance became gradually foreclosed. In the meantime, buoyed up by a temporary recovery in commodity prices in the mid-1920s, settler farming began shifting to mixed farming which required more land and labour.

All this led to reductions in the size of squatter plots, and increases in the amount of time they were obliged to work for the settlers, which by 1925 meant a minimum of six months, up from three months in 1918. So began a period of intense crisis in the squatter system and protracted struggle between squatters and settlers, which was to end violently in the Mau Mau war and the demise of the settler regime itself.

The household structures that emerged on the settler estates in the White Highlands were quite varied and complex. Kitching's contention that nearly all men who became squatters 'had their wives and children with them',[39] is not correct. According to Kanogo, settler farmers employed considerable numbers of contract workers, mostly Luo, Luyia, Gusii, Maasai and some Kalenjin.[40] Rarely did these labour migrants bring their families with them. In fact, Kanogo asserts that even among the squatters themselves, it was only the Kikuyu who almost invariably brought their families with them to the settler farms, and for whom migration was regarded as permanent.[41] This might have been due to the relative intensity of land alienation in Kikuyuland. Commodity production in Kikuyuland grew in the context of restricted land resources, as was not the case in Nyanza, for example. The problems of land shortage were, therefore, more pressing in Kikuyuland than in Nyanza. This meant that pressures for land privatization and concentration in Kikuyuland were more manifest as well. Thus, while increased commodity production was evident in both Kikuyuland and Nyanza, in Kikuyuland it took capitalist forms relatively faster than in Nyanza.[42] In other words, while agrarian changes in Kikuyuland and Nyanza generated in both regions cash-cropping households and labour-exporting households, it was only in Kikuyuland that squatter households emerged.

Clearly, the imperatives of production and reproduction differed for squatter households and contract labourers, whose families were in the reserves. Their respective economic opportunities and responses and cultural values and social integument also differed in quite important, if often subtle, ways. Since the settlers' labour requirements from squatters tended to coincide with the squatters' own labour requirements on their plots, squatters with family members on the estate were better placed than those without to ensure that both the settlers' and their own labour demands were met. The larger the squatter household, the more it was able to maximize the benefits of the squatter system. When conditions for squatters began to deteriorate sharply, it meant that the households that were entirely dependent on squatting also had more to lose. No wonder that when the Mau Mau explosion came, Kikuyu squatters were among those in its vanguard. And Mau Mau ushered in processes that, among many things, transformed the social and institutional basis of the colonial state, contributed to settler economic and political demise, and introduced important changes in the labour process, all of which culminated in the drama of decolonization.

Conclusion

In this paper, I have discussed the nature of the labour process in early colonial Kenya. I looked at the scope, dynamics and contradictions of forced labour and migration. In discussing the colonial labour process, attention should be paid both to forms of control and resistance. In the early colonial period, the practice of forced labour was widespread, but there was limited formal subordination of labour and, as yet, no real subordination.[43] This was not because the colonial state was not authoritarian enough, but because worker resistance was pervasive. Worker resistance encompassed both informal and organized, covert and overt, individual and collective opposition to state and employers in the labour process. It was inspired by both specific conditions at the places of work and the diffuse but no less compelling forces at work in the wider society.

The migrant labour system, I have argued, did not simply arise from the manipulative logic of capital. Neither was it uniform in its organization and development. It was a highly differentiated process. Different patterns of labour migration emerged depending upon the nature of the penetration of capitalism in each area, the particular political reorganization of each area, and local cultural and social traditions. Not surprisingly, distinctive types of households emerged. Each household type developed specific relations with the growing colonial economy and each required a particular set of practices to assure both household production and reproduction. By focusing on the organization and reorganization of households in the colonial labour process, the tendency to write labour history in terms of state policy, or to subsume it under structuralist paradigms, might be transcended. That would help us to see the labour processes during colonial rule in their bewildering complexity and contradiction.

Notes and References

1 R. M. A. van Zwanenberg, *Colonial Capitalism and Labour in Kenya* (Nairobi, East African Publishing House, 1975); A. Clayton and D. C. Savage, *Government and Labour in Kenya, 1895–1963* (London, Frank Cass, 1974).

2 Clayton and Savage, *Government and Labour*; van Zwanenberg, *Colonial Capitalism*; Sharon Stitchter, *Migrant Labour in Kenya, Capitalism and African Response, 1895–1975* (London, Longman, 1982); P. Collier and D. Lal, *Labour and Poverty in Kenya 1900–1980* (Oxford, Oxford University Press, 1986).

3 Stitchter, *Migrant Labour*, p. 25.

4 E. S. Atieno-Odhiambo, *The Paradox of Collaboration and other Essays* (Nairobi, East African Publishing House, 1974); R. D. Wolff, *The Economics of Colonialism, Britain and Kenya, 1870–1930* (New Haven, Yale University Press, 1974); E. A. Brett, *Colonialism and Underdevelopment in East Africa* (London, Heinemann, 1978).

5 Michael Cowen, *Wattle Production in the Central Province, Capital and Household Commodity Production, 1903–1964* (Nairobi, Institute of Development Studies, University of Nairobi, 1975); Gavin Kitching, *Class and Economic Change in Kenya, The Making of an African Petite Bourgeoisie, 1905–1970* (New Haven, Yale University Press, 1980); Nicola Swainson, *The Development of Corporate Capitalism in Kenya, 1917–1977* (London, Heinemann, 1980).

6 Crawford Young, 'The Colonial State and Its Connection to Current
   Political Crises in Africa', paper presented to the Conference on African
   Independence and the Consequences of the Transfer of Power, 1956–
   1980, University of Zimbabwe, Harare, 1985; Crawford Young and T.
   Turner, *The Rise and Decline of the Sairean State* (Madison, Wisconsin
   University Press, 1985).
7 van Zwanenberg, *Colonial Capitalism*, chapter 3 p. 82ff.
8 John Middleton, 'Kenya: Changes in African Life, 1912–1945' in V.
   Harlow and E. M. Chilver (eds), *History of East Africa* (Oxford
   University Press, 1965), vol. 2, pp. 341–5.
9 Wolff, *The Economics of Colonialism*, p. 60.
10 P. T. Dalleo, 'Trade and Pastoralism: Economic Factors in the History
   of Somali of North-Eastern Kenya, 1892–1948' (Syracuse University,
   PhD Dissertation, 1975).
11 van Zwanenberg, *Colonial Capitalism*, chapter 5; Clayton and Savage,
   Government and Labour, chapter 4.
12 Kenya Government, *Annual Reports* (Nairobi, Government Printer,
   1920–30).
13 Stichter, *Migrant Labour*, pp. 37–8.
14 Norman Leys, *Kenya* (London, Hogarth Press, 1924); W. M. Ross, *Kenya
   From Within* (London, Macmillan, 1927).
15 R. M. A. van Zwanenberg with Anne King, *An Economic History of Kenya
   and Uganda* (London, Macmillan, 1975), pp. 281–7.
16 S. H. Somjee, 'Kipande, the symbol of Imperialism, 1914–1948: A Study
   in Colonial Material Culture', Staff Seminar, Department of Literature,
   University of Nairobi, 1980.
17 Clayton and Savage, *Government and Labour*, p. 85.
18 S. Bowles and H. Gintis, 'The Labour Theory of Value and the
   Specificity of Marxian Economics', in S. Resmick and R. Wolff (eds),
   Rethinking Marxism: Essays for Harry Magdoff and Paul Sweezy (New York,
   Automedia, 1985).
19 M. Burawoy, 'The Contours of Production Politics', in C. Bergquist
   (ed.), *Labour in the Capitalist World Economy* (Beverly Hills, Sage
   Publications, 1984).
20 Wolff, *The Economics of Colonialism*; Stichter, *Migrant Labour*; C.
   Meillasoux, *Maidens, Meal and Money* (Cambridge, Cambridge
   University Press, 1981).
21 Jairus Banaji, 'Backward Capitalism, Primitive Accumulation and
   Modes of Production', *Journal of Contemporary Asia* 3 (4) (1973); Aidan
   Foster-Carter, 'The Modes of Production Controversy', *New Left Review*,
   No. 107 (1978); B. J. Berman and J. M. Lonsdale, 'The Development of
   the Labour Control System in Kenya, 1919–1929', *Canadian Journal of
   African Studies* 14 (1) (1980); W. van Brisbergen and P. Geschiere (eds),
   Old Modes of Production and Capitalist Encroachment (London, Routledge
   and Kegan Paul, 1985).
22 Tiyambe Zeleza, 'African History: The Rise and Decline of Academic
   Tourism', *Ufahamu* 13 (1) (1983). See the contributions in *Canadian
   Journal of African Studies*, 19 (1) (1985).

23 Frederick Cooper, 'Introduction', in F. Cooper (ed.), *Struggle for the City: Migrant Labour, Capital and the State in Urban Africa* (Beverly Hills, Sage Publications, 1983), p. 15.

24 Frederick Cooper, 'Introduction', p. 16; Frederick Cooper, 'Africa and the World Economy', Paper presented to African Studies Association, Bloomington, October, 1981, pp. 50–62.

25 Belinda Bozzoli, 'Marxism, Feminism and South African Studies', *Journal of Southern African Studies* 9 (2) (1983).

26 Kitching, *Class and Economic Change*, p. 251.

27 *Ibid.*, p. 19.

28 W. G. Martin, 'Beyond the Peasant to Proletarian Debate: African Household Formation in South Africa', in Joan Smith *et. al.* (eds), *Households and the World Economy* (Beverly Hills, Sage Publications, 1984).

29 Frederick Cooper, *From Slaves to Squatters: Plantation Labour and Agriculture in Zanzibar and Coastal Kenya, 1890–1925* (New Haven, Yale University Press, 1980).

30 Cynthia Brantley, *The Giriama and British Colonialism: A Study in Resilience and Rebellion, 1800–1920* (Berkeley, University of California Press, 1981).

31 Wolff, *The Economics of Colonialism*, p. 95.

32 Cooper, *From Slaves to Squatters*, p. 249.

33 Karim Janmohamed, 'A History of Mombasa, c. 1895–1939: Some Aspects of Economic and Social Life in an East African Port Town During Colonial Rule', (Northwestern University, PhD Dissertation, 1977).

34 On households as income-pooling units see I. Wallerstein, 'Household Structures and Labour-Force Formation in the Capitalist World Economy'; K. Friedan, 'Households as Income-Pooling Units'; and D. Wong, 'The Limits of Using the Household as a Unit of Analysis', in Smith *et. al. Households and the World Economy*.

35 Tabitha Kanogo, *Squatters and the Roots of Mau Mau* (London, James Currey; Nairobi, Heinemann Kenya, 1987), p. 21.

36 Clayton and Savage, *Government and Labour*, p. 128; van Zwanenberg, *Colonial Capitalism*, pp. 215–20.

37 Frank Furedi, 'The Kikuyu Squatters in the Rift Valley: 1918–1929', in B. A. Ogot (ed.), *Economic and Social History of East Africa* (Nairobi, Kenya Literature Bureau, 1976), pp. 181–2.

38 Kanogo, *Squatters*, pp. 5 and 29.

39 Kitching, *Class and Economic Change*, p. 244.

40 Kanogo, *Squatters*, pp. 30–1.

41 *Ibid.*, pp. 21, 42.

42 Tiyambe Zeleza, 'The Establishment of Colonial Rule in Kenya: 1905–1920', in W. R. Ochieng' (ed.), *A Modern History of Kenya: From 1895 to the Present* (London, Evans Brothers, forthcoming).

43 On the concept of formal and real subordination of labour see Paul Thompson, *The Nature of Work: An Introduction to Debates on the Labour Process* (London, Macmillan, 1984).

From Long-Term to Seasonal Labour Migration in Iringa Region, Tanzania: A Legacy of the Colonial Forced Labour System

C. M. F. Lwoga

Introduction

There have been changes in the pattern of labour migration from Iringa Region during the post-independence period in Tanzania, of which the most notable have involved the destinations and the duration of employment of the migrant labourers. The sisal industry which was, during the colonial period, the major destination of migrant labour, is threatened with collapse due to an acute shortage of manual labour. Long-term migrations of agricultural labour, which were common in the colonial period, have been replaced by short-term, seasonal migrations. What has not changed, though, is the source of the migrant labour.

In this paper I argue that the colonial state established labour reserves for the plantations through various coercive measures (economic, political/administrative, and ideological). These labour reserves became part and parcel of the socio-economic structure of Tanzania. Since the post-colonial state did not overhaul the colonial economic structure, peasants in the former labour reserves continue to reproduce themselves as cheap labour for the agricultural sector. Changes in destinations and duration of employment are in themselves not important for the purposes of this paper.

The Colonial Economy and the Establishment of the Migrant Labour System in Tanzania

The establishment of the colonial economy in Tanzania was begun by the Germans in the late nineteenth century. They established sisal plantations in the sparsely populated areas in the north-eastern parts of the country. In addition, German settlers established farms on which they grew food and export crops. Both the plantations and the individual settler farms required a large number of labourers to work them. Sisal became the most important crop during the German, as well as the British, colonial period, demanding more labourers than all other crops. Right from the initial establishment of plantations and of individual farms, the Germans were unable to attract sufficient wage labourers. One reason for this was that the wages offered by the plantations and settlers were very low. Another was that the Germans treated their wage labourers inhumanly. Peasants living in the neighbourhood of the plantations could also grow food crops which they then sold to the plantations for the feeding of the wage labourers.

As more labourers were required for the sisal estates, as well as for European farms, a demand local labour could not satisfy, recruitment had to be further afield. Initially, long-distance labourers were recruited in Unyamwezi (central-western Tanzania), Usukuma (north-western) and Iramba (central Tanzania). But after the people in Unyamwezi started producing cash crops (mainly cotton), thus reducing the number of labourers recruited for the sisal estates, the Germans extended their recruiting to other parts of the country, such as Ufipa, Tukuyu (both in south-western Tanzania), Songea and Lindi (southern Tanzania), and Singida (central Tanzania). Njombe District, which then included the present Ludewa and Makete districts, and is part of Iringa Region, was part of Songea District.[1] This was the beginning of the creation of labour reserves.

The British colonial administration inherited and strengthened this economic structure. The labour reserves had been created in order to ensure a constant labour flow to the plantations and mines.[2] Both the creation of the labour reserves and the maintenance of labour flow entailed the use of various coercive measures.

A dependency relationship developed between the labour reserves and employment centres, mainly the sisal, tea and tobacco industries, a relationship which, as has already been pointed out, was maintained throughout the colonial period through economic, political/administrative and ideological pressure. The political/administrative pressure was external to the labour reserves, as was part of the economic and ideological pressure. For example, peasants were coerced into wage labour through taxation (tax defaulters) and conscription (compulsory labour supply). Taxation was used as a convenient means of flushing out labour from rural areas. It was a method used by both the German and the British colonial administrations. It is noteworthy, for instance, that during British colonial rule tax collection coincided with demand for labour on plantations.[3]

Besides the revenue that accrued to the colonial state from taxation, the state also used cheap labour arising directly from the tax system. Peasants who failed to pay taxes in cash were sent to work in government undertakings, such as construction of buildings, roads, portage, and so on. Records show that during the great depression of the 1930s, when it was difficult for peasants to earn cash through wage labour or sale of cash crops, more people worked in government undertakings for failing to pay tax.[4] It should also be noted that tax defaulters working in government undertakings were paid lower wage rates than other labourers, forcing them, therefore, to work for longer periods. For example, in 1935, a tax defaulter in Njombe worked for 28 days in order to meet a tax obligation of sh.4.[5]

Economic pressure was applied through the tax system and also through denying the labour reserves alternative means of earning cash. Peasants in the labour reserves were compelled to sell their labour power because, for various economic and political reasons, they could not produce agricultural commodities. It is recorded, for example, that the colonial government was, as late as 1952, promising planters that peasants in the labour reserves would not be allowed to produce cash crops, adding that the labour reserves' role in the colonial economy was to provide labour for plantations.[6] Self-sustaining precolonial economies were also partially destroyed. This compelled peasants in the labour reserves to combine subsistence agriculture with wage labour as the only means of their reproduction. In the long run, part of the economic and ideological pressure became internal to the labour reserves. Pressure was applied on adolescent male youths through the reproduction of households (the dowry system). This internalization should be seen in the light of the development of the need for money in the various societies in the labour reserves.[7] It is easy to ignore the fact that the monetization of traditionally self-sustaining economies served interests that were external to the traditional societies. Whatever 'development' took place in the traditional societies, as a result of the monetization of their economies, was secondary to the main objective of the colonial capitalist economy.

The reproduction of the economies in the former colonies depends largely on intervention by the industrial Western economies. Hence, the economies of the post-colonial states go on fulfilling the requirements for which they were established, and the main points of the following (colonial) quotation still seem to apply:

> I believe we shall in future see the whole of our own cotton coming from our own Dominion [i.e. Empire]. I believe we shall thus secure cheaper cotton, cheaper raw materials for the use of our British manufacturers. I also believe that in doing that we will be supplying a market for our own people beyond the seas, and that the money they obtain from their cotton may to a greater extent be spent in making purchases from their mother country. It is an ideal for which we all ought to work, that the money obtained from us should in a different form come back to this country.[8]

Another important point that should be borne in mind is that production of agricultural raw materials confined the peasants to cultivation and the sale of their labour power. This situation remains the same today for the vast majority of the peasants. Social changes that have taken place in the rural areas have been based on these two activities. Cultivation of cash crops led to changes in land ownership and use, and as land in certain areas was turned into a marketable commodity, it resulted in enhanced development of commercial agriculture among the peasantry. Where land commercialization was held back, as in many parts of Tanzania, it stunted the growth of peasant commercial agriculture. In both cases, the changes helped the development of the migrant labour system. The reason for this was that in some of the areas where land was commercialized, land scarcity developed and the landless peasants had to migrate in search of either wage labour or new land. Where land was not commercialized, labour migration developed because of the lack of development of commercial agriculture. In this case, labour migration became a necessary supplement to food production. It is this structural linkage between wage labour and food production for household consumption that is ignored in labour migration theories that regard the movements of labour as taking place between dual economies ('traditional' and 'modern'). In theories of this kind, the 'traditional' sector is treated as a sector of low productivity from where the migrant labourers move, after weighing opportunity costs, to the higher productivity or 'modern' sector.[9]

My argument is that the development of commercial agriculture both on plantations and on peasant smallholding sectors, the geographical location of these employment centres and economic decisions made by those who control the economy, are central to the understanding of the persistence of labour migration in contemporary Tanzania. Taking these factors into account, it becomes possible to analyse how households conform to the economic structure in fulfilment of their economic needs. It is also possible to observe changes in the rate of migration, destination and types of labour migration, in accordance with changes in the economic structure; changes that may occur both as a result of the limited operation of the market forces and the allocation of development resources through development planning. It is true that the individual labour migrants make decisions when to migrate, where to go and for how long to remain in wage employment, but these decisions are made within the limits set by the economic structure in which they live. For example, the timing of out-migration often coincides with 'slack' periods in agriculture, a factor that merely suggests that it is the time when migration will cause the least damage to the agricultural cycle.[10]

Labour Migration in Iringa Region during the Colonial Period

As has already been pointed out, parts of Iringa Region became labour reserves under German colonial rule. During the British colonial period, Iringa was part of the then Southern Highlands Province, one of the provinces in the country that was settled by European farmers. The settlers established farms in the present Iringa Rural District (tobacco farming), Mufindi District (tea), Njombe District (pyrethrum and later, in the 1950s, wattle plantations) and in the northern parts of the present Ludewa District (pyrethrum and tea). There were no settlers in the present Makete District (then Njombe west). The reason for this was that land there was not considered suitable for European settlement. The same applied for the central and southern parts of Njombe District.[11]

The settling of Europeans in Njombe District would have meant wage employment nearer to home for the labour migrants of the district. But as it turned out, a larger number left the district and went to work in the sisal industry, on tea estates in Mufindi District, and tobacco farms in Iringa District. The settlers in Njombe District paid lower wages to the migrant labourers, making working for them an unattractive proposition. For example, in the 1930s, employers in Njombe District were paying sh.4 per month, compared with sh.30 in the sisal industry. The settlers in Njombe District supported the payment of low wages, arguing that 'cheap native labour is a requisite for successful European agriculture'.[12]

The male exodus from Njombe District was quite high, with an average of more than 50 per cent for the district as a whole. In Njombe west (Ukinga) the rate of absent males was 62 per cent; in Njombe central (Ubena) the rate was 60 per cent, and in Njombe south (Upangwa) it was 64 per cent.[13] Sometimes up to 400 men left the district for the sisal estates in Kilosa area in one month, and at other times over 100 people were recruited in a single day and were taken to sisal estates.[14]

During the Second World War, when sisal production was declared essential for the war effort, the industry had a higher priority than gold mining in the allocation of conscripted labour.[15] The Southern Highlands Province was required to provide 2,000 conscript labourers each year, and Njombe District's quota was put at 600 men. The Njombe District Commissioner complained about the 'unrealistic' quota, pointing out that the district had already been depleted of able-bodied men through normal labour migration and compulsory porterage. In some villages, only 33 per cent of able-bodied men were at home at the beginning of the cultivating season. The District Commissioner pointed out in 1944 that:

> Lorries from Kilosa [sisal estates] are picking up labour from Upangwa. Njombe District provides 80% of labour for Mufindi tea estates . . . a larger percentage of labour [from Njombe District] is working on sisal estates on the Central Line. A considerable number of natives go to Tanga for work on sisal estates. Tukuyu tea estates employ a large quantity of Wakinga from this district . . . the pyrethrum estates have 3000 natives employed by them. The Polish camp [detainees] has 500 natives employed. Government is employing 500 on Government works and the roads in the district. Finally this district has to supply a considerable number of porters [for the military] monthly.[16]

Desertion by 'duly conscripted' labourers was punishable by law. Moreover, chiefs or headmen in the areas where the deserters came from were required to replace each deserter with a new man from the same village.[17]

The District Commissioner's complaint above stopped labour conscription in Njombe District. The district was then, however, opened up for recruitment of labour by licenced recruiting agents. The Mbeya Recruiting Group, which was an affiliate of the Sisal Labour Bureau (SILABU) of the

Tanganyika Sisal Growers' Association, established a forwarding office in Njombe Town. A letter dated 10 January 1946 from the District Commissioner to the Labour Officer Mbeya, shows that a total of 2,880 labourers had been forwarded to the sisal estates through the Njombe office of the SILABU in 1945. Many more labourers found their own way to plantations.[18]

What is noteworthy in the opening up of the district to licenced recruiting agents is that, despite the existence of wage employment opportunities in the district and elsewhere, it was still necessary to push peasants into wage labour. Touts and recruiting agents flocked into the labour reserves and kept pressure on peasants to 'volunteer' for wage labour on plantations.

Migrant labourers from Njombe District found work in various areas of employment. The sisal industry was the destination of almost all the Wapangwa and the majority of the Wabena migrants. Tobacco and tea industries were the destinations of the majority of the Wakinga. Migrants from the Lake Nyasa area (the Wamanda) went to work on sisal estates, and others went to mines in South Africa (some Wapangwa went there too, as well as to Zimbabwe, then Southern Rhodesia). When gold was being mined in Chunya District (part of the then Southern Highlands Province), labour migrants from Njombe District went there too. They made up 5–10 per cent of the total labour force on the Lupa gold-field. One count in 1938 showed there were 900 Wakinga, 450 Wabena, 200 Wapangwa and 125 Wakisi (like the Wamanda, they are an offshoot of the Wapangwa) working on the gold-field and, in that year alone, 7,755 men from Njombe District were employed in gold mining at Lupa.[19]

Many of the migrants on the gold-fields were not paid for their labour and were merely given IOU chits. Sometimes the labourers received a token payment of sh.3–5 and a written acknowledgement of the debt. Usually, the labourers left without recovering their wages. The British colonial administrators blamed the labourers for not collecting their wages from their employers. In some instances, however, colonial officers helped in recovering wages due to labourers.[20]

The large exodus of men from Njombe District caused a shortage of labour within the district and the province. For example, in 1945 and 1946 there was a serious labour shortage in Iringa District, which depended on labour migrants from Njombe District. The labour shortage in Iringa was also due to low wages and to the increase of peasant marketable agricultural production, making it unnecessary for some peasants to earn money through wage labour.[21] To alleviate the problem, employers resorted to employing women and children, not only in Iringa District, but also in Njombe District itself. Three pyrethrum farms in Njombe District, for example, had employed a total of 238 men, 97 women and 342 children in December 1946. Another farm showed in its returns for the year a total of 7,375 days worked by the labour force on the farm, and these broke down to 3,404 days for men, 1,372 for women and 2,599 for children.[22]

Even the Lupa gold mines employed children. It was noted by the Labour Officer in February 1940 that the new labour gangs employed during that month consisted of 80 per cent juveniles (youngsters between the age of 13 and 16) and only 20 per cent adults.[23] Some employers asked specifically for child labourers in their requests for labour to the Njombe District Officer.[24]

Employment of women and children was not entirely due to shortage of adult male labour. It was also cheaper. Women and children were preferred by employers for jobs such as tea and pyrethrum flower picking. Whereas the adult male and female wage rates were fixed by the employers and were the same in all the farms, children's wage rates were left to the discretion of individual farm managers.[25] It should be pointed out that female and child labour was not confined to tea and pyrethrum industries. Tobacco farms in Iringa District used female and child labour. So did the sisal industry. As late as 1960, the sisal industry was using women and children in sisal production.[26]

Although the colonial government allowed child employment on condition that 'a child shall be accompanied by a parent or guardian', abuse of this practice was widespread.[27] This is recorded in correspondence between the Njombe District Commissioners, sub-chiefs, missionaries who were opposed to the practice because recruiting agents abducted children from mission schools, and the Labour Office responsible for issuing recruiting permits.[28] Employers used to send adult labourers to their villages with instructions to recruit as many children as possible, and were told not to return without juvenile recruits. Some of the recruited children were as young as seven or eight years old.[29]

The colonial district officials regarded child labour as an important source of wage labour and justified it by arguing that it was 'the main cash resource' of the Njombe people.[30] Action against child labour when occasionally taken, as a result of pressure from the missionaries, consisted of prosecution of the parents rather than of employers or recruiters. Occasionally, some of the children bound for wage labour were returned to Njombe town. At other times, the District Commissioner asked employers to 'return a few' of the child labourers to reduce the 'much unrest and ill-feeling caused among the inhabitants of this (Njombe) district by children running away from school.'[31]

The place of women and children as migrant labourers should be seen within the context of the reproduction of the migrant labour force. Children were being socialized in the labour process. Where schools existed (mostly run by religious institutions), the children were taken away, to grow up illiterate and believing that labour migration was the only way of earning money. Sometimes the entire family unit (man, wife and children) became labour migrants. When the children grew up and established their own families, the cycle was repeated. It is important to note how the colonial government treated the issue of child labour, as shown above. The long-term result of child employment was the denial of access to high-level decision-making positions to people in the labour reserves, thus further contributing to the perpetuation of labour migration. This was clearly noticeable after independence and the subsequent Africanization of high-level government posts. The preponderance of people from areas of cash-crop production in all top posts was justified by the argument that they were better qualified for the posts than people from the labour reserves, where very few individuals attained academic qualifications beyond primary education.

The Failure of Cash Crops as an Alternative to Labour Migration in the Last Years of Colonial Rule

Although Njombe District was regarded as a labour reserve, pockets of cash-crop production had developed in the 1930s, but were dominated by European farmers. Two major crops were grown in the district: coffee at Lupembe, east of the district headquarters; and pyrethrum, a few miles south of the district headquarters, in Uwemba and Mahenye areas and, later, further south at Lusitu and Madope in the now Ludewa District.

African farming of coffee and pyrethrum was limited to those few individuals who could obtain a licence for growing the crops. Various regulations governed the growing of cash crops by Africans, under the guise of quality control. One regulation required the approval of the Agricultural Officer or his nominee before coffee or pyrethrum could be grown thus making it impossible for many peasants in Njombe District to obtain approval for growing the crops as there were only a few 'nominees' of the Agricultural Officer in the district. In the 1950s, changes were initiated in Njombe District. Expansion of cash-crop production was encouraged, and attempts were made to change the status of the district from exporter of labour to exporter of cash crops. The changes were initiated by a new District Commissioner, who was strongly opposed to recruiting labour from the district. For example, when the Department of Labour suggested that more labour might be recruited from Upangwa (Ludewa District) and that a forwarding office should be opened there, the District Commissioner objected, arguing that:

> The Njombe Local Administration are now making intensive efforts to increase the wealth of the district by developing new cash crops, such as coffee, pyrethrum, wheat and peas ... which will begin in 1959 ... and which have the secondary objective of attracting back to the district some 15000 Africans who now find it necessary to seek work elsewhere. In the circumstances I cannot support any proposal which might aid in draining off still more of the areas's able-bodied men ... I am

particularly opposed to the establishment of any Forwarding Office in Upangwa, a backward area where
great efforts are to be made to develop an indigenous
coffee industry.[32]

Coffee production in Njombe District at that time was also
spurred on by success stories from other parts of the country:
the Kilimanjaro Native Cooperative Union and coffee development among the Chagga; the Victoria Federation of Cooperative Unions known for cotton production and development
among the Sukuma; the Rungwe Cooperative Union and
coffee development in Unyakyusa; the Ngoni-Matengo Cooperative Union which dealt with coffee and tobacco produced
in Mbinga and Songea Districts respectively; and within
Njombe itself, the Lupembe Cooperative Union dealing in
coffee produced in the district. All these inspired individuals,
especially in labour exporting regions, who wanted to see the
development of their own area. However, efforts to establish
cash-crop production in the district as an alternative to labour
migration did not succeed.

Government officials viewed cash-crop production from
their own perspective, and the amount of revenue that would
accrue to the government from the sale of the crops was of key
importance to them. At the same time, cash crops were
presented to the peasants as the best way of improving their
standard of living and accumulating wealth, and they were
expected to accept without question 'what was good for them',
as decided by government officials. When peasants failed to
do this, they were deemed to be irrational with regard to
money incentives, labour returns, labour demand and so on.[33]

Government officials did not look into the circumstances
that led peasants not to adopt coffee growing on a large scale.
One of the reasons for this was the cost of seedlings. Sold at 10
cents each, it was difficult for many peasants to afford enough
seedlings for just one acre (540 seedlings, i.e. sh.54). Furthermore, investment had to be made in equipment such as
secateurs, hand-pulping machines, pesticides and fertilizers.
It was then estimated by the Department of Agriculture that it
needed sh.1,000 to maintain just one acre of coffee trees and
that one man could not properly maintain more than one

acre.[34] In addition, the crop demanded much labour time, thus competing with food production, which for the peasants was the top priority. For many coffee growers, one member of the household (usually the man) had to devote his entire labour time to coffee production. During harvesting, every able-bodied member of the household had to join in picking the ripe coffee berries. Another constraint on peasants adopting coffee production was the lack of credit facilities that would have allowed them to obtain inputs and equipment for the development of their coffee plots. Thus for many peasants, coffee was not a paying crop, despite its high returns.

The lack of response to cash cropping was not confined to coffee production. The Department of Agriculture had problems in convincing peasants in Ukinga to adopt pyrethrum as the major cash crop in that area. Even in areas of Lupembe where coffee was already established, some of the coffee growers decided to change over to pyrethrum cultivation against the advice of the Department of Agriculture.[35] The reason for this was the short period (six months) it took for pyrethrum to mature as against three years for coffee.

In such circumstances (the unsuccessful attempt at cash crop growing on a large scale), peasants had to continue depending on labour migration as the only alternative means of earning cash. Indeed, while agricultural instructors were exhorting peasants to take up the growing of cash crops, the Department of Labour was issuing permits for labour recruitment in Njombe District, in spite of the opposition of the District Commissioner as quoted above.

Here, as later, one sees conflicting interests at work. The colonial state's interest was to raise production of plantation crops that depended on the availability of cheap labour. On the other hand, local interests in Njombe District aimed at increasing production of cash crops on smallholdings. This was important for the District Council's revenue, which could then be used for the funding of various socio-economic development plans in the district. Settler farming in Njombe District was failing as a result of the declining price of pyrethrum, and smallholder pyrethrum growers were now producing more than the settlers. For example, in 1955, smallholder farmers produced only 2 tons of pyrethrum but, by 1961, their production had reached 350 tons, while estate production stagnated at 175 tons. Not long after, estate pyrethrum farming was abandoned.[36]

Labour migration in Njombe District continued because the local authorities did not recognize, and thus failed to deal effectively with, the problem of rural poverty that made it difficult for peasants to take up cash-crop production. Poverty reinforced and reproduced conditions for labour migration.

Professional recruiting was stopped in Njombe District in 1957, but other kinds of recruitment were allowed, such as the recruiting of voluntary labourers who presented themselves at the work place or at the office of a recruiting agent, such as SILABU. Another kind of recruitment was by the employer applying for a Worker Recruiter's Permit and then despatching some of the labourers to their villages to recruit labour. This method was widely used in Njombe District. Until the late 1950s, however, Njombe District was still a labour reserve, and was not regarded as a potential cash-crop producer.

What is noted here is the conflict between efforts to establish cash crops as an alternative means for peasants to earn cash and the need to supply labour to plantations. Both the attempt to establish cash crops and the continuation of labour migration took place for reasons external to Njombe itself. Labour migration was established in the district at the advent of colonialism, so were cash crops in those areas where they were allowed to be grown. Investment in roads and social services was channelled into cash-crop producing areas, while labour-exporting areas were left to deteriorate as a result of the exodus of able-bodied men. At independence, the labour-exporting areas were grossly under-represented at all import-ant levels of decision making, further contributing to their lagging behind. They could not attract sufficient develop-mental resources from the socio-economic development planners.

Labour Migration in Iringa Region after Independence (1960s–1970s)

The discussion above has shown that although efforts were being made in Njombe District to persuade peasants to produce cash crops as an alternative source of income, the outcome was disappointing to the district authorities. At the time of independence in 1961, Njombe District was still a major labour reserve for the sisal estates and tobacco farming. At the same time, changes were taking place in the sisal industry, the largest employer of migrant labour, which led to the reorganization of production using a smaller, stabilized, labour force. For the first time in the history of sisal production, there were more labour migrants than the industry could absorb. Redundant labourers were sent back to their villages, or settled in villages in the neighbourhood of sisal plantations, and new-comers were being turned away. Immediately after independence, the post-colonial state embarked on a programme of rural development which involved intensification of cash-crop production. Three years after independence, the post-independence government decided to stop labour recruiting both from outside and within the country.

The government's step to check labour migration did not, however, take into consideration the fact that so long as cash crops had not taken root in the labour reserves, there was no alternative by which peasants in those areas could earn money. Furthermore, when labour recruiting was stopped, no measures were taken to ensure labour supply to the plantations from other sources. The post-independence government had apparently not realized that the labour reserves had been established during the colonial period precisely because of the failure to obtain voluntary labour for the plantations. Throughout the colonial period, there existed a strong relationship between the labour reserves and the plantation sector, a relationship which the post-colonial government was now breaking. As already pointed out, in 1964 (when the government stopped labour recruiting for plantations) the labour position in the sisal industry was a good one, but that was only temporary. Soon the labour shortage problem reappeared, as labour lost through desertion, retirement, illness and death could not easily be replaced.

Perhaps the post-colonial government had expected that job seekers from all over the country would look for jobs in the plantation sector, attracted by the wages, as was the case with other kinds of employment. But the nature of jobs in the plantation sector, especially in the sisal industry, made wage labour on plantations the last resort of job seekers. The reappearance of the labour shortage problem was not confined to the sisal industry. Almost all kinds of plantations experienced labour shortage, and the problem persisted throughout the late 1960s and 1970s. For example, in November 1966, Iringa Region alone had 9,550 vacancies for labourers on the tea estates in Mufindi and Njombe.[37] The Department of Labour had by then taken over the role of recruiting labour for various employers in the country, by advertising vacancies where employment opportunities were available for job seekers. Almost always, however, the vacancies on plantations were difficult to fill.

Expansion of cash (export) crop production did, to some extent, reduce labour migration from Njombe District. The reduction of labour migration to the plantations, especially to sisal estates (sisal was the largest crop which earned the post-colonial government foreign exchange) was a headache to the Department of Labour. The Department continued to issue recruiting permits for recruitment in Njombe District, despite vigorous opposition by the post-independence authorities in the district. Scenes that had taken place during the colonial period were repeated, i.e. the clash of interests between the central government at the regional level, on the one hand, and the district and lower level officials, on the other. For example, in September 1966, the Regional Labour Officer at Iringa wrote to his junior, the District Labour Officer at Njombe that a recruiter had been issued with a permit to recruit labour in Njombe District.[38]

The fact is that job seekers were not looking for work on plantations, hence the view of employers and those at the higher levels of decision making that it would be easier to recruit labour from the former labour reserves than elsewhere. This view also reflects the fact that no qualitative change with regard to agricultural labour policy had taken place since independence. That is, agricultural labour was still poorly paid and badly housed, and no efforts had been made to attract it through material incentives. Despite acknowledgement by the economic development planners that labour migration was responsible for the stagnation of the labour reserves, they encouraged recruitment there regardless of economic development programmes being implemented in those areas. Part of the Regional Labour Officer's letter read: 'Since the local leaders are not too happy about the continuous male exodus from the district, which they claim to be causing some social and economic imbalance there, please make sure that all these voluntary workers are taken through the Employment Exchange, Njombe, and keep me informed to that effect.'[39] Social and economic imbalance between labour supply and labour receiving areas would not, however, be redressed merely by having labour migrants registered with the Employment Exchange. The local leaders in Njombe District were resisting the recruitment of labour in the district because it depleted the labour force needed for development programmes within the district. The leadership pointed out to the regional authorities that labour for tobacco and tea estates in Iringa District should be recruited within Iringa District itself.[40]

The conflict of interests between the local authorities in Njombe District and the Department of Labour went on throughout the late 1960s and the 1970s. The Department of Labour argued that peasants were free to go to work anywhere in the country and that if permission to recruit labour in Njombe District were refused, the national economy would be adversely affected. Disagreeing with the Department of Labour, the Njombe local leaders argued that freedom to work did not mean recruitment by a third party.[41] For the Njombe local leadership, the issue was not merely one of wage employment for the peasants of Njombe, but concerned the misplaced views of the higher authorities that the former labour reserves should continue to provide cheap labour to the plantation sector at the expense of economic development within those areas. Much to the annoyance of the Department of Labour, recruiting in Njombe District was banned in 1971. The lowest government representatives (ward secretaries) were required by the district authorities to ensure that the ban was effective. It was possible to expect the ward secretaries to enforce the ban because in most cases they were appointed locally; and since labour migration was stigmatized (through political education campaigns and the news media, especially after the Arusha Declaration of 1967), they would see to it that their fellow tribesmen refrained from labour migration and tried to earn money through other 'honourable' means.

The Department of Labour's attitude towards labour migration in Njombe District was reinforced by declining tobacco production in Iringa District. Tobacco was one of the major foreign exchange earning crops in Tanzania. Labour shortages in the 1970s led to a sharp decline in tobacco production in Iringa Region from 4,261,685 kg in 1976–7 to 2,300,000 kg in 1980–1.[42] The government decided to intervene in order to ensure labour supply to the tobacco farms, thus ending opposition against labour recruitment in Njombe District. Despite this intervention, however, labour supply to the tobacco farms continued to decline. Because of this persistent labour shortage, some tobacco farmers had to abandon tobacco farming and turn to maize production.

The tobacco growers (most of whom were of Greek origin) had always depended on one source of labour supply – Ukinga – which was guaranteed during the colonial period. With changes after independence it was, however, difficult for the tobacco farmers to get labour supplies from the 'traditional' source. After the creation of Makete District in 1979, the problem became worse for the tobacco growers. The authorities in the new district banned recruitment in the district. The ban was more effective because control of the area was no longer directed from a distant headquarters at Njombe. Moreover, the district leadership, especially at the political level, was mainly local, and the economic development of the district was for them more important than labour requirements of plantations elsewhere in the country.

Neither the local authorities in Njombe District (including Ludewa District which was created in 1975, and Makete) nor the higher authorities and employers could, however, effectively control labour supply. The local authorities could not prevent individuals from migrating in search of wage labour, although they could, and did, turn back recruiters. Nor could the higher authorities make individuals go to work on plantations against their will by disguised means of compulsion, as had been the case during the colonial period.

Throughout the colonial days and in the period immediately after independence, peasants' attitudes towards labour migration had been undergoing change. Wage rates, working and living conditions on the plantations, export crop production, trade unionism, the politics of nationalism, and the ideological exhortation against labour migration, all played a part in shaping peasants' attitudes with regard to labour migration, especially that which led to working on plantations. It is true that economic reality forced peasants in the former labour reserves to combine food production with wage labour, but they were not compelled to remain in wage employment for longer than a few months, as they were no longer tied to employers by contracts whether they liked the job or not. Moreover, surplus food production was also becoming an alternative source of cash to labour migration. Thus, sometimes, employers in the plantation sector saw their demand for labour nearly fulfilled, whereas at other times labour supply was so low that it threatened some sections of the plantation sector with collapse.

On the other hand, local leaders in Njombe District were disappointed when some peasants continued migrating in search of wage labour instead of taking up export crop production. The local leaders had not realized that the agricultural policies being pursued contributed to the demand for labour, and also that the imbalance in economic development between regions forced peasants in the former labour reserves to go on depending on wage labour in distant places. The relative poverty of the labour reserves had become a vicious circle from which the trapped peasants could not escape without government assistance in the form of investment in infrastructures. For most of the peasants, labour migration was not a transition to a better life brought about by investing in agriculture money they earned in wage labour. Labour migration was an end in itself, as a necessary part of subsistence.

The Government's Position on Labour Supply to Plantations

The state can only intervene in the labour cycle at the level of circulation, neither employers nor the state are involved in the reproduction of the migrant labour force. Employers in the various sectors (including smallholder peasants) and the state itself (through intensification of export crop production in labour supply areas) compete for migrant labour. The state intervenes at the level of circulation of labour on behalf of the employers (excluding smallholder peasants). This is done in various ways, for example, by direct recruiting through the Labour Division (formerly Department of Labour) or the Ministry of Labour and Manpower Development. It can also be done through various regulations designed to flush out labour from the rural areas or the urban unemployed (cf. the Human Resources Development Act of 1985, and the reintroduction of taxation in the name of 'development levy').

Government policy with regard to labour supply from the former labour reserves has, at the very least, been ambivalent. This can be properly understood by an analysis both of the shift in its ideological stance and of the functioning of the Tanzanian economy, a task outside the scope of this paper. 'Socialist' rhetoric (after the Arusha Declaration) has been in contradiction with the capitalist relations of production that prevail in the plantation sector.

The government changed its position from opposing labour migration to encouraging it in the late 1960s, when the problem of labour shortage became very pressing in the plantation sector. Pressure was applied to the government by the managers of plantations both parastatal and private (including large-scale tobacco producers) for permission to recruit labour in the former labour reserves. In fact, as has been pointed out, the government itself became a recruiter (through the Labour Division) of migrant labour for various employers. It is to be noted, for example, that when large-scale tobacco farmers in Iringa District complained, in 1971, to the government about labour shortage and the measures taken by the village governments in Makete District to stop peasants from going to work as migrant labourers, the government intervened on behalf of the tobacco farmers. The intervention took the form of forcing village governments to sign a recruitment form prepared by the Labour Division, which authorized labour migrants to be recruited in the villages and forwarded to tobacco farms in Iringa District.

In addition, while researching in Njombe in June 1978, I observed that the Labour Division was recruiting migrant labour on behalf of various employers. The following advertisements (translanted from Kiswahili) were displayed at the Njombe Labour Division Office (which then catered for Ludewa District too):

> Mtibwa Sugar Estates require 600 sugar cane cutters at sh.380 per month. Required to cut three tons of cane per day. Transport arranged at employer's expense. Interested parties should report at the Njombe Labour Office on June 25th.

This advertisement was prefaced with an appeal to nationalistic sentiments to the effect that the nation's sugar supply was at its lowest level. The second advertisement required:

> Lumberjacks with own tools to work in Songea District. Should have long experience. Employer will refund fare to Songea. Applicants should report to the Labour Office by May 25th. Freedom is Work.

The third advertisement went:

> Sisal cutters required by Lugongo Sisal Estate Ltd. The estate is situated 28 miles from Tanga township. Fare to Tanga will be refunded *after two months of work*. A hardship advance of sh.30 *deductable from the first month's wages*, will be given to each cutter immediately on arrival at the estate. [Emphasis added.]

The advertisements were addressed to the Divisional Secretaries in Njombe (which included Makete District) and Ludewa Districts, who were asked to forward labourers to the Labour Office in Njombe.

In 1978, the Minister for Labour and Social Welfare was given permission by the National Assembly to authorize recruitment of labour from 'anywhere in the country'. In reality, it turned out to be recruitment in the former labour reserves. Moreover, in 1979, the government, in a bid to get away from its earlier opposition to recruitment of labour in the former labour reserves, rationalized the recruitment of sisal cutters by arguing that sisal cutting was not different from any other kind of employment, such as working in a textile factory.[43] Before that, the Tanzania Sisal Corporation (later Authority) used to ask for permission to recruit sisal cutters from the 'traditional sources', i.e. the former labour reserves.

The central government's opposition to recruitment of labour in the former labour reserves had died down by the early 1980s. The national political campaign against large-scale use of wage labour in agriculture (it was against the ideology of Tanzania's version of socialism, Ujamaa) was given a blow by President Nyerere in 1981. Nyerere said that large-scale farmers were welcome in Tanzania, 'provided they did not encroach on village land and uproot villagers for cheap labour', although he also argued that by 'allowing a capitalist to open a large plantation in a village, you create a landless class of people,' with whom the government would not know what to do. He said the government had not denied large-scale farmers the right to employ labour, 'provided the labourers were adults'.[44] It is also interesting to note that as recently as 1986 the Minister for Agriculture threatened to take action against regional authorities who refused to allow recruitment of labour in their areas for the sisal industry. The threat was made during the Minister's tour of sisal estates in Tanga Region, when he was informed about the serious labour shortage facing the industry.

The government's change of position from opposing to encouraging labour recruitment for plantations, should be seen in the light of capitalist relations of production. The state became, through the nationalization of sisal estates in 1967, the largest employer of migrant labour. The Arusha Declaration, which was supposed to put the country on a 'socialist' path, did not bring about any structural changes in the management of plantations. Plantation production still relied on the system of cheap labour for maximization of profit and, despite 'socialist' rhetoric about the dignity of work and equality, manual labour, especially agricultural labour, was still accorded the lowest status and paid the lowest wages, making it unattractive to job seekers. These factors, plus the deteriorating working and living conditions on plantations (as a result of the loss of workers' ability to confront employers directly through negotiations, after the abolition of the Tanganyika Federation of Labour in 1964), led to serious labour shortages in the plantation sector. The labour market was being regulated by so-called market forces, and the state-owned plantations had become a less attractive sector of the market, hence the government's condoning of the recruitment of labour in the former labour reserves.

Before the Arusha Declaration, the government had waged war against the migrant labour system, especially as it related to working on sisal plantations. This may be explained as 'class struggle' being identified or confused with the colour of the antagonists. Employers of migrant labour in the sisal industry were of European and Asian origin. After nationalization, in the wake of the Arusha Declaration, the state claimed to represent the interests of 'all Tanzanians'. For the wielders of state power, exploitation in the public sector did not exist.

Another point with regard to state intervention in the procurement of labour for the plantations concerns the nature of the plantation system in Tanzania. This system, as has already been pointed out, operates through capitalist relations of production and is inherently contradictory for a government with an ambivalent ideological orientation. Profit maximization in labour-intensive production techniques is only possible by either intensification of the labour process or extensive land use. There is a limit to which intensification of the labour process can be used, and extensive land use means displacement of the population from the alienated land. This creates more contradictions between capital and the state, on the one hand, and the population, on the other. As capital cannot hire the dispossessed peasants at the full cost of reproduction of the labour force (it would defeat the logic of cheap labour), and since they would be a liability to the state, land alienation is ruled out. Moreover, extensive land use demands a large labour force which, as I have argued, has to be coerced by the state to work on plantations. Despite government intervention in the procurement of labour for the plantation sector, however, labour has continued to be in short supply.

Modern Migrations in Iringa Region

Although plantations, especially sisal estates, are unable to attract sufficient labour from the former labour reserves, labour migration has not stopped. It is still taking place, albeit in a different form. Labour migration in contemporary Tanzania (from the former labour reserves) is seasonal and short term. Most of the labour migrants now look for wage labour with smallholder peasant farmers, many of whom need extra labour during peak periods. Such farmers are to be found both within and outside the districts of the migrant labourers, many of whom prefer to look for wage labour in the neighbouring region of Ruvuma to the south. Some migrants still go to work for short periods in plantations, especially sugar estates in Morogoro Region. However, it seems the sisal industry has been completely unable to attract migrant labour from Iringa Region.

The reduction of labour migration to plantations, the change from long term to short term, and the change of destinations are in themselves not important. The question is, Why are the former labour reserves still a major source of agricultural labour? In trying to understand the persistence of labour migration in these regions, it is useful to consider the position of the major participants in the migrant labour system, namely the migrants, the employers and the state. In the case of the migrants, it is an economic issue involving cash earnings as a complement to subsistence food production: there is still no better alternative to labour migration. Labour migrants have defied measures taken by their village governments to cut them off from wage labour. For example, village governments in Ludewa and Makete Districts impose a fine on returning migrants, the amount of the fine varying from

one village to another. But labour migrants take the risk of
paying the fine rather than remaining at home with no money.
I also observed in Iringa in 1979 that when the district
officials in Mufindi District refused entry to labour recruiters
from Mtibwa Sugar Estates, the would-be migrants simply
travelled to Iringa Town and reported to the Labour Division
where the recruiters were signing up labourers.

The choice of destinations by the migrant labourers is
influenced by several factors. The most important is the
amount of money to be earned during the short period of wage
labour. Another factor is the distance to the employment area
and the cost involved in getting there. Living and working
conditions also influence the choice of employers. From
records kept at the Labour Division at Njombe, it appears
that Mtibwa Sugar Estates was a more popular destination
with the seasonal labour migrants than the sisal estates or
Kilombero Sugar Company (both are in Morogoro Region).
For example, in April 1980, Mtibwa Sugar Estates had
applications from 170 labour migrants for the 150 vacancies
which were available. In May 1981, 300 labour migrants went
to the Labour Office to sign up for work with the Mtibwa
estates. On the other hand, Kilombero Sugar Company,
which had 400 vacancies for cane cutters in the 1980 season,
had applications from only 50 migrant labourers.

I also made an interesting observation with regard to
division of labour among migrant labourers who went to look
for wage labour in Mbinga District: it was according to the
districts of origin of the labour migrants. Migrant labourers
from Njombe District were engaged in brick making and
masonry, those from Makete were employed as lumberjacks,
while labour migrants from Ludewa District were employed
as farm labourers and had the lowest status, even among the
migrants from the other two districts.

In the case of employers, the issue concerns institutional
structures – economic, political and social. If labour migrants
are taken as a category of peasant in a socially differentiated
system, then migrants cannot be equal to those who purchase
their power or who direct the use of labour power in the
economic structure. The plantations' insistence on recruiting
labour from the former labour reserves should be seen in this

light. It is noteworthy, for example, that in September 1978, when Mtibwa Sugar Estates needed sugar-cane cutters and artisans (masons and carpenters), two separate advertisements were broadcast over the radio. The first concerned the sugar-cane cutters, and the advertisement said that lorries would be despatched to Iringa, Njombe and Ludewa Districts to facilitate their transportation. The second advertisement, which was for artisans, was broadcast on the following day and announced that recruiting officers would visit Arusha, Kilimanjaro and 'neighbouring' (unspecified) regions to interview those who would like to be employed at the Mtibwa Sugar Estates.

The impression given by the advertisements was that the districts producing cane cutters could not produce artisans, and vice versa. Thus it did not surprise the author when a Senior Labour Officer in Iringa said that 'different tribes were suited for different jobs'. The remark was in answer to the question why plantations insisted on recruiting labour from former labour reserves. But it should be pointed out that the issue of who migrates in search of wage labour cannot be understood in terms of the migrants' background. This masks other differences between areas, determined by the places they occupy in the economic structure as a result of their participation in the monetary sector, which can only be understood by analysing how the various parts of Tanzania were incorporated into the world market after the advent of colonial rule. This is further borne out by the current labour shortage in the plantations, for with the disappearance of the political and administrative compulsion that kept labour flowing to the plantations during the colonial period, the 'tribes which were suited for plantation work' no longer want to work there.

The persistence of labour migration in the former labour reserves is indicative of the unchanged nature of the economic structure which gave rise to labour migration in the first place, and still reinforces the uneven development of the rural areas, which in its turn reproduces poverty and labour migration. In the circumstances, labour migration cannot be ended solely by political and administrative measures as the government (district level) as well as village governments seem to believe.

Economic reality obliges many peasants in the former labour reserves to go on earning cash income as labour migrants. This is because the failure of the former labour reserves to raise their capacity for earning foreign exchange for the country through export crop production makes them an obvious target for recruitment of migrant labour. This may be compared with the economic planners' view of the unemployed in urban areas who have from time to time been rounded up and taken to plantations to work as wage labourers, only to desert and return to the urban areas after a short time.

The reproduction of peasants in the former labour reserves, who are compelled to combine subsistence agriculture with wage labour, and the lack of opportunity to break out from this cycle was observed during my research in three villages in Ludewa District in 1981. It was noted that the village (Milo) with the lowest number of grown-up children in the sample who were peasants (following their parents' footsteps) had 23.7 per cent of the total of grown-up children. The other two villages (Mapogolo and Maholong'wa) had 62.5 per cent and 69.6 per cent respectively. Milo village had the highest number of white-collar workers in the sample households (47.4 per cent), and in other non-agricultural wage labour (21 per cent). Mapogolo village had 16.7 per cent white collar workers, with no grown-up children in other non-agricultural wage labour. Maholong'wa had 9.1 per cent white-collar workers and 6.1 per cent in other non-agricultural labour. Milo's village position is historically determined as a result of mission influence (it was the Lutheran and later the Anglican mission headquarters for the area during German and British colonial rule). It had the least number of labour migrants who worked in the sisal industry, and was the only village whose migrants had been employed as domestic servants in hotels and European households.

Other data show the rate of migration in 1980 from the same villages. It was 7.7 per cent for Mapogolo; 28 per cent for Milo and 46.6 per cent for Maholong'wa. The rate of migration was higher in 1981 (53.3 per cent of Mapogolo; 85.3 per cent for Milo and 69.7 per cent for Maholong'wa). The majority of the migrants were on seasonal wage labour, i.e. for periods of less than one year (46.2 per cent for Mapogolo; 55.2 per cent for Milo and 78.3 per cent for Maholong'wa). In all the villages only a minority of peasants had not participated in labour migration (14 per cent of the sample for Mapogolo; 6 per cent for Milo and 14 per cent for Maholong'wa. In an earlier investigation at Lugalawa village the non-migrants in the sample were 22.2 per cent). In the current migrations none of the labour migrants in the sample went to the sisal industry (the major destination during the colonial period).

The data presented here show how difficult it is for peasants in the former labour reserves to escape from labour migration. There are three options for peasants in the labour reserves to earn cash income. One is to produce for the market, either export crops or surplus food crops. The second option is to combine subsistence agriculture with wage labour, as is the case now. The third is to break away from the land completely and join the bureaucracy with secure employment and provisions, in the event of unemployment due to illness or old age, made through pension schemes and the National Provident Fund.

The first option demands a high level of government investment in infrastructural networks and agricultural inputs. So far the government has been unable to undertake such investment.[45] The third option is only possible through education and unfortunately not all villages in the former labour reserves have opportunities like Milo village. It is true that the Tanzanian government has made it possible for all children of school age to obtain a minimum education (primary). But this cannot change the position of peasants from the former labour reserves within the economic structure. What is likely to happen given the present circumstances is that peasants in the former labour reserves will in future be semi-literate, but will still be unskilled and will therefore continue to be migrants. On the other hand, where more opportunity of access to the means of opting out of the combination of subsistence agriculture with wage labour as a way of earning a living exists, such areas will produce urban-destined migrants as is the case with Milo village.

Conclusion

In this paper I have shown that four districts (Njombe, Mufindi, Ludewa and Makete) in Iringa Region became labour reserves during the colonial period. Coercive measures (open or disguised) were used in the creation of labour reserves and in the maintenance of labour flow to plantations. Force (long contracts and prosecution of deserters) was also used to keep labour migrants in wage employment. The participation of peasants in the world market through labour migration became in the long run part and parcel of the economic structure of Tanzania. Peasants in the labour reserves could not grow export crops as a means of escaping from labour migration because their cultivation in labour reserves was initially forbidden. When export crops were eventually allowed to be grown there, the peasants were ill-equipped to undertake production of them.

Attempts to end labour migration after independence failed because the Tanzanian economy was agriculturally based and required a large labour force to work the plantations. Moreover, expansion of cash crops through smallholder production, including the former labour reserves, created a demand for extra labour which could only be met from households which could not themselves produce export crops or marketable surplus food crops. The majority of such households were to be found in the former labour reserves. I have also argued that the maintenance of the function of supplying labour to commercial agriculture, most of which is outside the former labour reserves, is a result of the unchanged nature of the Tanzania export-oriented economy, inherited from the colonial period.

What is important is that while on the surface labour migration seems to be a free choice on the part of labour migrants, it is in reality a manifestation of a compulsion inherent in the economic structure, i.e. the cash needs of the migrants and the lack of alternative means of acquiring cash income. Moreover, the state, as has been shown in this paper, uses open (recruiting by parastatal plantations) and disguised coercion from time to time. In this way, labour migrants are forced to provide cheap labour for commercial agriculture, while having the lowest status in the socio-economic structure. The raising of the standard of living of those involved in commercial agriculture thus takes place through the use of wage labour from poor households, which further enhances the differentiation between households and between areas of labour supply and the destination of migrant labour.

Notes and References

1 Iringa Region comprises Iringa Urban, Iringa Rural, Mufindi, Njombe, Ludewa and Makete districts. Njombe, Ludewa and Makete (Njombe District during the colonial period) was an important labour reserve for the sisal, tobacco and pyrethrum industries.

2 For details of the creation of the labour reserves in Tanzania see, for example, E. Lumley, *Forgotten Mandate* (London, C. Hurst, 1976), pp. 25–7, 68–9; L. Cliffe, 'Rural Class Formation in Africa', *Journal of Peasant Studies*, 4 (2) (January 1977), pp. 195–224; C. M. F. Lwoga, 'Integration of labour reserves into cash crop production' (University of Dar es Salaam, unpublished MA dissertation, 1977).

3 Tanzania National Archives (hereafter TNA), File No. 178/17/17; D. M. P. McCarthy, 'Organising underdevelopment from the inside: the bureaucratic economy in Tanganyika 1919–1940', *Journal of Historical Studies*, 10 (1977), p. 594.

4 C. Leubuscher, *Tanganyika Territory* (Oxford, Oxford University Press, 1944), p. 13; Lord Hailey, *An African Survey* (Oxford, Oxford University Press, 1958); p. 658; Rhodes House (RH), Mss. Afr. s 1218.

5 TNA, 155/AGR/1/18/6/II. Wages in the sisal estates were then sh.30.

6 TNA, 178/L.12/17.

7 See, for example, C. M. F. Lwoga, 'Labour migration and rural development in a former labour reserve in Tanzania', (University of Cambridge, unpublished PhD thesis, 1985), pp. 41–65.

8 Quoted in E. A. Brett, *Colonialism and Underdevelopment in East Africa: The Politics of Economic Change 1919–1939* (Nairobi, Heinemann, 1973), p. 72; see also M. R. M. Babu, 'An Alternative Policy for Africa', *New African* (August 1980), pp. 55–7; and remarks by a Provincial Commissioner in Kenya in the 1940s that it was highly questionable whether what was ostensibly being done in Kenya by the white man, in the name of 'modernity', was really good for the lasting benefit of the African, in N. Farsons, *Last Chance in Africa* (London, Victor Gollancz, 1949), p. 283.

9 See, for instance, M. P. Todaro, *International Migration in Developing Countries* (Geneva, ILO, 1976), pp. 36–7.

10 The term 'slack' in its general usage can be misleading when applied to the agricultural cycle of some societies, e.g. among the various ethnic groups in southern Iringa Region. Cultivation there goes on throughout the year. Absence of able-bodied male members from a household

reduces the number and size of the cultivated plots and can affect
(adversely) the timing of some agricultural tasks. It should also be noted
that the 'slack' period in agriculture is usually the time when many other
important tasks have to be undertaken, e.g. repairing of houses,
construction of animal sheds, grain storage huts, and the like.

11 TNA, 28/2.
12 *Ibid.*
13 TNA, 178/22/5.
14 *Ibid.*
15 Public Records Office, London, CO 852/608/8.
16 TNA, 178/22/5.
17 *Ibid.*
18 TNA, 22/3/Vol. III.
19 J. D. Graham, 'Changing patterns of wage labour. A history of relations
    between African labour and European capitalism in Njombe District
    1931–1961', (University of Northwestern, unpublished PhD
    dissertation, 1968), p. 117.
20 TNA, 178/17/7.
21 TNA, 178/9/35.
22 *Ibid.*
23 TNA, 177/17/7.
24 *Ibid.*
25 TNA, 576/L.1/9.
26 RH, Mss Afr. s. 1174.
27 See TNA, 178/9/35; TNA 178/L.1/5/III.
28 *Ibid.*
29 TNA, 178/L.10/20.
30 TNA, 178/9/35.
31 TNA, 178/L.10/20.
32 TNA, 178/L.1/5/III.
33 See, for example, TNA, 178/A3/17/III.
34 TNA, 178/D3/57.
35 *Ibid.*
36 *Ibid.*
37 TNA, 576/L.1/9.
38 *Ibid.*
39 *Ibid.*
40 *Ibid.*
41 TNA, 576/L.10/5/III.
42 Uhuru (Dar es Salaam), 13 April 1981, p. 3.
43 *The Daily News* (Dar es Salaam), 25 June 1979, p. 1.
44 *Ibid.*, 6 June 1981, p. 3.
45 See, for example, C. M. F. Lwoga, 'Labour migration and rural
    development in Tanzania', pp. 129–67.

Women's Resistance in 'Customary' Marriage: Tanzania's Runaway Wives

Marjorie Mbilinyi

Issues

A fictional account of country life permeates colonial defences of migrant labour policy in Tanganyika:

[1] Throughout the tropics . . . nature is so bountiful and the actual necessities of life are so simple and so easily procured that hardship is rare.[1]

The migrant labour system allegedly caused no harm to the local community nor to the wives left behind:

This article is based on a paper presented at the Oxford Centre for African Studies Workshop on 'Forced Labour and Migration', February 1987. I am grateful for the comments received from participants and from reviewers of the *International Journal of the Sociology of Law* 16 (1) (1988), where the revised article was first published. Much of the material is based on archival and oral history work conducted in 1985 and 1987. Funding was received at different stages of the work from the following organizations: IDRC, SIDA, Dartington Hall Trust, Leonard Cohen Fund, Fund for Human Need of the Methodist Church (London) and the Women's Research and Documentation Project (University of Dar es Salaam). Grateful acknowledgements to the personnel of the Tanzania National Archives, the Public Records Office and Rhodes House Library for their assistance. The late David Miller supported my enthusiasm about the significance of the Batungulu Mboneke 'case' and urged me to 'do something with it'. I am also indebted to the many people of Rungwe who have shared their time, knowledge, food and homes with me.

[2] An Ngoni wife is less dependent on her husband than
her European counterpart and she is able with relatively
little difficulty to maintain the food supply of her home in
his temporary absence. She is able to continue her
relations and mutual assistance with her feminine kin
and neighbours and, by the nature of the economy, and
low demand, she and her children can comfortably
continue with little or no money income.[2]

The stability of rural marriage was contrasted with town,
where

[3] One of the most noticeable aspects of life in town is
the licence with which men and women cohabit, without
the formal bonds of marriage and dowry, the uniting of
two families, which is obligatory in most tribes upcountry.[3]

These quotations reflect contradictions that developed within
and between the three different colonial labour regimes:
migrant, casual and peasant labour.[4]

The first refers to the 1920s, when the Tanganyikan Labour
Commissioner, Orde Browne, was faced with conflicting
demands for labour from plantations, mines and farms owned
by European-based corporations and private companies, local
companies, and private individuals (including white settlers)
and from the peasant and petty commodity production
sectors. This conflict was projected as a 'labour shortage' that
could only be resolved by increased extra-economic coercion
such as the strengthening of the Masters and Native Servants
legislation. Siding with companies and settlers, the Labour
Commissioner denied the potential effectiveness of wage
increases and improved social welfare. He projected the
imagery of a 'self-sufficing existence' in which, 'producing
themselves almost all that their simple needs required',
African workers were allegedly unresponsive to wage or other
economic incentives.[5]

The government sociologist, Gulliver, conducted surveys in
the 1950s of two labour reservoirs of Southern Africa – Songea
and Rungwe, in response to criticism of the migrant labour
system from missionaries and some government officials,

including Native Authorities. The second quotation above reflects his apologetic denial of any harm resulting from the absence of men from peasant farming systems, homes and communities. It also reveals government awareness of the significance of female labour in maintaining the migrant labour/reserve system.

The colonial administration grew alarmed at the level of militancy in urban working class communities in the post-war period. New forms of social cohesion and new cultures were developing among women and men in town that were not subordinated to Native Authorities nor to any other branch of the colonial administration.[6] Their volatile and potentially revolutionary character heightened during the post-war period, when 'riots' and strikes occurred frequently enough in towns and plantations to threaten the administration's capacity to rule. One of the government measures adopted at this time was 'influx' control to restrict African settlement in towns. Unmarried women were targeted as 'undesirables', rounded up, and 'repatriated' to their 'home', 'tribal' areas.[7]

A District Officer was directed to carry out a survey of Africans in Dar es Salaam, the major urban centre, after the 1950 riot there. In his report,[8] he emphasized the different positions of women in the countryside (productive) and in town (parasitic), and the lack of marital and community stability on town (see the third quotation). This partly justified the colonial policy of restricting women's migration and settlement in towns, mines or plantations.[9]

Colonial imagery of tranquil country life was belied by the turmoil expressed in the records of colonial native courts. The predominance of marriage and marriage-related cases in the courts, and the high proportion that involved women 'runaways', are testimonials to the level and intensity of women's resistance. The discourse used in the courts reflects the repressive reality of the colonial marriage system. The women who left their husbands or parents were called 'runaways'. Their action was defined as 'desertion' or, remarkably, 'escape'. The records document the strenuous efforts of the colonial state to forcibly keep women in the countryside, on the farm and subjugated to local chiefs, district officials and male 'guardians'.

I use native court records in this paper to illuminate the problematic nature of the concept of 'customary marriage'. Marriage politics were significant in the development of a new politics associated with indirect rule.[10] The system of indirect rule developed in the context of local struggles to regulate and control the three labour regimes noted above and to govern at local level. The authority and power of local authorities partly depended on their success in enforcing colonial systems of marriage, family and inheritance.

My analysis of marriage politics has benefited from the recent work of several other scholars.[11] They have examined the relationship between colonial legal and judiciary systems and changing relations of production and reproduction in different countries of Africa during different periods. In this paper, I want to focus further attention on the struggles that underlie marriage politics and that ultimately led to the colonial state's promotion of 'customary marriage' for Africans. In particular, I want to examine the forms of women's resistance pertaining to marriage that became problematic to the colonial authorities and investigate its origins.

I also intend to challenge colonial imagery of city and countryside in Africa that persists today, and to readdress our attention to the labour reserve that sustained the colonial labour regimes. This corresponds to the effort by many feminists to examine the relationship between relations of production and reproduction.[12] At the same time, I reject the tendency to reduce the politics of the Tanzanian economy to that of the 'peasant household', and Tanzanian history to the study of 'peasants', without the colonial administrators, missionaries, corporation managers, settlers and workers who helped to shape it. The significance of 'marriage politics' can only be properly understood by situating household and family in the context of wider social relations.

Rungwe District

This analysis focuses on Rungwe District, a part of the Southern Highlands in south-west Tanganyika, during the British colonial period, with special attention to the post-war years. Some women villagers in north Rungwe provided casual labour in coffee and, later, tea production on estates that were owned initially by white settlers and taken over later by George Williamson Corporation (UK). Others worked as peasant and casual labour in peasant production of coffee for export and of cheap food crops to feed wage labour in the mines and plantations of Rungwe and other nearby districts. All women worked as domestic labour in reproducing waged and peasant labour.

Rungwe had become a major labour reservoir for the labour force of Tanga sisal plantations and the Lupa Goldfields in the 1920s and 1930s. During the 1940s, more men were conscripted as forced labour into the British armed forces or into civil employment in 'essential' industries, namely sisal. After the war, Rungwe migrants shifted south to the Copperbelt in Northern Rhodesia and the South African gold mines. By 1954, one-fourth of Rungwe adult men were absent at any one time, 90 per cent of whom worked in the south.[13] 85 per cent of all young men (17–35 years) had worked as migrant labourers at least once.

Gulliver characterized this as a young, 'bachelor' labour force but, in fact, one-fourth of the married migrant labourers travelled with their wives according to his statistics. Gulliver recommended that the government should block women's migration from Rungwe, on the grounds that they learned 'bad' habits down south and the costs involved were too high.[14]

An immediate consequence of the migrant labour system and of other forms of out-migration in search of land or wage employment, was the development of a high female–male ratio. According to the 1932 Annual Report of the Southern Highlands Province, there were 70,905 women and 37,573 men, compared with 41,959 girls and 44,625 boys.[15] After 1932, provincial statistics lumped children and adult population figures together and made this comparison less possible.

The withdrawal of male labour from peasant production intensified female labour, and led to a drop in cultivated acreage. Land was more intensively farmed, however, partly due to population growth within this area and partly due to growing land alienation. By 1954, 17 per cent of the total land surface in Rungwe was alienated; the proportion of total cultivated land would have been much greater.[16] The government intensified peasant labour in cash crop production during the 1940s, in order to sustain England's war effort. Intensified land use, the depletion of local livestock, and a major decline in traditional manure practices combined to cause falling soil fertility.[17]

By the 1930s, monetary relations had pervaded many spheres of life. Both subsistence and cash crop production depended on cash purchases – for clothing, hoes, other implements, salt, medicines, schooling, church, food during times of food shortage for the poor, and rental of land. A labour market developed locally for casual labour in peasant production, as well as on the larger settler farms and company estates. Hired labour substituted for absent household members, at sh.2 per month with food ration.[18]

During the 1940s and 1950s, higher inflation rates and an intensification of commoditization made Rungwe households more dependent on cash for their reproduction. Wage remittances, local casual labour, proceeds from cash crops and brewed beer, increased bridewealth for daughters – all became part of the necessary reproduction of local households.[19] Women's labour was relied upon in household crop production for domestic use and for sale, tea plucking on Brooke Bond tea plantations, and other forms of casual labour. Commercial and capitalist interests were openly aware of their dependence on peasant food production and reproduction for cheap labour. Women and children were the major source of casual labour during labour peaks in the Rungwe tea industry and the Mbosi coffee industry; Mbosi coffee farmers used Rungwe migrants as squatter and casual labour: 'The wages paid on Tea and Coffee Estates are still remarkably low and were it not for the fact that the natives prefer to work close to their homes, these employers would find great difficulty in obtaining labour at the present rate of wages.'[20] It was known that peasant family labour helped to ease the upward pressure on the wage: 'Native foodstuffs are still easily procurable, plentiful and cheap and as long as a labourer is independent of wages for his food, it is unlikely that he and his fellow workers are going to make any general demand for an increase in wages.'[21]

The labour requirements of corporation and settler agriculture and mines were given first priority during and after the Second World War. This was consistent with past government support-policies in agriculture. Every effort was made to increase soil and labour productivity in corporate and settler agriculture through state and private investment and regulation. African peasant and commercial farmers increased crop production without major capital investment or infrastructural support. Increased output was based on the intensification of family and wage labour, female labour most of all. Indeed, African agriculture received no notable investment until the late 1950s, and even then only a small fraction of total agriculture expenditure.[22] Instead, labour in most rural areas was exploited in order to supply the major employment centres in Tanganyika and the south. The Provincial Commissioner was provoked to say in 1953 in a letter to the Member for Local Government that the Province's labour supply was 'over-exploited'.[23]

Bridewealth rates and adultery fines rose during the 1940s and 1950s.[24] This enabled chiefs and rich male elders to accumulate wealth because of the control they had over access to women, livestock and land.[25] This put them in an advantageous position when local society became transformed by the development of the migrant labour system and the cash nexus. The system of land allocation and inheritance based on male siblings of the deceased was transformed into a more individualized system. Inheritance moved from brothers of the deceased to the senior son. Previous systems of reallocating entire villages to the younger male generation ceased, and male heads of extended families retained control over land, trees and livestock. This enabled wealthier male elders to consolidate individual land holdings and ownership of coffee trees, trees used for fuel and other assets. The labour service of unmarried sons was prolonged (and probably intensified), which provoked sons and other dependent males to migrate in search of independent sources of cash. A large portion of wage earnings was used to purchase cows.[26]

One significant result of the above was the shift in control of the labour proceeds of dependent male labour from kin elders to in-laws. Most male elders would retain an interest in reinforcing the bridewealth system because of their control over dependent females, including wives, sisters and daughters. Another significant result was an increased drive to accumulate dependent women in order to accumulate the proceeds of bridewealth and desertion and adultery payments. This would explain the large number of cases that involved disputes over 'ownership' of young girls and widows in the 1940s, which the courts categorized as bridewealth and inheritance cases.[27] As dominant men lost control over the labour of dependent men, their interest in controlling female labour in production also rose. Women represented both a source of labour input and a source of bridewealth and other proceeds of marital disputes. Women's resistances against these oppressive bonds would heighten the conflict over control of women and increase the possibility of alliances and shared interests between young women and men. The runaway cases usually involved older husbands and younger male lovers. Higher bridewealth rates made it more difficult for poor men to marry or for wives to pay desertion penalties, repay their bridewealth or get a male lover to do so (see below). Both would have an interest in escaping the control of male elders and evading court regulations that reinforced bridewealth and other payments.

The monetization of bridewealth payments along with general commoditization transformed the social significance of bridewealth, marriage and women. Bridewealth had become a commodity, women had become objects of purchase and sale, and marriage and adultery had become moments of commodity circulation and accumulation. The term which was used to signify the act of payment of bridewealth was 'kulipa' (to pay). The same term was used for market transactions.

Given the centrality of female labour in domestic, peasant and casual labour in Rungwe, women's resistances against colonial marriage and residence systems had great economic, ideological and political significance for employers and administrators, as well as for dominant male elders in the community. I explore the resistance of running away in the next section.

'Runaway' Wives

The most prevalent form of women's resistance that appears in the native court records was to run away from husbands, fathers or other male guardians (*kutoroka*). This was a limited form of resistance, conditioned by the circumstances in which women lived. Women were discouraged by legal and administrative measures from residing in towns or mining camps unless they were attached to a real or fictional husband. There were major social sanctions and economic barriers against single women living alone in the countryside. Rungwe was a strongly patrilineal society, which meant that women had no independent access to land or other productive property. It is understandable, therefore, that most women ran away from one man to join another one. The second man was expected by all of the actors in the situation, including the courts, to pay the fines and bridewealth payments that were owed to the injured parties.

Violent, confrontational forms of female resistance did, however, occur and were a potential course of action for women and a threat to men. There were cases of women murdering their husbands, such as the one a provincial administrator named F. J. Bagshawe wrote about in his diary on 7 October 1922: 'a woman up for killing her husband by rupturing his penis, which she pulled in a matrimonial brawl'.[28] On 26 April 1928, Bagshawe noted another case where a woman was sentenced to three years' imprisonment for killing her husband by beating him over the head with a log after towing him out of a building by his 'genitals'.[29] On the other hand, women were frequently killed by their husbands. For example, on 17 April 1928, Bagshawe wrote that a 'man beat his wife with a stick for running away: saw stick, which was quite a reasonable weapon for the purpose. She died: no evidence as to why: obviously a grievous hurt case.'[30]

District authorities regularly commented on the high rate of divorce, adultery and general marital discord in Rungwe in the Southern Highlands Province Annual Reports during the period from 1931 to 1943.[31] According to the 1935 Annual Report, 'Adultery constitutes one of the greatest difficulties with which Native Authorities in the Rungwe District have to contend, since *popular opinion is lax in this respect*'.[32] This suggests that marriage bonds were not as tightly woven in the countryside and local opinion about female sexuality was not as conservative as many colonial commentators were wont to argue.

In 1936, the Provincial Commissioner attributed 80 per cent of all native court cases to adultery and seduction.[33] In 1939, alarm about the situation forced the provincial administration to investigate the prevalence of these cases in more detail. In North and East Rungwe (including the mountain areas around Tukuyu, Pakati and Mwakaleli), 70 per cent of all court cases were concerned with marriage. Of these, 22 per cent were about adultery and seduction, 32 per cent about bridewealth, and 16 per cent about other marital problems.[34]

The concept of male seduction as projected in the records implied female passivity. The actual accounts which are presented in the records of appeal cases to the Provincial Administration portray an opposite image, however. Women commonly left their husbands for other men because of personal preference. In a 1945 adultery case, for example, it was noted that 'the lady admits that the occasion on which appellant was caught was the fifth incident in the series. She lay with him she says because she liked him.'[35] In another case, a man's

> wife Timu admits quite frankly not only that she committed adultery with Anyimike in the manner described but that she [did] so often that she cannot count the times. She did it because she liked him. She has also done it since that case began but nowadays does not do so because her husband and she have moved to another village.[36]

According to court practice, by 1945 a marriage was considered broken if a wife had committed a second adulterous act with the same man.[37] Women could not get a divorce on the grounds of their husband's adultery, but they found other ways of surmounting the double standards: Committing adultery had obviously become a frequently used method for women to acquire a divorce from an unwanted marriage.

The frequency of such cases in the court records indicates that multiple divorce and remarriage were common, if not the norm. The movement of women in and out of marriages was conditioned by the fact that their freedom from an undesirable marriage partner necessitated repayment of bridewealth and payment of damages, the compensation for 'desertion' owed to husband or father, as the case might be. Most women lacked independent means to make these payments, and parents rarely paid them according to court records. Instead, women found another man who was willing to pay the damages (usually three cows in the 1940s) and the bridewealth.

The intricacies of such circumstances were revealed in a 1942 case involving a primary school teacher in Njombe named Anyitike Nsusa Mwakatuma, and Lebeka Nkuga, the daughter of Chief Mwankuga II. Mwakatuma, the presumed 'seducer', explained to the court that he had 'agreed' to 'give' the woman in question a divorce from her husband, i.e. to pay for the expenses involved in 'freeing' herself from the husband, at her urging. In his own, recorded words,

> She begged me to give her divorce (cows) because she did not get along with the youth, and I agreed to give her the divorce payments on the grounds of our love agreement.

After their arrival later in Njombe,

> she began immediately to jump around and to develop a relationship with a soldier. . . . After two days I heard the woman say, 'I see that you will not be able to marry me and to pay all the cows.' She said, 'There's one man here, Tom Mwakabumbe, who will marry me and finish [paying] the wealth of my first *bwana* [master].' I, I was left to wonder since by this time, I had already paid a total of seven cows, that is, the three cows of divorce and the bridewealth cows.[38]

A similar case reached the Governor of Tanganyika on appeal in 1945.

> The claim in this case was for the return of three head of cattle which the plaintiff paid to the defendant – the woman in question – to enable her to obtain dissolution of her marriage with one Harrison with intent that she should thereafter marry the plaintiff. It appears that the defendant obtained her *freedom* from Harrison, but her father prevented her from marrying the plaintiff . . .
>
> The defendant's contention appears to be that the claim should have been instituted against her father and not against herself, whereas her father says that he was not called as a consenting party to the dissolution of the defendant's marriage with Harrison. However this may be it is clear that the defendant obtained her divorce from Harrison by payment of cattle obtained from the plaintiff and, since the consideration for that payment has wholly failed, the plaintiff is entitled to recover it from the defendant to whom he paid it. The appeal is dismissed.[39]

This small segment illustrates that it was government policy to reinforce male authority over women, to block women's freedom of choice in marriage and to curtail the relatively high female mobility of marriage and residence. The rejection of the woman's defence suggests that the Governor's judgement was not based on contemporary 'customary' practice, which, given his obstruction of the marriage, held the father responsible for damages and bridewealth.

Women faced more severe parental sanctions for running away. In a 1939 case, a father denounced his daughter in the most devastating way possible under local conditions: 'I, M. Mwankenja, agree to return all the bridewealth given for my daughter, Batamaga, to Chief Melele: but, if I do so, Batamaga binti [daughter of] Mwankenja cannot be my daughter until my death. I will not think of her as my daughter commencing with today's date of 25.8.39. I completely renounce her.'[40]

What were women running from? Forced marriages, child betrothals, physical violence, failure of migrant labourers to remit wages home, dislike, impotency – a variety of reasons propelled women to leave their husbands. Wife beating was a common accusation, which reflected the level of male violence against women. It also reflected women's success at manipulating the courts system, however. Extreme wife beating was one of the few grounds for divorce for women that was acceptable in the courts, and some women undoubtedly manipulated that fact. Several women got divorce without damage payments after their accusations were accepted in court. Others were told to return to their husbands after they had paid fines.[41] Women sometimes returned unwillingly, such as the wife who came to the District Officer in 1939, 'seeking protection and advice' because of her fear of her husband.[42]

Another woman was accused in court three times by her husband of running away. In 1949, the wife, Tukagilwa Mwakang'ata, accused her husband, Katamba Mwaisunga, of wife beating and humiliating her: 'on my return from Mpugoso, I went to Katamba's house. Katamba started abusing me, spitting on my face and beating me.'[43] She was granted a 'free divorce' and did not have to pay any desertion damages. Labour migration provided an escape route for many other women. The DC noted in a letter to the Assistant Native Commissioner of Mashaba, Rhodesia, that 'The proclivity of Nyakyusa here to proceed south with other men's wives is a problem which we are finding it very difficult to solve'.[44] Here, again, the provincial administrator projected male agency and female passivity. The quote also illustrates the way that supposedly 'domestic' issues were perceived in a broader context by colonial administrators. The impact of the personal on political economic relations had become a problem which required pan-territorial cooperation and coordination of administrative and legal mechanisms.

Copperbelt corporations actively encouraged miners to reside in married quarters with their wives and families, in contrast to government policy which tried to keep miners' wives in the reserves in Tanganyika and Northern Rhodesia.[45] Utter confusion reigned on the copper mines in Northern Rhodesia when two or more men claimed the same woman as their wife, because management could not sort out who was married to whom. In 1956, for example, the Chingola (Northern Rhodesia) District Commissioner (DC) wrote to

the Rungwe DC that Lohelo Makunge said she was married
to one man, but another one claimed to be the husband, and
urged his counterpart, 'Can you please find out who married
whom and let me know?'[46]

Mining companies lost time and money because of the
amount of litigation involved with marriage cases and the
frequent requirement that miners return to their 'native' location
to settle them. Unstable marriage relations threatened law
and order in the mining compound in two ways. The personal
conflicts involved were a source of tension that could easily
spread, given the close living conditions in the compounds.
More significantly, however, the capacity of company management to control the labour force and the entire community
of the miners was challenged. Residence was officially
restricted to bona fide wives or relatives. Companies became
increasingly concerned about the large number of single
women who supported themselves in the compound. They
were perceived to be a source of disorder and militancy in
confrontations between the companies and the miners and
their communities in the 1950s.[47]

The state of flux in marriage reflected in the frequency of
such cases challenged the capacity of colonial chiefs and male
elders to rule. Christian converts were a special challenge to
the colonial authorities. Many cases were recorded of young
Christian converts who succeeded in winning missionary
support against their parents and husbands or fiancés. They
usually claimed that they were being forcibly married (to a
pagan, never another Christian) or expressed the desire for
advanced education or both.[48] The following exemplary case
was reported to the DC by a missionary at Kisa Roman
Catholic Mission:

> A Roman Catholic Girl, Teresia . . . has been betrothed
> to a son of Chief Kasambara. The parents of the girl,
> having got the dowry, are now repeatedly urging her to
> marry that young man, although the girl herself objects
> strongly to such a marriage. The reason is, that she is in
> love with another boy, a Christian one, by name
> Philippo, whom she intends to marry as soon as possible.
> Moreover, the Catholic Church objects to a marriage

between Teresia, who is a R. Catholic and the son of
Kasambala, who is a pagan . . . Teresia is staying with
the White Sisters at Kisa, she would like to be
summoned alone in order to state her case with full
liberty.[49]

State Responses to Women's Resistances

Customary laws and practices pertaining to marriage, family,
and residence were officially the business of Native Authorities
– they provided a rationale for indirect rule. In reality, the
provincial administration directly participated in the creation
of laws and procedures of enforcement at the local level. The
local balance of power between provincial administrators,
Native Authorities and other groups varied during the
colonial period according to place and time. There was never
any pretence of representative or electoral democracy at local
or territorial level. However, as long as the centre relied
locally on Native Authorities, the latter had a certain leverage
that depended on their relative success in winning obedience,
if not support, from their followers.[50]

Rungwe was renowned as a difficult government post in the
English colonial service. The Provincial Commissioner reported
in 1931 that the local people (Wanyakyusa) 'need careful and
patient handling', being a 'fractious people' given to countless
law suits over cattle theft, dowry and adultery.[51] The policy of
indirect rule was difficult for district officers to implement:
'The head Chiefs of the Wanyakyusa and Wakukwe [all
Rungwe residents] are only so in name, and there is little
prospect of the natives recognising them as such.'[52]

Partly at issue were different notions of local government,
the one which existed at the time of colonial conquest and the
one imposed later by the British colonial state. Immediately
prior to the German conquest, two forms of local leadership
existed: the 'princes' (*abanyafyale*) and the 'great commoners'
who represented the commoners to royal clans.[53] Chiefly rule
was not absolute, nor were commoners bound by territorial or
other constraints. Households and clans or sub-clans moved
frequently in protest against a mediocre or oppressive prince

or clan leader. The relatively high mobility of women in residence and marriage had its grounding in a more general openness in local society.

The British tried to create a more tyrannical form of chiefly rule, in consonance with the colonial authoritarian state.[54] They had simultaneously to subjugate the chiefs to British rule and increase their local power *vis-à-vis* other social forces. This led to contradictory actions: at one moment supportive of subversive behaviour directed against chiefs or against 'customary' beliefs and practices, at another moment reinforcing chiefly authority.

Marriage politics provided a significant arena for both tendencies, and ultimately contributed to the social reproduction of colonial relations. District officials used marriage cases to define the boundaries of power and authority between themselves and chiefs and others (namely women).[55] In this process they tried to consolidate and reproduce the greater power of the central secretariat and the overall provincial administration. The marriage cases cited here are a good indication that their efforts were not always, or readily, successful.

The hierarchical structure of the court system was critical to the reproduction of colonial relations. Civil cases of Africans were allocated to the local native courts, with right of appeal to higher native courts, and then to the District Commissioner (hereafter DC), to the Provincial Commissioner (hereafter PC), and finally to the Governor. Some of the earlier quotations illustrate the extent to which district administrators (and even the Governor) delved into the finer intricacies of local marriage politics in evaluating the judgements of lower courts. The significance of this structure of appeals was emphasized by the Provincial Commissioner in 1942, in response to criticisms by the Rungwe DC about the amount of time and energy absorbed by numerous and 'petty' appeals – 'subject-matter which is less than Shs 50/–'.[56] The PC replied that the Government did not wish to limit appeals, 'although it is realised that the amount of work is considerable. It is held to be a very necessary and important item of district work and in view of the fact that a number of these appeals are allowed no limitation can be sanctioned.'[57]

District and higher authorities reversed the judgements of Native Authorities, or insisted on the enforcement of rulings they resisted. In 1944, for example, there were a series of cases in which the DC protected the rights of women to be heard in local court. In one such case, the Masebe authorities were commanded as follows:

> this woman, Bikubunna Kamomonga, has come to speak before me many times and said that many times she has come before you, wanting to divorce her husband, but that you do not listen to her case. I want you to take her case immediately, moreover I don't want to see her here again. Let them divorce if she has cause.[58]

Similar commands were made to several other chiefs at this time. Such cases illustrate the way women manipulated the native court system and the district administration in their favour, while the chiefs tried to regulate women's movements in apparent conflict with the district administration. The provincial administration became directly involved in enforcing customary systems of marriage and the regulation of women's movements. Contrary to the liberal position taken by the DC in the above case, however, the provincial administration generally acted as a repressive and conservative force.

District officials carried on extensive correspondence on the subject of women 'runaways' with officials in other Tanganyikan districts, and in other territories. Once their whereabouts were discovered, 'runaways' were forcibly returned to Native Authorities and husbands 'under escort'.[59] Husbands were officially allowed to enter mining compounds on the Copperbelt to look for runaway wives.[60] It is difficult not to compare the plight of runaway wives with that of runaway slaves in nineteenth-century Tanganyika.[61] The adoption of the same term to denote runaway slaves and runaway wives reinforces the comparison.

The spirit of the chase is revealed in a 1948 case in Mwaya in which the chief concerned wrote to the Rungwe DC to ask his assistance for a husband's search for his runaway wife. He urged that the woman 'should be caught with government force' (*akamatwe kwa nguvu ya serekari*).[62] The DC replied that

force could not be used. Instead, the husband would have to
bring charges in the native courts of Songea, where she had
'absconded'.[63]

The provincial administration generally upheld male parental
authority *vis-à-vis* women, and was not obverse to repressive
means if necessary. An example can be seen when a father,
Mwakyambiki, came before the DC accompanied by his
daughter, Hana Kahusi, with a report from Itagata court
stating that he

> demands that his daughter be jailed for causing trouble
> by roaming with many men, therefore let her be jailed for
> one month. He has paid the Tshs 15/50 prison fee for
> subsistence.[64]

The DC replied:

> I have given Hana Kihusi [sic] permission to stay home
> because she has asked for an appeal – if she loses . . . she
> will be jailed as you have sentenced. This woman does
> not have permission to do any roaming nor to leave her
> father's place until her appeal is finished. If she does not
> listen and starts roaming before the appeal, let her be
> caught and I will put her in jail until the appeal date.[65]

Women's freedom of movement was also restricted through
de facto pass systems that were specific to women. All women
who entered towns, plantations or mining compounds within
the territory, or who crossed the border into Northern
Rhodesia, were forced to carry either marriage certificates
(rare items in the colonial period) or travel certificates called
cheti cha njia.[66] In 1946, a Labour Officer confirmed that with
respect to labour recruitment, 'No woman will be allowed to
accompany a contract labourer unless in possession of a valid
marriage certificate or letter of authority from the Native
Authority and bearing the seal of the same.' He urged labour
recruiters to 'do your utmost to prevent the illegal movement
of women by your contract labourers'. [67]

The provincial administration used the Rungwe African
District Council to tighten the grounds for divorce for women

in 1957, in line with the recommendations of Gulliver. District officials had urged the Council to limit the grounds for divorce to three: desertion (for 18 months instead of the previous 12 months); adultery; or cruelty.[68] The increased period of time required for desertion charges reflected the impact of the migrant labour system on marriage relations in the reserves. The Council reduced the grounds for divorce to two, desertion and cruelty, and excluded adultery. The DC's explanation to the Provincial Commissioner is an apology for gender relations that oppressed women:

> the Council after all decided to omit adultery as grounds for divorce. This may seem strange but the reason lies in the fact that by tribal custom while a tribal offence is committed when a woman commits adultery, no such offence is committed on the part of the man; i.e. a wife can fetch her husband a spare lover without cause of complaint by herself, whereas the converse does not apply. The Council felt that to introduce adultery as grounds for divorce at this stage, would merely benefit the Christians and more enlightened.[69]

By the 1950s, a change had occurred in the definition of marriage politics and their outcome in the courts. In previous years, cases of adultery and runaways far outnumbered divorce. They were usually resolved through compensation payments and fines, and there was considerable repetition of the same 'offence' by men and women. In some cases, women returned to their husbands and in others they remained with their new mates, partly depending on how much payment had been made. In the 1950s, however, divorce cases outnumbered adultery and runaways and frequently centred on bridewealth disputes. Chagrined husbands demanded a return of their bridewealth and not of their errant wives.

The change may connote a simultaneous weakening of familial and marital bonds and government success in restricting women's sexual autonomy of change. The process partly resulted from government promotion of 'customary' marriage for Africans. Its conservative position was in contrast to that of many Christian missions, which acted as a 'modernizing' and subversive influence.[70] Indeed, substantial conflict occurred between government administrators and missionaries and educators over marriage politics and other aspects of government policy towards women. The government often upheld the power and authority of Native Authorities, parents and husbands, even when it meant sacrificing women and antagonizing missionaries and feminist educators. The provincial authorities' ambivalence towards educated and/or Christian women was partly due to the real threat they posed towards indirect rule.

The case of a schoolgirl named Edina Korneli reflects these considerations. The feminist educator, Mary Hancock, who was closely identified with Kyimbila Girls School in Rungwe and with Loleza Girls School in Mbeya town, wrote about it to the DC (Z. E. Kingdon) on 13 April 1948:

> School girl, Edina Korneli, whose case was heard at Ushirika a short time ago, is adamant in her decision she cannot go to her 'guardian' Jonas for the school holidays . . . She was in great distress about the matter yesterday as she is certain Jonas will give her a very rough time . . . Edina wants to go [to Mbeya] and stay with some of her friends from school . . .
>
> Can you send for Jonas and tell him his 'daughter' will go to Mbeya for the holidays? I do not want him in the school as he causes fear in the hearts of many![71]

The DC replied on 18 May 1948:

> Re Edna – no I have not contacted Jonas. As he has not turned up to collect her I see no objection to her going to Mbeya for a visit, but I think it most unwise for her to attempt to break away from her guardian altogether, and should certainly give her no support as far as that is concerned. She has got what she wants so far as the proposed marriage is concerned, and she has very definite duties to her 'ukoo' [clan] by tribal custom just as the 'mkubwa wa ukoo' [clan head] has to her, and she is his responsibility the moment she is not in your care.
>
> I think Jonas should be informed that she has gone to Mbeya for a visit and that she is willing to join her family for the holidays if they will arrange to collect her.
>
> If she does not do this I shall have no sympathy with

her when she gets into trouble (as she will, eventually!). *It is a very different matter obtaining a legal decision as to her liability to get married whilst being educated, and flouting traditional social law under European protection*, and I will not be a party to it. I am sure she is capable of standing up for herself, and insisting upon the rights which she has secured. I am perfectly willing to tell the local lifumu [village headman] what the present position is if she wishes, so that she can go to him if any undue pressure is put upon her.[72]

In other conflicts that arose over interpretation of Christian marriage for Africans, district authorities upheld the letter of English Christian law, which was highly restrictive, whereas both missionaries and African clergy espoused a more lenient, flexible point of view. For example, in 1944, a Lutheran woman from Manow named Situagile Mwaigalili wanted to divorce her husband Selka on several grounds. According to the missionary's report, she claimed that she had been forced to marry by her father, who had received partial bridewealth payment; her husband was sterile; and 'she hates her husband . . . [would] rather prefer to kill herself than live together with him'.[73] The father agreed that he had forced her to marry Selka, and favoured her claim for divorce. The DC replied as follows:

> I fear that the grounds given by you are insufficient for divorce; if it can be proved that the woman Situagile Mwaigalili was forced to marry then the marriage *might* be annulled but it would take a lot to prove this . . .
> This is just another case, and I get dozens of them, where natives get married by Christian rites and then want a divorce thinking it will be as easy as getting one in the native courts. If the man commits adultery or marries again then she can get a divorce.[74]

Colonial authorities eventually adopted a dual interpretation of Christian marriage for Africans and for non-Africans by reforming marriage law according to the concept of 'native Christian marriage'.[75] Legal reform opposed the Tanganyika Divorce Law of 1929, which had repealed the Tanganyika

Native Christian (Divorce) Law of 1923 and erased all distinctions between racial groups in grounds of divorce. A husband could petition for divorce on grounds of his wife's adultery. A wife could petition on the grounds of her husband's polygamy after their Christian marriage; rape; adultery with cruelty; adultery with desertion without reasonable excuse for two years or more.[76] According to 'native Christian marriage', which had become standard practice by the 1940s, the marriages of African Christians were solemnized in church but were not bound by Christian principles pertaining to grounds for divorce. Ministers could only bless marriages which had first been performed and validated according to customary law. This reinforced the power of chiefs and elders over rebellious young women and men, missionaries and local church leaders.

One of the most significant aspects of this reform is that it was implemented during the 1940s without territory-wide legislation. The reform was carried out administratively by simply not registering the marriages of African Christians. It followed lengthy consultation within the Secretariat and between the government and the missions. When the matter of legal reform of 'native divorce legislation' was discussed in the Governors' Conference in Nairobi in June 1937, it was concluded that 'The matter is acutely controversial and very strong feelings are aroused when it is raised, in which, in many cases, native opinion is at variance with one or other, or all, of the churches.'[77]

When views of the Provincial Commissioners were solicited, the majority urged the adoption of the reform in order to reimpose 'native customary marriage' on Christians. Cultural relativism justified the adoption of this dual racist structure of marriage. The Deputy of Lake Province expressed this most succinctly in his 1938 memo: 'I fail to see why a native should be divorced from native custom regarding these matters because he happens to be a member of a religious body which is controlled by non-natives.'[78] Several of the cases used to support the reform involved Christian men who were unable to divorce their reportedly 'wayward' wives because of Christian ethics.[79] The reform specifically targeted women as a problem, as was revealed in the memorandum sent by the

Provincial Commissioner of Southern Highlands Province: 'I think we are storing up trouble for ourselves in the future by allowing all these Christian marriages to take place unless they are recognised by native laws. I believe I am correct in saying that most of the prostitutes amongst the Haya and other tribes in Bukoba come from the so-called Christian women.'[80]

There were few voices that represented the views of Christian women, or even stopped to consider them. The Deputy Provincial Commissioner of Tabora was an exception. He argued that Christian Africans might want to follow universal Christian principles:

> There are many Christian women who object to be one of two or more wives of the same man. I used, therefore, always to rule that if a Christian man married a second wife this gave good grounds for the first wife to sue for and obtain a divorce without any liability to pay damages or compensation to the husband . . . But *could one rely on the Native Courts thus modifying native law?* I doubt it and I feel that it is for this reason that the Missions now find the 1923 Ordinance to be unsatisfactory.[81]

The significance of colonial state intervention in regulating, indeed, inverting 'customary' African marriage is illustrated by the case of Batungulu Mboneke presented below.

The Case of Batungulu Mboneke

The controversy that surrounded the case of Batungulu Mboneke illustrates both the reality and the fiction attached to the concept of 'customary' marriage practices. This 'rather curious case' was minuted in the Secretariat as being 'interesting' (read 'disturbing') because 'the order which has aroused such indignation apparently originated with the District Commissioner, and *not* the Court'.[82] In March 1947, Batungulu Mboneke was imprisoned for six months by the DC because she refused to return to her husband or to pay the three cows divorce damages.[83]

On 15 July 1946, Mpuguso Federation Court (of appeal)

ordered Balungulu Mboneke to return to her husband, Mwilubi Mwamwenda, because of her failure to pay divorce damages.

> It is heard that the woman named Balungulu Mboneke has lost the case and has been ordered to return to her husband Mwilubi, but the woman strongly refuses to return to her husband Mwilubi. Therefore the court orders her that she must go with her husband, because she has nobody who can pay divorce damages for her, and also her father refuses to take her to his home.
>
> In accordance with our custom, if a woman wants to divorce her husband, she must name a new husband who can pay 3 cows for her divorce damages. But the woman has no new husband, that is the reason why the Court orders her to go with her husband. Shs 2/ costs to be refunded to plaintiff by the woman.[84]

According to the, minute of a secretariat official (signed 'T. J. R. D.'), 'Such a judgment is of course unenforceable, as is any contract for personal service, resumption of cohabitation, or slavery'.[85] Mwamwenda appealed to the DC's court in order to claim desertion damages of one cow from Mboneke, should she return to him, which had been overlooked by the Mpuguso court.[86] The DC ignored his claim for one cow and the possibility that Mboneke might return to him, and instead demanded that she pay her husband three cows. This completely transformed the character of the case: 'Respondent Batungulu before the Court states that *on no account will she return to her husband* appellant Mwailubi [sic]. Batungulu is therefore breaking the marriage and she must therefore pay the usual 3 cows to her husband. Appeal allowed with costs.'[87]

Whereas the chiefs had ordered Mboneke to return to her husband because she could not pay the three cows, the DC, C. F. Beauclerk, ordered her to pay because she refused to return to her husband. The case was transformed into a question of 'judgement-debtor' rather than that of (forced) marriage as described by the DC later.

> In District Commissioner, Rungwe Native Court Appeal Case No. 133/46, it was proved that this woman ran

away from her husband Mwilubi s/o Mwamwenda and refused to return to him. In accordance with Kinyakyusa law and custom she was ordered, on 24/9/46, to pay her husband compensation amounting to 3 cows for breaking the marriage, and she was also ordered to refund the costs of the case, Shs. 24/– to her husband. She was given 1 month to lodge an appeal but did not do so. A few months later the husband came to see me and complained that this woman refused to carry out the judgement. She was sent for and I warned her that refusal to comply with the judgement could only result in civil imprisonment.

On 5/3/47 the *husband* came to see me again accompanied by this woman and *applied for her to be detained* in the civil prison as she refused to pay 3 cows to him as ordered by the Court. The woman was again warned by me but she flatly refused to pay. She was accordingly committed to the civil prison until the 3 cows and the sum of Shs 24/– had been paid but in any case to civil imprisonment not exceeding 6 months.

This is in accordance with Kinyakyusa law and custom and is not repugnant to British justice or morality.[88]

The wording of the DC's judgement suggests that Mboneke persisted in her resistance to being forcibly returned to her husband and that she voiced her refusal to the DC in no uncertain terms. It also suggests that he was personally affronted by her behaviour.

The Commissioner of Prisons queried the judgement on the grounds that women might not be legally imprisoned as 'judgement-debtors', and pressed the Chief Secretary to pursue the matter further.[89] This was in October 1947, after Mboneke had already completed her six months' jail sentence.

The Secretariat Official, T. J. R. D., wrote on 29 December 1947, 'I consider this deplorable and repugnant'. Next to the last sentence of the DC's report quoted above, he added, 'It is to my way of thinking wholly repugnant'. In his minute of the same day he wrote,

This case fills me with revulsion.

I doubt the legality of the imprisonment, I doubt the propriety of the District Commissioner's action, and it is

in my view wholly repugnant to British justice and
morality.

To imprison a woman who runs away from her
husband – and this is in reality what this amounts to – is
tantamount to making her the physical slave of the
husband.[90]

He pointed out later that 'there is no record of any single
enquiry by the D. C. as to why she left him which would
surely be of major relevance'.[91]

T. J. R. D had worked his way up to his Secretariat post
from the provincial administration and had, himself, once
been a DC in Rungwe. He stated that he had witnessed a
number of other cases similar to this one,

They are nearly always characterised by unadulterated
venom and sustained malice on the part of the husband.
I have always taken the same line and informed the
husband that he is entitled to recover by attachment any
damages or costs, but that if these are irrecoverable,
under no circumstances would I sign a warrant of
imprisonment in default.[92]

Another Secretariat official named Whitlamsmith supported
the judgement of the DC:

I am afraid I do not share the revulsion in the previous
minute. The woman was not imprisoned for running
away from her husband (*although that would do some women,
and not only native ones, a great deal of good*) but for refusing
to obey a court order for payment which it appears was
in her power to obey (i.e. she did not deny she had toe
[sic] cows.[93]

Endorsing this view, the Solicitor General argued that since
women in England were imprisoned for debt, Mboneke's
imprisonment was 'not repugnant to justice and morality'.[94]
The PC also supported the DC's action in his garbled account
of events riddled with factual errors and conservative value
judgements.[95] He revealed, however, the DC's error in
holding Mboneke individually responsible for damages, given

the sexual division of labour which dispossesses women of productive property like cows. His account deepens our understanding of her predicament and courage:

> By tribal custom, *cows are family property and cannot be owned by an individual woman.* The woman's course was to draw 3 cows from the family property by approach to the head of the family i.e. the man who was also liable to refund the bride-price to the injured husband . . . Usually in such a case as this, a woman obtains the cattle required, in practice, from her new husband, so that family cattle affected in theory, are not touched in practice since the new cattle go direct from the new husband to the old.
>
> It is quite exceptional for a woman to object to her family's natural wish to *preserve her as an asset.* . .
>
> Custom in this case is clearly admirable as it aims at the preservation of the marriage tie. *A woman is a family asset in that she brings in bride-price* and, in the circumstances in the Rungwe District, a family will almost never fail to raise any cows that are necessary, by loan, if it has not got the correct number of beasts in hand. *It is clearly necessary that, since a woman may not own cows some sanction should be available to compel her to follow the marriage customs of her tribe.*[96]

The Attorney General's office decided that the judgement had been incorrect, but excused the DC for his actions on the grounds of ignorance of Kinyakyusa law and custom.[97] The Attorney General noted that the native courts never ordered Batungulu to pay three cows, and that the DC failed to call assessors to interpret 'native law and custom'. It doubted that there were grounds under local law to hold a married woman personally accountable to pay divorce damages or to imprison her for non-payment of a judgement debt. Moreover, 'in England, justice and morality and the law speak with the same voice' against the imprisonment of a man or a woman for debt.

A circular letter was sent to all Provincial Commissioners by the Chief Secretary, stating that the imprisonment of Batungulu Mboneke was illegal on the grounds that the courts could not order the arrest or detention of a woman on account of debt.[98] The circular specifically singled out women and remained silent about men, who were being imprisoned in colonial courts for 'debt', contrary to British 'justice and morality and the law'. It also remained silent on the question of the right of African women to reject an unwanted marriage.

The opposing views on the ethics of this judgement demonstrate that there were real differences of opinion and ideologies pertaining to marriage and women in the Secretariat and in the Provincial Administration. They also illustrate the moral conflict experienced by those colonial authorities who adopted universal values in matters pertaining to African women and rejected the racist relativism of their peers.

It is evident that the irony of the Mboneke case – 'The order which has aroused such indignation apparently originated with the District Commissioner, and *not* with the Court' – disturbed several officials.[99] It conflicted with their belief that British rule promoted modern development and enlightenment.

Batungulu Mboneke also upset colonial imagery about passive, downtrodden, obsequious African women. She was insubordinate to the DC, to the Mpuguso Court, to her family and to her husband. She chose imprisonment for six months rather than be bound to a husband she obviously rejected or to any other man. Her action also challenged the legitimacy of colonial ideology and practice about 'customary marriage'. Her open defiance of 'custom' and the authorities demonstrated that she was *not* a slave, either of her husband or of the colonial state. The outcome proved that resistance without accommodation was possible and potentially successful.

Marriage Politics on the International Stage

Local level politics about marriage found a much grander echo on the international stage. They were inflated into a major debate on 'customary marriage' in Britain's colonies which was coordinated by the Colonial Office and publicly discussed in the British Parliament and in other forums. The debate was initiated by missionary support groups led by Revd Owen in Kenya and a group of progressive and socialist MPs whose Parliamentary spokesperson was Miss Rathbone.[100] The case of a young woman in Kilimanjaro (Tanganyika), named Kekwe Muningafi was used in Britain to lobby against polygamy, bridewealth, physical coercion and female circumcision. Muningafi had been imprisoned for 15 months hard labour for manslaughter in the early 1930s after killing a man named Ndemfoo Nshau who tried to force her to go to her fiancé's house to be wed.[101]

The issue of forced marriage received international prominence at a conference organized in London by the British Commonwealth League, and reported locally in *East Africa*.[102] Spokespersons for 'customary marriage' included such notable Kenyan personalities as Dr L. S. B. Leakey and Johnston (Jomo) Kenyatta. Cultural relativism was used to justify oppressive marriage systems. For example, Leakey argued that women from different countries had different ideals, and that British feminists should not impose their ideals on African women. He opposed the registration of African marriages, which would only benefit 'detribalized' or Christian 'Natives', but 'which could not but be a burden of misery on the great mass of their own tribe.' He defended bridewealth, 'a guarantee of good behaviour, a security, a form of marriage insurance'.

Kenyatta presented a typical bourgeois nationalist position. He argued that critics like Owen had exaggerated on the basis of *isolated* cases of wife-beating, and that women's oppression was a secondary issue. He was quoted as saying, 'What the African needs is economic emancipation. You can help us in the bigger things of life and the smaller social questions will solve themselves.'[103] He also challenged the validity of European critics speaking on behalf of African women, who were absent from the conference, despite their presence in London. The absence of African women 'spokespersons' was a powerful point to make in liberal white circles. It aroused a defensive reaction from the chair that 'a number of African women had been invited to attend, but that no replies had been received'. However, Kenyatta was also accountable for not ensuring adequate female participation. Moreover, the presence of students and other middle class women who lived in Britain would not have resolved the question of whose was the authentic voice of the African women masses.

A more progressive position was presented by Dr Norman Leys, who related marriage politics to other factors, 'the Christian missions, schools, and modern industry, under which the individual, and not the family, became the unit of production'. He argued that

> British governments in Africa ought to abandon the policy of trying to keep tribalism intact, and encourage and make provision for those who wished to escape from tribalism. That would allow the old way of life to die gradually out in the reserves, would give town-dwellers healthy conditions, and, by providing individual holdings, give country dwellers the opportunity of a free life.[104]

In reply to Colonial Office queries about forced marriage in August 1936, which were based on the foregoing debates in conferences and in the press, most Tanganyikan Provincial Commissioners denied that physical coercion was used.[105] The events in Kilimanjaro were excused as harmless ritualized dramatizations of force and reluctance to marry which got out of hand.[106] Critics were accused of exaggerating the problem of forced marriage. At the same time, the arguments of cultural relativism were reproduced in apologetic defence of forced marriage and the oppression of African women. There was no denial that 'moral coercion' was common, but this was considered to be normal, acceptable and similar to Europe.[107] Provincial Commissioners were convinced of the accessibility of the 'native' court system and the courts of appeal to African women. The Provincial Commissioner of Western Province argued that 'The tribal court is a great protection to women in such matters: few men will face in open native courts a description by a woman of the reasons why she does not want to marry a particular individual.'[108] His humorous complacency would not have impressed Mboneke or the countless other women who failed to win their cases in the courts, let alone those who never dared try.

Martin Kayamba, a member of the new African middle class who worked in the Secretariat, compiled the Provincial Commissioners' returns. His long apologetic minute exhibited the paternalism and patronization that characterized colonial ideology about women.

Personally as an African I do not think there is much in the talk about physical coercion, which is really not coercion at all in the real sense of the word but parental advice to daughters.

It is the family emancipation and independence of children from parental authority which is creating all this trouble today. In the olden days it has been customary with all African tribes . . . for parents to advise their daughters as well as their sons as to who they should marry . . . They know who are enemies of the family and which families are friendly and also who are the best husbands, or husbands equal status . . .

It was considered that a girl who has no experience of the world was not in a position to select a suitable husband without someone to guide her and the best guide was her parents . . .

Today in certain tribes trouble sometimes occurs when the girl thwarts the advice of her parents because she is already in love with someone else who her parents disapprove. She could not do this openly in the olden days for fear of acquiring the displeasure of her parents and a bad name outside and inside the family circle; and she was especially afraid of the curse that would probably be pronounced on her by her parents and which would affect her whole life.[109]

Kayamba employs the 'olden days' imagery of a 'golden past' identified with 'tribe' and 'the countryside', which was an important part of colonial ideology and indirect rule.[110] A harmonious, albeit unequal society of the past was contrasted with the present 'transitional period through which Africans are passing today to civilisation'.[111]

There were a few dissenting voices in the administration at this time, as well as later. The Acting Provincial Commissioner of Tanga Province, for example, projected a more positive image of African women as active subjects and not passive victims. He also analysed the relationship between marriage politics, individual geographical mobility, and the development of a territorial labour market.

The present untrammelled freedom of movement to all parts of the Territory is a way of escape from any

uncongenial surroundings at home, when she feels
inclined to run away from them, freely used by the
increasingly independent native female today, *who is well
aware of the individualistic nature of western concepts*, in regard
to marriage particularly. Indeed, it is the constant cry of
family and tribal elders that parental and tribal discipline
cannot be enforced as of yore and that diminishing
respect for indigenous convention and institutions is the
rule amongst the younger generation. These conditions
are alone sufficient guarantee that any force majeur
prevailing will steadily give way to diplomacy on the part
of the heads of families, and mutual consent. *It is widely
known that errant wives cannot be recovered by force and that
forced marriages are not countenanced by Government when they
are brought to its knowledge.*[112]

Governor Harold MacMichael supported 'customary marriage' and reproduced the complacent acceptance of moral
coercion.[113] He explained that the Tanganyikan Government
was opposed to compulsory marriage registration (which
included obligatory assurances that the bride married of her
own free will) because 'It would certainly not achieve its
purpose unless it had the support of native opinion and unless
the move for its introduction came from within the tribe and
not from outside it.'[114] This kind of authentification process
which deferred to 'native opinion' and 'tribal' initiative
provided a useful diversionary tactic when the government
faced progressive critics. It projected the imagery of homogeneous 'native opinion' and common 'tribal' interests, while
repressing the views of rebellious women and other dissidents.

The replies from the different African colonies resembled
that of the Tanganyikan Governor. Most Governors insisted
that drastic action to reform 'customary marriage' would have
undesirable effects. The Kenyan Governor's argument that
'any sudden removal of parental control would have disastrous
results and might in fact shatter the tribal social system'
clearly related marriage and family politics to indirect rule.
The most outrageous view was that of Nyasaland's Governor,
who argued that women had very high status, and that the
'whole system [of bridewealth and marriage] is aimed at

guarding the interest of the women, who are honoured tribally as the mothers of the people.'[115]

The Colonial Office was forced to re-examine the question of forced marriage and women in response to the agitation of a feminist organization named St Joan's Social and Political Alliance in 1937.[116] St Joan's Alliance rejected the Colonial Office's reply to the earlier queries,[117] and took the issue to the Eighteenth Assembly of the League of Nations in 1937. The 'Statement of St Joan's Social and Political Alliance on the Status of the Women of Native Races' argued that 'the status of women would be raised by the adoption of an International Convention granting to women equality of rights and responsibilities' worldwide, 'of whatever race'.

The Alliance rejected the imperial justification of colonial marriage systems as a necessary aspect of indirect rule:

> To those objectors who tell us that if customs like the dowry system and polygamy disappear it will upset the family system of the African, it may be pointed out that slavery was once part of the family system; that the abolition of ritual murders and magical rites is said by some to have undermined the authority of the chiefs . . . We must be on our guard against maintaining inhuman customs on any pretext whatever.[118]

Education and 'paid work' were regarded as essential for women's emancipation. African women were responsive to both and had proven themselves to be

> grateful for emancipation and capable of taking advantage of it, and it remains for Governments and public opinion to encourage and support such work for 'on the woman depends very largely the future of Africa'.[119]

St Joan's Alliance also challenged the legitimacy of colonial rule:

> No Administration can be called just which governs a territory where a woman is treated like a chattel to be sold by her father or alleged proprietor to a polygamist or anyone else. We claim that every woman must be

permitted to choose her own partner in life despite any contract entered into in her name by any other person.[120]

Their report recognized the more advantageous position of Islamic women, particularly with respect to control over earnings and private property and inheritance, but noted that Islam 'is affected by tribal law and in its turn affects tribal law. This inter-diffusion tends to the deterioration of both customs.'[121] It directly criticized the racist policies of South Africa and the underlying migrant labour/reserve system. According to St Joan's Alliance, South Africa was the 'most aggravated form' of a general 'process of social disintegration, evident wherever an alien civilization based on competitive commercialism [capitalism] has been imposed on a primitive [precapitalist] society based on agriculture'.[122] St Joan's expressed *solidarity* with the struggles of African women, not just charitable concern for the downtrodden victim, and linked women's oppression to other forms of oppression and exploitation. It won the cooperation of people like Revd Owen who had already been active on the issue of 'customary marriage'. Moreover, it took marriage politics to the international stage of the League of Nations, and criticized all the imperial states and colonial administrations of Africa.

On 12 December 1937 St Joan's Alliance organized a public meeting in London on the subject of 'Forced Marriages of African Girls'. They requested a special meeting with the Secretary of State for the Colonies to present the meeting's resolutions but this was turned down, and they were invited instead to have an informal talk with the Parliamentary Under-Secretary of State for the Colonies.[123] Amongst their resolutions was the demand that the Colonial Secretary reopen inquiries and seek the evidence of women. A uniform Ordinance was proposed for all 'Dependencies' that made marriage or betrothal illegal below the age of 14 years; required a woman's consent for any marriage or betrothal contract; made forced marriage an offence and the resulting contract unenforceable by the courts. Recognizing the probable resistance of imperial machinery to these proposals, St Joan's Alliance later recommended that the Colonial Office authorize the Chief Justices of each colony to inform all administrators that 'forced marriage is repugnant to natural justice and morality, and therefore illegal'.[124] This could be implemented without further legislation.

Special pressure was put on the East African administrations. The appointment of the first high-level woman's officer in the Tanganyikan Government, Miss M. F. E. Pelham-Johnson, as Supervisor of Female Education in 1939 may have been one response to this pressure – it certainly was offered to St Joan's Alliance as evidence of political will by the Secretary of State.[125]

The Secretariat in Dar es Salaam was negative about the whole exercise. One official minuted that there had been 'a great deal of "hot air" ' on the subject, including the last meeting of the Permanent Mandates Commission.[126] The Chief Secretary was present at the meeting with the Parliamentary Under-Secretary of State and negated the efforts of St Joan's Alliance by saying 'they obviously have no first-hand knowledge' of the matters in question. The Secretariat decided to 'stifle such criticism as this and place Government in possession of uncontrovertible evidence of the true position' by inviting missionaries to submit the names of girls who had been forced into marriage.[127] These girls would be 'examined' by DOs, and a report compiled on the basis of their 'investigations'.

There were obvious problems of 'reliability' and 'validity' with the investigation procedures proposed. Only women associated with the missions would be sought; and they would be alienated by the form of investigation adopted. The whole procedure seemed intentionally structured to minimize the resulting 'evidence'. Moreover, the circular letter that initiated the survey instructed participants that a distinction should be made between 'real coercion' and ' "capture" by the bridegroom [which] is a part of tribal marriage ceremonies and that it is proper for the bride to "resist" '. It also distinguished between 'moral coercion' and 'physical coercion'. Only the latter was 'real' coercion.[128] According to the law officers, moral coercion was not an offence unless a woman was less than 12 years: 'It may be repugnant to natural justice and morality, but that is all'.[129]

Not surprisingly, only 6 cases of physical coercion were identified in Tanganyika, however these were all situated in

Lake Province. There were 9 cases of moral coercion (5 in Lake Province and 3 in Southern Highlands Province) and 12 cases that had been 'disproved' (of which 5 in Lake and 6 in Southern Highlands Province). The Chief Secretary reported to the East African Governors' Conference that 'The situation at present is not unsatisfactory in view of the general standard of civilisation of the inhabitants of the Territory, and is improving: accelerated improvement will be more successfully effected by education than by further legislation.'[130]

The Secretariat repressed the more critical missionary reports, such as that of Paul Rother of the Leipzig Lutheran Mission in Marangu:

> Chagga custom adds to this view the real conviction of the young girls that married life is more burdensome than maiden life. And really you notice that the duties of a young girl are much easier than those of a married woman.

Rother also wrote about collective resistance:

> it even happened in some chiefdom or another that girls made a kind of conspiration not easily to become married. They then refused so long until the chief himself ordered the young men to carry their fiancées off by force. So there were times when mass marriages were forced upon certain districts.[131]

The District Officer of Moshi discounted Rother's evidence, saying it was 'an unduly gloomy view of the position'. He relied on the more conservative views of Dr Guttmann, another German missionary and anthropologist, who was a well-known proponent of cultural relativism.[132]

The Secretary of State sought the views of the Tanganyikan Governor about the possibility of establishing a Commission of Inquiry on African marriages that consisted of government, missionary and non-official members.[133] Governor Young replied that during the war period there were 'far more pressing' problems to be solved than forced marriage.[134] He would not recommend such an inquiry in peacetime, either, because of the relative backwardness of Tanganyikan 'natives'.

The official who drafted his reply was none other than Whitlamsmith, the same individual who endorsed the imprisonment of Batungulu Mboneke for resisting forced marriage. The real reasons for rejecting a territorial inquiry are found in the Secretariat files. The chief voice was that of A. E. Kitching, then Provincial Commissioner of Southern Province. He argued that the government must not antagonize African men who 'are particularly sensitive in all matters relating to their womenfolk'.[135] This argument assumed that all Africans were male; no concern was expressed about African women's sensitivity about 'their menfolk'.[136] Kitching also feared that German missionaries would use the inquiry to 'stir up trouble in the native areas'. Maintenance of indirect rule was the main priority:

> nothing should be done which may give currency to the impression that Government extends to the missionaries a measure of confidence which it is not prepared to extend to the Native Authorities or that it encourages missionaries to be informers and tale-bearers . . . it will be exceedingly difficult to restrict the enquiry to 'forced marriages' only. Child marriages, bride price, divorce, and what not, will all be brought up before we are out of the wood. Unless we are careful it will come to be believed in the native areas that Government is prepared to give sympathetic consideration to representations from any woman who has not been allowed to marry in accordance with her wishes.[137]

The subversive potential of an inquiry about 'customary marriage' confirms the significance of marriage politics in colonial history. The spectre of widespread female rebellion and the decline of patriarchal rule threatened the entire structure of colonial society.

Marriage Politics Today and Yesterday

African women were *hostages* of colonial, indirect, rule. Colonial and imperial governments gave men control over women, particularly wealthy men or Native Authorities, as a form of security or pawn in exchange for male obedience and cooperation.[138] In Tanganyika, this emerged as a coherent policy during the inter-war period, but more research is necessary to periodize the different struggles that led to this outcome. The actions of Batungulu Mboneke and other rebellious women indicate that women resisted their hostage status. Given these conditions women from rural areas were potentially the most resistant and subversive force in colonial society, because of the multiple forms of oppression that they experienced. Recent studies have examined the history of women's resistance and organized struggle in Africa, but this is an area that invites new work.[139]

Research on the history of 'customary marriage', the pawning of women, and women's resistance is necessary to inform the present struggles of African women (and men) against oppression by class, nation, race and gender. African women continue to be oppressed by ideologies and practices associated with 'customary marriage', including forms of cultural relativism and nationalism that are reminiscent of Leakey, Kenyatta and Kayamba. The resolutions of St Joan's Alliance were ahead of their time and were never met during the period of colonial rule. Similar regulations against forced marriage were incorporated into the reform of 'customary marriage' law in Tanzania in 1971. The White Paper on which the new family law was based became the subject of intense national debate at local and national level.[140] Many of its sections would not have passed the National Assembly without the political activity of the national women's organization, Union of Tanzanian Women. The conditions of the debate had changed by then, however, in that the proponents of 'customary marriage' faced the growing consciousness of organized Tanzanian women who spoke for themselves. Nor are women complacent about the present situation. There are moves afoot to seek more radical changes in the laws pertaining to marriage, inheritance and children.

The social significance of women's struggles against oppression cannot be over-emphasized. One reason for the perpetuation of 'customary marriage' is the perpetuation of the three colonial labour regimes in independent Africa: migrant, casual, and peasant labour. All of these labour regimes

depend heavily on female labour in production and reproduction. The significance of casual and peasant labour has
increased relative to migrant labour in Tanzania. As male
labour was increasingly absorbed into regular and casual
employment in the organized sector of the economy, women's
labour was intensified in petty commodity production and
trade, and in production of essential reproduction requirements. Some 63 per cent of waged and unwaged agricultural
labourers between the ages of 15 and 29 were women in 1978.
The female ratio of regular and casual labour in the organized
sector also increased during the 1970s.[141] The regulation of
female labour in production and reproduction is, therefore, as
significant a problem for capital today as it was yesterday.
This was revealed in the 'round-ups' of unmarried women and
those without 'reasonable' employment in towns during the
nguvu kazi campaign and other attempts to erect barriers
against female migration from rural villages in the 1970s and
early 1980s.[142] 'Customary marriage' remains a central
component of the organization of the labour process and the
reproduction of social relations of production and reproduction. More recent struggles involving women suggest that
marriage politics will become even more intense and popularly
based in the future.[143]

Notes and References

1 G. Orde Browne, *The African Labourer* (London, Frank Cass, 1967), p.
   88. Originally published in 1933.
2 P. H. Gulliver, 'A Report on the Migration of African Workers to the
   South from the Southern Highlands Province, with Special Reference
   to the Nyakyusa of Rungwe District' (Tanganyika Provincial
   Administration, 1955), p. 37.
3 J. A. K. Leslie, *A Survey of Dar es Salaam* (London, Oxford University
   Press, 1963), p. 220.
4 Marjorie Mbilinyi, 'Agribusiness and Casual Labour in Tanzania',
   African Economic History 15 (1986), pp. 107–141.
5 Orde Browne, *African Labourer*, p. 26.
6 See J. Iliffe, *A Modern History of Tanganyika* (Cambridge, Cambridge
   University Press, 1979), for detailed descriptions of the post-war era. I
   also discuss the 'city' and 'countryside' imagery as employed in
   colonial Tanganyika in M. Mbilinyi, ' "City" and "Countryside" in

Colonial Tanganyika', *Economic and Political Weekly*, XX (43) (1985), WS, pp. 88–96.

7 Mbilinyi, 'City and Countryside'.

8 Leslie, *Dar es Salaam*.

9 Mbilinyi, 'City and Countryside'.

10 Karen E. Fields, *Revival and Rebellion in Colonial Central Africa* (Princeton, Princeton University Press, 1985); Ann Whitehead, 'The Effects of Political and Socio-Economic Change on the Politics of Marriage in North-East Ghana', paper presented to the Association of Social Anthropologists, Cambridge, 1983. Whitehead has developed the concept of marriage politics in a valuable study of their past and present significance in the Ghana case. I am grateful to her for sharing this work with me.

11 Janet M. Bujra, 'Women "Entrepreneurs" of Early Nairobi', and 'Postscript: Prostitution, Class and the State', in Colin Sumner (ed.), *Crime, Justice and Underdevelopment* (London, Heinemann, 1982); Martin Chanock, 'Making Customary Law: Men, Women and Courts in Colonial Northern Rhodesia', in Margaret Jean Hay and Marcia Wright (eds.), *African Women and the Law: Historical Perspectives* (Boston University Papers on Africa, 1982), VII, and *Law, Custom and Social Order* (Cambridge, Cambridge University Press, 1985); Margaret Jean Hay and Marcia Wright, *African Women and the Law*; Whitehead, 'Politics of Marriage' [note 10].

12 Lourdes Beneria and Gita Sen, 'Accumulation, Reproduction, and Women's Role in Economic Development: Boserup Revisited', in Eleanor Leacock, Helen I. Safa, et al., *Women's Work* (Massachusetts, Begin and Harvey Publishers, 1986).

13 Gulliver, 'Migration of African Workers'.

14 *Ibid.*, A12. These costs were not elaborated in detail, but they were real, and had ideological, political and economical dimensions.

15 Tanzania National Archives (hereafter, TNA), Accession (hereafter, ACC) File Southern Highlands Province, 23/1/32.

16 TNA ACC Southern Highlands Province, 157/L2/11/f 62.

17 Green manure is produced by placing weeds and grasses of certain crops in a big pit to decompose over time. This has been used by Wanyakyusa to fertilize banana fields and garden plots along with ashes, mulchings and animal dung.

18 Monica Wilson, *Good Company* (Boston, Beacon Press, 1963). First published in 1951.

19 TNA ACC 23/14/43.

20 TNA ACC 23/9/1939, Southern Highlands Province Labour Report 1939, p. 6.

21 TNA ACC 77/40/12, Labour Annual Report 1940, f. 9.

22 Marjorie Mbilinyi, 'Agribusiness and Casual Labour in Tanzania', and 'Agribusiness and Women Peasants in Tanzania', *Development and Change*, 19 (1988), pp. 549–583; Philip Raikes, 'Rural Differentiation and Class Formation in Tanzania', *Journal of Peasant Studies*, 5 (3) (1978), pp. 285–325.

23 TNA ACC 157/L1/7/f 47, dated 5 February 1953.

24 The argument in these two paragraphs is based on my interpretation of Iliffe, *Modern History of Tanganyika*; Godfrey Wilson, '*The Land Rights of Individuals Among the Nyakyusa*', The Rhodes Livingstone Papers No.1 (1938); Wilson, *Good Company*; and the tentative results of ongoing archival and oral research.

25 Wilson, 1938.

26 Gulliver, 'Migration of African Workers'.

27 TNA ACC File Rungwe District Office, 18/27/4/1944–46 and 1946–48.

28 Francis John E. Bagshawe, 'Diaries', Vol. VI, 1 September 1922 to 31 December 1924, Oxford, Rhodes House Library, Mss Afr s 279.

29 Francis John E. Bagshawe, 'Diaries', Vol. X, 27 March 1928 to 31 December 1929, Oxford, Rhodes House Library, Mss Afr s 279.

30 *Ibid.*

31 TNA ACC 23/10/31–23/23/54.

32 TNA ACC 1935 Annual Report, 23/4/1935. Emphasis added.

33 TNA 1936 Annual Report of the Southern Highlands Province, 25/25/36.

34 TNA ACC 23/9/1939.

35 TNA ACC 18/27/9/II/f 417, PC appeal 34/1945.

36 *Ibid.*, f 422, PC appeal 29/1945.

37 *Ibid.*, f 394.

38 TNA ACC 18/27/1/f 578, my translation. I am aware of the problem of interpretation in the process of translating Swahili records into English. This refers both to my translations and the official ones. Translation compounds the methodological problems that already exist with such 'evidence', based as it is on official records, court cases and the particular cases and issues which received official attention. Nevertheless, the problem becomes an object of study, in that the behaviour and ideology of government officials and others are also analysed.

39 TNA ACC 18/27/9/II/f 449, appeal 10 of 1945. Emphasis added.

40 TNA ACC 18/27/1/f 427.

41 TNA ACC 18/L4/2/f 229 of 1958; 18/27/1/f 394 of 1939.

42 TNA ACC 18/27/1/f 394.

43 TNA ACC 18/27/9/IV/58B, Katumba Court Case No. 289/49.

44 TNA ACC 18/LA/2/f 2.

45 Jane L. Parpart, 'Class and Gender on the Copperbelt', in Claire Robertson and Iris Berger (eds), *Women and Class in Africa* (New York, Africana Publishing Co., 1986).

46 TNA ACC 18/LA/2/f 32, 25.1.56.

47 Parpart, 'Class and Gender'.

48 TNA ACC 18/50/1/II, 18/27/4/46–48.

49 TNA ACC 18/50/1/II/f 513.

50 Fields, *Revival and Rebellion*.

51 TNA ACC 23/10/1931.

52 TNA ACC 23/1/32, Annual Report 1932.

53 S.R. Charsley, *The Princes of Nyakyusa* (Nairobi, East African Publishing House, 1969).

54 Chachage Seithy Loth Chachage, 'Socialist Ideology and the Reality of Tanzania' (Glasgow University, unpublished PhD thesis, 1986) See note 116.

55 This argument has also been made independently by Whitehead, 'Politics of Marriage'. I have adopted her terminology here concerning the definition of boundaries of power and authority.

56 TNA ACC 18/27/1/f 564.

57 *Ibid.*, f 619, 16.10.42.

58 TNA ACC 18/27/4/f 527.

59 E.g.TNA ACC 18/27/4/1944–46/f 49A.

60 *Ibid.*, f 135.

61 Marcia Wright, 'Bwanikwa: Consciousness and Protest among Slave Women in Centra Africa, 1886–1911' in Claire C. Robertson and Martin A. Klein eds, *Women and Slavery in Africa* (Madison, University of Wisconsin Press, 1983).

62 TNA ACC 18/27/4/1944–46/f 263.

63 *Ibid.*, f 264.

64 TNA ACC 18/27/4/46–48/f 236, 20.1.48; my translation.

65 *Ibid.*, f 237, 20.1.48; my translation.

66 TNA ACC 77/16/5/f 313, DC Njombe–PC 18.3.46.

67 *Ibid.*, f 307, 28.2.46.

68 TNA ACC 18/L4/2/f 131, DC–PC 15.1.57.

69 *Ibid.* f 141, 13.3.57.

70 Karen E. Fields, 'Christian Missionaries as Anticolonial Militants' *Theory and Society* 11, 1982: 85–108; *Revival and Rebellion.*

71 TNA ACC 18/27/4/46–48/f 313A.

72 *Ibid.*, f 314. Emphasis added.

73 TNA ACC 18/50/1/II/f 542, Nordfeldt to the DC, 28.10.44.

74 *Ibid.*, f 543, 30/10/44. Emphasis in original.

75 TNA Secretariat Minute Papers (hereafter SMP), 25040/I/II.

76 *Ibid.*, f 32.

77 TNA SMP 25040/I/f 20.

78 *Ibid.*, f 61.

79 TNA ACC, 18/27/4/46–48; TNA SMP, 25040 Vol. I.

80 TNA SMP 25040/I/f 64, 27.2.39.

81 *Ibid.*, dated 25.10.38, emphasis added.

82 TNA SMP 18844/II/m 33, 7.9.48. Emphasis in original.

83 *Ibid.*, f 9, 19.12.47.

84 *Ibid.*, case 134/46, f 23A.

85 *Ibid.*, m 24, 21.4.48.

86 *Ibid.*, f 23A, DC Appeal No. 133/46.

87 *Ibid.*, f 23A. Emphasis added.

88 *Ibid.*, f 3.

89 *Ibid.*, f 9. 19, 12, 47, (as shown) emphasis added by Secretariat official and initialed T.J.R.D.

90 *Ibid.*, m 10.
91 *Ibid.*, m 24, 21.4.48.
92 *Ibid.*, m 10.
93 *Ibid.*, m 11, 30.12.47. Emphasis added.
94 *Ibid.*, m 14, 5.1.48.
95 *Ibid.*, f 23, 10.4.48. The errors are pointed out in marginal notes by TJRD, and confirmed by my examination of other documents in file including the court records themselves.
96 *Ibid.*, f 23, 10.4.48. Emphasis added.
97 *Ibid.*, m dated 3.9.48.
98 *Ibid.*, 19.10.48, f 40.
99 *Ibid.*, m 33, 7.9.48.
100 TNA SMP 24450/I, II.
101 TNA SMP, 24450/I, f 14.
102 *Ibid.*, I/f 6, excerpt *East Africa* 14.11.35. The article's title, 'Happiness or Slavery? The Status of African Women', nicely projects the mechanical, undialectical, nature of most of the views expressed about African women on 'both' sides. Would Batungulu Mboneke have been able to fit herself into either of these categories?
103 *Ibid.*
104 *Ibid.*
105 *Ibid.*, vol. I.
106 *Ibid.*, f 34, District Officer Moshi to PC Northern Province, 17.11.36.
107 *Ibid.*, f 30, PC Western Province, 24.12.36.
108 *Ibid.*
109 *Ibid.*, m 38–39, 31.12.36.
110 Mbilinyi, 'City and Countryside'.
111 *Ibid.* I am grateful for having been allowed to read and cite Chachage's unpublished PhD thesis, 'Socialist Ideology and the Reality of Tanzania', which provides a detailed critique of Kayamba's work.
112 TNA SMP 24450/I, f 23, 2.11.36. Emphasis added.
113 *Ibid.*, f 43, 6.2.37.
114 *Ibid.*
115 Colonial Office 'Correspondence Relating to the Welfare of Women in Tropical Africa 1935–37', London, 1937, African No. 1162 in TNA SMP, 24450/I/f 61.
116 TNA SMP 24450/II, m 1, f 1A.
117 Colonial Office 'Welfare of Women' correspondence, TNA SMP 24450/I/f 61.
118 TNA SMP 24450/II, m 1, f 1B, p.2.
119 *Ibid.*, p. 4.
120 *Ibid.*, p. 2.
121 *Ibid.*, p. 13.
122 *Ibid.*
123 *Ibid.*, f 1A, letter from Colonial Office to Secretary of Conference of East African Governors, 27.3.39.
124 *Ibid.*, letter to Secretary of State for the Colonies, 27.1.39.

125 *Ibid.*, f 3B, 12.12.39.
126 *Ibid.*, m dated 16.3.40.
127 *Ibid.*, m dated 1.3.40.
128 *Ibid.*, f 4, 19.3.40.
129 *Ibid.*, m dated 1.3.40.
130 *Ibid.*, f 20, 4.11.40.
131 *Ibid.*, f 11A, 24.5.40.
132 *Ibid.*, f 11, PC Northern Province to Chief Secretary, 3.6.40.
133 *Ibid.*, f 21, 6.3.41.
134 *Ibid.*
135 *Ibid.*, f 8, 16.4.40; a similiar view is regularly expressed today by donor agencies.
136 This nullification of African women's existence is also typical of American history and in much mainstream women's studies with respect to Black women. Gloria T. Hull, Patricia Bell Scott and Barbara Smith, *All the Women are White, All the Blacks are Brave: Black Women's Studies* (Old Westbury, NY, Feminist Press, 1982).
137 TNA SMP, 24450/II, m 1, f 8, 16.4.40.
138 According to the *New Collins Concise English Dictionary*, a hostage is 'a person given to or held by another as a security or pledge'.
139 See Bujra, 'Women Entrepreneurs' and 'Prostitution, Class and the State'; Chanock, 'Making Customary Law' and *Law, Custom and Social Order*; Hay and Wright, *African Women and the Law*; Whitehead, 'Politics of Marriage'; Mbilinyi, 'City and Countryside'; Robertson and Klein, *Women and Slavery in Africa*; Claire Robertson and Iris Berger, *Women and Class in Africa*; and Susan Geiger, 'Women in Nationalist Struggle: TANU Activists in Dar es Salaam', *International Journal of African Historical Studies*, 20 (1) (1987), pp. 1–26. There are very few Tanzanian women historians (i.e. including those like myself who lack formal training in historiography). The History Department at the University of Dar es Salaam has had very low female enrolment at undergraduate and, especially, post-graduate level and has never employed women lecturers. Members of the Women's Research and Documentation Project (WRDP) are presently writing life histories of women in Dar es Salaam, Tanga and Rungwe. The Union of Tanzanian Women sponsored a book on the history of women's struggles in Tanzania, which seven Tanzanian women (including myself) have jointly written. It will be published in Kiswahili and English, which is also true of some of the WRDP life histories. It is hoped that many others will be stimulated to 'make history'.
140 Ophelia Mascarenhas and Marjorie Mbilinyi, *Women in Tanzania* (Uppsala, Scandinavian Institute of African Studies, 1983), Part One.
141 Mbilinyi, 'Agribusiness and Casual Labour' and 'The Big Slavery'.
142 Donna O. Kerner, ' "Hard Work" and Informal Sector Trade in Tanzania', paper presented to the American Anthropological Association, Philadelphia, 7 December 1986.
143 Mascarenhas and Mbilinyi, *Women in Tanzania*, Part One.

Forced Labour and Migration in Senegal

Babacar Fall and Mohamed Mbodj

From the end of the nineteenth century the labour system of Senegal presents a special picture when compared with the other territories of West Africa. Free labour seems dominant there, whereas elsewhere the mobilization of the workforce was effectuated principally by administrative coercion. This special trait has often masked the operation of forced labour within the former colony. It is true that enforced recruitment in Senegal never attained the level found in the Sudan, in French Guinea, Ivory Coast or in Upper Volta, but a proportion of the labour force was nonetheless mobilized under coercion and consigned to various works.

This paper proposes to shed light on the peculiar characteristics of the labour system in Senegal, to analyse several significant forms of forced labour in this region, and to highlight the demographic impact of such forms of labour organization.

Peculiarities of the Labour System

In Senegal, a region dominated by the groundnut economy, the labour system was not subject to heavy administrative constraints in regard to the high degree of monetarization of both social relations and the special and longstanding methods used in implanting groundnut culture.[1]

The overall condition of labour is marked by several

characteristics. In fact, with the increased integration of the Colony into the market economy, the system of free labour seems dominant throughout the process of causing the peasantry to submit to the production of surplus value within the framework of the groundnut economy. Bernard Founou-Tchuigowa points out that 'before 1930 three essential factors were simultaneously in play: (1) tax constraints, (2) construction of the transportation infrastructure and (3) prices' in order to assure the development of the groundnut economy.[2] All these factors worked together to bring about the monetarization of social relationships in order to remove non-economic constraints.

It would seem that these factors encouraged the peasants to disengage to a large extent from subsistence economy, a trend favoured by the fact that the so-called 'liberal period' (1840–1930) corresponded with the growth of the groundnut economy, a period of 'prosperity' for the peasant, whose income was largely superior to that of the Dakar labourer.[3] This explains why the labour force was still largely connected to the rural world and consequently appeared to fluctuate. This mainly concerned unskilled labourers who would gravitate towards urban centres during the dry season in order to earn extra income. Certainly during this 'flourishing' period of the Senegalese economy the Colonial Administration refrained from intervening in the process of direct production.

It was nontheless aware of the weakness of the production forces and of the attraction held by cash gained from groundnut production for the population of the neighbouring colonies. Thus, basing itself on the economic solidarity of the West African colonies, the Colonial State favoured conditions for the free circulation of agricultural labour. The groundnut basin of Senegal became an economic pole, seasonally attracting workers from the adjacent colonies of the Sudan and French Guinea. This migratory flow, known as *navétanat*, consisted with few exceptions of free labourers attracted from neighbouring colonies in order to participate in the cultivation and harvesting of groundnuts, in return for a salary which enabled them to pay their taxes and buy imported goods. Intervention was generally limited to adjusting the size of this work force according to demand,[4] as this migratory movement was largely determined by price fluctuation in the groundnut market.[5]

Moreover, it should be noted that as a result of the early urbanization of Senegal certain labourers on worksites were able to acquire specialized skills. Salaried labour was comparatively well developed in towns such as Saint-Louis, Dakar and Rufisque. The existence of this salaried workforce was able to meet the demands of entrepreneurs and worksites within Senegal, which was even able to supply specialized labour to the other colonies of the federation of French West Africa and AEF. Such recourse to Senegalese workmen is comparatively old and regulations attempting to protect Senegal from a loss of skilled labour through emigration go back as far as 1895. Overall it is this category of skilled labourers that formed the nucleus of the free labour market.[6] From this it follows that only the fluctuation of the workforce can explain forced employment in the towns. Indeed, it was often the case that Senegal was confronted with an inadequate workforce owing to the constant fluctuation, resulting from population movements from rural labour reserves to urban centres. A report on the workforce of French West Africa recognizes the need of the Administration to requisition labour between May and October in order to assure the proper functioning of the port of Dakar and the railway workshops at Thiès.[7]

According to all evidence, the practice of forced labour in Senegal was more limited and far less intense than in Guinea or Sudan. The most striking characteristic of its mobilization, however, arose from the violent methods of recruitment and the almost military organization of the work, proceeding from a class alliance embodied in the collaboration between the Administration and the native authorities.

The classification of forms of labour is often taken to be dependent on the nature of the employer, i.e. whether public or private. Thus certain analysts will only consider the term 'forced labour' applicable to corvée exactions when these are assigned to private interests. This approach unilaterally drains forced labour of its essence, namely the application of an extra-economic constraint, whether administrative or political, in order to force an individual to work.

Some Forms of Forced Labour

In Senegal between 1900 and 1936 the colonial administration was principally engaged in directing the indigenous workforce towards building and maintaining a transport system. The reluctance of the population to take up such work was to be overcome not by offering attractive wages but by constraint. The violence which had brought about the submission of the country was now employed to mobilize the labour force in order to establish an economic tool. The supply of workers to private enterprises was also satisfied by the same mechanism.

Labour and the Road Network:

1. Regulation and Significance of corvée Exactions

Originally the system of Corvée exaction aimed at remedying, as far as possible, the inconveniences and abuses of requisitioned labour, the oldest method of applying coercion to the mobilization of indigenous labour. In a letter dated 31st October 1912, the Minister for the Colonies observed that the corvée labour demanded by French West Africa had no basis in law. A local decree issued on 25th November 1912 filled this gap.

Corvée labour consisted in demanding of tax payers, in addition to taxes paid in cash, a fixed number of days labour assigned to local public works. In other words it was a tax in kind, a sort of exaction contributing to the solution of labour problems in colonies where waged labour was not yet well developed. Corvée exaction appeared at a time when metropolitan public opinion and the Colonial Ministry were opposed to the use of requisitioned labour.[8]

The general decree of the 25th November 1912 which regulated the system of corvée labour in French West Africa, stipulated that every healthy adult male belonging to the indigenous population (except for the elderly, those in military service, provincial guards, those working in customs and forestry) should be subject to the system. Corvée labour was not, however, to be exacted during periods of agricultural activity or harvesting. Nor were corvée labourers to be assigned to work more than five kilometres from their village without being assigned rations, in cash or kind. The length of corvée labour depended on the colony. In 1926 the rate was eight days a year in Senegal, ten days a year in Guinea and twelve days a year in Sudan and Mauritania.

In 1930, following the Geneva conference on forced or obligatory labour, which had defined the corvée labour system as a disguised form of unwaged forced labour, the French Government reacted promptly with the general circular of 12 September 1930. This made the 'native contribution exacted hitherto a direct tax exactable from all men aged between 18 and 60 years irrespective of status and payable in cash or kind, certain tax payers however being subject to obligatory payment in cash'.[9] The length of the period was reduced from twelve to ten days under Governor General De Coppet. The circular of 3rd of November 1936 further reduced the number of days exactable each year, this varying between two and ten days: 4 in Senegal and Mauritania, 8 in Guinea, 7–9 in Sudan, and 8–10 in the Ivory Coast.[10]

Corvée labour was responsible for all roadworks and for the maintenance of airfields. Generally speaking the road system was developed rather later in the Federation of West Africa compared with the colonial penetration effected at first along rivers and, after 1895, by rail. The construction of roads was further delayed by a persistent desire to eliminate any rivalry with the railway. From 1916, however, it was observed that the construction of a railway system, required not only improvements to be made to the dirt tracks leading to the stations but also the construction of new earth roads to facilitate transportation and reduce costs. Commercial interests had already expressed the wish to see the construction of a whole network of roads conferring 'that value to the railways that they cannot acquire without this natural and indispensible complement.'[11] Considering that it was up to the Administration to construct the road system within the provinces and to ensure its upkeep at the beginning of the dry season, the Provincial Governor charged with building these roads, but with limited financial means at his disposal, soon had recourse to mobilizing the population by making use of corvée labour.

In Senegal it was from the beginning of 1920, at the time of the 'course de l'arachide' and the triumph of the truck, that the road network, by virtue of its flexibility, became increasingly more important in the distribution of grain. The creation of the necessary road infrastructure took part in two stages.[12]

From 1900 to 1928 the pre-existing network of roads and tracks was improved – in order to ensure connection between urban conglomerations and the economic zones – through local resources and corvée labour. Roads remained the creation of the province; the Administration opened up and maintained tracks thus making it easier for it to perform tours of duty within the region. By 1918 all centres of any economic importance were joined either directly or by connecting roads to one of the principal axes. By 31st December 1926 the total length of the network was 11,155km, of which only 38km had paved surfaces.[13] During this period both the Administration and commercial interests exerted pressure for the construction of roads in order to satisfy their own requirements. The Administration, however, having inadequate financial and material resources, relied heavily on corvée labourers.

Between 1928 and 1940 traffic increased by virtue of developing economic activity, particularly groundnut cultivation, and increasingly important links with other colonies of the group, most importantly with Sudan, Mauritania and Guinea. Meanwhile, the increased numbers of heavy vehicles in use required the construction of permanent roads. The desire to improve the quality of roads and other types of civil engineering was made easier by the important financial and material contribution assigned to roadworks from the local budget. The Department of Public Works was responsible for constructing the colonial road system, but until 1936 the work force was mainly unskilled and provided by the Provincial Governors from corvée labourers. From 1937 the corvée system was reformed, and cash payments were substituted for labour due throughout the colony and the whole of French West Africa, which enabled machinery to be purchased and road workers often to be employed as salaried free labourers.

2. Organization of Corvée Labour

The inadequacy of financial and material resources and the absence of skilled labour explain why, until 1928, the tracks and roads were seasonal.[14] At the end of each rainy season the Provincial Governor summoned the district and village heads to carry out the programme of upkeep and construction of the road network within their region. As from 1912, the Council of Elders permitted the Provincial Governor to draw up a general plan of campaign. Each district was then responsible for seeing the work done and sharing it among the various villages supplying corvée labour.

After adopting this programme the members of the Council expressed the wish that a worker with specialized knowledge of roads should be assigned to each district, or even sub-district, in order to survey the roads, carry out repair work, draw attention to weak points requiring partial rebuilding, extinguish straw fires and search out the culprits.

In general, it fell upon the tribal chiefs in consultation with the village elders to select the corvée labourers who were to form the team responsible for the maintenance or construction of a given section of road or track. The Administration made judicious use of the authority of the chiefs in claiming the recruitment and dispatch of corvée labour to be a 'purely native affair'. Thus each family unit called upon by the chief supplied one or two members to fulfil the work requirements entrusted to the village. The family had to make up the loss of manpower for one or more weeks according to the nature of the work and the distance of the worksite. The chiefs and elders chose supervisors from among their relations, who were charged with overseeing labour at the site. It was not unusual, therefore, to see minstrel-magicians and tam-tam players entrusted with creating an atmosphere which would stimulate the zeal of the workmen. The Provincial Governor made sure the work was supervised by means of auxiliaries, translators and provincial guards. The corvée labourers were to weed the road bed along the length of the section assigned, all trees or shrubs on the track were to be uprooted, anthills flattened, holes filled and rises levelled. In order to complete these tasks, the workmen, who were simple unskilled labourers, were provided with rudimentary tools: machetes, hatchets, spades and baskets. Whenever the provincial guards or other officials charged with overseeing the work thought the corvée labourers had not done their job properly they would order them to start all over again as a punishment. Such sanctions obviously prolonged the stay of workers at the site.[15]

By definition, this type of labour was unpaid but the Administration was supposed to provide rations in cash or in kind whenever a labourer was called upon to work more than 5km away from home. Provincial Governors often mentioned in their reports that provisioning the labour force took up a large part of the credit assigned for this purpose. A gulf separates evidence drawn from the archives and reality, for everyone questioned on this point agreed in contradicting the Provincial Governors. In their opinion, the corvée labourers were not fed and the workforce was obliged to bring its own provisions to the worksite which was often a long way from the village (up to 50km on occasion). When provisions taken along proved inadequate to cover the period of forced work at the site, the corvée labourers appealed to their relatives in the village. In difficult situations solidarity was established among the corvée labourers by pooling their food in common, in order to prevent any of their number starving.

Assessment of the quality of corvée labour was unequivocal: everyone agreed that it was mediocre, which is hardly surprising considering it was unpaid and obligatory. Rudimentary techniques and the almost permanent absence of specialized personnel scarcely contributed to improve the quality of work achieved. These results, however poor, did nonetheless meet the immediate objective, namely to get the roads, tracks and bridges into a state where they could cope with seasonal trading traffic and administrative movements.

The inadequacy of the financial resources invested and the nature itself of corvée labour also explain the many cases of unfair exaction and abuses to which attention has been drawn by corvée labourers, some colonial advisers and even by high-ranking adminstrators such as Governor General De Coppet. It is through certain complaints addressed to the Administration that one can find occasional glimpses of the numerous abuses practised in the utilization of corvée labour. From the establishment of the Colonial Council in 1920 the administrative authorities were increasingly called upon to explain themselves. One may note the letter of protest sent on 21st February by Galandou Diouf as Colonial Councillor to the President of the Colonial Council, in which he denounces the bad treatment corvée labourers had been subjected to in the Province of Louga. Diouf starts by observing that the corvée labourers working on the road from Louga to Saint Louis had accomplished 'a Herculean task' since for more than 30km they had managed to cover the road with sand and millet stalks until the roadbed had become drivable. 'But', he continued, 'these people are more than 10 or 15km from their villages and they are receiving no food allowance. Moreover, they start work at 7am and work without a break until 6pm, (i.e. nearly 11 hours per day).'[16]

Moreover, based on the report drawn up by Governor General De Coppet, Marius Moutet, the Colonial Minister, made an important resumé of the abuses arising from the system of corvée labour. 'In a word, the regulations form a facade behind which unjust and abusive practices are still taking place. The desertion (abandonment) of villages along the length of the major highways attests in concrete form the disastrous results of this policy.'[17]

The permanent recourse to corvée labour with its attendant unfair exactions and ill treatment brought about forms of resistance in the native population which, taken together, amounted to a refusal to fulfil the quota of corvée labour, or brought ill-will to the execution of the work. In various parts of Senegal, but particularly in the regions of Saint-Louis, Diourbel, Eastern Senegal and Casamance these reactions of collective refusal occasionally even manifested themselves as hostile demonstrations against the auxiliary agents of the colonial administration. These incidents were, however, mostly scattered and of short duration and of limited scope; and their resonance was diluted by various factors, such as the role of the native authorities, the social structures and the recruitment methods for corvée labour.

Forced Labour in Private Enterprise:
A number of private enterprises were content for a long time

to rely on the Administration for the provision of labour. These included the Compagnie des Cultures Tropicales en Afrique (CCTA), established at Wassodou (Tambacounda Province); La Société de Plantation de la Haute Casamance (Kolda); La Société des Salins du Sine-Saloum (Kaolack); La Société Agricole de Lat-Mingué (Kaolack), and La Société Industrielle des Mines du Falémé-Gambie. All these companies encountered to various degrees a shortage of labour. Their situation in south-east Senegal where population density is low, the painful and distasteful nature of salt extraction and low wages, are so many factors explaining the difficulty experienced in recruiting the required workforce. In order to assure their functioning the Administration itself intervened, so as on the one hand to 'encourage' the natives to take up employment with the above mentioned companies, while on the other transporting contingents of workers from Sudan and Upper Volta as members of the 'deuxième portion militaire.'

In the case of the CCTA the recruitment of workers was effected with the aid of the Administration, which even undertook to convey employees to the concession at Wassadu. Propaganda was organized by the office of the Provincial Governor of Tambacounda. When the CCTA succeeded in recruiting workers, it put into operation a policy of domestication. This policy, whose very name is expressive of attitudes towards native labour, consisted of putting into practice a special form of sharecropping which bound the labourers to the concessions by giving them, alongside their activity within the factory, a financial interest in the groundnut economy.

Such a system allowed stabilized workers to dispose of supplementary income while acting as instructors to the labourers who formed the bulk of the workforce and who were extremely difficult to recruit, according to reports from the Governor of Tambacounda Province. As a result of this, recourse was made to the colonies of Upper Volta, Sudan and the Ivory Coast in order to meet the requirements of the CCTA.

Within the framework of experiments in the mechanization of groundnut culture in Lat-Mingué, forced labour came to the rescue of a technology which was supposed to have eliminated direct exploitation of the peasantry. This experiment, which lasted from 1921 to 1925, was in response to several requirements of which the most important were maximization of profits and the reduction of costs to a minimum. Moreover, the First World War had suggested the possibility of mechanization being integrated into the colonies in order to speed up the reconstruction of capital. Other more conjectural reasons are the rivalry between Bordeaux and Marseilles in dominating French colonial interests, the high market price of groundnuts and the cost of freightage. The experiment was undertaken by the CFAO (Companie Francaise de l'Afrique Occidentale) the showpiece of Marseilles interests in tropical Africa, on 200 hectares at Lat-Mingué, within the heart of the groundnut basin and accessible to river transport. Despite the use of heavy machinery (more than 20 engines were brought from the USA) the experiment failed: returns were too low compared with the costs of investment. The experimenters then struck on the idea of utilizing forced labour to complete mechanized work (weeding, uprooting, clearing ground etc.). More and more it became necessary, however, to make up for the defects of inadequate machinery and the Administration provided the required workforce from corvée labour.[18]

The reaction of the population was varied, for initially it had hoped to take advantage of the experiment to supplement income with work during the dry season and piecework. It soon became obvious, however, that the agricultural calendar would force a choice between their own fields and the CFAO. The latter, moreover, intended to pay occasional workers only with 'gifts' such as cola nuts and sugar, whence the necessity of obliging peasants to offer their unwaged corvée labour.[19]

Demographic Impact

A variety of factors explain the low rate of population increase in Senegal, which is estimated at 1.8 per cent p.a. between 1900 and 1946, while the direct influence of forced labour on demographic developments remains to be explained. Senegal was indeed thought to possess an adequate labour force, but this did not prevent recourse to workers from neighbouring colonies. The migratory movement of *navétanes* towards the groundnut basin was a permanent phenomenon, whereas displacements brought about by coercion were comparatively limited in scope. In fact the principles of labour employment utilized had a stabilizing influence. Each province could only call upon workers within its administrative boundaries to complete local work and, except for major projects such as railway construction, the indigenous inhabitants were seldom forced to leave their native province in order to provide forced labour. Moreover, corvée labourers were kept at the worksite for only three or four weeks, and the amount of work assigned seldom required a prolonged absence from the village. In the north of Senegal, however, important displacements of the Toucouleur people from the left bank to the right bank were reported. From 1911 onwards administrators at Matam and Ponor were troubled by large scale desertion of the Senegalese Fouta who, among other reasons such as recruitment being enforced in Senegal but not in Mauritania, and differences in the rate of taxation, fled to avoid the haulage duties and corvée labour imposed on them.

It is plausible that this tendency, already observed in 1911, would have continued or even intensified given the increasing importance of the migration of the Toucouleur into Mauritania. The strong presence of this people in the neighbouring colony could be explained as part of the consequence of the intensity of forced labour in Senegal. The same hypothesis may be advanced to explain migratory movements of population into Gambia. From 1910 on significant movements of population from Sine-Saloum were noted by the Administration who have explained it by the differing price of groundnuts and rates of salary operative in Gambia. It is equally probable, however, that faced with multiple corvée labour on roads, railways and wharves and the use of force to obtain this – as had been the case under the administration of Brocard – the population reacted by slipping away to the more liberal British colony of Gambia.

Moreover in Sine between 1934 and 1936 the hand of the Administration was clearly to be seen in the migratory movements towards the east which occurred within the framework of the 'Terres Neuves' (New Lands) operation. But here one should talk of organized migration rather than the impact of forced labour. Taking an overall view, it may be said that in Senegal the consequences of forced labour on migration were rather limited. It remains for more detailed studies to determine the part forced labour played in motivating certain internal migrations, or which led part of the Senegalese population to settle in Gambia and Mauritania. It is already clear, however, that it cannot on its own explain these movements.

Notes and References

1 Bernard Founou Tchuigoua *Fondements de l'économie de traite au Sénégal* (Paris, Silex, 1981) pp. 52–53.
2 *Ibid.* p. 52.
3 André Vanhaerverbeke *Rémunération du travail et commerce extérieur – Essor d'une économie paysane exporatrice et termes de l'echange de production au Sénégal* (Louvain, 1970) p. 176.
4 Philippe David *Les Navétanes* (Dakar-Abidjan Nouvelles Editions Africaines, 1980) p. 523.
5 Later the collapse of the price of grain in 1932 brought about a considerable reduction in the number of *navétanes*. The Administration introduced measures to encourage the flow of migrants by providing movement permits and free transport. Bassemba Keita *L'evolution de la population et la production agricole du Sénégal (1920–1968)* (Dakar, Université de Dakar, Faculté des Sciences Juridiques et Economiques) *Mémoire D.E.S.* 1970.
6 Monique Lakroum 1979 p. 26.
7 A.N.S.-K55 (19) *Rapport sur la main d'oeuvre* (A.O.F., 1915).
8 Réné Mercier *Le travail obligatoire dans les colonies Africaines* (Paris, Cerf, 1933) p. 7.
9 Jules Ninime *La main d'oeuvre dans les colonies Africaines* (Paris, Jouvé, 1932) p. 55.
10 Nicole Bernard-Duguenet 'Le Front Populaire et le Probléme des Presétations en AOF' *Cahiers d'études Africaines* XVI (1–2) 61–62 (1976) p. 163.
11 A.N.S. 2G 16/4 Sénégal *Rapport politique annuel* (1916).
12 Serigne Bamba Ndiaye *La mise en place du réseau routier au Sénégal 1900–1940* Mémoire de Maitrise Université de Dakar, Départment d'Histoire, 1977–78 pp. 19–24.
13 A.N.S. 2G 27/21 A.O.F. T.P. *Rapport d'emsemble* (1927).
14 A.N.S. Sénégal Ancien T.P. Dossier No. 70 *Etat des routes dans le cercle de Louga 1924–1925*.
15 Serigne Bamba Ndiaye 1977–8 *op.cit.* p. 14.

16 A.N.S. Sénégal Ancien T.P. Dossier No. 70 *Lettre de Mr Galandou Diouf au President du Conseil Colonial 21/02/1925.*
17 A.N.S. K8(1) Lettre du ministre des Colonies à M le Gouverneur de l'AOF, Paris le 09 mars 1938.
18 A.N.S. 2G 25/29 *Rapport agricole annuel 1925.*
19 R. Mannoury 'Essai de culture mécanique de l'arachide au Sénégal' – *Bulletin des Matiéres Grasses* (1921) pp. 195–7.

Manifestations of Forced Labour in Senegal: as Exemplified by the Société des Salins du Sine-Saloum Kaolack 1943–1956

Babacar Fall

Introduction

It has long been held at Kaolack that the returns from the salt works of the Société des Salins du Sine-Saloum have never been good. It is as if the salt-workers were pursued by a curse, whose origins lie in a conjunction of poor salaries and, above all, the composition of the work-force between 1943 and 1956. The greater part of the permanent work-force employed by the company during this period was provided by prisoners condemned to hard labour and engaged in the disagreeable, harsh and underpaid task of salt extraction. This provided the motive for the establishment of the prison camp at Koutal in 1944, a paradoxical solution to the shortage of labour in a colony where forced labour played so small a part when

I would like to thank Mr Pipien, Administrative Director of the Société des Salins du Sine-Saloum who suggested this line of research and provided valuable information about the identities of my informants. I am also grateful to my colleagues Doudou Gaye, Abdoul Sow and Mohamed-El-Bachir Diop and to Babacar Ndiaye, employees of the salt works, who offered great assistance during the course of my enquiries.

This article is based on information gathered between 18 and 21 April 1987 at Kaolack and Koutal from former and present employees of the Société des Salins du Sine-Saloum. Consultation of documents series K, particularly K334: Labour situation of the Salins du Sine-Saloum 1945–1963 (National Archives of Senegal) has enabled me to place many items of information within context.

compared with other territories of the Federation of French West Africa, such as Sudan, Guinea or the Ivory Coast.

One fact, however, is indisputable: the case of the Société des Salins du Kaolack offers a clear illustration of the survival, reincarnation one might say, of forced labour in Senegal ten years after its official abolition by the enactment of the Law of Houphouët Boigny on 11 April 1946. The need to supply the colonies of the Federation of French West Africa with salt was advanced as an official justification for using governmental coercion rather than offering good wages as a means of recruiting labour. This archaic procedure of making prison labour available to private enterprise, as exemplified by a study of the salt works of Kaolack, throws an unexpected light on social problems in the Federation.

The reconstruction of the period when forced labour predominated in the Société des Salins de Kaolack comes up against a certain silence of shame, as many former prisoners who chose to continue working with the company after completing their sentences are at pains to hide their convict past. This is understandable, as their social status is at stake. The difficulty, however, is less serious than it might be as those who claim to have been contract labourers admit that they shared the same working conditions as the prisoners from Koutal. The only information concerning direct implication in the system of forced labour is likely to be censored.

The Importance of Salt and the Crisis of Labour

Kaolack's vocation as an exporter

Founded in 1914 on the initiative of the French company, les Salins de Midi, the Société des Salins du Sine-Saloum was devoted to the extraction and sale of sea salt from the left bank of the River Saloum, 4 kilometres to the south of the town of Kaolack. From the beginning, the company was beset with difficulties and, between 1914 and 1924, salt production was less than 5,000 tonnes per annum. Only after 1940 did production exceed 10,000 tonnes.[1] The growth of the port of Kaolack, which was the most important groundnut exporting port in West Africa from 1931 on,[2] and its connection to the Dakar–Niger railway, provided an important market for the Société des Salins, namely, Senegal and, above all, French Sudan. In fact, the requirements of Senegal were largely met by traditional salt-workers exploiting the salt marshes of the Gandiolais, Bargny and the Lower Saloum Valley, production varying between 9,000 and 12,000 tonnes p.a.[3]

In 1940, the war situation proved most favourable for developing the activities of the salt works at Kaolack, and its role as an exporter was rapidly clarified thanks to a dynamic commercial policy taking advantage of the fact that European coasts were blockaded. The opportunity was, therefore, provided for the Kaolack salt works to substitute its product for rival salt originating from Spain, and to undertake supplying the West African coast. The new commercial policy was, however, successful only as a result of the intervention of the colonial government from 1943 on. The High Commission of French Africa raised the status of salt to that of a strategic product and decided that the Kaolack salt works should be responsible for supplying salt to the Federation of French West Africa. A note from the Directorate General of Economic Services, dated 14 December 1943, gives formal notice of the decision of the federal authorities, who considered it essential for the economy of the Federation that its colonies, particularly those lying to the south (Guinea, Ivory Coast, Togo and Dahomey) should be regularly and copiously supplied with salt. It was the war situation that determined the value of salt, as it was felt that distribution of large quantities of this commodity on the market would stimulate the local population to bring in raw materials essential for the war effort.[4]

There was, however, a considerable difference between the demands of the Federation for salt, estimated at 95,000 tonnes in 1944, and the stagnant production of the Kaolack salt works. It is true that in 1944 the company achieved a record production level of 22,957 tonnes compared with 14,118 in 1943, 13,433 in 1942 and 13,727 in 1941.[5] Nevertheless, the shortfall was still greater than expected by the federal authorities. The solution to the problem seems to have been sketched out in correspondence exchanged between the Director of the Société des Salins du Sine-Saloum and the

Governing Secretary General of the Federation towards the
end of 1943. In a letter dated 5 December 1943, M.
Mondeil, Administrative Director of the Kaolack salt works, pointed
out to the Governor General of the Federation of French West
Africa that to meet the salt requirements of the Federation
would require the political will to take 'appropriate measures
at the right time'.[6]

Labour: a source of difficulties

For Mondeil, the difficulties of the company had arisen at
least in part from damage to factory machines, bad weather
conditions having prevailed in 1941 and 1942, but the
principal troubles arose from labour problems. By the
beginning of the 1943 season, defective machinery had been
repaired, but problems of labour recruitment remained
dominant, all the more so as Mondeil's request for aid from
the local administration at Kaolack and from the government
of Senegal had proved ineffective.[7] As a result of this shortage
of manpower, the company was obliged in 1942 to abandon
20,000 tonnes of salt to the rain. In the opinion of the
administration of the salt works, the lack of support from
government authorities lay at the heart of the problem of the
shortage of local workers. State intervention in the recruitment
of labour was seen as the key that would enable the company
to meet the salt requirements of the Federation of French
West Africa. On many occasions, Mondeil forcefully underlined his willingness to undertake joint studies with the public
authorities of such working conditions and salaries as might
attract labour to the salt works.[8]

Government assistance had, however, already been deployed
in the season of 1943 to help the company's recruitment
problem, a fact which Mondeil glossed over in order to bring
pressure on the new Governor General to provide continuing
assistance for the company in recruiting necessary labour after
that year. In fact in 1943 the Governor General, Hubert
Deschamps, had already supported Mondeil's analysis that the
principal difficulty to be overcome was that of the labour force.[9]
As a result of the difficulties the company had experienced in
recruiting a voluntary labour force to engage in the huge task

of salt extraction, the Governor General had exceptionally authorized the Commandant of the administrative district of Kaolack to make 100 prisoners available to the company.

In order to expedite the suitable exploitation of the salt marshes and to maintain the prompt despatch of salt stored on the banks of the Saloum, the administrative authorities inclined towards the employment of civilian conscripts. This first attempt concerned a small contingent of some 50 conscripts raised from members of the local population not engaged in agriculture.[10] For Hubert Deschamps, this system was by its very nature provisional, and the salt works were expected to recruit voluntary labour after the end of the agricultural season.

The harmony of views between the Governor General and the administration of the salt works only lasted long enough to ensure one successful season, as Mondeil knew perfectly well that he was in no position to fulfil his promise to attract voluntary labour to the works. Poor pay for hard labour held no attractions for the local population. Only government intervention could assure a supply of local labour.

This situation may be considered typical of cases when the attempt to establish capitalist enterprises near populous areas comes across the difficulty of attracting voluntary labour from the working population. In such cases, mediation by the colonial government proved necessary for the enterprise to attain the stage of development required before it could switch to voluntary recruitment and do without government help with the work force. It is strange that such a case should occur in Senegal as late as 1940–50.

A number of factors explain why, in general, forced labour played such a small part in Senegal, among them being the early establishment of the French presence, the political life of the four communes (Saint-Louis, Rufisque, Gorée and Dakar) and, above all, the role played by the groundnut economy in the increased development of trade.

As early as 1933, the Governor General noted that Senegal was living largely under a system of free labour, and salaries were determined according to the law of supply and demand.[11] When forced labour was formally abolished in 1946, a large labour market was established. This freeing of the work-force was marked even in rural sectors, despite the instability of labour. Some manifestations of forced labour, however, continued in the form of using men of the deuxième portion, that part of men enrolled in the army who were not required for military duties. Thus, on 20 September 1946, a total of 3,024 men were being forcibly employed on two work sites. In Dakar, work at the Yoff airport, drain construction in the suburbs of Fann and the construction of the northern section of the port employed 1,524 deuxième portion men. At the same time, a further 1,500 were employed at Richard Toll between 1943 and 1947 in order to overcome the difficulty of finding local labour for the works of the Mission d'Aménagement du Sénégal (MAS) owing to the low local population density and, above all, to its antipathy to being engaged in earth construction works.[12]

This attempt to avoid the provisions of the Law of Houphouët Boigny by maintaining the men of the deuxième portion was vigorously denounced, and between 1944 and 1946 the forced labourers themselves were engaged in active protests. The most impressive demonstration occurred on 27 September 1946 on the public highway and involved workers barracked at the camp at Yoff.[13] Their protests were also picked up in France. 'Is Forced Labour Abolished?' was the title of the issue of A.O.F., organ of the French section of the workers international (S.F.I.O.) dated 21 March 1947.[14] Political and social agitation finally forced the government to put an end to the practice of keeping men of the deuxième portion. The Decree of 18 November 1948 determined on the early liberation of the last recruits to the deuxième portion, starting from 15 February 1949.[15]

Curiously enough, no mention was made in the Decree of the forced labourers working at the Kaolack salt works and the fate of these penal labourers was enveloped in silence. Thus the hell of these salt-workers continued because public opinion was quiet. The government, and still less the Société des Salins, had not run into opposition as a result of using this type of forced labour. This shows how vulnerable and voiceless were those detainees who were in a state of moral rupture from society. They were available to be worked as hard as their employer chose.

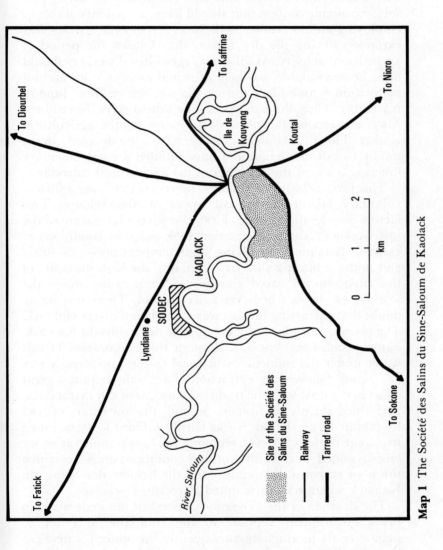

Map 1 The Société des Salins du Sine-Saloum de Kaolack

Ineffective solutions to the labour problem

The establishment of the salt works company occurred in a socio-economic context that should have proved favourable to employing an indigenous work force. In Senegal, sea salt was extracted during the dry season that follows the period of agricultural activity. At this time, agricultural workers should have been available, as their principal activity – groundnut cultivation – took place during the wet season from June to November. Thus, the active season for salt-workers (November–May) corresponded with a slack season for the agricultural worker. This time could, in theory, have been devoted almost totally to salt extraction and have fulfilled a complementary function, *vis-à-vis* the activities of the agricultural calendar.

This favourable context failed, however, to release a flow of voluntary labour to the salt works of Sine-Saloum. Two factors are significant here. First, the particular nature of the salt workers' labour. Extraction took place in conditions of extreme harshness, involving high temperatures (35–40°C) and under a blazing sun. In addition to the high humidity of the environment, rapid changes of temperature made the working of the salt beds yet more painful. There can be no doubt that extracting the salt was a harsh and distasteful task. The process introduced by the Société des Salins du Kaolack, namely 'culturing' the salt through the evaporation of salt water under the influence of natural factors, principally sun and wind, followed by extraction of sea salt, required great effort in contrast with the traditional means of salt extractions, performed mainly by women. Second, the low salary offered for labouring on the salt works hardly sufficed to attract men to engage in the work even temporarily. Low remuneration for labour added to difficult working conditions thus explained the poor response that confronted the Société des Salins du Kaolack whenever it attempted to recruit workers.

The decision of the Governor General of the Federation to bring government support to the company in order to maximize its production consequently introduced a new era into the life of the enterprise. From 21 December 1943, the Governor General insisted that the Head of the Colony of Senegal should study with Mondeil the company's labour problems, as they had not yet been satisfactorily resolved.[16] According to Mondeil it was indispensable that there should be 250 permanent workers at the site from December each year in order to ensure packaging and distribution, while an additional 400 men would be necessary temporarily from mid-April in order to maximize salt production, i.e. a total of 650 workers per season.[17]

The Governor General agreed that recourse to civilian conscripts should only be a last resort because of the very nature of the salt extractions. It was also felt that this method might adversely affect the labour market and the morale of the local population, particularly if conscripts were called on to perform harsh work that prisoners had not completed adequately.[18]

It was decided, then, to follow up the experiment of using penal labour but on a more rational basis. The new procedure that was promoted consisted of two complementary strategies. The first consisted of assigning a contingent of workers from the penal work-force to labour at the salt works. The company would, thus, be able to call on a stable work force of 150 to 200 men originating from the prison camp at Kelle, which was to be transferred to Koutal in the suburbs of Kaolack. This work-force could also be augmented by a certain number of prisoners of better condition coming from Kaolack prison. The second strategy consisted of progressively encouraging the salt works to conform to the laws of the labour market. In order to achieve this, the company was to put into practice methods that had proved successful at Dakar and elsewhere and that entailed the employer progressively providing food, clothing and accommodation for unconscripted labourers.[19] In this way, the company would be able to build up a body of voluntary workers capable of forming a stable nucleus for the work-force.

This approach largely determined the composition of the work-force of the Kaolack salt works until 1953, when recourse to penal labour was abandoned.

Convict Labour on the Kaolack Salt Works

It was established practice in Senegal to assign convicts to various public works. These workers were used for a variety of tasks: constructing tow-paths, repairing quays, constructing and maintaining the network of roads, as well as working on official buildings and accommodation. However, they had never before been used as supplementary labour. Use of convicts for public works had been classified by the International Labour Office (ILO) as a form of forced labour. Unlike views on the use of workers of the deuxième portion, this position held by the ILO was never contested at Geneva.[20] This throws yet more light on the obsolete nature of prison labour being made available to the Société des Salins du Kaolack.

Fluctuating work-force

The need to provide workers for the salt works led to the decision of the authorities to establish the Koutal prison camp, situated on the road between Kaolack and Nioro, 5 kilometres from the salt works. The position of the camp was determined by the need to provide labour for the works, while avoiding land subject to flooding. The government of Senegal notified the Société des Salins that the camp would be operative from 14 April 1944 and would hold 200 prisoners.[21] The camp was to intern able-bodied prisoners condemned to hard labour, dangerous re-offenders and certain other internees.

In addition to this measure, the Commandant of the administrative district of Kaolack was authorized to give his official support to the company in maintaining its voluntary work-force. The euphemism of 'official support' amounted to heavy-handed pressure on the local population to engage in work in the salt works in exchange for a derisory salary, food, commodities and 10 metres of cloth at the end of the season as a gratuity.

The efforts deployed in setting up the Koutal camp did not, however, have the desired results. A report drawn up a month after the opening of the camp shows a startling failure. Out of a total of 214 prisoners, only 87, that is to say 40 per cent, were still available for work at Kaolack. The remaining 137 were either ill, incapable, or employed in work required to maintain the camp.[22] The report of the Inspector of Administrative Affairs and the Governor of Koutal camp showed that improvization and haste had presided over its establishment. Old materials had been used, and the corrugated iron had holes in it. This was enough to justify using a contingent of prisoners to rebuild the camp.[23] The disappointment of the company at this was all the greater because the rate of defection of voluntary workers greatly accelerated at the same time. Of 800 men engaged at the beginning of May 1944 there remained only 300 on 12 May, which was further reduced to 200 by 17 May.

To try to overcome this difficult labour situation, the Governor of the administrative district made available 100 new prisoners from the civil prison at Kaolack. In the opinion of Mondeil, however, this supplementary force was totally inadequate. For, if during April 1944 the company had been able to raise 45,000 tonnes and put 12,000 tonnes under shelter, while preparing to pack and ensure the despatch of 6,000 tonnes, it was probable that the company would not be able to achieve half that figure for May unless the labour situation were corrected. The company ran the risk of having to abandon half of its production on the banks of the River Saloum.[24]

Two factors together explain the serious defection of labourers from the salt works. First, the instability of the work force was accentuated with each agricultural season. The voluntary workers were demobilized at the approach of the period of cultivation. Mondeil recognized that as soon as the rates of purchase for the next groundnut harvest were announced, together with the food grants for the producers, the rate of desertion of workers would increase greatly, with the work-force falling from 800 men to only 200 within a fortnight. The policy of trying to motivate salt workers had had hardly any effect. This is not surprising since, despite the harsh and distasteful nature of the work, the company did not seem disposed to offer attractive salaries. In consequence, it was unable to face the rivalry of the local labour market.

Secondly, the harsh working conditions encountered in salt working made their effects felt on the workers from the prison camp. There was a long working day, from between 10 to 11 hours, inadequate quantities of food of poor nutritional value, and a disciplinary system based on humiliating the worker. It is easy to understand the high level of unavailability of workers from the Koutal prison camp.

The only reaction of the authorities was to be disturbed about the inadequacy of the work force. From Alger, the Commissioner for the Colonies claimed to be troubled about the repercussions on the work force following the arrival of *navétanes*, migrant workers arriving in Central Senegal from Sudan and French Guinea. On 25 May 1944 only 200 prisoners were still working in the salt works. This number was clearly insufficient, all the more so as harvesting continued until July, and a minimum of 400 more workers was required if the salt supply was not to be jeopardized. This necessitated the provision of yet more labourers by the colonial administration if the anticipated production was to be maintained.[25] Confronted with the forceful instructions of the Governor of Senegal, the Commandant of the administrative district of Kaolack resorted to the customary practice of conscripting civilians to satisfy the requirements of the salt works.

With the completion of works on the prison camp of Koutal in 1945, the number of men available stabilized at 200 prison labourers divided into three camps, named A, B and C respectively. The prisoners were made available to the Kaolack salt works from February until July.

Draconian working and living conditions

Every morning at dawn the prisoners were taken from the camp at Koutal to the salt works, a distance of 5 kilometres. In close file and chained two by two the prisoners were submitted to a forced march under the vigilant eyes of the official guards. On arrival, they were separated into teams of 20 to 30 men and assigned to different production tasks.[26]

The first stage was harvesting or extracting sea salt from the salt tables. This was the most gruelling task. The thick layer of salt was scraped up by hand or with the help of a shell. This operation was known as 'battage'. The salt was then put in moderate sized baskets and carried 200 or 300 metres from the salt tables before being poured out in small heaps. The second stage was to wash the salt, a process aimed at separating sodium chloride from impurities. After washing, the salt was stocked in mounds known as 'camelle'. Sifting and crushing took place at the base of the camelles. These were the only two stages of the process that were mechanized. Lastly, the salt was placed in sacks and weighed before being carried by hand to the quay for transportation. An account of the working conditions prevalent in the salt works between 1943 and 1956 reveals a horrifying picture. Public opinion accommodated itself to the spectacle of this living death only because such purgatory was sanctioned by the crimes of the prisoners. The exceptional nature of this work force was accentuated by the repressive nature of control and surveillance of the work force.

The general rule was to apportion labour to fulfil tasks in a given time. Workers were thus driven to the very limit of their strength. The work rhythm was controlled by the demands of the task. The working day was long, never less than 10 hours, according to a former prisoner.[27] Moreover, the system practised to discourage desertion was fearful. The prisoners were chained at all times, and wore fetters to which a heavy ball was attached. Their food was provided by the company. Twelve prisoners whose conduct had inspired confidence were assigned to the kitchen. Large casks were used as cooking pots, and when cut served as huge bowls. The ration consisted of maize-flour soup.[28]

In this area, the difference between practice and theory is striking. In theory, the prisoners had a right to two meals a day, and the Assistant Public Attorney thought it desirable that those employed in particularly heavy labour should be provided with a hot drink on awaking.[29] According to regulations, meat should have been provided five times per week (350 gm per day for workers, 250 gm for non-workers). The monotony of this diet was to be varied twice weekly by the distribution of fish. The cereal ration for each day was as follows: rice or millet for workers was 375 gm and for non-workers, 250 gm; barley or semolina for workers was 340 gm and for non-workers, 225 gm. In addition, they were entitled to 60 gm of oil per day. As in the case of other forced labourers, however, these rations were not provided. All witnesses agree that the rations were inadequate. Overwork was not compensated for by a correct diet. A mission of inspection by the assistant procurator complained of the lack of protein. Many men were found sick or dead in the work place. Some canals were used as cemeteries according to a former prisoner.[30]

The shocking allegations collected by the mission of inspection were corroborated by a check report on the prison camp drawn up by Assistant Public Attorney Cosson. The report reveals certain characteristic aspects of prison life. Sanitation was defective. Out of a total of 203 prisoners, 23 were ill in hospital, of whom 15 were suffering from influenza. Two deaths from pneumonia were recorded on 4 October 1945 and 30 December 1945. This hardly surprised the mission of inspection, who had noticed in the courtyard a prisoner lying naked under a blanket against a wall and spitting blood. On their authority they had insisted that he should be taken to the quarantine hospital 350 metres from the camp.[31] The camp did not itself have an infirmary, and those who had fallen ill were sent to the quarantine hospital. Serious cases were treated at Kaolack. In principle, the camp should have been visited by a doctor every week, but as the mission found out, according to reports in the special register, the last visit had taken place on 14 June 1945, which is to say six months previously.[32] Hygiene also left much to be desired. There were three wells in the camp, one of which was so polluted it was unusable. These conditions explain the high levels of morbidity and mortality.

Many prisoners had no clothing other than a thin blanket to protect them against the local cold and humidity. In the opinion of the Assistant Public Attorney the complaints of the prisoners about the lack of clothing were perfectly justified. After the intervention of the Prison Surveillance Commission and a visit by the Médecin-Colonel, Head of Sanitary Department of Kaolack, the camp Governor said he hoped suitable clothing would at last be distributed to prisoners.[33]

The overall impression gained from the inspection of the camp strongly suggested that the system ought to be abolished, all the more so as production, which had risen to

45,000 tonnes in 1945, no longer corresponded to demand, and the employment of voluntary labour should have sufficed to produce adequate salt to meet purchasers' requirements.[34] The Governor General, Pièrre Cournarie, did not however agree with the views of the Commission supporting the abolition of the Koutal prison camp. According to him, the maintenance of the camp would be justified for years to come as the production of the salt works ought not to fall below 50,000 tonnes. He felt that in 1946, the Société des Salins du Kaolack ought to supply the colonies of the Federation with 68,100 tonnes. Besides, there were still difficulties in recruiting voluntary labour. The regulatory intervention of the state would remain essential even if, as Cournarie acknowledged, it was obvious that at a time when France was proclaiming the doctrine of free labour in West Africa, it was neither possible nor desirable for the government to procure forced labour for a private enterprise.[35] The only possible form of government assistance that could be envisaged was to maintain the camp at Koutal while improving conditions. Thus, the privilege granted to the Salins du Kaolack was to provide a special work-force flying in the face of social development already sanctioned by the provision of the 1946 Law of Houphouët Boigny.[36] An island of forced labour thus benefited from government protection, which guaranteed low wages and withdrew the enterprise from the need to face competition in the labour market. For, during the period between the end of the trading season and the beginning of agricultural activity, that is to say when the salt works were active, a large number of navétanes and unemployed hastened to the commercial port of Kaolack to assure the despatch of groundnuts until the beginning of the winter season. They were not attracted by offers of work at the salt works, however. Moreover, even when there was a serious increase in unemployment from 1950 on, which was only partly absorbed by the annual groundnut and trading season, the unemployed did not seek work with the Société des Salins du Sine-Saloum.[37]

Thus, despite the legal suppression of forced labour, coercion was used between 1946 and 1956 to assure a supply of workers at the salt works from February until the end of July each year. The Société des Salins du Kaolack employed an average of 300 workers, between 150 to 208 being provided by the prison camp of Koutal. During the period when salt was harvested, the salt works employed up to 500 workers for three months.[38] The non-prison labour was recruited thanks to the propaganda of recruiting agents supported by the administration, the targeted population consisting of penniless *navétanes* who had had a bad season.

The Société des Salins only modified its policy of forced employment from 1956 when mechanization of salt harvesting was introduced. Moreover, the opportunity of progressively establishing a stable core of voluntary workers allowed the company to build up a work-force whose destiny was identified with its own. The majority of these men were former prisoners who had served out their sentences and whose conduct and experience of the salt works led to them being taken on as contractual labourers. To this category of workers, who had broken off relations with society and often with their families, the Salins du Kaolack offered accommodation within the work site. This form of reintegration established firm links between the labourers of the salt works and the enterprise itself. The change in the regime of labour was completed in 1956, when the mechanization of salt harvesting effected an 80 per cent reduction in the normal labour force.[39] The Salins du Kaolack were then able to dispense with penal labour from Koutal. The prison, nonetheless, was not closed down. Prisoners were sent to work in quarries and in public works at Kaolack.

Conclusion

The case of the Société des Salins du Sine-Saloum illustrates well that industrialization started early in the colony of Senegal. The administrative district of Kaolack, situated at the heart of the groundnut basin, had already extended a welcome to the Lyndiane Cannery, established two years before the salt works. This agro-industrial unit was first devoted to the production of preserved meat before orienting itself rather to the canning of fish. It is true that the experience of this enterprise did not prove profitable,[40] but it is indicative of French imperial policy in introducing processing industries into Senegal. If this liberal strategy which assigned to overseas territories the function of producing the greatest amount of raw material at the lowest cost developed in Senegal,[41] it is necessary to note that one of its characteristics was the minimization of labour costs. This practice, however, seldom harmonizes with the principle of the freedom of labour. On the contrary, state intervention in the recruitment of the work force acts as a break on the development of social legislation. Moreover, by offering a protective wing to certain enterprises unable to face competition, the government may be considered to have hindered technological innovation. This paradox of colonial policy is manifest in the case of the Salins du Kaolack.

Compared with other colonies of French West Africa, the labour regime in Senegal was peculiar in one respect – free labour was dominant, whereas elsewhere mobilization of the labour force, at least until 1946, was assured by government coercion. This has often served as a screen hiding from view the practice of forced labour in the colony.

In Senegal, as elsewhere, government intervened in the recruitment of labour for private enterprises. From 1920 till 1940, the Société de Plantations de la Haute Casamance (Kolda), the Compagnie de Cultures Tropicales en Afrique, established at Wassadou (Administrative District of Tambacounda), the Société Industrielle des Mines de Falémé-Gambie and the Société Agricole de Lat Mirque (Kaolack) were all content for a long while to rely on the government for the supply of labour.

In the case of the Société des Salins du Kaolack, however, the peculiarity of the procedure lies in the composition of the work-force assigned to the salt works and the long duration of this practice. Recourse to this type of forced labour had been officially deplored since the Geneva Conference of 1930, but attempts to justify it were based on the importance of supplying the Federation of French West Africa with salt. This reveals the social conservatism flourishing within certain enterprises. The coercion of labour to supply the salt works with a work-force necessary for its operation was not an exceptional procedure arising solely from the war situation, however. The use of penal labour and government assisted recruitment lasted until 1956, ten years after the provisions of the Law of Houphouët Boigny legally suppressed forced labour.

Thus, the intervention of the colonial state enabled the Salins du Kaolack to continue with this cheaper solution rather than totally mechanizing the harvesting of salt. The maintenance of this social cancer was only possible because those condemned to hard labour were, in the public mind, worthy objects of opprobrium. As a result, a certain complicity underlay relations between government and public opinion. The prisoners were exposed to horrific working conditions, and held in conditions that were an affront to the rights of man. As labourers, they were subject to both physical and moral distress. Humiliated, underpaid and worked to the limits of their endurance, the salt-workers seemed to be damned souls labouring under a curse that darkened for many years the fate of those at the salt face.

The mechanization of salt harvesting, brought about in 1956, marked a turning point in the social policies of the Salins du Kaolack. From then on, a new era opened up for the enterprise which was now forced to face competition in the labour market. The myth of the curse, born of its past, however, has not as yet faded completely from the consciousness of Kaolack.

Notes and References

1 Ibrahima Diouf, 'Position of Salt in the Senegalese Economy', (University of Dakar, submitted for Masters Degree in Geography, 1977).

2 A. Dessertine, *A Secondary Port on the West African Coast* (Senegal, Kaolack Chamber of Commerce, 1959).

3 National Archives of Senegal (hereafter NAS), K334 (26), 'Labour Situation Salins du Sine-Saloum – 1945–46'. Letter from the Governor of Senegal to the Governor General of the Federation of French West Africa concerning the labour force of the Salins du Sine-Saloum, St Louis, 27 February 1944.

4 NAS, K334 (26), Note on salt from Sine-Saloum – Labour – Dakar 14 December 1943.

5 NAS, K334 (26), Administrative letter from the Director of Salins du Sine-Saloum to the Governor General of the Federation concerning salt supply for the Federation, Kaolack, 17 May 1944.

6 NAS, K334 (26), Administrative letter from the Director of Salins du Sine-Saloum to the Governor General of the Federation concerning salt supply to the Federation, Kaolack, 5 December 1943.

7 *Ibid.*

8 *Ibid.*

9 NAS, K334 (26), Note from the Governor General of the Federation concerning transportation of salt from Kaolack to the Southern colonies, Dakar, 19 July 1943.

10 *Ibid.*

11 NAS, K19 (1), Letter from the Governor General of the Federation to the Minister for the Colonies, Dakar, 3 February 1933.

12 NAS, K335 (26), Letter from the Direction Generale de A.P.A.S. to the Minister for France Overseas, Dakar, 19 April 1946.

13 NAS, K360 (26), Report of the Commandant of the Gendarmerie Section of Dakar, Dakar, 28 September 1946.

14 NAS, K360 (26), SAR (Amadou Babacar) 'Is Forced Labour Abolished?' in *A.O.F.*, 21 March 1947.

15 NAS, K260 (26), Note for the High Commissioner concerning the employment of the deuxième portion, Dakar, 5 January 1949.

16 NAS K334 (26), Letter from the Governor General of the Federation to the Governor of Senegal concerning the work force of the Salins du Sine-Saloum, Dakar, 21 December 1943.

17 *Ibid.*

18 *Ibid.*

19 *Ibid.*

20 Babacar Fall, 'Forced Labour in the Federation of French West Africa: The Case of Senegal, Sudan and Guinea' (University of Dakar, PhD thesis, 1984), pp. 258–9.

21 NAS, K334 (26), Letter from the Governor of Senegal to the Governor General of the Federation concerning the labour force at Salins du Sine-Saloum, 27 February 1944.

22 NAS, K334 (26), Administrative letter from the Director of the Salins du Sine-Saloum to the Governor General of the Federation concerning the salt supply to the Federation, Kaolack, 17 May 1944.

23 NAS, K334 (26), Report to the Governor General of the Federation and the Governor of Senegal concerning the situation of the Prison Camp of Koutal, Koutal, 6 June 1944.

24 NAS, K334 (26), Letter from the Director of the Salins du Sine-Saloum to the Commandant of the Administrative District of Kaolack, Kaolack, 12 May 1944.

25 NAS, K334 (26), Telegram from the Directorate of Colonies to the Governor General of the Federation, Algiers, 25 May 1944.

26 Conversation with A. G. who entered the salt works in November 1950 and has worked there 35 years, Kaolack, 17 April 1984.

27 Conversation with D. S., workman third class at the time of his retirement in 1977; taken on in 1946; fetter marks were still visible on his feet, Kaolack, 20 April 1984.

28 Conversation with I. S., typical of the second generation of workers at
    the salt works, born in the works compound in 1940 and employed under
    contract since 1968. His father had to work at the salt works for 30 years.
29 NAS, K334 (26), Report on the condition of the Prison Camp at Koutal,
    Koutal, June 1944.
30 Conversation with A. G., Kaolack, 19 April 1987.
31 *Ibid.*
32 *Ibid.*
33 *Ibid.*
34 NAS, K334 (26), Letter from the Governor General of the Federation to
    the Governor of Senegal concerning the Prison Camp at Koutal, Dakar,
    30 March 1946.
35 *Ibid.*
36 *Ibid.*
37 NAS, 2G 52/71, Regional Labour Inspectorate of Southern Senegal,
    Kaolack Annual Reports for 1952–53.
38 NAS, 2G 56/30, Regional Labour Inspectorate of Southern Senegal,
    Kaolack Annual Report, 1956.
39 *Ibid.*
40 Mohamed Mbodji, 'Attempt to establish an Agro-industrial Plant in
    Senegal: The Cannery of Lyndiane (Sine-Saloum) 1912–1919', in
    Enterprise and Entrepreneurs in Africa XIX–XXth Centuries (Paris,
    L'Harmattan, 1983), Vol. 1, *Laboratory 'Knowledge of the Third World'*,
    pp. 351–65.
41 Jacques Marseille, *Colonial Empire and French Capitalism – History of a
    Divorce* (Paris, Albin Michel, 1984), p. 275.

Ngoanyana: The Story of a South African Farm

Colin Murray

The point of departure of this story is the eviction at gunpoint of eighteen black families from a small white-owned farm in the eastern Orange Free State in October 1979. They were dumped in Onverwacht, which was at that time a newly established sprawl of tents, shacks, and tin toilets in the barren veld to the west of the Thaba 'Nchu district of Bophuthatswana (see figure 1). Now, officially known as Botshabelo, it is the largest relocation slum in South Africa, having well over half a million people in the late 1980s.[1] The purpose of this study, however, is not to explain this small episode of forced relocation in terms of the macro political economy of the present phase of reform and repression in South Africa.[2] Rather, it is to reconstruct some of the important socio-economic changes that have taken place in this part of the South African countryside through an intensely parochial focus on the history of one farm over a period of exactly 100 years. Incidentally, it will suggest that 'patterns of dispersal' in the eastern Free State have long and complex historical roots that can only be analysed adequately in the context of a detailed regional study.

There are two dominant landmarks in this undulating landscape: the looming bulk of Thaba 'Nchu itself (2,138 m) and the slightly lesser Thaba Phatshwa (2,049 m), 21 km to the south-east. Halfway between them lie two roughly conical bumps. The larger is Ngoana ('Child'); the smaller is Ngoanyana ('Little Child'). The farm with which this story is

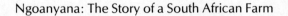

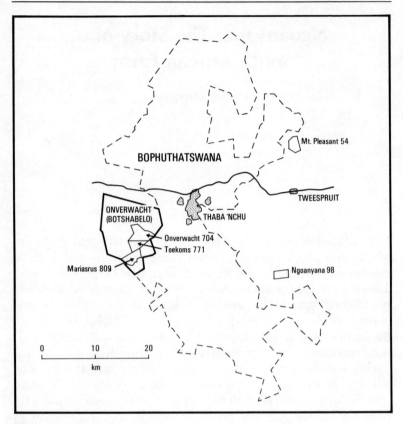

Figure 1 Thaba'Nchu, 1986

concerned is registered as Ngoanyana 98.[3] It was part of the old Thaba 'Nchu district but is now incorporated in the Excelsior district. The title dates from 1886. As one result of the discovery of gold on the Witwatersrand in that year, a wave of speculative capital washed over the Thaba 'Nchu district in the late 1880s. Ngoanyana 98 – much larger then than it is today – passed rapidly from black ownership into the hands of a land speculator who made his money in the Kimberley diamond mines. He sold his large estates in the district in 1901 to the Orange River Colony government, which established a substantial land settlement scheme for settlers of British stock on relatively small sub-divisions of the original large farms. This was the foundation of a self-consciously imperialist English-speaking farming community in the Tweespruit area, which survives today in the heart of a predominantly Afrikaner political constituency. Ngoanyana 98 belonged for nearly 80 years, until 1980, to the family of the Irish settler to whom the farm was allocated in 1902. It was the home base of an outstandingly successful farming enterprise that expanded rapidly through the first half of this century but which, after the death of its founder in 1951, fell into decline in the 1960s and 1970s. The old man's grandson went bankrupt early in 1979, and this was the most important circumstance which led to the eviction of the eighteen families in October of that year.

The detailed history of transmission of the title over this period is only of interest in so far as it leads us to explore the dynamics of particular socio-economic transformations. Three major themes emerge that are closely interconnected empirically and analytically. The first theme is the predominance of share-cropping, through the last decade of the nineteenth century and the first decade of the twentieth, as a relationship between white landowners and black peasant cultivators with their own ploughs and oxen. The second theme is the trajectory of capital accumulation which was launched by generous state assistance to white farmers in the period following the Anglo–Boer War, and which ultimately destroyed the possibility of an independent livelihood for black people on the land. The third theme, although this is implicit rather than explicit in the evidence presented here, is the capital intensification of white agriculture through rapid mechanization in the 1960s and early 1970s. This had two significant effects. On the one hand, most farms were increasingly heavily mortgaged to the Land Bank and the insurance companies. Combined with a strategy of excessive specialization in winter wheat, this left some farmers in the Tweespruit area dangerously exposed to the risk of insolvency, a risk sharply exacerbated by the drought of the early 1980s. On the other hand, mechanization was accompanied by a dramatic increase in black structural unemployment, manifest in the last two decades, in particular, through relocation on a massive scale from white farms to the Bantustans.[4]

The story of Ngoanyana is intended, then, to illustrate some of the themes that must loom large in any comprehensive history of agrarian change in South Africa from the late nineteenth century. Immensely valuable foundations for such a history have been established through a series of recently published regional studies: notably, *Putting a Plough to the Ground*, edited by Beinart, Delius and Trapido; Keegan's *Rural Transformations*; and Bradford's *A Taste of Freedom*.[5] These regional studies have themselves provoked a wide-ranging and vigorous critique of the methods and assumptions of a generation of social historians, on the grounds that they have failed to specify precisely the significant points of transition to capitalist agriculture and the political implications of this.[6] This study extends the chronological range up to the present but offers an extremely narrow focus on one farm and thus skates very lightly over the analytical problems and the deficiencies of empirical evidence that would need to be confronted in order to develop a comparably nuanced understanding of agrarian transformations in this part of the eastern Free State.

Land Alienation

The Barolong territory of Thaba 'Nchu comprised more than 1,000 square miles of valuable wheat, maize and pasture lands that adjoined the Conquered Territory taken by the Orange Free State republic (OFS) from the Basotho in the second Sotho–Boer War of 1865–8. Surrounded by the Boer republic, the Barolong political community maintained a precarious independence until 1884. In that year, a bitter succession dispute was brought to a climax when the incumbent chief Tshipinare was murdered by his rival Samuel Lehulere Moroka. President Brand of the OFS immediately annexed the territory. After protracted commissions of enquiry, freehold titles to 95 farms were granted to members of the Barolong aristocracy, mainly the sons and daughters of Tshipinare and close collateral relatives. Many other farms, however, were appropriated directly by the government of the OFS, and two reserves were set aside for African occupation (see figure 2).

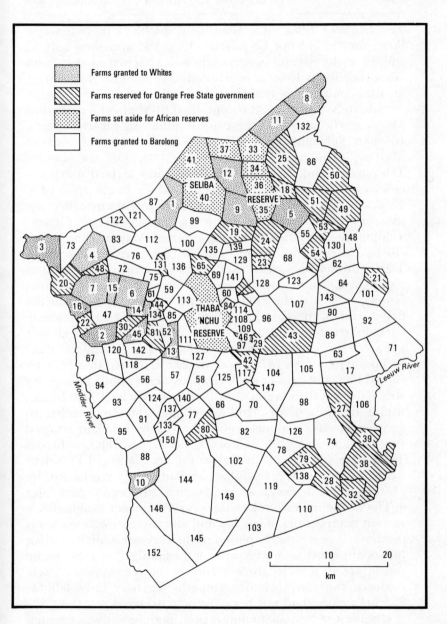

Figure 2 Thaba'Nchu, 1886

The freehold titles were nominally qualified in two ways. First, they could not be sold for 15 years, and then only to white people. Second, a servitude was attached so that bona fide residents in 1884 were entitled to remain on those farms for the remainder of their lives.[7]

Title to Ngoanyana 98 was granted to Michael Tshabadira Moroka, who also held the two neighbouring farms, Ngoana 104 and Springhaannek 105, and, in the name of his wife Majang, Groothoek 125 (see figure 2). On the day of Tshipinare's murder, Michael Tshabadira arrived much too late to be of assistance to his chief,[8] which might reflect the distance of his lands from the capital but might also reflect his thoroughly equivocal position in the royal genealogy. He was Tshipinare's son-in-law, having married Majang, one of the chief's daughters in his fourth house (see figure 3). His father Tshabadira, who died in 1874, had been half-brother both to Tshipinare (same mother) and Samuel Lehulere (same father), who was the only surviving male descendant in the first house of the old chief Moroka. Majang had previously been married to Motlhware, Moroka's grandson and heir apparent in the senior house, but he predeceased the chief without issue in the 1870s, and Moroka arranged that Majang should be taken over in the levirate by her cousin Michael. By strict custom, then, a son of Majang's by Michael Tshabadira would be 'raised for Motlhware' and thereby entitled to succeed Moroka. Samuel argued that Tshipinare had usurped the chieftainship on Moroka's death in 1880, whereas Tshipinare's claim, confirmed by the arbitration of President Brand of the OFS, was that he had been nominated by Moroka as his successor and had in any case been *de facto* ruler of Thaba 'Nchu in Moroka's last years.[9] Michael Tshabadira's various complex ties of kinship and affinity (figure 3) made his position more delicately poised in the succession dispute than that of any other senior member of the family. The fact that he was granted title to three farms is, however, prima facie evidence that any private sympathy he may have felt for Samuel's cause had not been publicly declared.

Despite the non-alienation clause, permission was granted by the Volksraad in 1887 to Richard Maramantsi (see figure 3) and Michael Tshabadira to sell their farms, on condition that

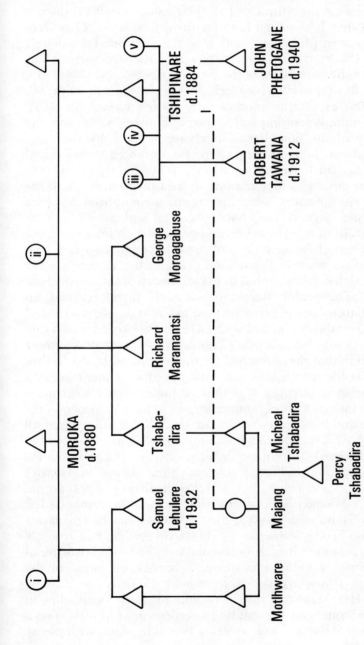

Note: Chiefs at Thaba 'Nchu in capitals

Figure 3 Partial genealogy of the Barolong aristocracy

they released their titles and all their followers left the district or that they left enough land for them to remain. They were the two most prominent landowners apart from Tshipinare's eldest son and heir, Robert Tawana. Richard owned four farms in the south-west of the district (figure 2, Nos. 144, 145, 146, 149) and Michael a block of three in the east (Nos. 98, 104, 105) as well as another in his wife's name (No. 125). Their initiative prompted a flurry of other sales and the waiving of the non-alienation clause, so that by the early 1890s about three-quarters of the land granted to individual Barolong had been sold to whites. Why did alienation take place so rapidly? Three reasons suggest themselves. First, the prominent grantees were profoundly demoralized by Free State rule. Second, they had no capital with which to farm successfully. Third, however, and perhaps most important, the millers and grain merchants of the Conquered Territory who handled the trade in Basutoland grain for the Transvaal were awash with surplus capital in the aftermath of the discovery of gold.[10] The senior Barolong notables, therefore, had an immediate incentive to realize their assets in the short term and to try to establish a better life elsewhere. They could reasonably expect to buy land in other regions at a substantially lower price than that they obtained for their farms at Thaba 'Nchu.

By far the most significant early speculative incursion into the Barolong territory was that of James Robertson, miller and grain merchant of Jammerberg Drift near Wepener on the Basutoland border. In November 1887, Robertson bought all of Michael Tshabadira's farms for £6,162, and in December all of Richard Maramantsi's farms for £10,380. Six months later, in June 1888, he sold all these lands to Charles Newberry (see below) for £24,262, realizing a substantial profit.[11] Michael Tshabadira and Richard Maramantsi left Thaba 'Nchu with some of their followers and bought farms near the Setlagole reserve in the territory that had recently been proclaimed British Bechuanaland. The Administrator of that territory found this move 'a remarkable proof of the estimation in which the Natives hold the privilege of living under Her Majesty's rule'. We find Michael Tshabadira in the late winter of 1889 building a settlement at Malibane on a tributary of the Setlagole river, 'a beautiful place, with plenty of trees'.[12] Later, however, he moved to the Bechuanaland Protectorate and became headman of a section of Samuel's impoverished refugees at Ramokgwebana in the Tati district. His son, Percy Tshabadira, succeeded to the chieftainship of the exiled Samuel on the latter's death in 1932. Percy Tshabadira, described by the anthropologist Isaac Schapera in 1943 as 'weak, ignorant and backward',[13] was sponsored by a populist opposition movement in Thabu 'Nchu in the late 1930s as the rightful chief there.[14]

Charles Newberry and his elder brother John were immigrant carpenters and builders who arrived in Natal in the early 1860s. After five or six years of persistent work at the Kimberley diamond diggings in the 1870s, they held eight full claims and their joint estate was worth about £25,000. As the process of company amalgamation gathered pace, the brothers added their claims to those of the Kimberley Central Diamond Mining Company, in which their joint shareholding in March 1881 was £71,660.[15] Charles built an impressive estate at Prynnsberg in the Clocolan district and invested in land on a large scale, initially in the Thabu 'Nchu district and later in Gordonia in the northern Cape. John built the mill at Leeuwrivier in the early 1890s, the largest of its kind in the OFS.

The Newberry estates at Thaba 'Nchu in the 1890s embraced not only the eight farms purchased from James Robertson in the transaction described above, but also Wonderkop 17, Lovedale 89, Eden 96 (together with a small portion of Egypte 107) and Kopjeskraal 150 (see figure 2). Some of the titles had been transferred free of servitudes, implying that no indigenous residents remained. Ngoanyana 98 was one of these. But many heads of families did not wish to leave the farms with Michael Tshabadira and Richard Maramantsi, and a list of their names was passed to James Robertson.[16] In addition to the 'insiders' who remained, it seems clear that the Newberry estates provided an opportunity for access to land for 'outsiders' also. Many of these were probably Barolong and Basotho who had been displaced from government farms leased to whites in the 1890s. Others may have 'spilled over' from the two reserves set aside for African occupation under the terms of the 1885 land disposition. An

OFS commission of enquiry into 'native squatters' in the Moroka district reported in 1890 that 'There are already many Kaffirs, who are entitled to reside on locations, but who are hiring ground from Newberry and other owners'. In respect of the potential threat to servitude rights that arose when land was sold to whites, the commission also noted that 'natives resident on farms sold in the district could have matters made so unpleasant for them by the owners, that they would rather waive their rights and simply reside with persons of their own tribe on farms such as Newberry's, where they would not be daily interfered with.'[17] More than 10 years later, Newberry's agent Harry Hanger recalled that Newberry had never taken any steps to find out how many people living on his land did not have servitude rights or were otherwise not entitled to live there.[18]

The Newberry estates, then, were representative of the large holdings of absentee landlords with no interest whatever in applying the anti-squatting regulations. The dominant contractual relationship was undoubtedly share-cropping.[19] There were also considerable opportunities for transport-riding.[20] Although share-cropping continued after the Anglo–Boer War, the relative security of tenure that applied in the 1890s was decisively subverted by new conditions. In the first place, both black and white inhabitants of the district were removed to concentration camps in the guerrilla phase of the war, and much livestock was stolen or dispersed. This caused such chaos that it was extremely difficult afterwards to assert servitude rights successfully. In the second place, the bulk of the Newberry estates, amounting to 45,446 morgen, was sold to the new colonial government in October 1901 for £90,891.[21] Land Settlement was to prove a very different regime for black share-cropping peasants.

Land Settlement

Land settlement was one of Lord Milner's particular schemes for reconstruction of the two new colonies (the former Boer republics) of the Transvaal and the Orange River, which had been devastated by the war. Its political object was to dilute

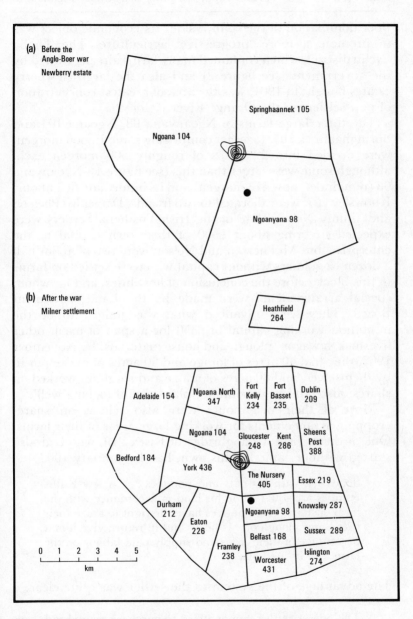

Figure 4 Milner's land settlement
(a) Before the Anglo-Boer war: Milner's Newberry estate
(b) After the war: Milner settlement

Boer domination of the countryside. Its economic object was to promote a more 'progressive' agriculture. The Thaba 'Nchu district, which contained many farms already owned by the government (see figure 2) and also the large Newberry estates bought in 1901, was the area of greatest concentration of new settlers in the Orange River Colony.

The three large farms of Ngoanyana 98, Ngoana 104 and Springhaannek 105, together comprising some 13,600 morgen, were divided into 22 farms of roughly 500 morgen each, although some were larger than this (see figure 4). Ngoanyana 98 (remainder, now 473 morgen) and its immediate neighbour, Knowsley 287, were allocated to two friends, Daniel McPherson and Jimmy Nelson, late of the Irish Fusiliers. Settlers were expected to bring about £500 of their own capital to the enterprise, but McPherson and Nelson were two of about half a dozen ex-soldiers without capital who were settled on farms in this block before the conclusion of hostilities, and for whom special arrangements were made by the Land Settlement Board. They were advanced what was judged to be the minimum working capital of £350 for a span of oxen, other livestock, a wagon, plough and house materials. By November 1902, they had 40 acres of forage and 30 acres of maize put in by themselves, and 80 acres of maize and sorghum worked on shares; also '100 bags potatoes, planted and looking well'.[22]

Most of their neighbours were also reliant on share-cropping arrangements for working large areas of their farms. One of them, Ernest Langbridge of Essex 219, who had also started without capital of his own, had by January 1903

> done well with his oats and potatoes . . . A few Kaffir families are squatted on his land in accordance with the local custom. These natives have the right to graze their cattle and plough on his farm, and in return give him a percentage of their crops and supply paid labour on the farm and in the house.

The advantage of the system to the settler was quite clear:

> The poorer settler cannot afford to purchase many head of cattle, but with natives on his land who plough for him with their own oxen, and who ride transport for him with

their own wagons, he is enabled to bring much more of his land under cultivation than would otherwise be possible.[23]

Fred Nicholson of Heathfield 264, which was a sub-division of the government farm Alexandria 43 to the north of Ngoana 104 and Springhaannek 105, started accumulating animals on a small scale from September 1903 through the sale of sorghum grown on the half-share system. His diary for this period contains a series of laconic entries to this effect: 'Bought a cow in calf for 5 sacks kaffir corn'; 'Bought two ewes for sack kaffir corn'; 'Bought a cow from Kaffir for 6 bags corn'; 'Bought 6 sheep from Kaffir for 3 bags corn. Kaffirs all drunk and one of my sheep missing in evening'. This enabled him to start ploughing with a single furrow plough.[24]

Thus the settlers were dependent on share-cropping arrangements in the difficult early years. They had to contend with drought, locusts and labour shortages; and many of their enterprises did not survive. The Secretary of the Land Settlement Board reported on a tour in April 1906:

> The Thaba 'Nchu and Ficksburg settlers, taken as a whole, continue to have the worst of luck . . . The general opinion was that the only solution, and the only way to get them out of their difficulties, was for the Government to assist them with a further issue of breeding stock on the share system, which had answered so admirably up to date, both in the interests of the Government and themselves, and to continue the development of their farms, principally as regards permanent water supply for stock and domestic purposes.

Specifically, the Board recommended that the assisted settlers – including McPherson and Nelson – should not have to pay interest on the £350 advance and that the principal should be repayable at settlers' convenience during the 30 years' period of purchase.[25] The Board operated a system of issuing livestock to settlers on shares; of carrying out water-boring operations at no cost to the settler; and of advancing fencing materials on loan repayable at 4 per cent interest over 10 years. In due course, some settlers reported enthusiastically on the progress they had achieved.[26]

The self-image transmitted to their descendants emphasizes the rugged virtues of the frontiersmen engaged in a struggle with a difficult environment. But the settlers recognized, of course, their dependence on a sympathetic state. At the time of the movement towards Responsible Government for the new two colonies in 1906, with a Liberal administration returned to power in London, the Thaba 'Nchu settlers were acutely anxious about the implications of a take-over of their affairs by a Dutch-dominated government. Their agitation was successful to the extent that a Land Board was constituted in 1907 that was accountable to the imperial and not to the colonial authorities for the administration of the settlers' affairs. In 1910 and 1911, the interest per annum payable on the original valuation of the farms was reduced from 4 per cent to 3 per cent, as was interest due on subsequent loans.[27] The standard terms included an additional 1 per cent p.a. payable for redemption, but many settlers had successfully applied to forego the redemption element until they were firmly established. In 1912, the new Union government passed an Act giving settlers in the OFS the absolute right to a Crown grant of perpetual quitrent tenure (virtual freehold), provided they entered mortgage bonds in favour of the government to cover the repayment of the balance of the purchase price of their farms. Much later, the original 30-year leases were due to expire in the depths of the severe economic depression that accompanied the great drought of 1932–3, and many settlers found themselves unable to meet the redemption payments. Fred Nicholson of Heathfield and Leonard Flemming of the farm Geluk near Dewetsdrop, who both knew Jan Smuts personally, successfully appealed to the government for legislation that extended the redemption dates of the settlers' mortgages.[28]

All this capital assistance and political indulgence gave decisive impetus to the passage of the 1913 Land Act that prohibited share-cropping. Plaatje observed the devastating effects of the Act throughout the Orange Free State in the same year that most settlers in the Thaba 'Nchu district obtained title to their farms. About half the black residents on

white-owned farms in the district were evicted as a direct
result of the prohibition of share-cropping.[29]

Accumulation and Decline

Daniel McPherson obtained title to Ngoanyana 98 in 1914.
He came to prosperity in the period between the First and
Second World Wars, a period remembered by the settler
families as one of strong rivalry between two 'Potato Kings' in
the area south of Tweespruit. McPherson was one of these
kings. The other was Jacob Boris Lurie, a Lithuanian
immigrant who arrived in South Africa in 1892 with £2 10s.
He worked as a butcher during the Anglo–Boer War and
served Tempe refugee camp outside Bloemfontein. He specu-
lated in produce and then grew potatoes on half-shares with
the settler who had been placed on Kent 286. In 1907, Lurie
rented Fortuinspruit 233 from its owner, and later bought that
farm and others nearby – Lovedale 89 and Prospect 649 –
making a total of 4,000 morgen. In the late 1920s, his farming
operations were conducted on a massive scale: 700 oxen, 56
ploughs, 70 cultivators and 24 harrows. 'On these farms he
has three large locations as in his busy season he employs up
to 600 natives.'[30] All were wage labourers, it appears, since
Lurie did not allow African-owned cattle on his land.
Interestingly, Lurie's labour arrangements were singled out
for admiring and yet also disparaging comment in the oral
evidence submitted to the Native Economic Commission in
February 1931. The majority of his labourers were alleged to
be women from Basutoland, more or less 'loose' in their
marital and sexual commitments. In response to questions
from the commission as to why Lurie could obtain all the
labour he wanted, despite not allowing African-owned cattle
on his farm, Dr James Moroka acknowledged that he paid
higher wages than generally applied but laid more emphasis
on the 'fact that, at Lurie's place, any Native can go there and
get a wife any day he likes . . . that is why Lurie has no
difficulty'. 'When a woman goes to Lurie's place, she is never
asked anything. She simply goes there and stays there and, as
long as she can go and cart wheat or scoffle potatoes or reap
mealies, no questions are ever asked of her.'[31]

There are no comparable figures on McPherson's operations based at Ngoanyana in the 1920s and the 1930s, but he was probably farming on a similar scale. An almost exclusive concentration on potatoes over more than 20 years enabled him to buy up the following farms: Belfast 168 in 1916, Worcester 431 in 1919, Schuinsekop 126 in 1921, Kent 286 in 1923, Merrydale 638 in 1927, Cranborne 190 in 1931, Sussex 389 in 1935 and various sub-divisions of Maseru 64 in the late 1930s (see figure 5). He was buying land in the 1930s when many others were being forced to sell up. When he died in 1951, his property in land comprised roughly 5,600 morgen and his estate was valued at over £100,000.[32] More significantly, he had no debts. This must be an unrivalled record of accumulation for a Milner settler in the Thaba 'Nchu district. He was, as his grandson John Nieuwenhuysen remarked, a 'most careful and excellent businessman'. Potatoes were his working life, but he also developed an interest in water-boring machines and indulged a passion for race-horses.[33]

Like Lurie, McPherson also employed hundreds of seasonal labourers at the height of the potato season. One of them, MT, who was born and brought up on Ngoananyana, recalled her experience as an adolescent in the late 1930s:

> We worked the potatoes. It was very hard. We got up in the dark, as soon as the call reached the village, and went off to work. And the papa [maize porridge] we took with us, there was nothing inside it, we ate it just as it was. Apart from that we used to steal his potatoes and cook them and hide the billycans where we were working so he wouldn't see them, [otherwise] he'd have a look inside to see if there were potatoes there. We worked the potatoes on all his farms – the lands to the south, Dawn, Kent Farm, Merrydale, all of them. It was tough. We had no blankets, we had nothing. We wore sacks. In the evening when we went to sleep your mother would take the sacks and sew them together, sew them together, to make a single cover. You got in a line and she'd cover you up with the sacking to go to sleep. That's how it was all the time we were growing up. And as you grew up you got a bit more money, up to R3 a month, £1 10s! They gave us rations of four tins of maize flour in the evenings.[34]

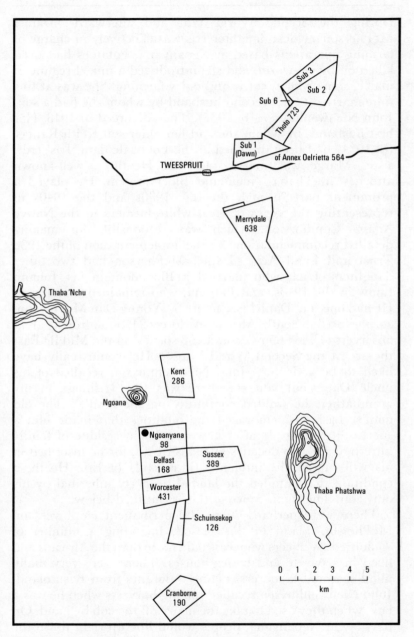

Figure 5 Daniel McPherson's estate, 1951

During the Second World War and afterwards, Daniel McPherson's eldest daughter Iris was effectively in charge of farming operations based at Ngoanyana. Potatoes had been killed off by eel-worm, and she introduced a mixed regime of maize, some wheat, cattle and dairy farming. She was at this time married to her second husband by whom she had a son, John Nieuwenhuysen (b. 1937). They divorced in 1948. Her first husband, by whom she had her elder son Keith Ranger (b. 1934) had been drowned in the Lovedale dam. Iris' half-sister Marge was married to Eric Heath, a well-known attorney in Thaba 'Nchu and Bloemfontein. He played a prominent part through the late 1930s and the 1940s in representing the views of local white farmers to the Native Affairs Commission, which was responsible for making detailed recommendations for the implementation of the 1936 Trust and Land Act.[35] Daniel McPherson had two other daughters: Una, who married a Bloemfontein vet Johann Louw in the 1940s; and Patricia, who remained unmarried. He had one son, Daniel (see figure 6). Young Dan McPherson, as one of the South African Airforce 24 Squadron's 'great observers . . . led 65 raids and 108 sorties' in the Middle East theatre of the Second World War.[36] 'He would really have liked to be a doctor,' John Nieuwenhuysen recalled of his uncle Dan, 'but you see there was this Irishness in my grandfather, he wanted continuity on the land'.[37] The old man's 'Irishness' embraced the qualities that made him a successful farmer. It also, however, left a residue of family bitterness for two decades after his death, for he inscribed in his will, under the influence (it is said) of Eric Heath, a condition that entailed the landed property inherited by his only son. The significance of this is outlined below.

There were perhaps 70 to 100 permanent employees on McPherson's land in this period, including a number of 'Coloured' overseers who were paid more than the Africans and lived in separate and better houses. There were very many more seasonal labourers, mainly migrants from Basutoland. John Nieuwenhuysen recalled the big harvests when he was a boy, when they used to take the maize off the cob by hand. On pay-day at Ngoanyana, people would line up right down the drive and receive their wages in cupped hands through the

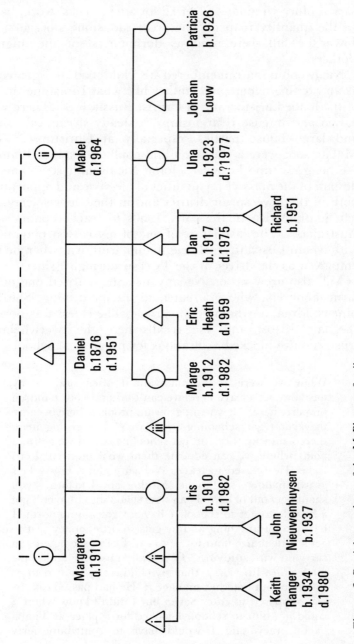

Figure 6 Partial genealogy of the McPherson family

barred office window – £1 or £2 for a few weeks' work, based on the quantity reaped. The great sandstone storage sheds down the hill were used as dormitories for the migrant workers.

Nieuwenhuysen remembered his childhood at Ngoanyana as an exciting experience, 'rather like what I imagine the life of the landed aristocracy in Czarist Russia was'. There were varied and intense relationships, a steady stream of visitors and large house parties, especially at Christmas.[38] The McPhersons were a close-knit and ebullient extended family. As he grew up, however, John Nieuwenhuysen came to despair of the massive inequalities of life-style and opportunity both in the Tweespruit district and in the wider society. He left South Africa in the early 1960s to teach economics in Australia.[39] 'The last I saw of one of my closest playmates, with whom I used to steal neighbours' fruit, was when he was employed as the driver of the Tweespruit night (shit) cart.'[40]

MT also grew up on Ngoanyana. She married one of the farm labourers, who graduated to tractor driving. She had nine children, of whom eight survive. The eldest was born in the late 1940s, and she recalls here the overwhelming frustration of blocked aspirations for progress at school:

> While we were at Ngoananyana I often said to my husband, let's leave here, we can't bring up our children properly here. They can't grow up properly here because they can't get schooling while we're just sitting here, there's no way they can get schooling, when we get to a point where we can educate them we'll be tired! Let's leave. He refused to leave. Well, my eldest boy – he's grown up now – said to me, 'Mother, speak to father, you should get out of here, I can't get schooling, I haven't got a bicycle to get to school, I haven't got any uniform. I haven't got anything and he gets so little money just to get a little maize flour for us to eat. I can't see how I can carry on with studying.' That really upset me and made me feel ill with worry, that my child really wanted to go to school but couldn't manage it. He had passed Six, he was supposed to enter Seven but I didn't know where I could get him to school. I looked for a place at Thaba 'Nchu, they said I would have to contribute forty

[?fourteen] rand for the building fund. I hadn't got
fourteen rand. So my child couldn't go to school.[41]

In the late 1950s and 1960s, more and more people moved
in to live on the farm in response to the increasing severity of
influx control elsewhere. Iris Nieuwenhuysen had to engage in
'fearful administrative procedures' with the Bantu Administration and Development (BAD) officials who attempted to
enforce formal registration of every resident. Acute official
anxiety in this period about *beswarting* ('blackening') of the
platteland is reflected in the 1959 Du Toit Commission's
publication of a map showing the extent of unsupervised
occupation by Africans of white-owned farms in three districts
of the OFS to the south-west of Thaba 'Nchu.[42] Although it
was possible for farm owners, if they chose, to resist state
pressure to reduce 'squatting', 'it was the easiest thing in the
world to get people off the farm'; and rapid over-crowding
made it very difficult to improve living conditions for Africans.
Keith Ranger, who took over the management of Ngoanyana
from his mother, never attempted to control the number of
residents. 'When the BAD officials came, there'd be people
drifting off into the veld or up the mountain or round the
corner into the woods, you see, they'd be living like fugitives to
a certain extent.'[43] Many of them depended on wage
remittances from the mines or towns.

By this time, the estate had been divided. Daniel McPherson
died in 1951. His estate passed to his children in equal
undivided shares, but there were restrictive conditions placed
on the shares of Dan, Una and Patricia (see figure 6). The
portions of the estate inherited by Una and Patricia were to be
administered in trust on their behalf by Eric Heath. Dan's
portion – the northern block of Dawn, etc. – was entailed by
the condition that 'in the event of his dying without lawful
descendants then such fixed property shall revert to the
estate', apparently because, as Dan himself expressed it with
bitter understatement years later, 'my marriage had not met
with universal approval'.[44] The old man feared that his
daughter-in-law, an English woman, would otherwise induce
Dan to sell his land and give up farming. The practical effect
of this attempt to 'rule from the grave' was to impose a heavy

constraint on Dan's farming operations, because he could not raise a mortgage bond on property entailed in this way. Dan felt that Eric Heath had usurped the role of paterfamilias through his effective control of four-fifths of the estate. The question of Eric Heath's allegedly misdirected influence over old Daniel McPherson remained, therefore, an extremely sensitive one within the family. Eric Heath's death in April 1959 was followed by the startling revelation that his trust account was in deficit to the amount of R30,000. Suspicion came to rest on his partner, however, who was some years later convicted for trust account fraud.

The ultimate irony of this part of the story is that the property of the two older McPherson daughters, Iris and Marge, on whose titles no conditions were imposed, has been lost to the family. Marge sold Merrydale in the 1960s. Iris and her son Keith Ranger, who inherited the block of land around Ngoanyana, went bankrupt in the late 1970s. By contrast, the northern block of Dawn and portions of Maseru, inherited by Dan McPherson and subsequently relieved by legal action of its onerous entailment, is the only part of the old man's estate that remains substantially intact. Heavily mortgaged, it is farmed today by Dan's son Richard. Una's land is still farmed by her husband Johann after her death in the late 1970s. Part of her sister Paddy's ground was bought by Bill Morgan who married Marge and Eric Heath's daughter Judy. She keeps up the McPherson tradition of Christmas hospitality.

The decline of Ngoanyana may be attributed to several factors. Along with other farmers in the district, Keith Ranger over-committed himself to the 'wheat revolution' launched by Sam Bairstow of the nearby farm Jevington: a decisive shift in the 1950s to mono-cropping of winter wheat on a summer fallow system, involving caterpillar tractors to plough in the stubble and more intensive use of fertilizers.[45] This experiment was initially successful but ultimately produced a fragility of soil condition that made mono-cropping of wheat very vulnerable to drought. Other factors were more personal. Keith Ranger was slow to shift to sunflowers. He was not temperamentally suited to farming. He was also, in common with many others in the district, a heavy drinker. The farm

never really paid its way. In the end they depended on his wife
Ann Ranger's salary as a teacher in Tweespruit.

Eviction

Keith Ranger and his wife and children left the farm at the
beginning of 1979. His mother Iris remained, married now to
her third husband, a retired Dutch sea captain named
Jordens. The bankruptcy put the farm workers and their
families in a desperate situation. They were not paid for eight
months, from January 1979 until their eviction in early
October. They were harassed by the Tweespruit municipal
police. MT takes up the story:

> Then this white man – what was his name? who was that
> Baas? Baas Fanthonnoro [van Tonder], he came and
> ordered us off. We didn't go, we refused. He shut the
> water off. He said we shouldn't use it, we should pay for
> his water. We refused. We got up at night and took the
> water anyway when he wasn't around. Another time he
> came and waved a gun at us, and fired it tuu! tuu! a few
> times. We scattered. Then we went to tell Mrs Jordens.
> 'Hela! This Baas is provoking us, he is shooting at us
> with a gun and ordering us off the farm.' She said tell
> him to come here. But he didn't turn up again. The next
> thing was the police came and took us all, they came and
> rounded us all up. Some got away, others went to gaol.
> Kids were just left in the huts with nobody to look after
> them. Someone from central government came and
> asked us what was the problem? We told them. We were
> just staying there but we had nothing, there was nothing
> we could do. So they phoned up Qwaqwa to come and
> get us. The commissioner just told us get your stuff
> together, tomorrow I'm going to fetch you, you are going
> to Onverwacht because you're in a real mess here. Yes,
> we said, we were. That's how we came to Onverwacht.[46]

Who was Baas van Tonder? Baas Johannes Hendrik van
Tonder was a victim of forced relocation. To explain this, let
us look westwards for a moment to a block of white-owned

farms lying between the Modder river and the boundary of the
Thaba 'Nchu district of Bophuthatswana (see figure 1): the
twelve farms identified in a press report of September 1978 as
due to be compulsorily expropriated by the central government
to create a vast new black township.[47] The farm Onverwacht
704 was owned by Ignatius (Naas) du Plessis, who had
bought it only the previous year. He was the butcher in Thaba
'Nchu until 1985, when he sold the business to his son. He has
lived there for 40 years and is known as Tsotsi to local
Africans. The adjoining farm, Toekoms 771, belonged to Coen
van Tonder, and Mariasrus 809 to Johannes Hendrik van
Tonder (apparently no relation). The owners were outraged
to discover the imminent loss of their land. There were
protracted negotiations with government officials, involving
no less than three valuations and argument over how much of
the compensation would be payable immediately in cash. Du
Plessis and Coen van Tonder were given seven days' notice in
May 1979 to leave their farms. 'On Tuesday this week,
government trucks rolled on to the farm of Mr Naas du Plessis
and workers began building a township to house 3,000
people.' Eventually the question of compensation was settled
out of court and those who were removed at a week's notice
received 100 per cent of the farm valuations in cash, by
contrast with the standard arrangement of 40 per cent in cash
and 60 per cent in government securities. Naas du Plessis was
reported as not unhappy since he made a profit of R15 per
morgen.[48]

Johannes Hendrik van Tonder bought Mount Pleasant 54,
north of Tweespruit (see figure 1), with cash from the
compensation for Mariasrus 809 and a loan from the Land
Bank. He then tried to buy Ngoanyana 98 for his son but
could not raise a bond on the property. Pending his failure to
do so, however, he evicted the 18 families from Ngoanyana
in the manner described above. He had a row with Iris
Jordens over his treatment of the people on the farm. He is a
man of formidable size and weight, and he personally
supervised the eviction from Ngoanyana. He then pointed
out to the refugees, when they were dumped in the D section
of the new slum, where his farmhouse had been on Mariasrus
809. One portion of the D section lies on a corner of his old

property. MT and her neighbours commented bitterly on the irony of this.

There is another small irony in the tail of this story. J. H. van Tonder failed to negotiate a bond for the purchase of Ngoanyana 98. The farm was bought, instead, by Naas du Plessis with a bond of R110,000 from the Bloemfontein Board of Trustees, whose chairman (an ex-mayor of Bloemfontein) he knows.[49] The transfer was registered in June 1980. Keith Ranger died in the same month, and MT was describing the desperate circumstances of the family in Onverwacht:

> I'm running about even at night, I lie awake the whole night worrying about how we can survive, what I can do, what I can sell in order to look after these mites deserted by their menfolk. They depend on me, if I don't get up even at night, they don't eat, they just stay as they are. So I get up and go to this white man and beg him, 'Hao! Baas, if you would only give me meat on credit, I'll pay you when I've finished selling it.' Well, he hands it over, so that I can sell it and pay him off, and struggle to find maize meal for my children. He writes me down in his book, that I'll pay him another time when I've sold the meat, and with what's left I buy maize meal. That's the truth, there's no-one who can say I'm lying.[50]

The white man concerned was the butcher in Thaba 'Nchu, Naas du Plessis. His manners were rough, she said, but he helped her by extending credit in this way. Having been brutally evicted from the farm where she had grown up and spent her working life, MT could get a dead sheep on credit from Naas du Plessis with which to struggle for a very marginal livelihood in the informal sector of a huge rural slum. He borrowed R150,000 in 1985 from the Standard Bank of Bophuthatswana on the security of his title to Ngoanyana 98.[51] The contrast provides a starkly appropriate index of their respective opportunities to improve their lives. Naas du Plessis has allegedly ruined good land at Ngoanyana by overloading it with stock reared for the slaughter-house. He is a butcher by profession, after all, not a farmer. Old Daniel McPherson must have turned in his grave. He lies in a small eucalyptus grove less than a stone's throw from the lovely sandstone mansion which he built in 1926, and which was destroyed by fire on 13 March 1982. His eldest daughter Iris Jordens sustained third degree burns in the fire and died of a heart attack on the following day.

Conclusion

The fortunes and misfortunes of the white and the black families who have lived and worked at Ngoanyana over 100 years have been inextricably intertwined. The particulars of the story are, of course, unique, but they encapsulate many significant changes that may be observed more generally across the southern highveld. Thus, events and experiences at the micro level reflect and illustrate structural tendencies at the macro level in the political economy of agrarian transformation in the region.

In this case, the annexation of African territory coincided with South Africa's second mineral revolution. This released a flood of 'English' speculative capital on to the land and led to the rapid alienation of African-owned farms. Black share-croppers survived and prospered, briefly, before they fell victim to various forms of imperial intervention and were displaced, in this district, by Milner's Land Settlement scheme and the state-sponsored capital intensification of white agriculture in the first and second decades of the twentieth century. As the white settlers acquired title to their farms, the remnants of a semi-independent black peasantry were dispersed and undermined. The enterprise at Ngoanyana in the 1920s and 1930s is a prime example of rapid capital accumulation based on a differentiated labour force of permanent wage employees and seasonal migrants from Basutoland. Wages were very low in cash and kind. Influx control tightened in the 1950s, mechanization proceeded apace in the 1960s, and commercial agriculture became saddled with a burden of debt in the 1970s that, for many white farmers, proved overwhelming. Some farms became, in effect, dumping grounds for a black population that was 'surplus' in two senses. First, it was very difficult for families to find anywhere else to live, and many drifted on to farms although they were primarily dependent on urban wage incomes. Second, a squeeze on black employment in white agriculture inflated the number of 'squatters' vulnerable to eviction either by landowners or by state agencies. Hence the flood of refugees into rural slums such as Onverwacht/ Botshabelo in the 1970s and 1980s.

Notes and References

1 For an account of Onverwacht/Botshabelo in the early 1980s, see *Forced Removals in South Africa* (Cape Town, The Surplus People Project, 1983), vol. 3, *The Western & Northern Cape & Orange Free State*, pp. 166–74.
2 See C. Murray, 'Displaced urbanization: South Africa's rural slums', *African Affairs*, 86 (1987), pp. 311–29; W. Cobbett, 'Behind the "Curtain" at Botshabelo: Redefining the Urban Labour Market in South Africa', *Review of African Political Economy*, 40 (December 1987), pp. 32–46.
3 Ngoanyana is the Serolong equivalent of the Sesotho Ngoananyana. The registration of the farm as Ngoanyana reflects the local domination of Serolong political culture in the late nineteenth century and original ownership by a member of the Barolong aristocracy. Sesotho-speaking inhabitants of the area refer to the hill and its immediate environment including the farm as Ngoananyana. My usage of the two terms in this paper consistently follows this small difference.
4 The first two themes above are explored for the southern highveld region as a whole in T. Keegan, *Rural Transformations in Industrializing South Africa* (Johannesburg, Ravan Press, 1986). The third theme is examined in M. de Klerk, 'Seasons that will Never Return: the Impact of Farm Mechanization on Employment, Incomes and Population Distribution in the Western Transvaal', *Journal of Southern African Studies*, 11 (1984), pp. 84–105.
5 W. Beinart, P. Delius and S. Trapido (eds), *Putting a Plough to the Ground: Accumulation and Dispossession in Rural South Africa 1850–1930* (Johannesburg, Ravan Press, 1986); Keegan, *Rural Transformations*; H. Bradford, *A Taste of Freedom: the ICU in Rural South Africa, 1924–1930* (New Haven, Yale University Press, 1987).
6 M. Morris, 'Social History and the Transition to Capitalism in the South African Countryside', *Africa Perspective*, New Series 1, 5 & 6 (1987), pp. 7–24.
7 For full details of land dispositions, see C. Murray, 'Land, Power and Class in the Thaba 'Nchu District, Orange Free State, 1884–1983', *Review of African Political Economy*, 29 (1984), pp. 30–48.
8 Parliamentary Papers C.4263 [December 1884], Enclosure E with Despatch No. 67, Resident Commissioner, Basutoland, to High Commissioner, Cape Town, 17 July 1884, *Colonies: Africa 17* (Irish University Press edition), p. 497.

9 For various accounts of the genealogical intricacies of the argument, see
   S. M. Molema, *Chief Moroka: His Life, His Times, His Country and His
   People* (Cape Town, Methodist Publishing House, 1951); J. Wales, 'The
   relationship between the Orange Free State and the Rolong of Thaba
   'Nchu during the Presidency of J. H. Brand 1864–1888' (Rhodes
   University, unpublished MA thesis, 1979), chapter 7; R. L. Watson,
   'The Subjection of a South African State: Thaba 'Nchu, 1880–1884',
   Journal of African History, 21 (1980), esp. pp. 360–2.
10 T. Keegan, 'Trade, Accumulation and Impoverishment: Mercantile
   Capital and the Economic Transformation of Lesotho and the
   Conquered Territory', *Journal of Southern African Studies*, 12 (1986), p. 205.
11 Orange Free State Archive, Bloemfontein (hereafter, OFSA), AKT
   2/1/144, Land Register Thaba 'Nchu.
12 Parliamentary Papers C.5363 [April 1888], Annual Report,
   Administrator, British Bechuanaland, to High Commissioner, Cape
   Town, 30 September 1887, *Colonies: Africa 44* (Irish University Press
   edition), p. 437; United Society for the Propagation of the Gospel,
   archive held in Rhodes House, Oxford, Missionary Reports E44
   (1889B), report of Revd Henry R. Bevan on St Michael's Phokoane for
   quarter ending 30 September 1889.
13 I. Schapera, 'The Native Land Problem in the Tati District',
   unpublished report to the Bechuanaland Protectorate Government,
   1943.
14 C. Murray, 'The Barolong Progressive Association: local politics and the
   struggle for land in the eastern Orange Free State', *Africa Perspective*,
   New Series 2, 1 (1988).
15 The first figure is Charles Newberry's own estimate, given in a few pages
   of parsimonious and moralistic reminiscences of his life which he
   compiled for his children in 1912. I am indebted to his grandson John
   Moffett of Kirklington, Clocolan, for access to this brief autobiography.
   The second figure is taken from R. Turrell, *Capital and Labour on the
   Kimberley Diamond Fields 1871–1890* (Cambridge, Cambridge University
   Press, 1987), p. 218.
16 OFSA, ORC 46 (1901), Report on the Moroka District, Annexure Z,
   evidence of Harry Hanger; DLS 2 A40, enclosures with letter from
   Hanger to Land Settlement Board, Bloemfontein, 3 April 1902.
17 OFSA, ORC 46 (1901), Annexure S.
18 OFSA, DLS 2 A40, H. Hanger to Land Settlement Board,
   Bloemfontein, 3 April 1902.
19 This did not, however, imply an absence of capital investment in
   farming operations on the part of Newberry himself. Roderick Finlay
   remembered, for example, that he and his brothers were taken to the
   concentration camp at Thaba 'Nchu in 1901 in wagons drawn by
   Newberry's steam-tractor. Marge Bairstow, letter to author, 2 April
   1985.
20 Keegan, 'Trade, Accumulation and Impoverishment', p. 207.
21 OFSA, DLS 4 A230, Purchase of Farms by Land Settlement Board.
22 OFSA, DLS 4 A294, DLS 17 A1213, reports of Walter S. Cohen, 1902;

DLS 117 A4340, memo K. Apthorp (Secretary Land Settlement Board) to Colonial Secretary, 26 June 1906.

23 E. F. Knight, *South Africa After the War: A Narrative of Recent Travel* (London, Longmans, Green & Co., 1903), pp. 147, 153. Knight was special correspondent of *The Morning Post*.

24 'Frederick Nicholson of Heathfield', *Africana Notes and News*, 22, 5 (1977), p. 208. I am indebted to his daughter Agnes Oats of Linksfield, Johannesburg, for access to her father's diary for the period September to December 1903. The entries quoted are for 2, 3 and 20 October and 12 November 1903.

25 Public Record Office, Kew (hereafter PRO), CO 224/20 f19936, Apthorp's report, 30 April 1906.

26 PRO, CO 224/30 f40222, Annual Report of Land Board 1908–9, including letter from W. A. Crout, Mount Pleasant, to Apthorp, 14 September 1909.

27 PRO, CO 224/33 f11300, memo Goold-Adams to Crewe, 28 March 1910; CO 551/9 f38606, Annual Report 1909–10.

28 Act 25 of 1932. 'Frederick Nicholson of Heathfield', pp. 209–10. Flemming was a writer whose light satirical style in verse and short stories conveys a strong sense of the desperate importunities of the early years of Land Settlement. See his *A Settler's Scribblings in South Africa* (London, Stephen T. Green, 1910) and his autobiography *The Call of the Veld* (London, Hutchinson & Co., 1924).

29 S. Plaatje, *Native Life in South Africa* (London, P. S. King & Son, 1916; reprinted New York, Negro Universities Press, 1969). The estimate of evictions in the district is derived from the magistrate's figures given in the report of the Beaumont Commission, U.G. 22–1914, p. 22; Appendix XI, p. 6.

30 Interview with Lul Lurie, J. B. Lurie's elder son, Fortuinspruit, 4 September 1983; 'Mass Production of Potatoes', *Farming in South Africa* (June 1928).

31 University of South Africa, Pretoria, Documentation Centre for African Studies, Native Economic Commission 1930–32, Oral Evidence, vol. 8, pp. 4882–3, 4918.

32 I am grateful to Richard McPherson of Dawn, Tweespruit, for access to papers relating to his grandfather's will.

33 Interview with John Nieuwenhuysen, Daniel McPherson's grandson, London, 1 December 1983.

34 Interview with MT, Thaba 'Nchu, 14 July 1986.

35 This is a separate and very interesting issue. In the late 1930s and late 1940s, respectively, there were two waves of purchase of white-owned farms by the South African Native Trust. On the one hand, farmers felt uncertain about the future market value of their property if it was adjacent to the 'released' areas, and so they felt impelled to resist expansion of those areas. On the other hand, once expansion was seen to be inevitable, many were anxious for their properties to be included in the 'released' areas because the rates of compensation proved attractive.

36 E. M. Tucker and P. M. J. McGregor, *Per Noctem Per Diem*, The Story of

   24 Squadron, South African Airforce (Cape Town, 24 Squadron Album
      Committee, 1961).
37 Interview, John Nieuwenhuysen, 1 December 1983.
38 Years later, at Onverwacht, the women who made enormous salads for
   Iris Nieuwenhuysen's house parties at Ngoananyana remembered them
   still. Some people's lavish hospitality was other people's unpaid
   overtime.
39 Hugh Macmillan has recently reviewed the circumstances that led 'the
   more critical younger economists', including Nieuwenhuysen, to leave
   South Africa in the early 1960s. See his paper 'Economics, *Apartheid*
   and the "Common Society" ', presented at the Conference on the
   Southern African Economy After Apartheid, Centre for Southern
   African Studies, University of York, 29 September to 2 October 1986,
   p. 27.
40 John Nieuwenhuysen, letter to author, 22 April 1987.
41 Interview with MT, Thaba 'Nchu, 14 July 1986.
42 *Commission of Enquiry into the European Occupancy of the Rural Areas*
   (Pretoria, Government Printer, 1959), reprinted in *The Oxford History of
   South Africa*, vol. 2, *South Africa 1870–1966* (Oxford, Oxford University
   Press, 1971), p. 105.
43 Interview, John Nieuwenhuysen, 1 December 1983.
44 Papers in the possession of Richard McPherson relating to the
   administration of Daniel McPherson's estate.
45 E. B. Dickinson, 'Wheat Development in the Orange Free State: Some
   Recollections', *Fertilizer Society of South Africa Journal*, 2 (1978), pp. 73–8.
46 Interview with MT, Thaba 'Nchu, 14 July 1986.
47 *Volksblad*, 9 September 1978.
48 *Sunday Tribune*, 6 May 1979; *Friend*, 14 May 1979. Interview with Naas
   du Plessis, Thaba 'Nchu, 9 July 1986.
49 Deeds Office, Bloemfontein, MB 8011/1980. Interview, Naas du Plessis,
   9 July 1986.
50 Interview with MT, Onverwacht, 13 June 1980. The circumstances of
   this household in Onverwacht/Botshabelo over the years 1980–6 are
   described and analysed in C. Murray, 'The Political Economy of Forced
   Relocation: A Study of Two Households Through Time', in J. Suckling
   and L. White (eds), *After Apartheid: Renewal of the South African Economy*
   (London, James Currey, 1988), pp. 36–46.
51 Deeds Office, Bloemfontein, MB 6357/1985.

The Administration of Resettlement in Ethiopia Since the Revolution

Alula Pankhurst

Prior to the Revolution in 1974, resettlement in Ethiopia occurred largely on an *ad hoc* basis, through the individual initiative of local governors, without any centrally coordinated policy.[1] By the time of the Revolution, 20 settlement sites had been established, including some 7,000 household units, which represented less than 0.2 per cent of rural households.[2] This slow rate of resettlement has been attributed mainly to a lack of commitment to changing the land tenure system which hindered the implementation of Government plans.

After the Revolution, resettlement became far more important. By the end of the first post-revolutionary decade, some 45,000 households, comprising 180,000 people and representing 0.68 per cent of total rural households, had been resettled on 88 sites in 11 regions.[3] Three main factors explain this six-fold increase. First, the Land Reform Proclamation nationalizing rural land removed the greatest obstacle impeding the implementation of earlier plans and proposals. Second, two successive nation-wide famines within the span of a decade

This paper is based partly on a study of earlier reports and government documents, and partly on fieldwork in Western Wellegga from October 1986 to June 1988. The research was made possible by a grant from the Economic and Social Research Council of Great Britain. Thanks are due to the Ethiopian Government Relief and Rehabilitation Commission for facilitating travel and providing data, to Addis Ababa and Manchester Universities, and to the aid agencies Irish Concern and Secours Populaire Français for their support.

highlighted the need to seek long-term solutions. Third, the Government established the Relief and Rehabilitation Commission in 1974 and the Settlement Authority in 1976, finally merging the two organizations and the Awash Valley Authority to form a new integrated Relief and Rehabilitation Commission (RRC) in 1979.[4]

Resettlement since the Revolution can be divided into three phases: (i) the first decade (1974–84) during which the RRC organized resettlement; (ii) the emergency phase (1984–6), organized by the Workers' Party of Ethiopia; and (iii) after a 'consolidation period' (1986–7), a small-scale resumption of resettlement (1987–8). A new settlement authority is to be set up to take charge of further resettlement. Since government policy regarding this new phase is still in the process of finalization, and the exact nature and powers of the resettlement authority are not yet clear, the present discussion will be confined to reporting details of settler movements between November 1987 and May 1988 after the 'consolidation period', without speculating on possible future policy changes.

After discussing the history of post-revolution resettlement, this paper seeks to classify schemes by type of settler, motivation, settlement environment and external organization. Differences between high-cost 'conventional' settlement clusters in the lowlands, and low-cost 'integrated' settlements in the highlands are considered with reference to scale, concentration and inputs.

Social and economic considerations are the subject of the final section. Demographic trends are discussed, and the inverse correlation between previous density and resettlement is explored. Various types of interaction with the local population are classified according to the degree of contact and exchange between settler and local communities. Economic performance is measured in terms of area of land and production per household in order to assess self-sufficiency. Finally, issues raised by the need for longer-term sustainability are considered.

The First Decade (1974–84)

The Relief and Rehabilitation Commission (RRC)

The drought in the early 1970s and the *ancien régime*'s neglect of the issue provided an important stimulus for preventive action. As a result, the RRC was set up by Order no. 93 of 29 August 1974. The famine situation led the new Ethiopian Government to investigate the underlying problems of production. A World Bank mission participated in the enquiry, and concluded that: 'If major resettlement and land use improvement programmes were not implemented within the next decade, increasingly severe famines and further deterioration of living standards would follow.'[5] The single most important measure that facilitated further resettlement was, however, the Land Reform Proclamation no. 31 of 5 March 1975, which paved the way for Government use of under-utilized land for further resettlement. From 1975 to 1977 the RRC was involved in seven settlement sites comprising some 17,000 settler households.[6]

The Settlement Authority (1976)

A sign of the Government's determination to push ahead with resettlement and give it more prominence was the establishment of the Settlement Authority by Proclamation no. 78 of 4 February 1976. The Authority, which was an autonomous unit within the Ministry of Agriculture, had a specific brief to take charge of all resettlement activities. All pre-existing schemes, including those run by non-governmental organizations, were accordingly handed over to the Authority. It took over 28 settlements with a population of almost 13,000 households and resettled an additional 30,000 households between 1976 and 1979 in over 80 sites.[7] A plan was formulated to resettle 20,000 families per year.

The new Relief and Rehabilitation Commission (1979)

Three years after the setting up of the Settlement Authority, this body was merged with the former RRC and with the

Awash Valley Authority to form a new institution with the old name of Relief and Rehabilitation Commission. This change was effected by Order no. 173 of April 1979. The new RRC was an autonomous body accountable to the office of the Chairman of the Council of Ministers. The merger had the effect of linking relief in the famine zones in the north more closely with rehabilitation efforts in resettlement areas in the south and west. In 1979, some 5,000 settlers from famine areas in Wello were resettled in Wellegga and Bale administrative regions (as provinces were renamed after the Revolution). A plan was put forward to resettle 40,000 households annually.

Numbers of settlers

Despite confusing figures, a clear trend of increasing numbers of settlers is discernible. The first RRC was responsible for seven sites with some 17,000 households. In 1976, the Settlement Authority took charge of 28 settlement sites with some 13,000 households and resettled a further 30,000 households. By the time of the setting up of the new RRC in 1979, some 30,000 new families had been resettled. In 1980, the RRC was responsible for some 40,000 households,[8] in over 80 sites, a figure which rose to almost 46,000 by 1984. Estimates for the total settler population, which are usually derived from numbers of household heads, range between 140,000 and 200,000.

Since the Revolution, the number of settlements increased four-fold to 88 sites, situated in 11 administrative regions. By January 1985, just over 35,000 families were receiving assistance from the RRC. This represented a total population of about 123,700 persons, or an average of 4 persons per household living in 74 settlements. The decrease in numbers is due to the integration within the local administration of 11 settlements that had become self-reliant, and the conversion of two which became part of state farms. Of the 74 settlements, 57 were assumed to have become self-reliant in food and clothing, based on 1984 yields.[9]

Financial costs of resettlement

Estimating costs of resettlement poses difficulties given scarce and conflicting data. Nonetheless, a considerable and steady increase in expenditure is clear. Annual expenditure on resettlement before the Revolution was less than US$1 million.[10] This figure rose to $5 million during the Settlement Authority administration and, with the amalgamated RRC, reached $24.6 million in 1979.[11] In the first three years of the 1980s, the annual average was almost $31 million. Expenditure on resettlement had, thus, increased six-fold in the decade since the Revolution. Government expenditure on settlements prior to the Emergency Phase was assessed at $100.1 million for the period 1980–7, suggesting an average annual expenditure of $14.3 million.[12]

The question of expenditure per household is complicated by the difficulties of establishing population figures, keeping track of changes, and comparing estimates. A number of assessments have been put forward, ranging from $1,800 to $5,200 per household or $400 to $1,100 per settler.[13] Actual government expenditure from 1980 to 1987 on previously established settlements was estimated at $3,160 per household or $734 per settler,[14] which would suggest a running cost of $450 per household or $105 per settler, per annum.

Assessments

Resettlement during the first phase (1974–84) was criticized in several reports on a number of counts.[15]

1   The pace of resettlement was considered too slow to have a significant impact on population pressure in the highlands. Although close on 46,000 settlers had been relocated by 1984, this represented a mere 0.6 per cent of total rural households. According to the Ethiopian Highlands Reclamation Study, 4.3 million people or 860,000 families will have become landless in the highlands by the year 2010.[16] The Resettlement Strategy Proposals suggest the need for 645,000 families to be resettled over 25 years, i.e. an average annual need for rural resettlement of approxi-

mately 25,800 families or 129,000 people.[17] The plan set out by the new RRC in 1979 to relocate 40,000 settlers per year was clearly beyond its means. In fact, the annual resettlement rate achieved by the RRC, during the first decade of its existence, was only 4,500 families.

2 Evidence of high costs and low productivity, particularly in the high-input schemes, gave rise to concern about their economic viability and sustainability. Moreover, ten years after they were set up, only about a quarter of the original tractors were operational in a number of mechanized sites,[18] and in some sites declining yields posed a threat to long-term agricultural sustainability.[19] However, based on 1984 yield production, 57 out of 74 settlements were considered 'self reliant in terms of the ability of settlers to cover food and clothing requirements for their families'.[20] A more recent report that assesses self-sufficiency in terms of the average required household land and yield suggests that, with the exception of irrigated lowland schemes, most old settlements are well on the way to food self-sufficiency. Out of 14 rain-fed resettlement complexes, 11 produced above the annual nutritional household requirement of seven quintals.[21]

3 Certain unpopular policies led to desertions and account for the lack of success of some schemes. In particular the element of coercion, especially of unemployed urban youths with neither the motivation for nor the experience of agriculture, is held to account for the failure of such schemes. Another unpopular policy was the settling of single male household heads without their families, with the intention that they would clear the land and receive their families once they were established. However, the hardships in the initial stages were compounded by both the psychological stress of isolation from wives and families and, perhaps more importantly, the added practical difficulties for men unused to domestic work such as fetching water and firewood, and cooking. As a result, desertion rates were high until the families were brought to join the settlers.[22] Family reunion, therefore, became a priority and the policy of settling men first was discontinued by the RRC.

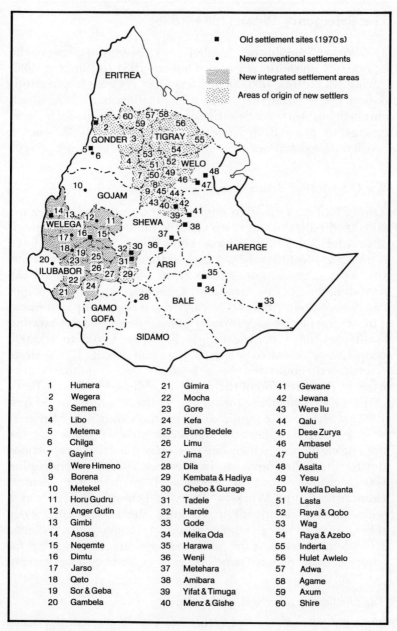

Map 1 Location of settlement sites

1	Humera	21	Gimira	41	Gewane
2	Wegera	22	Mocha	42	Jewana
3	Semen	23	Gore	43	Were Ilu
4	Libo	24	Kefa	44	Qalu
5	Metema	25	Buno Bedele	45	Dese Zurya
6	Chilga	26	Limu	46	Ambasel
7	Gayint	27	Jima	47	Dubti
8	Were Himeno	28	Dila	48	Asaita
9	Borena	29	Kembata & Hadiya	49	Yesu
10	Metekel	30	Chebo & Gurage	50	Wadla Delanta
11	Horu Gudru	31	Tadele	51	Lasta
12	Anger Gutin	32	Harole	52	Raya & Qobo
13	Gimbi	33	Gode	53	Wag
14	Asosa	34	Melka Oda	54	Raya & Azebo
15	Neqemte	35	Harawa	55	Inderta
16	Dimtu	36	Wenji	56	Hulet Awlelo
17	Jarso	37	Metehara	57	Adwa
18	Qeto	38	Amibara	58	Agame
19	Sor & Geba	39	Yifat & Timuga	59	Axum
20	Gambela	40	Menz & Gishe	60	Shire

The Emergency Phase (1984–1988)

This phase should be divided into three sub-phases: the emergency phase proper from October 1984 to January 1986, during which time 600,000 settlers were relocated, a 'consolidation phase' from February 1986 to October 1987, which entailed no further resettlement, and a small-scale new emergency phase from November 1987 to May 1988, when a further 10,000 settlers were relocated.

The October 1984 Action Plan

The 1984 Ten Year Plan envisaged the resettlement of some 800,000 families in stages up to 1994, involving the movement of around 3–4 million people altogether.[23] This would have represented less than 10 per cent of the population. However, the worsening famine situation in the north led to the abandoning of this gradual approach in favour of an emergency programme to be carried out on a campaign basis. The emergency phase proper began as the second devastating famine within a decade struck Ethiopia. Close to 600,000 people were relocated within a year and a half. The scale of resettlement could not have been increased to that extent without the direction of the newly established Workers' Party of Ethiopia which organized the entire venture. In March 1983, a high-level committee under the Council of Ministers was set up to plan the Government's response to the impending famine which began to take on crisis proportions during the following year. In October 1984, an action plan was formulated by the Political Bureau of the Central Committee of the Workers' Party of Ethiopia.[24] This was a wide-ranging document envisaging short-term emergency relief, as well as a whole range of longer-term projects. Resettlement was but one of several options. It accounted for a quarter of the planned expenditure on emergency development.

The resettlement component of the plan

The section of the October Action Plan dealing with resettlement proposed that 300,000 family heads (an estimated

1.5 million people) be resettled over two years in two phases. Phase 1 would cover 50,000 families (half from Wello, half from Tigray). Phase 2 would cover 250,000 families (125,000 from Wello, 75,000 from Tigray, 50,000 from Gonder plus an undetermined number from Shewa). The settlers were to be relocated in Wellegga, Ilubabor, Kefa, Gojjam and Gonder administrative regions. 300,000 hectares were to be cultivated with 540 tractors and 150,000 plough-oxen, and produce an expected yield of 5.34 million quintals.[25]

Financial costs of the emergency programme

The emergency plan set out a budget of $265.96 million for development, excluding emergency daily assistance in the famine areas.[26] The settlement component represented just over a quarter of the proposed expenditure ($61.72 million) and was to be financed from Government reserves (76.2 per cent) and internal loans (23.8 per cent). The breakdown of the resettlement expenditure was to be as follows: 37.8 per cent on agricultural equipment, 35.7 per cent on oxen, 10.4 per cent on implementation, 8.1 per cent on transport and 8 per cent on land preparation and construction. The RRC estimate was slightly higher: $86.4 million (excluding transport). The breakdown was to be as follows: 60.2 per cent on oxen and agricultural implements, 26.9 per cent on agricultural machinery and services, 6.2 per cent on agricultural inputs, 3.4 per cent on salaries and 3.3 per cent on oil and lubricants.[27]

Actual government expenditure for part of the resettlement component alone far exceeded the total emergency budget. In the three year period 1985–7, expenditure on the new resettlement sites amounted to $282.2 million, or $90.5 million per annum for 176,000 households.[28] Some 45 per cent is accounted for by the Ethio–Italian Tana–Beles project. The remaining expenditure was spent as follows: food, utensils, clothes and agricultural equipment, 65 per cent; Ministry of Agriculture expenses, 24 per cent; transport and administration, 8 per cent; and State farm at Gambella, 2 per cent. RRC expenditure of $113.5 million accounted for 73 per cent.[29] The above estimate of $155 million spent by the

Government does not, however, take into account input by the Ministries of Construction, Health, Education and Water Resources. Total expenditure was, therefore, considerably higher. Government expenditure may be estimated provisionally at some $200 million. Foreign assistance may account for another $200 million (including the $150 million Italian-funded project). Expenditure, including foreign assistance, would, therefore, be $2,285 per household or $755 per settler for three years, i.e. $761 and $251 annually. Expenditure in areas without foreign assistance would be about half the above figures.[30]

Implementation of the plan

In less than a year and a half, between October 1984 and January 1986, two-thirds of the target had been reached. Over 200,000 households consisting of nearly 600,000 people from five regions in the north, resettled to six regions in the west and south-west. The vast majority of settlers (96 per cent) originated from three areas: Wello (63 per cent), Shewa (18 per cent) and Tigray (15 per cent). The bulk of the settlers (96 per cent) were relocated in four regions: Wellegga (42 per cent), Ilubabor (24 per cent), Gojjam (17 per cent) and Kefa (13 per cent) (see table 1).

Table 1 Settlers by region of resettlement and region of origin

Area of resettlement			Area of origin					
Region	Settlers	%	Wello	%	Shewa	%	Tigray	%
Wellegga	253,282	42.7	220,636	87.11	11,279	4.45	21,367	8.43
Ilubabor	146,216	24.7	72,226	49.39	28,275	26.17	45.715	31.26
Gojjam*	101,122	17.1	29,839	29.50	54,858	54.24		
Kefa	79,828	13.4	50,690	63.49	6,514	8.15	22,634	28.34
Gonder*	6,397	1.1						
Shewa	6,149	1.0			6,149	100		
Total	592,994	100.0	373,392	63.0	107,075	18.1	89,716	15.2

Note: The total of 101,122 settlers from Gojjam includes 16,425 settlers (16.24%) resettled within the same region; all the settlers from Gonder were resettled within the region.

Source: RRC,unpublished figures provided by the RRC for the year 1986.

Some changes took place during the execution of the plan. Only two-thirds of the proposal was put into practice in the year and a half from October 1984 to January 1986, when the programme was halted for a consolidation period. Over 200,000 families were relocated, but this represented only 600,000 people, as the actual average household size was around three persons rather than the estimated five.

The administration of resettlement

The emergency phase of resettlement required considerable effort and involved large areas of the country. The programme was planned and supervised by the Workers' Party of Ethiopia (WPE), and all sections of the population from the local peasant associations to university students and staff were mobilized in a series of campaigns to prepare temporary shelters and build rudimentary housing. The WPE issued overall directives to the Ministries of Agriculture, Health, Construction, Transport and Communications, and to the National Water Development, and Relief and Rehabilitation Commissions. The RRC was responsible for the transport of settlers and provision of food, basic clothing, household utensils and agricultural hand tools. Over 25,000 personnel from government departments and mass organizations were mobilized on a full-time basis to take part in the Action Plan. In February 1985, a new law required all working Ethiopians to contribute one month's salary over a twelve month period to combat drought.[31]

International assistance

Significant assistance has been provided by five foreign governments: the Italian, Soviet, Canadian, East German and North Korean.[32] The Italians are financing the multi-million Tana–Beles project.[33] The Soviet Government assisted with the transport of settlers by providing planes and the transport of food by supplying trucks and drivers. They also financed a hospital in the Asosa region.[34] The Canadians are partly funding the aid agency Concern.[35] The German Democratic Republic assisted in transport of settlers by plane and funded a hospital for the Metemma resettlement scheme.[36] The Democratic Republic of North Korea is providing labour for an irrigation project in the Gambella settlement area.[37]

Over a dozen non-governmental agencies were involved in supporting the earlier resettlement during the first decade of post-revolution resettlement.[38] However, the subsequent Emergency Phase resettlement was perceived as controversial and politically sensitive. The US Government was opposed to any resettlement and its lead was followed by the UK, FRG and several other EEC countries. The major aid agencies 'did not want to go against the policy of the USA from which many of them got their resources'.[39] Only four secular aid agencies became involved in the emergency phase resettlement. The French Secours Populaire Français was the first to become involved in March 1985. It was followed by the Austrian/ West German Menschen für Menschen in May 1985 and the Irish Concern in November 1985. The Norwegian Save the Children, Redd Bàrna, started a programme in January 1987. In addition, four religious organizations became involved: Jesuit Relief Service, the Mekane Yesus Evangelical Church, the Catholic and the Adventist missions.[40] Several international organizations including UNESCO, UNICEF, UN Development Programme (UNDP), Food and Agriculture Organization (FAO), World Health Organization (WHO) and World Food Programme (WFP) have also assisted or are considering assisting resettlement with limited indirect aid as part of their country-wide programmes.[41]

The consolidation period and the 1977–8 resettlement

The resettlement programme was temporarily suspended at the end of January 1986, precisely when the famine threat was coming under control. The timing of the halt to resettlement was no doubt due to internal reasons related to the famine and production cycle rather than, as some commentators have assumed, to external pressure.[42] As the famine became widespread and more severe, most peasants had no alternative but to sell their plough-oxen, thereby losing their stake in the land. Those who managed to survive without doing so regained hope when the next rains came, and fewer of them were willing to leave. At the same time, the Government became less concerned with trying to do something to counter the crisis, since it was subsiding. The logic of government response has, in fact, been closely correlated to the intensity of famine. As the situation worsened, the Government became more anxious to do something long-term; moreover an awareness of dependency on external aid and a sense of frustration was generated and, in the face of disaster, resettlement was perceived as a purposive, positive and hopeful step, irrespective of what the outside world thought. It is, therefore, not surprising that resettlement was resumed at what, to foreign eyes, seemed the worst possible time, when resources were most stretched, as a new famine was expected. To predict the likely extent of resettlement, we therefore need to look at the early warning indicators for drought.

For almost two years after the suspension, no further resettlement took place, and government efforts were directed towards extending support to settlements through the Ministries of Agriculture, Health and Education. Other issues, most notably villagization, came to the forefront of government social and economic policy, and resettlement received little publicity. However, resettlement still remained a national priority and is referred to in the new constitution.[43] In the last quarter of 1987, harvests were poor, and the possibility of a famine of equal proportion to the 1984–5 famine was considered by the Government and by aid agencies. The resettlement programme was resumed in November 1987 amid reports of impending famine. The new famine did not, however, take on the proportions of the 1984–5 one, and the pace of resettlement correspondingly slackened. In the six months from the end of November 1987 to the end of May 1988, some 10,715 settlers forming 4,265 households were relocated. The breakdown was as follows: 2,501 households comprising 5,352 people were moved from Wello to Pawe settlement in Gojjam, and 3,599 households comprising 5,363 people were moved within Gonder to Metemma settlement.[44]

Types of Settlement

Resettlement can best be conceptualized by taking into account the three factors that make up organized schemes: settler backgrounds and motivations, settlement environments, and external inputs.

The settlers' background

Three main types of settler may be considered according to occupational background: peasants, nomads and urban dwellers. Resettlement during the first post-revolutionary decade involved all three categories of settlers, although the composition changed. The Settlement Authority took over a variety of schemes, and in 1976 the composition of settlers was as follows: 43 per cent were urban, 23 per cent peasants with little or no land, 18 per cent nomads, 9 per cent agricultural labourers, and 7 per cent charcoal producers or retired soldiers.[45] By 1981, over half were from the famine-prone and overcrowded highlands (39 per cent were drought victims and the rest came from densely populated areas) The rest were composed of nomads (26 per cent) and urban unemployed (20 per cent).[46] The emergency phase was concerned predominantly with peasants and not with nomads or urban settlers.

In terms of the reason for their resettlement, settlers may be divided into three categories. They were victims of (i) drought and famine; (ii) overpopulation and land degradation; and (iii) conflict and warfare. While resettlement during the first decade after the Revolution rehabilitated war victims from the Ogaden conflict, the emergency phase was concerned predominantly with famine and drought and, to a much lesser extent, with overpopulation and land degradation. (A small proportion of the settlers from Shewa came from the densely populated areas of Kembata and Hadiya in southern Shewa.)

Resettlement motivation

International media coverage of resettlement in Ethiopia during the emergency phase was predominantly concerned with the issue of coercion. The controversy surrounding a number of incidents succeeded in conveying the image that the entire programme was an exercise in coercion.[47] In fact, government criteria for selection included willingness of heads of households to be resettled, to bring along their dependants and to engage in agriculture, as well as their satisfactory physical condition (age and health).[48] According to Kurt Jansson, head of the UN Emergency Office in Addis Ababa:

> during the first phase of the resettlement programme in the winter and spring of 1985 most observers agreed that the programme was voluntary.[49]

However,

> in the second half of 1985 it became difficult to find people willing to be resettled, partly because of the beginning of good rains and much improved food distribution. The local authorities had problems filling their planned targets of settlers. It was during this stage that force and coercion were being used, although this was against the announced policy of the government in Addis.[50]

> Regional authorities in Tigray and Shoa had ceased to select settlers by September 1985, very few still wanting to go. In Wello settlers were still being selected, but once the rains began there was great reluctance to move.[51]

> Regional administrators thought it appropriate to select families whose *meher* crops had failed completely, or were in debt and unable to repay, or were cultivating slopes above 30 degrees. Others included people who had migrated to a feeding centre.[52]

Concern about coercion has, however, obscured the fact that the majority of settlers came 'voluntarily' or, rather, were forced by the famine to take up the Government's offer of a new life elsewhere. In fact, settlers often contrast the emergency phase, when they volunteered for resettlement, with the earlier resettlement of the late 1970s, which they refer to as *giddaj* or forced resettlement. Willingness to resettle did not mean that settlers were not reluctant to leave their homes, nor that the decision was an easy one. Peasants were faced with a desperate situation as the famine worsened: the longer they tried to keep their oxen, in the hope of being able to last out until the next ploughing season, the more the price of oxen decreased, and the terms of trade between livestock and grain became unfavourable. Once peasants were forced to sell, however, or let their animals die for lack of fodder, they no longer had a stake in the land. Even if they could have survived until the next rains, they would not have had oxen with which to plough and would have become dependent. This explains why so many were willing to leave when given another chance to become productive farmers. The motivation of settlers who were famine victims was, however, by no means straightforward and often involved difficult choices.[53] The most common expression used by famine victims who resettled was '*Yeihil wiha gudday new yassaddeden*', i.e., 'It was a matter of grain-water [grain and water] that sent us into exile.' Closer examination usually reveals, however, that the motivation was far more complex. Many who could have relied on relatives chose not to, in accordance with the ethos of independence which states, 'We won't beg from their hands.' Some settlers showed signs of great altruism in accordance with the ethic of kinship. As one young man who left his father and sister succinctly explained, 'What I eat could be for my sister.' Others left for the sake of a relative as expressed in the oft-heard saying, '*issu yebellaw amora yiblagn*' ('Let the kite that eats him eat me'). Large numbers left in response to peer and/or community pressure: as one man expressed it, '*gorfu neddan*' ('The torrent drove us'). Others responded to the fear of a worsening situation. As one man who still had reserves of food explained, 'I had sold my oxen and heard that those who had done so should resettle; when you say "wush" to a donkey all the others' ears stand up.'

What is more surprising is that a considerable proportion of settlers were not famine victims, but opted for resettlement, without being destitute, in the hope of better opportunities. Resettlement attracted large numbers of young people who led a marginal existence in the northern highlands and who chose resettlement often without informing their parents, who would have tried to dissuade them. Large numbers of settlers fit the classical image of migrants dissatisfied with the old world and seeking a new world on the frontier.[54] The most common statement by such migrants when asked about their motives for resettling was '*zim biyye mettahu*', literally 'I came silently'; the term has lost its original literal sense and has come to mean: 'I simply came', or 'I just came'. This initial response is in itself significant as it distinguishes this category clearly from those who came because the famine had reduced them to destitution. The next most common statement was '*tegibbe*', literally 'I was full' or 'satiated', though the metaphorical meaning which has become the current one is to be arrogant, conceited, perhaps even unruly, irresponsible and lacking in maturity and respect. This word is of interest in that it defines people who are non-conformist. It is highly significant that it was used in a famine situation since it highlights the diametric opposition between those who came because they had too little in their stomachs (*yeihil wiha gudday*, a question of 'grain-water') and those who came because, as it were, they had too much (*teggebu*). With hindsight, several young men saw their decision to move as impetuous and ill-considered. They describe it as '*yelijinnet neger*', 'an act of youthfulness'.

Many young men left for resettlement with ambitions of self-improvement, some with hopes of furthering their education, others with illusions of participating in town life, many wishing to become soldiers.[55] Some settlers stressed that they took a sudden, spur-of-the-moment decision. Statements such as '*fentirre*', literally 'I leapt up', or '*biddig biyye*', 'I got up suddenly' or '*bedinget, salassibew mettahu*', 'I came suddenly, unexpectedly', were frequently used. These young people often left suddenly or surreptitiously to prevent relatives from dissuading them. Others, on the other hand, did not bring their whole family because they 'wanted to see the land first', with a view to bringing their relatives, after they felt established.

Some of the youngest settlers had lost their parents or had parents who were too poor to support them and had, therefore, placed them in *yesew bet*, '[other] peoples' houses', in other words not with relatives, in houses where they became virtual servants. Before the famine, in cases where the

children were small the parents would receive some remuneration and, if they were older, they could hire themselves out
for a modest sum. During the famine, no such payments were
made and many 'orphans' decided to take the opportunity to
leave. As one young lad explained: 'I had no one responsible
for me and decided I wouldn't be ruled over in some one else's
house.' Young people even left without their parents' consent
and/or without telling them. In one case a young man recalled
how his father 'picked up a stick' to try to prevent him. There
are a variety of escape stories with the common statement,
'*tefiche mettahu*', 'I disappeared' or 'I escaped and came.' Some
had quarrelled with their parents. As one young man
succinctly put it: 'We clashed on "I will go out of the hut, no
you won't" ', i.e. whether the son would or would not set up a
separate homestead. A large number of young people left
partly because of family disputes, often with step-parents. As
the saying goes, '*innatiyya tirraggetalech inde ahiyya*' ('The step-
mother kicks like a donkey'). A number of poor young men,
who had married wealthy women and worked for their affines,
also decided to leave. Many of those who had been married
were parted from their spouses in the famine when conditions
worsened. Often one spouse would go to look for wage labour
or relief food, while the other, generally the woman, would
stay at home, but would be unable to survive until the spouse
returned and, therefore, joined the resettlement. A few even
decided to split up or left their spouses when the situation
became difficult.

The decision to leave often involved painful choices and
inevitable separations. Many old people refused to come,
saying 'What use is someone else's land to an old woman' or
'May the earth of my homeland clothe me.' Peoples'
allegiances to parents and spouses were put to the test.
Sometimes a spouse would refuse to go, deciding to remain to
look after an elderly parent. In some cases, a wife would leave
her parents to go with her husband, while in others she would
leave her husband to go with her parents. As one woman
commented, 'You can always find another husband, you can't
find another father.'

The settlement environment

Resettlement is affected by both physical and human environments. The most important physical factors are availability of water and altitude. The vast majority of the resettlement projects established in the emergency phase were rain-fed; however, large-scale irrigation projects were set up in Gambella, Ilubabor region and in Metekkel, Gojjam region.

As far as altitude is concerned, there is a significant difference between land below 1,500 metres, traditionally designated as *qolla*, and that above, termed *weyna dega*. A little over half the emergency phase (55 per cent) took place in the lowland regions. The prevalence of several major diseases is closely correlated to the physical environment. The lowland resettlement schemes required considerable malaria control programmes, and some attempts are being made to counter the tsetse fly challenge in altitudinally marginal areas (such as Jarso and Qeto),[56] in order to permit ox-drawn plough cultivation.

The human environment is closely interrelated with physical factors. Historical patterns of spontaneous settlement were largely determined by physical constraints, and density correlates closely with altitude.[57] The lowlands and river basins have been inhabited by a number of ethnic groups practising different types or combinations of modes of production. These semi-nomadic groups live in scattered, sparsely settled communities. The populations include hunter-gatherers, pastoralists, hoe-agriculturalists and fishermen.[58] The more densely-populated highlands are inhabited by sedentary crop-growers.[59] After the Revolution the population in the highland areas was organized into peasants' associations and is currently being regrouped into villages.[60] The emergency resettlement was carried out in both zones with a slight preponderance in the lowland areas.

External organization

The level of government intervention in resettlement schemes has been the subject of several classifications, all of which hinge on the extent of governmental or non-governmental input. Simpson distinguishes between high inputs (full-time on-site extension staff), medium inputs (part-time staff), and low inputs (no resident staff).[61] The RRC made use of two different sets of distinctions: first 'low cost' (labour intensive) as opposed to 'special' settlements and, second, resettlement schemes 'under budget' (where the RRC has full economic responsibility) as opposed to those 'under technical assistance' (where inputs are more limited).[62]

In the present emergency phase the above dichotomies correspond to the distinction between so-called 'conventional' and 'integrated' schemes (see below). The bulk of the present phase of settlement (97 per cent) is in these two types. Conventional settlements represent 53 per cent of the total, and are located mainly in the lowlands of Gojjam, Wellegga and Ilubabor. Integrated settlements represent 44 per cent, and are mainly in the highlands of Ilubabor, Wellegga and Kefa. There is also a third type of settlement which is integrated into already existing settlement sites (mainly in Wellegga), which account for the remaining 3 per cent, or some 16,000 people.

Conventional and integrated schemes

Kuta gettem or *medebegngna*: conventional or combined settlements

Two Amharic terms are used to designate what has been termed conventional settlement. The first, *medebegngna*, implies 'allotted' or 'established' and hence 'conventional', while the second and more current term, *kuta gettem*, conveys the idea that individual plots are joined together to form one large unit as in a *kuta* or toga made of several pieces of cloth. Preferable translations, if the sense of the former term is desired, may be 'allocated' or 'designed' settlements. If the meaning of the latter term is to be emphasized, the translation might be 'combined' or 'unified' settlements. Conventional settlements involved mechanized agriculture and the linking of settlements into complexes located mainly in the sparsely populated western lowland, which required land clearance and disease and pest control.

Conventional settlements are in the process of becoming producers' cooperatives and were allocated a series of campaigners, including technical extension agents from the Ministries of Agriculture and Health, and the RRC, as well as cadres from the Workers' Party of Ethiopia, to organize the peasantry into peasants', women's, and youth associations, and to oversee resettlement administration.

Sigsega: integrated or insertion settlements

The Amharic word *sigsega* is used to designate what have come to be known as integrated sites. The term conveys the idea of filling in empty spaces and a better translation may be 'insertion settlements'. Integrated settlements receive much less costly and sophisticated equipment than conventional settlements, principally plough oxen and seed. Integrated settlements were initially assisted by the local peasants' associations which constructed shelters and ploughed the land for them in the initial year. Integrated settlements were scattered, mainly in the western highlands, and varied in size from a handful to a couple of hundred households. Integrated settlements received minimal overall government directives, tended to show a preponderance of private agriculture, and did not benefit from on-site technical support.

Differences between conventional and integrated settlements

The Amharic terms *kuta gettem* or *medebegngna*, and *sigsega* convey opposite meanings. The 'combined' settlements are planned with large areas set out or allocated for the settlers in largely unoccupied land, while the 'insertion' settlements seek slots of free land to fit settlers into an existing land tenure structure.

Since the terms 'conventional' and 'integrated' have gained currency, they will be used in this paper. The difference between these two types of resettlement could be conceptualized in terms of their most important links. Conventional settlements rely mainly on 'vertical' links with the state, while integrated settlements are supposed to have 'horizontal' links with the local peasants' associations. Three main differences between these two types of resettlement may be distinguished.

1 *Scale*. In theory, conventional settlements are made up of villages of 500 households while integrated settlements comprise about 50 households. In fact, conventional settlements are often slightly above the model and integrated settlements may comprise anywhere between 2 and 800 households. The distinction according to scale is, however, useful since most settlements fit this dichotomy.

2 *Concentration*. Conventional settlements are organized in complexes that comprise between 10,000 and 20,000 households, normally within a radius of 100 kilometres. The concentration justifies expenditure on mechanized agriculture, collective facilities such as schools, clinics, mills, cooperative shops, and campaigners living in the sites. Integrated settlements, by contrast, are scattered relatively inaccessibly and are often quite far apart.

3 *Inputs*. Members of conventional and integrated settlements received the same food ration (500 gm/person/day) in the initial stages of resettlement, but the former also sometimes obtained salt, pepper and a greater variety of food more regularly. Three main types of input may be considered.

a) *Personnel*. Both types of settlement are provided with extension staff, but conventional settlements have resident campaigners such as Workers' Party of Ethiopia cadres, health‹workers, agricultural extension staff, literacy campaigners, and RRC food distributors, while the integrated settlements do not have on-site extension staff, but receive visits from agricultural extension staff, each of whom supervises several sites. Three successive campaigns of cadres were assigned to conventional settlements on a yearly basis. Their role was to give overall direction, organize settlers into peasants', women's and youth associations, apportion the settlers into work teams, supervise agricultural and construction work and provide political education. The number of cadres was gradually reduced from nine per site in the first year to six in the second and three in the third. After the third year cadre campaigners were removed from individual conventional settlements. Each complex of about half a dozen sites is,

however, assigned a team of cadres who are located in one
site, which becomes the *wereda* or district headquarters.
Conventional settlements are due to become producers'
cooperatives; particular emphasis was, therefore, placed
on collective agriculture. In conventional complexes, each
settlement of 500 households was allocated two health
workers, and every three months two literacy campaigners
teach for a period of three months in accordance with the
national campaign system currently in its nineteenth
round. Two conventional settlements form a unit named
zerf which is allocated five or six agricultural extension
workers who specialize in different aspects, e.g. a *zerf* team
leader, a conservationist, a livestock expert, a cooperative
organizer and an 'all-rounder' for each site.

b) *Means of production.* Both types of settlement are
provided with agricultural hand-tools and seeds by the
RRC. Conventional settlements receive tractor services,
however, while integrated settlements are provided with
oxen. There are exceptions, though. The conventional
complex at Jarso has already successfully moved towards
considerable reliance on oxen while the Qeto complex is
also being supplied with oxen by the aid agency Concern.
Conversely, a few integrated settlements (for instance in
Dale Sedi wereda in the Qeto area) have benefited from
tractor services loaned from nearby conventional settlements.

c) *Infrastructure.* Both types of resettlement have grain
stores and buildings for literacy and health care, but
conventional settlements have been provided by the
Government with better health and educational facilities
since such settlements are larger and several sites may
share facilities. A couple of conventional sites are often
twinned and share a cooperative store and a grinding mill.
Feeder roads are built as well as offices for the peasants',
womens' and youth associations, craft workshops, model
houses and cultural centres. In the case of integrated
settlements, on the other hand, it was the local peasant
associations who were responsible for preparing pro-

visional housing before the settlers arrived, and ploughed land for them in the first year. In many cases, the peasants' associations did much more: providing food, cooking and household utensils and water carriers, providing seed and loaning oxen for ploughing, and treading in the *tef* after sowing. Close links often developed between the local peasants' association leadership and the settler executive committee.

As with government inputs, international assistance has concentrated on conventional settlements, notably the large-scale Italian project at Pawe, the Canadian-backed projects run by Concern in Wellegga, the Soviet hospital in Asosa, and the East German hospital at Metemma. The Jesuit Relief Service project at Kishe supports a small-scale conventional project in Kefa. Integrated settlements, on the other hand, are supported by the German agency Menschen für Menschen in Ilubabor, by the Norwegian Save the Children, Redd Barna, and several churches such as the Evangelical Church Mekane Yesus, the Catholic and the Adventist missions in Wellegga. The French agency Secours Populaire Français, based at Qeto, has a health centre, which was initially set up to assist the conventional settlements, but which also serves the nearby integrated settlements, as well as the local population.

Social and Economic Considerations

Demography

Sex ratios

The sex ratio in both conventional and integrated settlements is slightly unbalanced in favour of men. In 1977, 53 per cent of the population in conventional settlements and 53.1 per cent in integrated settlements was male. National figures show a slight preponderance of women, 50.1 per cent, as does a Wello figure of 50.5 per cent.[63] This would suggest that resettlement attracted more single men than women. The imbalance has, however, begun to even out, as earlier figures for 1986 reveal a slightly higher imbalance, with 55.2 per cent male in conventional settlements and 54.3 per cent in integrated settlements. This may be explained by a greater rate of desertion by men. The proportion of female-headed households has increased from 9.5 per cent in conventional settlements in 1986 to 9.9 per cent in 1987, and from 13.6 per cent in integrated settlements in 1986 to 14.9 per cent in 1987. It is unclear why integrated settlements should have a larger proportion of female-headed households, though this may be due to less pressure to get married.

Age composition

Figures for age breakdown provide the following percentages: 15.5 per cent for the 0–5 years age-group, 28.7 per cent for the 6–17 age-group, 52.8 per cent for the 18–60 age-group, and 2.9 per cent for the over-60 age-group. Comparison with the national average shows a lower proportion of small children and old persons: the national figure for the 0–4 age-group is 17.7 per cent and the over-60 age-group represent 6.2 per cent.[64] These figures correspond with what one would expect, since the birth rate was low in the initial stages and child mortality was high, many of the elderly people refused to leave, and those who did were probably more likely to suffer from difficulties in adapting and higher mortality rates.

Family size

The average resettlement household size is 3.2 compared with a rural average of 4.1 in Wello, and a national average of 4.4.[65] The size of conventional settlement households (3.24) is almost identical to that of integrated settlements (3.23). A number of reasons account for the small family size in settlements.

1 Many families lost members during the famine.
2 Many families chose a strategy of leaving employed family members behind or splitting the family in the hope that those who remained would have enough grain to survive without selling their oxen, thus avoiding destitution and dependency.

3 Some individuals, especially elderly persons, could not be persuaded by their families to leave their homes.

4 Some individuals saw resettlement as a chance to leave families with whom they were in conflict (notably adolescents and people who had disputes with their spouses).

5 There were a number of involuntary family separations, either due to incidents of coercion or when family members entered shelters at different times and/or boarded different buses, on the assumption that they were going to the same place; some failed to find each other in large transit shelters, which partly explains the existence of 'orphans' in the sites.

6 Many peope had to make difficult choices, when some members of their family were in favour of resettling and others opted to remain. There were cases of women leaving their parents behind when their husbands chose to move and vice versa. The RRC family reunion programme is working on reuniting separated family members and has a special orphan programme. In addition, many settlers have managed to establish contact with relatives elsewhere and correspond with them regularly. In a number of instances, individuals or families have undertaken their own family reunion by moving to join members of their family in other settlements. However, the issue of family separation remains one of the strongest grievances of many settlers who have otherwise adapted to a new life.

Natality

Figures for the conventional sites provide a birth rate of 36 per thousand compared with 31 per thousand in the integrated sites.[66] The difference may be explained by better ante-natal and post-natal health care in conventional sites, and possibly by more rigorous accounting. These figures are, however, low in a country with a birth rate of 47 per thousand, and can be explained by the fact that births were few in the first six months of resettlement, no doubt for a combination of nutritional and emotional factors. In the Qeto settlement complex, there were 10 times as many deaths as births during the first three months, and five times as many in the next three.[67] Within the first year, the number of births exceeded the number of deaths and, in 1988, there were four times as many births as deaths. The crude birth rate of 41 per thousand in Ethiopian Calendar 1979 (ending September 1987), though not quite up to the national average of 47 per thousand,[68] is higher than the rate for Wello (where most of the settlers originated), which was 39 per thousand in 1981. Recent increases in the birth rate have given rise to some concern and the Ethiopian Family Planning Association has started a programme which is proving very popular. Births show seasonal variations, with 70 per cent occurring in the six-month period from April to September.[69] This could be explained by higher fertility during the nutritionally optimal late rains and harvest period.

Mortality

Deaths were frequent in the first few months of resettlement, not on account of lack of food, but because of poor sanitation and epidemics in crowded shelter conditions. However, the arbitrary claim by the French aid agency Médécins sans Frontières that 100,000 people died is neither credible nor based on any facts.[70] Current figures from the RRC suggest a death rate of 10 per thousand in conventional settlements and 12 per thousand in integrated settlements.[71] The difference can probably be explained by better health care in conventional settlements. Although these death rates could be accurate for the present situation with improved health conditions, they are far too low for the entire period when compared with a national average of 18.4 per thousand.[72] This may be explained partly by under-reporting of deaths, particularly in the early phases. In the Qeto complex, for which more detailed figures are available, the death rate over the past two and a half years fell from 41 per thousand in the first year to 10 per thousand in 1987.[73] Some 63 per cent of the deaths in the first two and a half years occurred in the first three months, and 72 per cent in the first six months; only 13 per cent occurred in the last year. Infant mortality is still, however, a

Table 2 Local and settler population, percentages and changes in density

Region	Area (km²)	Population	Density	Settlers	(%)	New pop.	Set. (%)	New den.
Wellegga	70,481	2,488,891	35.3	213,581	42.4	2,702,472	12.5	38.3
Sub-region								
Asosa	15,270	239,536	15.6	48,973	9.7	288,509	16.9	18.9
Horo Gudru	16,578	481,394	29.0	24,671	4.9	506,065	4.8	30.5
Neqemte	7,009	345,765	49.3	17,146	3.4	362,911	4.7	51.7
Qelem	10,739	470,409	43.8	59,217	11.7	529,626	11.1	49.3
Gimbi	16,828	746,192	44.3	30,097	6.0	776,289	3.8	46.1
Arjo	4,073	205,707	50.5	4,505	0.9	210,212	2.1	51.6
Ilubabor	46,367	964,325	20.8	144,943	28.8	1,109,268	13.0	23.9
Sub-region								
Gambella	24,276	69,464	2.8	51,531	10.2	120,995	42.5	5.0
Sor+Geba	3,935	245,761	62.4	38,023	7.5	283,784	13.4	72.1
Buno	7,541	417,527	55.3	21,386	4.2	483,913	4.8	58.2
Gore	4,020	114,545	28.5	23,784	4.7	138,329	17.2	34.4
Mocha	6,594	117,143	17.7	10,209	2.0	127,352	8.0	19.3
Gojjam	61,224	3,199,413	52.2	76,644	15.2	3,276,057	2.4	53.5
Sub-region								
Metekkel	28,681	223,453	7.8	76,644	15.2	300,097	25.5	10.4
Kefa	56,633	2,456,722	43.3	56,958	11.2	2,513,680	2.2	44.3
Sub-region								
Limu	7,672	485,612	63.3	12,095	2.4	497,707	2.4	64.8
Jima	8,897	950,454	106.8	11,643	2.3	962,097	1.2	108.1
Kulo Konta	6,704	287,025	42.8	654	0.1	287,679	0.2	42.9
Kefa	11,174	540,373	48.3	15,953	3.1	556,326	2.8	49.7
Gimira	7,383	132,488	18.2	14,004	2.7	149,108	9.4	20.2

Gonder Sub-region	79,579	2,869,269	36.0	4,816	0.9	2,874,085	0.1	36.1
Chilga	21,280	350,042	16.4	4,816	0.9	354,858	1.3	16.6
Shewa Sub-region	85,093	7,911,492	92.9	6,149	1.2	7,917,641	0.07	93.0
Chebo	9,144	1,247,236	136.4	6,149	1.2	1,253,385	0.5	137.0
Total for all sub-regions with settlers	217,785	7,669,899	35.2	503,091	100	8,172,990	6.1	37.5
Total for all sub-regions minus Shewa & Gonder	187,361	6,072,621	32.4	492,126	97.8	6,564,747	7.5	35.0

Sources: (1) Provisional Military Government of Socialist Ethiopia, *Ethiopia 1984: Population and Housing Census Preliminary Report* (Addis Ababa, Office of the Population and Housing Census Commission, 1984); (2) Provisional Military Government of Socialist Ethiopia, *Population of Weredas and Towns by Sex and Average Household Size Based on the Preliminary Census Results and Population Projections by Age, Sex and Rural and Urban for Total Country and Regions 1984–1995* (Addis Ababa, National Committee for Central Planning/Central Statistical Office, 1985); and (3) Provisional Military Government of Socialist Ethiopia, *Area by Region, Awraja, Wereda in Sq. Km., Gasha, Hectare* (Addis Ababa, Central Statistical Office, 1986), *Statistical Bulletin* 49; and (4) RRC figures. This table was compiled using area figures in (3) excluding decimal points; rural population projects for 1986 in (2), part 3 (figures for *awrajas* were calculated from these projected increases for the relevant regions); and RRC figures for 1986.

cause for concern. The number of child deaths increases during the 'hunger season' in the late dry season and during the early rains.[74]

Departures

Current RRC data for people who have left resettlement provide figures of 4.7 per cent for conventional and 4.6 per cent for integrated settlements.[75] These figures are probably too low, given high rates of population decrease, especially in the early stages, when accounting was least rigorous and discontent highest. A tentative estimate of the number of people leaving resettlement sites in Qeto suggests a figure of about 8 per cent over the first three years.[76] Circumstantial evidence, however, suggests a slowing down of the departure rate in 1988. Many of those who leave resettlement sites do not return to the north but remain instead in the west; the men work as seasonal wage-labourers during the harvest and coffee-picking season, while the women become servants or work in bars. A number subsequently return to the settlements.

Settler percentage of the population and changes in density

Resettlement has taken place in six regions of Ethiopia. Settlers overall represent 6 per cent of the population of the *awrajjas* or sub-regions in which resettlement has been carried out. This ranges from 13 per cent in Kefa to less than 0.1 per cent in Shewa. A more accurate picture emerges, however, if one focuses on *awrajjas* in which settlement occurred. For instance, settlers represent as much as 25.5 per cent of the population of Metekkel but only 2.4 per cent of the total population of Gojjam region (see table 2). Similarly, settlers represent 1.3 per cent of Chilga *awrajja*, but only 0.1 per cent of Gonder region as a whole. If one excludes Shewa and Gonder, where little resettlement took place, the settler percentage rises to 7.5 per cent for settler-inhabited *awrajjas* in the other regions. Settlers represent over a quarter of the population in two *awrajjas*: Gambella with 42.5 per cent and Metekkel with 25.5 per cent, and more than 10 per cent in four others: Asosa and Qelem in Wellegga, with 16.9 per cent and

11.1 per cent respectively, and Gore and Sorinna Geba in Ilubabor with 17.2 per cent and 13.4 per cent. Settlers represent less than 1 per cent in two *awrajjas*: Kulo Konta in Kefa, with 0.2 per cent, and Chebonna Gurage in Shewa, with 0.5 per cent.

Settler percentages need to be considered in relation to overall population density. The average density in the *awrajjas* with resettlement within the six regions prior to resettlement was 35.2 persons per square kilometre (or 32.4 excluding Gonder and Shewa). With the settler presence, these figures rose to 37.5 and 35.0 respectively. The density was above 100 per kilometre in only two *awrajjas*: Chebonna Gurage with 136 and Jimma with 106; these *awrajjas* received 1.2 per cent and 2.3 per cent of the total resettlement population. The third highest density was in Limu *awrajja* with 63; this *awrajja* received 2.4 per cent of the resettlement. Pre-resettlement density was less than 10 in two *awrajjas*: Gambella, with 2 and Metekkel with 7; these areas received 28 per cent and 15 per cent of the total resettlement population, resulting in the density doubling to 5 in the former and reaching 10 in the latter. The only other *awrajja* to receive around 10 per cent of the total, Asosa, had the third lowest density (15.8 per cent). It is thus evident that resettlement is inversely correlated with earlier population density.

Integration

A whole range of links, transactions and relationships between the settlers and the local population may be conceptualized, and different spheres or loci of contact distinguished.[77] At one extreme, in some conventional settlements without nearby local peasant associations there is hardly any contact, except at the market-place. In Wellegga, language difficulties create some constraints, although a fair proportion of the settlers from Wello are Oromo-speakers, and a number of locals, particularly in leadership positions, have learnt to read and write Amharic. At the other extreme, there are some integrated settlements where settlers have close friends among the locals and socialize with them. There have even been a few cases of intermarriage.

Market and labour

The market is the most important focus of contact and exchange. Because of the language barrier, settlers could at first be seen communicating with signs, but by now they will tell you 'We have enough words for market.' Occasional misunderstandings arise, for instance the Oromo traditionally count the number rather than the value of coins (so that 5 cents means five coins of 5 cents each, i.e. 25 cents).[78] The settler presence has led to an increase in the numbers and size of markets. The settler influx also resulted in changes in the terms of trade: the price of grain plummeted, the settlers needing to sell part of their food rations to buy other essentials, such as salt, pepper and soap. Conversely, the price of livestock rocketed since the settlers soon began to invest in the livestock ladder from chickens to goats and sheep. This is exactly the opposite of the famine pattern where grain prices rise sharply and livestock prices decline proportionally. In the first year, it was common for settlers to find daily wage labour among the local population during the peak agricultural seasons, at a rate of about 1 birr for a day's work. Now that they are more established, settlers tend to be too busy with their own work. Some of those who leave the settlements enter the employment of enterprising locals.

Exchange and gifts

Some settlers and locals have become good friends, particularly in integrated settlements. Local Oromo often give settler friends milk products, seeds, vegetables such as pumpkins, cabbages, gourds and sweet potatoes, with which the settlers were not familiar, as well as fruits such as bananas, mangoes and papayas to plant. Other gifts to special friends include tobacco and *chat* (a mild narcotic). Some locals have given bee-hives to settlers or shown them how to make them. The locals hang them in the trees while the settlers, who come from areas where trees are scarce, traditionally put them on a forked stick or hung them on the walls of their houses; however, the settlers know how to catch the queen bee and prevent the swarms from disappearing after the honey has been collected, an art some locals are learning.

Friendship and religion

In integrated sites, some close friendships have developed between settlers and locals. Both groups drink coffee at each others' houses and attend each others' funerals. In most areas of the west, the local population is predominantly Christian, as are most of settlers, apart from Muslims from some areas of Wello. Settlers sometimes go to the local church or mosque. In a number of places, Christian settlers have found godparents for their newborn among the local population.

Intermarriage and co-dwelling

Perhaps the most conclusive indicator of the degree of integration is intermarriage. In some areas, where most locals are Christian and most settlers Muslim, religion presents a barrier. Nonetheless, in several integrated settlements, there have been a few marriages between co-religionaries. In all known cases these have been between a local man and a settler woman, notably among the leadership (e.g. local youth association secretary marries settler women's association deputy chair). Striking examples of integration occurred in two separate instances of isolated families who had lived in the area selected for settlement. In both cases, the locals assisted the settlers, notably by allowing them to use their millstones. When the other locals were being grouped in villages during the villagization programme these families asked, and were allowed, to remain among the settlers who already constituted a village, rather than join the other locals. As one administrator commented: 'These families are the ones who are truly integrated and not the other way round.'

Costs and conflict

In the initial stage, the local population was mobilized to build and cultivate for the settlers. In some cases, though the land chosen for resettlement was not intensively or continuously used by the locals, it was, nevertheless, exploited for hanging beehives in the tall trees. Moreover, during the dry season the herds were taken to the rivers through land which has now been settled. In a number of cases, compromises were reached whereby the locals could leave their hives in the trees until they had harvested the honey and then take away their hives. Access to the rivers was also negotiated. Another area of conflict concerned the exploitation of wild coffee in the forests. Here the boundaries had to be defined so that settlers could be prevented from collecting coffee on the land of the local inhabitants. Despite boundary definitions, several incidents of settlers picking coffee on local land have occurred. In a number of cases, the market-place was the scene of fights between settlers and locals, which usually started either with an accusation by one side of not paying the agreed price or as a result of men drinking on money made at the market.

Benefits and examples

Despite the aforementioned problems, local Oromo peasants in many areas of Wellegga express support for resettlement because of several benefits that outweigh the disadvantages. Three factors are most commonly mentioned.

1 The settler influx is considered to have frightened away the wild animals, and reduced the threat to crops from pests such as baboons and wild pigs: 'Now the wild animals flee the scent of man and our crops are safer.' In addition, the settlers are perceived as having brought the wilderness under control and as having put dangerous unproductive land to good use.

2 The settler presence is believed to have brought the area to the attention of the central authorities: 'Now the Government has no longer forgotten us.' With the settlers have come better roads and improved services, such as schools and clinics.

3 No doubt most importantly, the settlers' presence has opened up the area to trade and dramatically increased the demand and consequently the price of cash crops, such as the narcotic, *chat*, and coffee and, especially livestock. Conversely, the local population is able to acquire 'aid items' such as blankets, clothing, household equipment and food at greatly reduced prices. Currently, the glut in the grain market, with no demand for the large quantities of cereals produced by the settlers, has allowed local

merchants to make enormous profits from buying grain at a third of Agricultural Marketing Board price, transporting it and selling it at high prices in the towns. In many resettlement areas, villages have turned into small towns largely as a result of the settler presence.

The settlers also provide an example of a hard-working group to the local population. The latter had a reputation of not exerting itself to produce surpluses for the market, which may be explained by the fact that demand was limited. Whether settler enterprise will have a demonstration effect or give rise to jealousy and bad feeling remains to be seen. No doubt the outcome will depend to a certain extent on whether regional development plans address the issues integration raises, and whether the provision of services reaches the local population as well as the settlers.

Economic performance (see table 3)

According to a government report,[79] the amount of land cultivated per household in the new settlements over the first three years (1985–7) was 0.9 hectares per household and productivity was 8 quintals per hectare. However, these

Table 3 Household production in new settlements

Year	Hectares	Quintals	q./ha.	ha./head	q./head
Conventional settlements					
1985	23,688	77,370	3.27	0.30	0.97
1986	67,338	547,917	8.13	0.86	7.0
1987	72,765	810,007	11.13	0.96	10.8
Integrated settlements					
1985	24,940	124,514	4.99	0.32	1.58
1986	47,931	293,090	6.11	0.68	4.16
1987	60,209	359,723	5.97	0.85	5.10

Source: People's Democratic Republic of Ethiopia Government, *Sefera bedihre abiyot itiyopia: witet, chigiroch, yewedefit aqtachcha* (Resettlement in Post-Revolutionary Ethiopia: Results, Problems and Future Direction) (Addis Ababa, National Committee for Natural Disaster Rehabilitation, Host Regions Study Committee, 1988) (Miyazya 1980 E.C. Amharic), p. 237.

averages conceal an improvement over the three years and differences between conventional and integrated settlements. Production figures in conventional settlements have increased over ten-fold from 77,340 quintals to 810,000 quintals; average household production rose from 0.97 quintals in 1985 to 10.80 in 1987. The amount of land under cultivation more than tripled from 23,680 hectares to 72,765, and the number of hectares per household increased from 0.3 to 0.96. In the integrated settlements, the increase was much smaller. Production figures doubled from 124,514 to 359,723 quintals, and the number of quintals per household increased from 4.99 to 6.11. The amount of land under cultivation rose from 24,940 hectares to 60,209, and the amount of land per household from 1.58 to 5.10. Conventional settlements would, therefore, seem to be producing almost twice as much as integrated settlements, though the difference may be explained partly by greater difficulty in obtaining figures for scattered integrated settlements with a greater variety of produce, and partly because the total household population decreased to a greater extent in conventional settlements. Productivity figures also reveal a considerable increase and substantial differences between conventional and integrated settlements. Average household production rose from 3.27 quintals per hectare to 11.13 in conventional settlements, and from 4.99 to 6.11, in integrated settlements. Greater output in conventional settlements is probably due to better Government agricultural extension support, particularly in the provision of fertilizers and advice from extension staff.

Self-sufficiency

Two criteria are used by a government report to assess prospects for self-sufficiency: the amount of land under cultivation per household, and the amount of produce per household per year. Self-sufficient peasants in the country as a whole cultivate between 1 and 3 hectares of land and produce between 6 and 12 quintals per year. Since considerable differences exist between types of settlement and between regions (see tables 3, 4 and 5), it is worth considering these issues in greater detail.

Table 4 Household production in conventional settlements by settlement (hectares and quintals)

	Gambella	Asosa	Anger	Jarso	Qeto	Pawe	Metemma	Total
1985								
ha./head	0.34	0.57	0.18	0.43	0.07	0.09	1.10	0.30
q./head	0.56	2.27	0.93	0.74	0.26	0.12	4.15	0.97
q./ha.	1.67	3.95	5.06	1.72	3.60	1.33	3.78	3.27
1986								
ha./head	0.99	1.06	1.10	1.04	0.94	0.47	0.32	0.86
q./head	4.67	11.18	11.22	9.36	11.77	1.55	1.29	7.01
q./ha.	4.71	10.60	9.88	9.00	12.10	3.29	3.80	8.13
1987								
ha./head	0.92	0.96	1.46	1.18	0.94	0.74	1.85	0.97
q./head	7.64	12.95	16.87	15.16	13.96	7.10	8.17	10.80
q./ha.	8.27	13.43	11.47	12.90	14.76	9.49	4.41	11.13

Source: As table 3, p. 114.

Table 5 Household production in integrated settlements by region (hectares and quintals)

	Kefa	Ilubabor	Wellegga	All regions
1985				
ha./head	0.23	0.20	0.49	0.32
q./head	0.74	1.42	2.33	1.58
q./ha.	3.25	7.05	4.72	4.99
1986				
ha./head	0.52	0.62	0.98	0.68
q./head	2.97	4.28	5.51	4.16
q./ha.	5.67	6.89	5.64	6.11
1987				
ha./head	0.61	0.97	0.88	0.85
q./head	2.49	7.40	4.34	5.10
q./ha.	4.09	7.57	4.96	5.97

Source: As table 3, p. 115.

There are five large-scale conventional settlements with 10,000–20,000 households and a smaller one, Jarso, with 3,500 households. In 1987, three of these six settlements did not reach the minimum recommended land holding of 1 hectare per household. However, two, Qeto and Gambella, almost attained it, for they were above 0.9. The worst performing settlement complex according to this criterion is Pawe, with 0.74 hectares per household, and the best, Metemma, has 1.85, approaching the national average guideline of 2 hectares per household. In terms of production per household, none of the six settlement complexes fell below the lower guideline of 6 quintals in 1987, but three of them, Gambella, Pawe and Metemma, were below the average guideline of 9 quintals. According to this criterion, the worst-performing settlement was Pawe, with 7.10 quintals per household, and the best, Anger Gutin, with 16.87. Four settlements, Asosa, Qeto, Jarso and Anger Gutin, were above the 12 quintal upper guideline. If these two criteria of land and produce per household are taken together, two settlement complexes, Gambella and Pawe, did not satisfy the lower guidelines of 1 hectare and of 6 quintals. If one considers the productivity figures, the average for the six settlement complexes is 11.13 quintals per hectare, the most successful settlement being Qeto, with 14.76, and the least successful being Metemma, with 4.41.

Integrated settlements exist in three regions: Wellegga, Ilubabor and Kefa. Production figures at the local level are not readily available but regional differences and overall figures are worth considering in comparison with data for conventional settlements. Average household land cultivated in integrated settlements in 1987 was 0.85 hectares, compared with 0.97 in conventional settlements. However, these figures conceal considerable variation between regions. The highest rate was achieved in Wellegga, with 0.98 hectares, which is above the conventional settlement average. The lowest rate was in Kefa with 0.61, which is lower than the worst-performing conventional settlement. Average household production was 5.1 quintals, slightly less than half the conventional settlements' average of 10.8. However, the Wellegga figure of 7.4 quintals is above the lower guideline of 6 per household, while the figure for Kefa of 2.97 quintals is clearly inadequate. Productivity at an average of 6.11 quintals per hectare is slightly over half the conventional settlements' average, varying from 7.57 in Ilubabor to 5.67 in Kefa.

There is much variety among integrated settlements. Some seem to be highly successful and may be considered more prosperous than conventional settlements, with settlers rapidly investing in livestock, while others face major problems and seem far worse off than conventional settlements.

Three major variables tend to affect the relative success of the integrated settlements.

1 *Plough-oxen*. The prosperity of the settlements is closely related to their number of oxen. A report in the Qeto area suggests variations ranging from 0.16 to 0.43 oxen per family.[80] Another study in Wellegga notes that in some cases there were as many as one pair of oxen per family, while in a few exceptional cases up to 25 households shared a pair of oxen.[81] Shortages of oxen were due to fatality in areas with Tsetse fly, as well as to lack of funds. Settlements with a ratio of above 10 families per ox-team experienced difficulties, and even those with less than 5 found it hard to make ends meet. In addition to

government assistance, a number of aid agencies and religious organizations have given assistance to purchase oxen.

2 *Type of land.* A study of integrated sites in Wellegga differentiates between two types: those on uncleared land and those on land which had been used, but was not then under cultivation.[82] In the first case, the initial effort required for land clearance was considerable; crop loss from wild animals (particularly baboons) was also a serious problem. In the latter case, these problems were insignificant, but in some places the land was no longer fertile and required fertilizers. In a few instances, local officials suggest that it may be necessary to relocate settlers to more productive land. The short-term disadvantages of sites on virgin land thus seem to be outweighed by the long-term advantages, and such settlements seem far more promising than the ones on land already cultivated.

3 *Settlement size.* According to the aforementioned study, the smallest sites seem to face most problems and the settlers feel more isolated and less optimistic than those in larger groups. On the other hand, in extremely large integrated settlements, there was a notable lack of services and facilities, which are the hallmark of conventional settlements, and settlers sometimes outnumbered the local population, thereby creating conditions that could lead to tension. Recommendations for alleviating these problems included amalgamating the smallest sites, as had been proposed by the administration in Gimbi, in order to reduce anxiety and increase production. Conventional status could be given to large integrated settlements, if situated near a conventional complex, as happened in the Jarso complex and could happen in Qeto; alternatively large integrated settlements could be considered as autonomous peasants' associations, as seems to be happening in Dale Wabera *wereda* of Qelem *awrajja*.

Long-term sustainability of the settlements

After almost three years, the settlers are about to obtain their third harvest and most of the new settlements are moving towards short-term agricultural self-sufficiency. In some areas, water-logging has caused problems while, in others, not enough water was found when bore-wells were dug. As a result, a number of sites have had to be relocated.[83] In many areas, further land needs to be cleared as the area per household has not reached the 1 hectare minimum guideline. Despite such problems, the short-term survival of what were hopeless famine victims has been assured and the settlers have enough to eat. A number of crucial longer-term issues need, however, to be addressed and policy choices need to be made.

Private versus collective agriculture

Most production in conventional settlements is on a collective basis while in the integrated settlements it is mostly private. Collectivization in the former has justified the provision of better communal facilities, such as clinics, mills, schools and establishment of cooperative shops run by service cooperatives for two producers' cooperatives. With the large numbers of settlers involved in conventional settlements, shops can run viably while subsidizing costs, since the service cooperatives can acquire goods cheaply from the Ethiopian Domestic Distribution Corporation.

Greater private incentive seems to have resulted in some differentiation in integrated settlements. A number of settlers have become more prosperous than others (for instance owning a dozen sheep and, in some areas, even cattle), while the conventional settlements are more uniform. The most successful integrated sites, where land is fertile and plentiful and sufficient oxen have been distributed, present an air of greater prosperity than the conventional settlements. However, the less well-off integrated sites, where these conditions do not obtain, are clearly much worse off than the conventional settlements.

An intermediate mixed strategy could combine the benefits of greater inputs and services in conventional sites with lower costs, less constraints and more initiative in integrated sites.

Ox-plough versus tractor-based cultivation

Until recently all the conventional sites relied on tractor services. In the old high-cost settlements established a decade ago, the settlers are now fully self-sufficient in food and can even pay for tractor spare parts, but they are unable to afford new tractors, which are badly needed. Only a quarter of the original number are operational, while the population has doubled owing to further resettlement. This would suggest that mechanized schemes may need to increase production of cash crops unless Government and aid agencies are to continue to subsidize such schemes.[84] Alternatively, partial reliance on ox-plough cultivation could be promoted, a move already begun in Jarso. Such a policy can be justified since resettlement is by definition a labour-intensive process and the main asset settlements have to offer is abundant person-power. However, if a more oxen-reliant policy is promoted, control of the trypanosomiasis caused by the tsetse fly in the riverine lowlands will need careful consideration.

In the integrated settlements the ratio of household to ox-teams varies considerably between sites, from the desirable one to one ratio to a disturbing 25 households to one pair of oxen. This is an area where assistance is required to even out discrepancies and ensure that the requisite means of production exist for all settlers.

Tsetse control versus forest conservation

The considerable amount of construction of houses and collective buildings, such as granaries, peasant's association offices, shops, mills, etc. in the resettlement sites, and the clearing of vast expanses of land for cultivation has had the positive result of reducing the tsetse fly habitat. Extensive clearance will, however, lead to deforestation and consequent soil erosion and land degradation, unless conservation measures are accorded a high priority. Special areas have been reserved for forest and grazing, and reafforestation campaigns have been launched. Nevertheless, with fuel and building construction needs, and a growing population, this could become a vital issue for the future.

Virgin land versus cultivated land

Conventional settlements were placed in lowland areas which had previously been sparsely inhabited, and where the land had not been used continuously or intensively. Land clearance was labour-intensive, though much clearance was done mechanically. The main problems were the threat to crops from wild animals during the harvest season, and diseases, notably malaria. Swamp clearance programmes, improved sanitation and spraying have considerably reduced the incidence of malaria. The long-term sustainability of intensive cultivation needs, however, to be assessed and agricultural conservation techniques applied to preserve soil fertility.

Clearance problems in integrated settlements were less acute but, in previously cultivated areas, fertilizers are required to improve yields. Where the density is already high, there may be little room for further expansion, given demographic growth. Both virgin and uncultivated lands, therefore, have disadvantages, but in most cases settlers can become self-sufficient within a few years, and, with adequate inputs and careful management, resettlement may be able to contribute to the local, and even to the national, economy.

Conclusions

Resettlement during the first post-revolutionary decade (1974–84) involved some 45,000 households or 180,000 people. Its slow pace, high cost and low productivity have been criticized in a number of reports. The main lesson learnt was the inadvisability of settling heads of household on their own. Although short-term food self-sufficiency is no longer a problem in most cases, the question of longer-term sustainability of mechanized agriculture and declining yields, raises important issues.

The emergency phase (1985–8) involved over 200,000 households or almost 600,000 people who were resettled in less than two years. This represented a 20-fold increase in the yearly rate of resettlement. Demographic data reveal a slight preponderance of men (53 per cent) and slightly fewer small children and elderly people than the national average. Although the number of deaths was high initially and the number of births low, current natality and mortality figures are below national averages but the birth rate is rising. Resettlement is shown to be inversely correlated to previous population density. The market-place is the most important locus for exchange with the local population. The settler influx resulted in an expansion of markets and a change in the terms of trade in favour of the local population: the price of grain and aid items decreased and livestocks and cash crops increased proportionately. Despite some areas of friction over natural resources, in some areas the settler presence is welcomed by the local population, in part because it has led to increased government assistance; there have already been some marriages between settlers and local people.

The two types of resettlement, large-scale conventional settlement complexes in the lowlands involving mechanized agriculture and disease control, and small-scale integrated settlements in the highlands, based on ox-plough private cultivation, present different characteristics. Conventional settlements rely on collective agriculture, which justifies considerable inputs from the Government in the form of agricultural, health, and education services. Integrated settlements receive oxen and seed and rely mainly on private agriculture and links with the local peasant associations. An intermediate mixed strategy could combine the benefits of greater inputs and services found in conventional settlements with the greater initiative and lower costs of integrated ones.

Although most settlements are moving towards short-term food self-sufficiency, the longer-term issues relating to sustainability mentioned in the case of the earlier settlements need to be considered and choices made. Mechanized agriculture may become viable if cash crops are introduced. In altitudinally marginal areas, a more oxen-reliant policy could be promoted if the tsetse fly challenge can be met. The reduction of forest cover for agriculture and building construction has undoubtedly reduced the tsetse habitat, but the long-term danger of deforestation, despite reafforestation efforts, cannot be underestimated. It remains to be seen whether the new settlements can avoid some of the problems encountered by the earlier resettlement of the 1970s.

Notes and References

1 For discussions of resettlement prior to the Revolution, see Eshetu Chole and Teshome Mulat, 'Land Settlement in Ethiopia: A Review of Developments' (Addis Ababa, unpublished paper, 1984); C. J. Samuel, *Ethiopian Highlands Reclamation Study: Resettlement Strategy Proposals* (Addis Ababa, Ministry of Agriculture, Land Use Planning and Regulatory Department/FAO, 1985); G. Simpson, *A Preliminary Survey of Settlement Projects in Ethiopia* (Addis Ababa, Institute of Development Research, 1975), Research Report 21; C. E. Van Santen, *Six Case Studies of Rural Settlement Schemes in Ethiopia* (Addis Ababa, Ministry of Agriculture and Settlement, 1978); A. P. Wood, 'Population Redistribution and Agricultural Settlement Schemes in Ethiopia, 1958–80', in J. Clarke, M. Khogali and L. Kosinski (eds), *Population and Development Projects in Africa* (Cambridge, Cambridge University Press, 1985).

   Resettlement was conceived primarily in terms of agricultural development, but also to provide land in lieu of pensions and to settle nomads. Resettlement planning was first officially considered in the Third Five Year Plan (1968–73) with a view to relieving population pressure in the northern plateau and to improving agricultural productivity (Imperial Ethiopian Government, *Third Five Year Development Plan 1968–1973*, Addis Ababa, Ministry of Planning and Development, 1968, pp. 373–4 and 425–6).

2 Wood, 'Population Redistribution 1958–80', p. 92.

3 Samuel, *Resettlement Strategy Proposals*, p. 51, quoting Relief and Rehabilitation Commission (hereafter RRC) headquarters, Department of Statistics, January 1985. Actual figures quoted were 45,849 household heads and 141,632 family members.

4 RRC, *The Challenge of Drought: Ethiopia's Decade of Struggle in Relief and Rehabilitation* (London, H & L Communications, 1985), pp. 156–8.

5 Samuel, *Resettlement Strategy Proposals*, p. 4, referring to World Bank, Agricultural Division, Report no. 444 a OT, June 1974.

6 RRC, *Challenges of Drought*, pp. 123–4.

7 *Ibid.*, pp. 157–8.

8 *Ibid.*, p. 161 (40,123 households and 12,900 settlers).

9 Samuel, *Resettlement Strategy Proposals*, p. 51.

10 All dollar figures refer to US dollars; figures in Ethiopian birr have been converted to US dollars at the official rate of 2 birr to the dollar. Pre-revolution resettlement has been estimated to have cost $8 million or roughly half a million dollars annually (Wood, 'Population Redistribution 1958–80', p. 92).

11 Wood, 'Population Redistribution 1958–80', p. 108, table 7.5; Eshetu Chole and Teshome Mulat, 'Land Settlement in Ethiopia', p. 48, table 15.

12 People's Democratic Republic of Ethiopia Government, *Sefera bedihre abiyot itiyopiya: witet, chigiroch, yewedefit aqtachcha* (Resettlement in Post-Revolutionary Ethiopia: Results, Problems and Future Direction)

(Addis Ababa, National Committee for Natural Disaster Rehabilitation, Host Regions Study Committee, 1988) (Miyazya 1980 E. C. Amharic), p. 122.

13 See Samuel, *Resettlement Strategy Proposals*, pp. 38–44; D. Hareide, *Report on the New Resettlements in Ethiopia 1984–6* (Addis Ababa, UN Office for Emergency Operations in Ethiopia, 1986), 11.2–6; Eshetu Chole and Teshome Mulat, 'Land Settlement in Ethiopia', pp. 43–8; K. Jansson, M. Harris and A. Penrose, *The Ethiopian Famine* (London, Zed Books, 1987), p. 65.

14 Ethiopian Government, *Sefera bedihre abiyot itiyopiya*, p. 122.

15 See Eschetu Chole and Teshome Mulat, 'Land Settlement in Ethiopia'; A. Pankhurst, 'Resettlement in Ethiopia: A Background Paper' (Addis Ababa, unpublished report, 1988); Samuel, *Resettlement Strategy Proposals*; Simpson, *Settlement Projects in Ethiopia*; Van Santen, *Rural Settlement Schemes*; Wood, 'Population Redistribution 1958–80'.

16 Samuel, *Resettlement Strategy Proposals*, p. 65.

17 *Ibid.*, pp. 65–6.

18 Eshetu Chole and Teshome Mulat, 'Land Settlement in Ethiopia', p. 51.

19 A. Pankhurst and Hezekiel Gebissa, 'Report on a Study Tour of Settlement Schemes in Wollega, 12 October–9 November 1986' (Addis Ababa, unpublished report, 1986), p. 12.

20 Samuel, *Resettlement Strategy Proposals*, p. 51.

21 Ethiopian Government, *Sefera bedihre abiyot itiyopiya*, pp. 238–9.

22 Samuel, *Resettlement Strategy Proposals*, p. 53, comments: 'Such a situation has affected the productivity of the settlers. It has also been a key factor in settler displeasure and discontent leading to the desertion of many of them during the first year.'

23 Provisional Military Government of Socialist Ethiopia, *Ten Years Perspective Plan 1984–5 – 1993–4* (Addis Ababa, Office of the National Council for Central Planning, 1984).

24 Provisional Military Government of Socialist Ethiopia, *Bedirq mikniyat yetekessetu chiggiroch lemeqwaqwam yetezegajje yedirgit program* (Action Programme Prepared to Solve Problems Arising from the Drought) (Addis Ababa, National Committee for Central Planning, 1984), (Hidar 1977 E. C. Amharic).

25 Maize would account for 70 per cent of crops to be sown and 78 per cent of the expected harvest; sorghum 20 per cent of crops sown and 16 per cent of the harvest; and vegetables, 10 per cent of crops sown and 4.5 per cent of the harvest.

26 The expenditure breakdown was to be as follows: 44.4 per cent to be used on smallholder development (agricultural equipment, seed, oxen); 25.7 per cent on the settlement programme; 13.6 per cent on state farms; 9.2 per cent on water development; and 77 per cent on livestock development.

27 RRC, *Challenges of Drought*, p. 200.

28 Ethiopian Government, *Sefera bedihre abiyot itiyopiya*, pp. 123–5.

29 According to requests to donors, the RRC had planned to spend $210

million on new settlements in 1986 alone (Hareide, *Resettlements in Ethiopia 1984–6*, p. 11.6).

30 G. Prunier, 'Population Resettlement in Ethiopia: The Financial Aspect' (Paper presented to the Tenth International Conference of Ethiopian Studies, Paris), like several other writers (see note 15), tries to guess at likely costs and comes up with a figure of $400 per person, which would add up to a total expenditure of $263 million. He then suggests that to have conducted resettlement properly about twice as much would have been required, i.e. $800 per settler. This is probably a closer estimate of actual expenditure.

31 J. Clarke, *Resettlement and Rehabilitation: Ethiopia's Campaign Against Famine* (London, Harney and Jones, 1986), p. 33.

32 RRC, *Review and Assistance Requirements (1986/1987)* (Addis Ababa, RRC, 1987), p. 8 mentions that: 'The governments of UK, Yugoslavia, Bulgaria and Romania, 12 Voluntary organizations and UNICEF have provided 37,471 MT of seed, 1,500 MT fertiliser, 2,681 oxen, 6,500 different types of hand tools and 67 various kinds of farm machinery.'

33 The Italian project involves some $190 million and assists 75,000 people with construction of roads and clinics, agricultural irrigated developments, water resources and supply, and rural electrification.

34 The Soviet Union provided 22 doctors for the 250-bed hospital they financed in Asosa, 12 Antonov planes, and 300 short-haul trucks and 700 drivers. Airplanes from Libya and the German Democratic Republic were also used for transport of settlers. No planes from Western donors were used for settler transport. (Jansson, Harris and Penrose, *The Ethiopian Famine*, pp. 37, 39; Hareide, *Resettlements in Ethiopia 1984–6*, p. 12–5.)

35 The Canadian contribution to Concern was around $4.5 million.

36 Hareide, *Resettlements in Ethiopia 1984–6*, p. 12–5.

37 *Ibid.*

38 Agencies assisting the earlier resettlement projects included: Catholic Relief Services, supplying oxen and fertilizers in Gamu Gofa at Manuka and Dana; Swiss Evangelical Nile Mission, Scottish Catholic International Aid Fund, and Christian Relief and Development Association, also at Dana; Catholic Mission (with Dutch Government support) in Kefa at Gojeb; Sudan Interior Mission in Gamu Gofa; Seventh Day Adventists, in Kefa at Gena; Redd Barna in Bale; World Vision at Gode; Save the Children in conjunction with UNICEF in Wello; Norwegian Church Aid, involving well drilling in Bale; Oxfam supplying pumps in Gonder at Metemma; Lutheran World Federation in Bale at Genale; and International Committee for the Red Cross supplying equipment and vehicles. (See RRC, *Challenges of Drought*, p. 140; and the UN Office for Emergency Operations in Ethiopia.)

39 Jansson, Harris and Penrose, *The Ethiopian Famine*, p. 67.

40 By March 1988, the German agency Menschen für Menschen had spent $15.5 million out of a total budget of $20.7 million. The project assists 91,000 people in integrated settlements in the Ilubabor highlands with

emergency supplies such as blankets, clothing and food; agricultural inputs such as oxen, seed, hand-tools and seedlings; infrastructure including mills, stores, schools and clinics.

The Irish agency, Concern, has two projects in conventional settlements at Qeto with 38,000 people and at Jarso with 13,000 in Wellegga. The budget for Qeto amounts to almost $3.5 million and the budget for Jarso is over $2.1 million. Most of the funding came from the Canadian Government agency, CIDA, and the voluntary agency, Band Aid. Funds were used on agriculture (seeds, oxen, fruit-trees, nurseries, conservation), infrastructure (stores, mills, schools, roads), spring protection, and preventive health. The planned expenditure was $5.6 million over 3 years.

The French agency Secours Populaire Français spent some $715,000 from March 1985 until September 1988 assisting 38,000 settlers and 12,000 locals with emergency supplies (blankets, food, utensils). A health centre was set up in Qeto. Nine site clinics are visited and immunization programmes carried out. A permanent health centre complex will be completed in 1989.

The Norwegian Save the Children, Redd Barna, has been assisting 2,050 settlers in an integrated settlement in Limu *awrajja*, Kefa region, starting January 1987 with an expenditure of $400,000 spent on agriculture (oxen, seed, tools, training), water supply (pump maintenance, spring protection), health education and community development.

Jesuit Relief Services are financing two integrated settlements in Jimma *awrajja*, Kefa region, assisting 15,500 people with $1.1 million spent in 1986 on agriculture and conservation (tools, seed, trees, seedlings, irrigation and tractor services), infrastructure (roads, stores), water (bore-holes and spring protection), and health (clinics, health education, orphanages). The total cost for 3 years is $3 million.

Several missions in western Wellegga, notably the Mekane Yesus Evangelical Church, as well as the Catholic and the Adventist missions, have been supporting integrated settlements with food, hand-tools, blankets and clothes.

41 Funding from UNESCO amounts to $4 million for the construction of 50 basic education centres as part of $56 million education programme. UNICEF has been providing material aid and supplementary food through its Regional Institutional Basic Services programme. FAO, partly with UNDP funding, has a number of projects of relevance to resettlement assessment and planning, including their Land-Use Planning Project, and Soil Survey Project. World Food Programme (WFP) is considering support for food-for-work programmes in Wellegga. WHO have submitted several projects for basic health support. (Hareide, *Settlements in Ethiopia 1984–6*, p. 12–6).

42 Kurt Jansson (Jansson, Harris and Penrose, *The Ethiopian Famine*, p. 68) writes that the programme was suspended 'not because of a change in policy and certainly not due to pressure from the West, but because of

lack of resources for agricultural inputs and a shortage of transport which had to be used for coffee export and the transport of food crops.'

43 Provisional Military Government of Socialist Ethiopia, *Revised Draft Constitution of the People's Democratic Republic of Ethiopia* (Addis Ababa, Ethiopian Herald, 30 January 1987), article 10.2.

44 RRC figures, July 1988.

45 RRC, *Challenges of Drought*, p. 157, compiled from Sahle Mariam Moges, 'Land Settlement as Rural Development Policy: The Ethiopian Experience' (University of Wisconsin, MSc thesis, 1982), p. 103.

46 RRC, *Challenges of Drought*, p. 161; Wood, 'Population Redistribution 1958–80', p. 105.

47 J. W. Clay and B. K. Holcomb, *Politics and the Ethiopian Famine 1984–1985* (Cambridge, Mass., Cultural Survival, 1985); M. Colchester and V. Luling, *Ethiopia's Bitter Medicine: Settling for Disaster* (London, Survival International, 1986).

48 Jansson, Harris and Penrose, *The Ethiopian Famine*, pp. 65, 173.

49 *Ibid.*, p. 66.

50 *Ibid.*

51 *Ibid.*, 1987, p. 173. By the end of May 1985, before the rains started, 75 per cent of the settlers from Wello had been moved (Clarke, *Resettlement and Rehabilitation*, p. 171).

52 Jansson, Harris and Penrose, *The Ethiopian Famine*, p. 173.

53 Pankhurst, 'Resettlement in Ethiopia', pp. 9–20.

54 This category accounts for more than one-third in a complete sample of over 1,000 adults in a village in Qeto resettlement.

55 Young men wanted to become soldiers partly because of the prestige of being a *balebiret*, 'owner of [an] iron [gun]', or a *tataqi* or 'belted [person]', i.e. soldier, but mainly because they saw it as an opportunity of escaping the drudgery of peasant life, and as a way of travelling to see the world. Moreover, they would add that those who return gain the status and respect of heroes and may be given pensions if wounded, or lighter work, such as serving as guards.

56 Getachew Tikubet and Mulugeta H. Sellassie, *Tse Tse and Trypanosomiasis Situation at Ketto Resettlement, Wellega Region, June 1988* (Addis Ababa, Report prepared for Concern, 1988).

57 Wood, 'Population Redistribution 1958–80', pp. 84–5.

58 The Gambella region is inhabited by Anuak and Nuer, the Asosa region by Berta and the Metekkel area by Gumuz (E. Cerulli, *Peoples of Southwest Ethiopia and its Borderlands* (London, International African Institute, 1956), pp. 12–38; M. L. Bender, *The Ethiopian Nilo-Saharans* (Addis Ababa, Artistic Printing Press, 1975), pp. 56–66).

59 The Oromo have inhabited most of the western highlands for several centuries (G. W. B. Huntingford, *The Galla of Ethiopia* (London, International African Institute, 1955)).

60 J. M. Cohen and N. I. Isaksson, *Villagization in the Arsi Region of Ethiopia* (Uppsala, Swedish University of Agricultural Sciences, 1987).

61 Simpson, *Settlement Projects in Ethiopia*.

62 RRC, *Challenges of Drought*, p. 160.

63 Provisional Military Government of Socialist Ethiopia, *Ethiopia 1984: Population and Housing Census and Preliminary Report* (Addis Ababa, Office of the Population and Housing Census Commission, 1984), p. 16; and *Population of Weredas and Towns by Sex and Average Household Size Based on the Preliminary Census Reoprts and Population Projection by Age, Sex and Rural and Urban for Total Country and Regions 1984–1995* (Addis Ababa, National Committee for Central Planning/Central Statistical Office, 1985), p. 137.

64 Ethiopian Government, *Population of Weredas and Towns*, pp. 166–7 (1985 figures).

65 Ethiopian Government, *Ethiopia 1984*, p. 71.

66 According to RRC figures for 1987, 10,264 births have been recorded in conventional settlements and 4,660 in integrated sites excluding Wellegga and Gonder.

67 Pankhurst, 'Resettlement in Ethiopia', p. 29.

68 Provisional Military Government of Socialist Ethiopia, *Report on the Results of the 1981 Demographic Survey* (Addis Ababa, National Committee for Central Planning/Central Statistical Office, 1985), *Statistical Bulletin* 46, p. iv.

69 A. Pankhurst, 'Seasonality of Infant Natality and Mortality in Ketto Settlements: Some Implications for Assistance' (Addis Ababa, unpublished report, 1987).

70 Kurt Jansson writes: 'MSF issued an arbitrary figure of 100,000 deaths having occurred in the resettlement programme; this was pure speculation. No one was then or now in a position to know casualty figures and no one will ever know how many settlers would have died in the relief camps at the height of the famine and outbreaks of disease which intermittently ravaged these camps' (Jansson, Harris and Penrose, *The Ethiopian Famine*, p. 25).

71 RRC figures in 1987 were 2,514 for conventional settlements and 2,030 for integrated settlements, excluding those in Wellegga, Kefa and Gonder.

72 Ethiopian Government, *1981 Demographic Survey*, p. iv.

73 Pankhurst, 'Resettlement in Ethiopia', p. 29.

74 Pankhurst, 'Infant Natality and Mortality in Ketto'.

75 RRC figures for 1987 suggest 11,664 for conventional settlements and 10,858 for integrated settlements, excluding Wellegga and Gonder regions.

76 Pankhurst, 'Resettlement in Ethiopia', p. 29.

77 This section is based on visits in 1986 to Gimbi and Qelem *awrajjas* of Wellegga region (see Pankhurst and Hezekiel Gebissa, 'Settlement Schemes in Wollega') and of more detailed knowledge of the Qeto area during residence there from January 1987 to June 1988. Impressions may not, therefore, correspond to the situation in other areas.

78 Pankhurst and Hezekiel Gebissa, 'Settlement Schemes in Wollega', p. 76.

79 Ethiopian Government, *Sefera bedihre abiyot itiyopiya*, pp. 100–23.
80 J. McGuire and Fesseha Asgaw, 'Integrated Villages in the Vicinity of Ketto Conventional Resettlement' (Ketto, unpublished report by Concern, 1987), Appendix 3.
81 Pankhurst and Hezekiel Gebissa, 'Settlement Schemes in Wollega', pp. 33–4, 53, 79.
82 *Ibid.*, pp. 24–5, 34, 78.
83 Pankhurst, 'Resettlement in Ethiopia', p. 33.
84 Plans for greater production of cash crops was announced by Chairman Mengistu in his report to the Sixth Plenum of the WPE Central Committee in 1988.

Egyptian Peasant Women in Iraq: Adapting to Migration

Camillia Fawzi El-Solh

In 1975, the governments of Egypt and Iraq signed an accord that served officially to initiate the sponsored migration of Egyptian peasant families to Iraq. A political background to this bilateral agreement is to be found in various addenda to the Charter of the League of Arab States, which provides the theoretical framework for regional cooperation between member states.[1] Political ideology aside, however, the socio-economic advantages of such a resettlement scheme were an equally, if not primary, motivating force behind the calculations of both governments. This resettlement project was essentially viewed in complementary terms. Underpopulated Iraq with its oil wealth, and its relatively unexploited agricultural resources, would benefit from the expertise with which the Egyptian peasant has traditionally nurtured his infinitesimal plot of land. In turn, overpopulated Egypt, with an economy afflicted by the dual problems of high population growth rate and lack of capital resources, would benefit from the export of its manpower surplus.

Accordingly, the Egyptian government initiated a campaign via agricultural cooperatives, village councils and the media to encourage Egyptian *fellaheen* (peasants) and their families

---

This paper is based on research carried out as part of a doctoral dissertation: Camillia Fawzi El-Solh, 'Egyptian Migrant Peasants in Iraq: A Case-Study of the Settlement Community in Khalsa' (University of London, unpublished PhD thesis, 1984).

to settle permanently in Iraq. For its part, the Iraqi government committed itself to shoulder the settlers' travel expenses, to build new village settlements and house them free of cost, and to hand over to them plots of land averaging between 16 and 20 Iraqi dunum or 5–7 Egyptian feddan.[2] In contrast to the official agricultural policy pursued in Iraq at the time, they would be allowed to cultivate these as individual holdings.[3] One hundred peasant families, recruited from various provinces in Egypt, arrived in the spring of 1976 in the Khalisah settlement, which had been built for them some 36 miles south of the capital Baghdad. They were to be followed by 'hundreds of thousands of *fellaheen*', as soon as arrangements for new settlement sites and the provision of cultivable plots of land were completed.[4]

The enthusiasm generated by this 1975 agreement rapidly deflated, however. Egypt's decision to seek a separate peace treaty with Israel in 1977 culminated in the rupture of political ties between it and most of the Arab world. The Iraqi government officially shelved the planned resettlement of other Egyptian peasant families.[5] Nonetheless, the deteriorating diplomatic relationship between both countries, which by 1979 had led to a suspension of direct flights between Cairo and Baghdad, did not stem the influx of Egyptian nationals into Iraq. On the contrary, this flow continued to increase, reaching a peak with the outbreak of the Gulf War in 1980, and Iraq's subsequent need for replacement manpower.[6] In fact, the Iraqi government made a point of facilitating the flow of Egyptian migrant labour by waiving such requirements as entry visa and work permit. For its part, the Egyptian government officially ignored the fact that its nationals were migrating temporarily to Iraq by using a third country (mainly Jordan) as a convenient transit route. Economic expediency could not ignore the, at least short-term, advantage of exporting the country's unemployment problem and of benefiting from the migrants' remittances.[7]

The majority of the Egyptian settler families in Khalisah have not failed to take advantage of the new economic opportunities that have come their way after resettlement, and were found to be enjoying a higher standard of living in comparison with their circumstances prior to migration. The adaptive mechanisms resorted to during this process appear to function in new situations mainly on the basis of established social norms. New expectations seek to reconcile a traditional socialization, which attributes a high value to hospitality and generally shuns solitude, with an incipient individualism that accords primary importance to one's own welfare. Where ideal and reality come into conflict, economic expediency is more often than not accorded priority, though the fiction of adhering to valued customs and traditions is upheld. This pattern of reflexive accommodation between what is economically necessary and what is socially desirable is particularly exemplified by the position of the Egyptian peasant women in the Khalisah settlement.

The Contemporary Egyptian Village and the Influence of Regional Factionalism

The heterogeneity in the region of origin of the Egyptian peasant families in Khalisah necessitates a digression into some aspects of their socio-economic backgrounds in order to appreciate more fully the dimension of the changes which have taken place· after migration. Up to the recent past, sociological studies carried out in rural Egypt have tended to adhere to the implicit assumption that, bar a few exceptions, the data compiled is also applicable to other village settings.[8] In fact, it is only during the past decade or so that social scientists interested in the study of Egyptian rural society have begun to realize that the near-famous remark, coined by Father Ayrout in the mid-1930s, to the effect that Egyptian villages are all alike,[9] is a fallacy that has for too long been permitted to influence social research in rural Egypt. Though, in contrast to a number of Arab countries in this geographical area, Egypt has historically never been divided into ethnic components, and though the majority of the inhabitants of the Nile Delta and Valley share a common history, language and culture, a pattern undoubtedly intensified through the collective experience of the 1952 Revolution and its social, political and economic consequences, there are nonetheless a number of differentiating variables attesting to the fact that the country is not a homogeneous entity. There are both inter-regional as well as intra-regional variations to be taken into account. One can, therefore, only speak of *the* Egyptian village in very general terms. Since this is not a place to delve extensively into these differentiations (and thus implicitly highlight the gaps in dire need of research),[10] the following discussion will concentrate on those deemed more-or-less relevant to the analysis of the post-migrational changes experienced by the Egyptian peasant women in the Khalisah settlement.

First, modernization and its cumulative influences have spread earlier in Lower (Northern) Egypt compared with the provinces south of Cairo. This is as much due to the Nile Delta's proximity to the administrative capital, as it is a result of this region's more intensive contact with innovations brought in by the many conquerors who have come and gone. One important indicator of this regional differentiation is the relatively higher literacy rate prevailing in Lower Egypt. However, the modernization process is also affected by such factors as village size and proximity to provincial urban centres. Larger villages are, for example, more likely to have a wide range of social services, and will tend to be socially stratified due to a higher percentage of non-peasant occupations.

Second, the introduction of cash crops (e.g. cotton, vegetables), and the shift from basin to perennial irrigation were introduced over a century ago in the provinces north of Cairo. This transformation began to take hold in Middle Egypt around the turn of the present century, while in Upper Egypt it was only completed by the early 1960s. Both the organization of agricultural production, as well as village social structure, were affected by these developments.

Third, though the influence and dominance of the consanguine institution appear to be gradually declining in Egyptian society as a whole, there is, nevertheless, a regional variation with regard to this trend in rural Egypt in particular. Thus, the decreasing dominance of the extended family has a longer history and has, furthermore, been more rapid in Lower Egypt, compared with the regions south of Cairo. The diminishing likelihood of land inheritance, the development of a settlement pattern, where population pressure and land scarcity combine to divide families spatially from their kin, the wider availability of social and economic services, as well as the villagers' more intense contact with the world beyond their social horizon, have all served to encourage the proliferation of nuclear families. Kin remain an important source of emotional support, however, and the wider family continues to determine a person's rank on the rural social ladder. Though all these facts are to some extent applicable within the social context of the southern provinces of Egypt, here the consanguine institution continues to be more dominant in the sense that individuals are generally held to be publicly responsible for the deeds and misdeeds of their kin. The blood feuds characteristic of community life in the provinces south of Cairo are a pertinent reflection of this reality, however much the increasing diffusion of governmental authority may be encouraging the decline of a tradition that for centuries has been an inherent part of 'urf (customary) law.

Fourth, peasant women in Middle and Upper Egypt generally do not work on the land, though they are expected to carry out specific tasks during the peak harvesting periods organized around the principle of sex segregation. It is believed that the type of agricultural system existing prior to the transformations described above, encouraged the practice of a relatively rigid female seclusion in the provinces south of Cairo.[11] By contrast, no such cultural constraint exists in Lower Egypt, except in the case of sedentarized bedouins who tend to stress their ethnic distinction from the indigenous inhabitants of the Nile Valley. Female seclusion is a cultural ideal in rural Lower Egypt, however, since it is an indication of higher social status in the village community.

This ideal reflects the notion that the duties and responsibilities traditionally attributed to the male gender role have been fulfilled. Not having to contribute her labour outside the home, a cherished dream of every impoverished peasant woman socialized since early girlhood to work whenever and (almost) wherever necessary, implies that her husband or male kin are able to secure the household's material welfare, leaving her to fulfil her natural role as wife and mother. Non-exposure of women outside the home also ensures the family's social standing in the village community, for the male head of the household thereby demonstrates his ability to protect the honour of his womenfolk. In all three regions, female circumcision is practised as a form of social control. Traditional Egyptian society defends this custom with the conviction that women by nature have strong sexual feelings which, being the weaker sex, they are incapable of controlling unaided.[12] Thus, men's honour which, as elsewhere in the Arab world, is defined primarily in terms of women's behaviour, is always at stake, unless the appropriate social control is enforced.

Regional variations, which are indicative of the differential rate of development held to exist between Lower Egypt and the rest of the country, are undoubtedly crucial factors which the Egyptian authorities must take into account when drawing up and implementing the diverse socio-economic policies needed to raise productivity and the standard of living in rural Egypt. With regard to the Khalisah settlement in Iraq, however, the influence of the variable of regional origin, purporting a differential rate of development in favour of Lower Egypt, was found to be negligible in so far as the settler families' productivity and pursuit of their economic self-interest was concerned. Though a settler household tended to concentrate its energies on cultivating those crops with which it was most familiar, it was generally also prepared to experiment with new varieties in response to market demand. In fact, the Khalisah settlement quickly established a reputation for the high quality and variety of its vegetable crops in particular.[13] Nearly all the settler families originated from the class of poor peasants in rural Egypt owning and/or renting less than one feddan, and were generally forced to supplement their income through wage labour. It was, therefore, not surprising to discover that over two-thirds of the settlers and nearly 90 per cent of the settler wives are illiterate.[14] Here again, however, no significant correlation between literacy level and productivity could be discerned. Rather, apart from the motivation to escape the vicious cycle of poverty back in the village of origin, it was above all the fact that migration involved a minimum of risk (given that the settler families not only received their homes and plots of land free of charge, but were also financially subsidized during the first few years), which was found to be the more influential variable.

During the initial post-resettlement period, the impact of
factionalism based on the consciousness of originating from a
particular province/region in Egypt tended to be counter-
balanced by the geographical remoteness of the village of
origin, as well as the settler families' social isolation in an
unfamiliar environment. Both these facts encouraged them to
identify with the settlement of which they had become a
physical part. Nonetheless, provincial consciousness has
tended to play a role within the context of community
relations in Khalisah, contributing to the periodical eruption
of conflicts between settler households. A particular example
pertains to the formation and development of leadership in the
settlement. Settlers from the same province/region back in
Egypt, who may entertain little if any social contact with one
another, would, during elections of the cooperative board,
form factions to ensure the nomination and election of a
baladiyat (one from the same area of origin), in order to stop
the *ghareeb* (stranger, i.e. one from a different province/region
of origin) from securing a position. Similarly, a settler would
tend to side with his *baladiyat* during fights over the allocation
of irrigation water, or priority in the use of agricultural
machinery supplied by the cooperative society, regardless of
who was at fault.

This sense of identification has, however, been gradually
receding in the face of the settler family's experience with the
novelty of economic success, measured in terms of the
standard of living prior to migration, which in turn has
increased its sense of security. The incipient individualism
that has become a predominant characteristic of the Egyptian
peasant family in Khalisah, and which has reduced the
importance of provincial consciousness, has been further
encouraged by the following.

To begin with, the settler household is to a large extent
economically self-reliant, in the sense that it can dispense with
the need for economic cooperation with others in Khalisah.
The latter's proximity to urban centres ensures that the settler
family can easily purchase all the requirements it does not
produce itself. This pattern of self-reliance has been indirectly
encouraged by the Iraqi authorities' initial prohibition of
employing non-family wage labour. The subsequent laxity in

enforcing this regulation did not, however, significantly alter this trend. Only a few settler households were found to be party to specific agreements involving the supply of labour in exchange for goods and, though to a much lesser extent, for cash. Furthermore, the Egyptian peasant family's security is not dependent on the goodwill of its co-patriots in Khalisah, since it is an external authority – i.e. Iraqi governmental institutions – which ensures its access to economic and social services. The patronage system which has historically been a part of the Egyptian village social structure, and which continues to remain vital to those situated on the bottom rungs of the rural social ladder,[15] is redundant within the resettlement experience in Iraq. In addition, the settler's social and psychological dependence on relationships with his fellow settlers has decreased more or less in proportion to his widening circle of social contacts outside Khalisah. However, these contacts are predominantly, if not exclusively, with the community of temporary Egyptian migrants living and working in the area in which the settlement is located. They serve to reinforce the links with the village of origin, thus psychologically shortening the geographical distance between Iraq and Egypt, while at the same time not only reducing the settler's reliance on the company of his co-settlers in Khalisah, but also the need to socialize with Iraqis in neighbouring villages or market centres. Either way, from the perspective of the individual household, social contacts are a matter of choice and not an imposed necessity, a fact which will be more fully discussed within the context of the women's social world.

This incipient individualism, which is so conspicuous among the Egyptian peasant families in Khalisah, is further exemplified by the type of kin relationships that have developed after migration. Around one-third of the settler families have agnates and/or cognates living in the settlement. But kin rarely cooperate economically with one another, even when they are on the best of terms and it would seem to be advantageous to both parties concerned. Economic self-reliance appears to have encouraged the relegation of these relationships to the social sphere. Since no household is barred from the possibility of maximizing its income, pursuing one's self-interest is not perceived to be at the expense of the welfare of others. In fact, it has become socially acceptable behaviour. Moreover, kin groups do not necessarily cluster in adjacent houses or the same alley-way, even though, at the time of resettlement, each family was free to choose in which part of the settlement it wished to live. Those who remain on cordial terms with their kin maintain social contacts of varying intensity with them. Participation in each other's life-cycle events remains imperative, since these provide occasions to display the ideal of kin solidarity. Confining the exchange of visits to the socially more important life-cycle events (e.g. the birth and circumcision of a boy) is an indication of a more distant relationship between kin. There are, however, also those who have seemingly not sought to resolve the strains marking their relationships prior to migration, or who have become estranged after resettlement. The ideal of kinship solidarity can, in fact, be all the more easily ignored given not only the settler household's relative economic independence of others, but also because of the lack of any future inheritance entanglements. In order to avoid the land fragmentation implicit in the application of the Muslim inheritance code, the Iraqi authorities have decreed that only one son (not necessarily the eldest) may inherit the settler parents' home and plot.[16] All other sons can secure their own house and land under similar conditions.[17] There are two kin groups, however, that appear to be functioning as extended families, in the sense of a common residence, commensality and the carrying-out of production tasks. In each case, dominant parents chose brides for their underage sons, who, though they may be chafing at the leash, appear nonetheless to accept the perpetuation of parental authority.

Of particular interest in this context is the fact that the variable of regional origin, according to which the consanguine institution is held to be more dominant in the provinces south of Cairo compared with Lower Egypt, was found to be largely insignificant in so far as the type/intensity of contacts cultivated between kin after migration to Iraq are concerned. Either way, this pattern reflects the reality that the settler family's social and economic circumstances after migration have reinforced the element of choice as a crucial variable. Relationships are to a large extent a function of the individual's preference and calculations, even though kinship bonds may be invested with more emotion and affective attachment than would normally be the case between non-kin.

Female Gender Role in the Khalisah Settlement

Extended families apart, the individual settler household functions as a separate production and consumption unit, whose members carry out specified tasks related to farming, and allocated according to age and gender. Cultivation is geared towards the production of surplus for the market and, secondarily, towards the satisfaction of some of the household's basic needs. Since, with the exception of the aforementioned extended families, there is no significant economic cooperation between households, be they kin or otherwise, it may be surmised that the majority rely on the labour contribution of immediate family members. Those who employ wage labour from outside the household, or who sell their produce to others at a reduced price in order to avoid the market place, remain very much a minority in the settlement. This pattern is particularly significant given the fact that the settler households are concentrating their efforts on the production of relatively labour-intensive vegetable crops and animal fodder. These crops are, however, lucrative to the extent that the settler household has calculated that it need only cultivate part of its plot in order to realize its income aims. The remaining land generally remains fallow, the actual extent of which depends on the amount of family labour available. This economic self-reliance has an important impact on the division of labour in the settler household, in particular with regard to the economic participation of settler wives.

The Egyptian peasant woman's traditional duties as wife and mother are similar to those in other Third World rural societies: housework, child-rearing, dairy production and, depending on economic status and regional origin, labouring in the fields and selling in the market place. Household responsibilities are perceived to be an inherent part of the female gender role, the assumption of which is the culmination of a pattern of socialization that begins early in the peasant

girl's life. As elsewhere in the Arab world, rural Egyptian
society offers no socially acceptable alternative to its women
other than the traditional role of wife and mother. It is her
success in these roles, rather than her economic participation
outside the home, that constitute a woman's status and
identity.

Turning to the Khalisah settlement, one may observe that
though a woman's traditional role inside the family continues
to function unchanged, the settler family's circumstances after
migration to Iraq have inevitably introduced certain modifications with regard to her role outside this sphere. The
regional variation regarding the peasant woman's economic
activities outside the household in rural Egypt is reflected in
table 1. Thus, around 89 per cent of all Lower Egyptian settler
wives were engaged in cultivation prior to resettlement; but 77
per cent of all Middle Egyptian settler wives, as well as all
those from Upper Egypt, claim they had not (though it should
be kept in mind that, given their socio-economic backgrounds,
these respondents must have worked during peak harvesting
periods, when even the most secluded women among the poor
peasant class have to contribute their labour). While little
post-migratory change is statistically discernible in the case of
those from the north of Cairo, i.e. 85 per cent work on the land
after resettlement, the change which has taken place with
regard to the other two regions is striking. Resettlement and
the settler household's primary reliance on the labour
contribution of family members have induced 81 per cent of
all Middle and 83 per cent of all Upper Egyptian settler wives
to work on the land.

This trend is more or less matched by an increase in
marketing activities after migration (see table 2). Around 41
per cent of all Lower Egyptian female respondents used to sell
in the market-place back in their area of origin in Egypt,
compared with 17 per cent from Middle and none from Upper
Egypt. After resettlement, 77 per cent of all Lower Egyptian,
as well as 87 per cent of all Middle Egyptian and 42 per cent of
all Upper Egyptian settler wives sell the household's produce
in the market-place situated on the outskirts of Baghdad.

The post-migratory changes depicting an increase in the
rate of female economic participation outside the household

Table 1 Settler wives' economic activities: cultivation (percentages)

Region	Egypt		Total	Khalisah		Total*
	Yes	No		Yes	No	
Lower Egypt	89	11	100	85	15	100
Middle Egypt	23	77	100	81	19	100
Upper Egypt	0	100	100	83	17	100

Note: * Total is 71 settler wives.

reflects the reality that cultural values *per se* are inadequate indicators of behaviour. As Youssef explains, 'behaviour is a function of the situation and is adjustive with regard to the eliciting situation.'[18] However, though Youssef also asserts that, compared to Latin America for example, there is in Middle Eastern countries nonetheless a 'close association between asserted ideals and actual feminine behaviour made possible through the explicit institutional arrangements which have cemented the cultural syndrome of female honour and female chastity',[19] there are arguably two particular variables which may contribute to a perceptible divergence between ideal and reality in Arab society, namely, poverty and economic expediency.

For example, those among the Middle Egyptian settler wives who have worked on the land and been active selling in the market-place prior to migration, even though their region of origin upholds the tradition of female seclusion, all indicated that the absence of adequate male support, i.e. poverty, had forced them to work outside the home in order to secure their family's livelihood. Though all the female respondents from Upper Egypt denied having worked outside the home prior to migration, one may surmise from the

Table 2 Settler wives' economic activities: marketing (percentages)

Region	Egypt		Total	Khalisah		Total*
	Yes	No		Yes	No	
Lower Egypt	41	59	100	77	23	100
Middle Egypt	17	83	100	87	13	100
Upper Egypt	0	100	100	42	58	100

Note: * Total is 71 settler wives.

personal accounts of the socio-economic conditions they left behind in their villages of origin that strict seclusion was very probably an ill-afforded luxury. (Though it should be noted that, in contrast to Lower Egypt, the labour of unmarried southern Egyptian peasant girls is rarely hired out.) Similarly, the striking post-resettlement changes with regard to the economic participation of Middle and Upper Egyptian settler wives illustrates the impact of the variable of economic expediency. A mixture of the life-long habit of frugality, which continues to encourage the avoidance of any expenses deemed unnecessary, and the novel taste of profit are the main factors discouraging the employment of non-family labour. Each and every able household member is expected to contribute his/ her labour, differentiated by age, to the common aim of income maximization, in order to realize the cherished plan of returning as successful migrants to Egypt. The geographical distance from the social judgement of the community back in the village of origin is undoubtedly an additionally important factor which has been encouraging women's economic activities outside the home.[20] Nonetheless, this pattern is considered to be temporary in a strange country where the family's situation differs, and where the husband has to rely on his wife's help. None of the settler wives who are economically active outside the home expect to be engaged in agricultural work or marketing activities once they have returned to Egypt, since it is anticipated that husbands will be able to fulfil their role as provider. Without exception, all these women look forward to a more-or-less secluded life, where they can concentrate on being *sitt al-beit* (housewife, implicit in which is the notion of being a lady of leisure), in accordance with the higher social status that successful migrants aspire to upon their return.

The settler's increased reliance on his wife's labour contribution and, by implication, women's increased involvement in some of the traditionally male spheres of activity, have, however, not been reciprocated by structural changes in the relationship between the sexes. Specifically, the boundaries demarcating gender-specific tasks within the peasant home have remained largely intact, and husbands avoid work customarily carried out by women (though some may keep an eye on pre-school children while their wives are selling produce in the market-place). Traditional notions of gender role attributes continue to be influential, and the male's position as household head remains undisputed. The ideal that equates the male gender role with that of provider, and that views women's work outside the household as an unavoidable and, hopefully, temporary necessity, is aptly reflected in the settler wife's disposition to describe such work as 'helping' rather than 'working alongside' her husband.

At first glance, this pattern would seem to imply that the settler wife in Khalisah has not benefited much from migration, since she is now burdened with the demands of land and market in addition to her household chores. But, in fact, such deduction is not necessarily applicable to each and every settler wife. Though over two-thirds of them work on the land and also take the produce for sale in the market-place, not every settler wife is necessarily burdened with the demands of the household. For it is pertinent whether or not there are one or more daughters, or other female kin, who can share in these responsibilities. This is where the cultural preference for male children is apparent, expressed through the parents' social mobility aspirations, which are primarily concentrated on sons. Boys are encouraged to excel in school, for educational success is perceived to be the key to social mobility out of the peasant stratum. No parent wishes to see a son follow in his father's footsteps, however attractive the Iraqi authorities' offer of free housing and plots of land.[21] It is only if a son cannot keep up with his peers in school that parents resign themselves to the fact that he is better off cultivating the land, rather than working as an unskilled wage labourer.

By contrast, settler parents do not envisage a role for their daughter other than the traditional one of wife and mother. Educating girls is not viewed as a priority. Rather, whether or not she may be receiving any schooling, which rarely goes beyond the primary level,[22] the unmarried girl's main responsibility involves helping her mother carry out the many household chores and sharing in the care of younger siblings. Though daughters may also help on the land during the peak seasons, they are at all other times confined to the home, and even discouraged from venturing into the alley-way once they have reached puberty. The girl's seclusion is justified by the higher social status she is, thereby, deemed to enjoy. It is also perceived to increase her chances of marrying a non-peasant, preferably a government employee because of the security of his regular monthly salary. Such a possibility is considered to be also enhanced by her brother's educational attainment. Thus, the fact that the Iraqi authorities have not decreed that a daughter has the same rights as a son with regard to house and land, is not regarded as being to her disadvantage. Apart from the fact that settler wives accept that property in the settlement is registered in their husbands' names, few settler parents wish to see their daughter marry a cultivator, anyway. In reality, this division of labour between a settler family's female members has the very practical immediate effect of enabling the wife to devote more time and effort to economic activities outside the home, thus playing an important role in improving the household's material welfare, without interrupting a son's education.

The settler family's continuing adherence to the cultural norm prescribing a more-or-less rigid differentiation between male and female gender roles characteristic of Egyptian peasant society, is implicit in the attitude of those families who only have male children. None of the sons, whether or not attending school, is expected to carry out household chores in order that the settler wife may devote more time to work outside the home. Though boys may tend the animals, help collect dried stalks for the bread oven, are expected to pitch in during peak harvesting periods, and may occasionally take care of younger brothers, none of these duties is allowed to interfere with their education. Where fathers are disinclined to help take care of children (because they consider it shameful to be seen doing women's work), settler wives will tend to work less regularly outside the home. In some cases, either the husband sells the produce in the market-place, or it is sold to other settler households at some loss of profit. Either way, women are the more flexible labourers, whose role varies according to the sex of their children and/or the attitude of their husbands.

The perpetuation of the traditional female gender role within the Egyptian peasant family in Khalisah, in spite of the

increased incidence of women's economic activities outside
the home, is, moreover, implicit in the continuing practice of
female circumcision. All the girls above the age of nine have
been circumcised. Those who reached this age after resettlement in Iraq were circumcised by a Lower Egyptian settler
wife, who apparently had carried out this ritual back in her
home village. Without exception, all mothers in Khalisah
believe that no respectable man would want to marry their
daughter if she remained uncircumcised, since her chastity
would always be questioned.[23] Fathers, brothers and husbands
would always have to worry about women's behaviour, given
the traditional belief that they are incapable of controlling
their sexuality unaided. According to one informant, there is a
reason why girls are usually circumcised at a later age than
boys, usually around the age of nine or ten, but before the
onset of menstruation, namely, in order not to forget the pain
associated with this part of their anatomy. However, it should
be added that, in contrast to the Sudan and a number of other
African countries, where infibulation is the rule, traditional
Egyptian society does not dispute a woman's right to sexual
gratification, so long as it is within the sanctity of marriage.
(In fact, by all accounts, this is an avidly discussed topic
among married women in village society.) Hence the stress on
the reduction, rather than the elimination of female sexual
desire, and the admonition that the midwife or gypsy who
performs this ritual take care not to cut away too much
tissue.[24] The continuing custom of female circumcision in
Khalisah must be viewed as an inherent part of the ideal of
female seclusion, and the settler parents' aspiration for higher
social status, dependent as this is on the chastity of women.

The incidence of female circumcision in Khalisah is of
further interest, since it has some implication for the
assimilation of these Egyptian migrant peasant families into
Iraqi society by way of the settler parents' choice of marriage
partners for their children. Settler wives are generally not in
favour of their daughters marrying Iraqi men, out of fear that
they may lose contact with them, an indirect reference to the
hope of eventually returning to Egypt. These women are,
however, much more adamant in their opposition to the idea
of their sons marrying Iraqi girls. While some concede that

Iraqi parents too may not wish to be parted from their daughters, and while reference will tend to be made to the differing customs between home and host countries, it is the fact that female circumcision is unknown in Iraq that appears to disturb these women the most. Though none made any explicit reference to the chastity or otherwise of Iraqi girls, the insinuation clearly was that uncircumcised brides could never really be trusted given female 'nature'.

The many post-migratory changes that have undoubtedly taken place have, thus, not perceptibly influenced traditional notions of male and female gender roles. In fact, migration has to some extent left the settler wife at a certain disadvantage. Apart from the expectation that she contribute her labour outside the home as much as her particular circumstances may permit, the settler wife who does not have any kin in or outside the settlement is, in effect, deprived of the traditional social support institutions that are an inherent part of village communal life back in Egypt. She is in this case more-or-less totally dependent on her husband's goodwill. In contrast to the peasant woman left behind in the Egyptian village by her migrant husband, the settler wife in Khalisah has, moreover, not experienced the need to head the household and take on many of the responsibilities traditionally held to be the man's affair.[25] Rather, she continues to remain subjugated to her husband's role as family-head.

Yet, there is another side of the coin to be considered. The absence of the traditional female hierarchy based on age and status can conceivably contribute to strengthening the wife's position in the nuclear family in Khalisah, in so far as she may be the only adult female in the household on whom the family-head can rely. Such reliance would be all the more pronounced given the settler household's aim of income maximization, as well as the social mobility aspirations for children, both of which have increased the woman's importance as an economic asset. A further post-resettlement change relates to the physical lay-out of house and yard, which, for example, renders it difficult for the settler wife to avoid all contact with male strangers. Indeed, in the husband's absence, it may well be the settler wife who has to deal with callers (for example, Iraqi livestock breeders who come to buy the clover crop direct from the settler family). It is conceivably also the husband's increased presence inside the home which encourages a greater degree of intimacy with regard to intra-family relationships. For, in general contrast to the Egyptian village, the home in Khalisah is no longer primarily the place where the family-head satisfies his physical needs. Rather, it has become the centre of the family's leisure-time activities, which mainly revolve around the television set. (Nearly every household owns one.) Resettlement can, thus, be said to have shortened the social distance separating the world of men and women. This may well be an explanatory factor for the relatively low incidence of polygamy in the settlement. Given the household's reliance on female labour, one would have assumed that a settler would perceive it to be advantageous to have an additional spouse, given his improved financial ability to fulfil any *mahr* (bride price) requirements. But, in fact, only four out of a total of sixty-nine settlers have a second wife.

To what extent these developments may have increased a woman's self-awareness may be indirectly discerned from attitudes to family planning. A third of the settler wives of child-bearing age were found to be using modern contraceptives (the pill), while another third claimed they were intending to do so as soon as they had weaned their youngest child (lactation continues to be regarded as an effective means of birth control). The rest either want more children, or tend to resort to abortions as a means of limiting their family size. The most frequently cited reason for the use of modern contraceptives was that 'no-one carries the other's burdens in a strange land,' implying that consecutive births are a burden which a settler wife has to shoulder on her own. What is significant here is that nearly all the women using modern contraceptives indicated it had been their own idea, subsequent to which they had convinced their husbands of the wisdom of this decision. However, it should be added that, apart from a relatively low child mortality rate in Khalisah, all contraceptive users have at least two sons, thus ensuring that the cultural preference for boys has been fulfilled. Equally significant, however, is the fact that, due to the country's under-population, the Iraqi government does not officially advocate birth control. In contrast to Egypt, where the authorities have for decades been waging a battle to control the population boom, the Egyptian peasant families in Khalisah have not found themselves subjected to such a campaign. In fact, couples using modern contraceptives have to go out of their way to secure their supply, mainly from Egyptian truck drivers commuting between Kuwait and Baghdad (up to the outbreak of the Gulf War), and between Jordan and Iraq.

The Social World of Settler Wives

The female social network operating in Khalisah is another pertinent example of how customs and traditions are subtly adapted to the realities of the way of life after migration. The social rules that have come into force in the settlement are a blend of what is traditionally perceived to be socially desirable, and what circumstances dictate to be economically expedient. Thus, the appropriateness of entering another woman's home is not only determined by the type of occasion or reason, but also by the degree of affective attachment inherent in kinship bonds, as well as the extent of familiarity characterizing a non-kin relationship.

The settler wife who has female relatives in the settlement with whom she is on good terms will generally be careful to visit them as a public expression of the ideal of kin solidarity. In contrast, where a certain formality or strain exists between female kin, then this will be expressed by the avoidance of visits on the occasion of life-cycle events deemed socially less significant (e.g. the birth or circumcision of a daughter, unless she is the first-born). Whatever the occasion necessitating a visit, female kin are expected to present one another with *nuqut* (money-gifts), based on the principle that they must be reciprocated at the very least in the equivalent amount. To give in excess of the amount previously received is an indication of a particularly close relationship between blood relatives. Generally, life-cycle events for girls involve smaller amounts than those celebrated for boys. However, though the actual sums exchanged have been increasing compared with the initial post-resettlement phase, reflecting the improving standard of living in Khalisah, in fact this exchange has a symbolic rather than a practical value. In contrast to the home village in Egypt, where the money-gift traditionally has the function of enabling the celebrating family to shoulder the burden of additional expenses, none of the settler families are in need of such aid. This is not so much due to financial ability. Rather, being in a strange land is perceived to be a valid reason not to incur any undue expenses during life-cycle celebrations, since the primary motivation of migration is the accumulation of savings.

The notion of social duty implicit in the act of making visits is also an inherent part of the social reciprocity expected between settler wives who are not related. However, the incidence of social interaction between non-kin women presupposes a familiarity established on the basis of relatively frequent face-to-face contacts. In fact, the settler family's conscious striving to implement the ideal of female seclusion as a correlate of their improved economic circumstances, means that women's physical mobility is very much restricted. Thus, very few settler wives leave the confines of their alley-way, except for a valid reason: be it to work in the fields, or to take the produce to market, or to visit the health centre, or to take some dress material to one of the four seamstresses in the settlement (all of them settler wives), or to fetch water from the main pump near the entrance into the settlement when the yard tap runs dry, or to visit kin living elsewhere in Khalisah. Therefore, it is female neighbours living along the same alley-way who tend to constitute a settler wife's main network of non-kin social contacts. Women living in the row of houses lying on the fringes of the settlement do not regard the path-way in front of their homes as their alley-way. Because fringe households border on to fields or waste-land, i.e. the pathways are more or less public thoroughfares, the settler wives concerned who are interested in socializing with other women will become part of the female social network in the adjacent alley-way.

Similar to the type of relations existing between close kin, the greater the degree of familiarity and affective attachment in a non-kin relationship, the more likely that the settler wives concerned will exchange visits on the occasion of all life-cycle

events, regardless of their social importance. Female non-kin
bound by such friendship ties will tend to refer to one another
as sisters, stressing the affection and esteem they hold for one
another by reciprocating money-gifts in excess of the amounts
generally exchanged between non-kin. Equally important, the
affective attachment between them implies the informality of
visiting each other's homes without prior notification.

In fact, however, very few settler wives claimed to have
such a close relationship with other non-kin women in the
settlement, indeed, not even in their own alley-way. Though,
when asked to name the non-kin women they socialized the
most often with, the majority of the respondents named their
female neighbours, they also stressed that these were *ma'reffa*
(acquaintances) rather than *sahbat* (Egyptian colloquial for
female friends). Similar to the case among kin, the more
formal a relationship, the less are visits reciprocated during
socially unimportant events. Though the custom of exchanging
money-gifts is adhered to, this is merely symbolic. The
amounts involved are relatively insignificant and are rarely
increased when reciprocated.

Visits between non-kin acquaintances to commemorate
ceremonial events are always announced beforehand and
always take place inside the home, where the guest is offered
some refreshment. By contrast, all informal contacts between
non-kin women are confined to the alley-way, a pattern which
appears to be influenced by a number of distinct considerations. To begin with, nearly all the settler families receive
visitors from among the community of temporary Egyptian
migrant workers employed in the area. Not all of these visitors
are necessarily a settler family's kith or kin (though they are
generally from the same area of origin back in Egypt), but
may have obtained the settler's name from mutual friends.
Either way, a settler wife will more than likely meet a male
stranger in her neighbour's home. Indeed, this was the most
frequently cited reason why female non-kin tend to socialize in
the alley-way and not enter each other's homes unannounced.
But none of these respondents appear to perceive it as
contradictory that they themselves may not be able to avoid
male strangers when their husbands receive and/or let a room
to temporary Egyptian migrants whom they may not have

known previously. By all accounts, it is the husband's presence inside the home that is perceived to mitigate the undesirability of this social exposure. For there is an unwritten rule in the settlement that non-kin male visitors and lodgers must not loiter in the home if the husband is absent. Thus, the family can maintain the fiction that its women are secluded, while at the same time securing an additional income through letting accommodation. By also enforcing the social rule that women avoid their neighbours' homes, other than on the occasion of ceremonial visits, the settler is in effect under-lining his wife's impeccable behaviour and, by implication, his own honour, in front of male visitors and lodgers. For it is the latter, in their role as a human channel of communication between Iraq and Egypt, who will report back to the home village on the exemplary behaviour of the settler wife. In the last resort, it is the village community of origin back in Egypt which continues to function as a social frame of reference, and whose approbation remains important.

Women sitting with other non-kin women in the alley-way, rather than in the privacy of the home, also appears to satisfy the male's prerogative to control his wife's behaviour outside the home. 'Men like to know what we are up to,' explained one informant with an unmistakable glint of amusement in her eyes. Even though squatting at either entrance into the alley-way is avoided, thus accentuating the women's distance from the public space beyond, its lay-out nevertheless leaves their behaviour open to scrutiny. At the same time, since the alley-way is considered to be the social space of its inhabitants, more specifically the social arena of women and children (men perceive it as shameful to be seen squatting there), the traditional value restricting female physical mobility is regarded as fulfilled. Thus strangers entering the settlement are discouraged from venturing into the alley-ways, unless they have specific business with one of its inhabitants. The guard-dogs, of which each alley-way seems to have at least one, enthusiastically help enforce this unwritten rule.

A third motive behind the confinement of informal gather-ings of non-kin women to the alley-way is related to the striving of the settler household to guard *sirr al-beit* (the secret of the house, i.e. its private affairs), from *'ain al-hasoud* (the evil eye) of its neighbours. The pretence that they are not well off, which settler households never tire of attempting to convey to anyone who will listen, must at all costs be upheld. This is not only due to suspicion of the outsider, but also reflects the Egyptian peasantry's traditional mistrust of governmental authorities. The fear that female neighbours may, out of envy, expose the family's private affairs, is a deterrent to allowing them unrestricted access into the home. The stress here is on female neighbours, for it is women who are believed to be particularly envious by nature, and it is they who are thought to have little compunction about evoking the evil eye. This is not only a male notion, but one that settler wives themselves unquestioningly accept as immutable wisdom.

This fear of the evil eye and of exposing the family's private affairs must be seen in relation to another reality regarding the way of life after resettlement. One particular means of conflict resolution that has evolved between neighbours is for one of the disputant parties to move elsewhere in the settlement. Though this practice has gradually been abandoned, partly because neighbours have over the years established a *modus vivendi* to minimize strife between them, the fact remains that moving house continues to remain a possibility. Any potential mistrust between neighbours is, thus, further accentuated by the lack of stability which can be said to be the predominant characteristic of a female social network in the alley-ways of Khalisah. This is, in turn, compounded by the settler family's plan to return to Egypt as soon as it has amassed enough savings. Such reality has encouraged a relatively calculating attitude. It has fostered a trend whereby relationships tend to be judged on the basis of short- rather than long-term rewards. Because membership in the alley-way's female social network lacks the durability normally attributed to relationships between those living in close proximity to one another back in the villages of Egypt, unrelated settler wives lack the certainty that the help and support they may extend to non-kin neighbours will be duly reciprocated in the long term. The fact that non-kin women reciprocate visits during ceremonial events is not a contradiction to such an observation. The socialization typical of Egyptian village society, which tends to instil a dislike of solitude and a need to share life's joys and sorrows, will also tend to encourage a settler wife to squat for a chat with her female neighbours in the dust of the unpaved alley-way.

Indeed, this network is perhaps all the more important given the geographical remoteness of the home village, and the fact that the settler wife is discouraged from venturing outside her alley-way unless there is a compelling reason to do so. In contrast to their menfolk, who have many contacts outside Khalisah, settler wives have developed few if any relationships outside the settlement, be it with wives of temporary Egyptian migrants (in fact, a minority), or with Iraqi peasant women from neighbouring villages. Upholding the tradition of reciprocating visits to mark life-cycle events is but one form of payment ensuring one's membership in the alley-way's female social network. The price demanded for the avoidance of social isolation is minimal, given the great similarity in the settler wives' way of life, which ensures an abundance of events during which visits can be reciprocated in the short-term.

Yet, the women concerned do not necessarily perceive themselves bound by the type of expectations implicit in relationships between neighbours in the contemporary Egyptian village. In spite of participation in each other's life-cycle ceremonies, these non-kin female relationships are not marked by closeness, though neither are they strictly impersonal. This is reflected by the general lack of communal activities and even cooperation between non-kin settler wives. For example, in contrast to the prevailing custom in the Egyptian village, baking does not provide an opportunity for socializing. The majority tend to bake on their own in the traditional oven, which every settler family has built in a corner of its yard. Sharing an oven with a neighbour would involve unrestricted entry into each other's homes, a possibility which female non-kin strive to keep to a minimum. Similarly, settler wives who view each other as acquaintances would not leave their pre-school children in each other's care. Each maintains she has enough burdens to shoulder *fi al-ghurba* (in a strange land), without taking on those of other women as well. Neither would they offer to breast-feed a neighbour's infant. The possibility of milk-kinship is not accorded much consideration.[26] Rather, most mothers feel that since a child can be given a bottle feed (powdered milk is freely available and well within the settler family's financial means), there is no reason to breast-feed *wilad al-ghareeba* (a female stranger's children). It is the use of the term stranger which perhaps best sums up the type of relationship prevailing between non-kin women, though they have been living over half a decade in close proximity.

Nor does membership in the female network of an alley-way demand or imply any undue display of loyalty. For example, those who live in the proximity of the settler wife functioning as a *daya* (traditional midwife), and who may even reciprocate visits with her during ceremonial celebrations, do not necessarily seek her services when giving birth. Instead, they may just as likely turn to the Iraqi midwife appointed by the authorities. Similarly, a settler wife will take her custom to a seamstress who suits her taste and financial means best, even if it means snubbing the one living next door.

Yet, in contrast to their husbands, who tend to rank themselves in relation to other men, members of a female social network in the alley-way in Khalisah do not consciously judge their relationships with other women in these terms. Specifically, they do not, in front of outsiders, attempt to inflate their own prestige at the expense of other non-kin women. This confirms the findings of a number of studies which suggest that female relationships in Arab society have traditionally tended to be less hierarchically organized than those involving males.[27] This lack of any overt social ranking may well be the perpetuation of conscious/unconscious attitudes in which these Egyptian peasant women have been socialized back in their villages of origin. This pattern would also, however, appear to be reinforced by the reality that the way of life after migration cancels the necessity of patron–client relationships. Essentially, there is no other pressure than the fear of social isolation to impel a settler wife to seek the company of others in the alley-way. This lack of pressure is implicit in the fact that there are a number of settler wives who are not part of this female social network: some because they consider the habit of squatting in the alley-way to be shameful and beneath their self-perceived status, others because they are not particularly interested in socializing with other women.

The development of social contacts among settler wives beyond the confines of the alley-way is not only hampered by the ideal of female seclusion, but also by the settlement's infrastructure. Thus, running water in every household has replaced the canal, well or public tap, where Egyptian peasant women traditionally meet to fetch water and wash household utensils. The closing down of the social centre (partly due to lack of interest in the sewing and handicraft classes which used to be offered), has in effect been another impediment in the way of wider social contacts between settler wives. Moreover, in contrast to the villages of Egypt, market day does not provide an occasion to socialize, either with Iraqi women, or with other settler wives living elsewhere in Khalisah, other than the opportunity to chat on the way to and from the market-place. Women are expected to return immediately they have sold their wares. Purchasing the household's needs is the husband's responsibility. Far from regarding this as male control over the family's finances, a wife feels cherished that her husband does not want to expose her to the necessity of haggling with vendors and shop-keepers. That she herself may be involved in just such haggling when selling the produce in the market-place is a carefully ignored reality.

The virtually irresistible attraction of the television has proved to be another effective barrier to wider social contacts between settler wives. Not only has television viewing become the predominant leisure-time activity regardless of age and gender, but because it is considered 'aib (shameful) for settler wives to leave their homes after dark, and since informal social contacts with other women are confined to the alley-way, television viewing has developed into a family rather than a female group activity. By contrast, men have a choice between watching television in the privacy of the home, or in the company of other men in one of the settlement's two coffee-shops (owned and run by temporary Egyptian migrants).

In addition, there is no cemetery in the vicinity of Khalisah, where settler wives could congregate on the occasion of anniversaries and religious festivals to honour the memory of the dead. Those who have died since resettlement have been buried near a provincial town some distance from Khalisah. Furthermore, there is no nearby saint's tomb or religious shrine around which settler wives could congregate, as is the tradition in rural Egypt. There appears to be little sense of identification with the Shi'a shrines in Najaf or Kerbalah, situated further south from Khalisah.[28]

Return to Egypt: Myth or Reality?

Reflected in the type of community that has been evolving in the Khalisah settlement is the settler family's attitude of viewing its stay in Iraq as temporary. Such an attitude is more-or-less typical of the first migrant generation and its continuing psychological attachment to the country of origin, regardless of the motives behind the decision to migrate. In the case of these Egyptian peasant families in Iraq, their possible assimilation into the host country – a crucial factor in postponing their departure and, eventually, abandoning the idea of return altogether – has undoubtedly been hampered by the relative ease with which they have been able to psychologically shorten the geographical distance between them and their villages of origin back in Egypt, be it through almost constant contact with kith and kin back home, or through daily exposure to Egyptian films and serials. Assimilation by way of more intensive contact with the indigenous population has also been at least partially hampered by the existence of the Egyptian migrant community in Iraq. A sizeable portion of this community is employed or self-employed in the services sector. This essentially means that the Egyptian settler in Khalisah can buy the household's necessities from an Egyptian grocer, have his hair cut by an Egyptian barber, his *galabiah* (traditional male garment) sewn by an Egyptian tailor, and enjoy a *shisha* (water pipe) or a game of *tawla* (backgammon) in one of the numerous Egyptian owned coffee-shops and food-stalls which have sprung up along the nearby highway leading into the capital.

Yet, whether or not these Egyptian peasant families in

Khalisah will remain or return will also largely depend on a number of factors. To begin with, there is the attitude of the host country towards migrant labour to be considered, specifically whether the Iraqi government will continue to facilitate the influx of temporary Egyptian migrants. There is also, however, the fact that the Egyptian village, which the settler family left behind in 1976, has undergone its own transformations by the 1980s, not least of which is an inflationary trend affecting each and every commodity which a returning migrant is likely to invest in. The settler family has no doubt been discovering that the savings it has accumulated since its migration to Iraq may be insufficient for fulfilling its social and economic ambitions back in the village of origin, and thus may continue to postpone its return until the desired optimum is achieved. But the prolongation of the settler family's stay in Iraq has implications for the second generation. With regard to the settler sons in particular, the greater educational and employment opportunities available to them may well encourage them to plan their future in Iraq.

Thus, the Egyptian settler parents in Khalisah will find themselves torn between, on the one hand, the desire to return as successful migrants and reap the rewards of higher status and prestige back in the home village in Egypt, as well as to secure Egyptian non-peasant husbands for their daughters and, on the other hand, to remain in Iraq where the future of one or more sons looks more promising.

Whatever the Egyptian peasant families may ultimately decide, a question mark appears to hang over the long-term viability of Khalisah. The planners of this resettlement project, who envisioned it in terms of permanency, have not taken the human element sufficiently into consideration, specifically what such a settlement can provide in terms of status, and the social aspirations of its inhabitants. These aspirations point to the significance of the operating stratification network in the Arab world. A value system which traditionally relegates the peasantry to the lower end of the social ladder, and which attributes higher rewards in terms of prestige to non-peasant occupations, has led the settler families in Khalisah to encourage the social mobility of their children out of the peasant stratum. Land ownership and the social position of small landholders have not functioned as sufficient incentives. Implicit in this sense of hierarchy is the belief that higher income without status is insufficient.

Concluding Remarks

The extent to which the Egyptian peasant families in the Khalisah settlement in Iraq have taken advantage of the range of economic opportunities that have come their way after migration undermines the notion of cultural determinism, positing the belief that it is generally the rural social structure *per se* that encourages behaviour resistant to innovation and impedes change. In fact, it is the element of risk reduction that is an important variable influencing the response to modernization. The negligible influence of the variable of regional origin, as well as that of literacy level, on the settler household's economic performance and productivity further substantiates this finding. Though post-resettlement changes in the Egyptian peasant family's social attitudes continue to be dictated by traditional norms and values, these have been subjected to some modification, regardless of the fact that the fiction of abiding by cherished customs continues to be upheld. In fact, these modifications are a particularly relevant illustration of how tradition and economic interests reflexively adjust to one another. This elective affinity between elements of peasant culture and elements of the economic base is a complex relationship, but it underlines the point that continuity, albeit modified, is not necessarily an impediment to change. In fact, it may well ease the almost inevitable strains during the process of transition until new behavioural patterns establish their legitimacy.

Notes and References

1 See A. M. Gomaa, *The Foundation of the League of Arab States* (London, Longman, 1977).
2 By Egyptian standards, this places the settler families in the category of small landowners. See S. Radwan, *Agrarian Reform and Rural Poverty in*

Egypt: 1952–1975 (Geneva, International Labour Organization, 1977). One Iraqi dunum is 1,500 m²; one feddan is 4,200 m², or 2.8 Iraqi dunum, or 1.038 acres.

3 The stress here is on 'official', for in Iraq as well as a number of other Middle Eastern countries, publicly proclaimed agrarian policies are often not strictly adhered to. Thus, there tends to be a mixture of state farms, agri-businesses, agrarian reform cooperatives and private farms. See R. Springborg, 'New Patterns of Agrarian Reform in the Middle East and North Africa', *Middle East Journal*, 31 (1977), pp. 127–42. In recognition of the need to increase productivity in the rural sector, and for a number of political reasons, the Iraqi government has been gradually encouraging private farming initiatives since 1979, a trend officially sanctioned by law 35/1983. See R. Springborg, 'Infitah, Agrarian Transformation and Elite Consolidation in Contemporary Iraq', *Middle East Journal*, 40 (1986), pp. 33–52.

4 As claimed in 1979 during interviews with Egyptian and Iraqi officials involved in the planning and implementation of this resettlement scheme.

5 One explicit indication of this policy reversal is the arrival in 1981 of some two hundred Moroccan peasant families in Iraq. They were housed in a newly established settlement in the Governorate of Wasit (some 200 miles south-east of Baghdad), which had originally been destined for Egyptian migrant peasant families.

6 No accurate data is available on the volume of Egyptian migrant labour in Iraq during this period. Estimates vary widely between 50,000 and 1.5 million for 1978. See N. Choucri, *Migration in the Middle East: Transformations, Policies and Processes* (Cambridge, Mass., Massachussetts Institute of Technology, 1983), vol. I, table C–1, and the Egyptian daily *Al-Ahram* of 18 September 1978. Other authors estimate that the number of Egyptian migrants in Iraq cannot have exceeded 223,000 by 1980. See J. Birks *et al.*, 'The Demand for Egyptian Labour Abroad', in A. Richards and P. Martin (eds), *Migration, Mechanization and Agricultural Labour Markets in Egypt* (Cairo, The American University in Cairo Press, 1983). By the early 1980s, government sources in Iraq were unofficially estimating the number of Egyptian migrant workers to be over one million. A verification of these estimates is difficult, since Iraqi statistics do not classify Arab migrants by country of origin.

7 This belief has since been disputed, for, in fact, the volume of migration had by the 1980s led to a shortage of skills in the Egyptian labour market, affecting even the rural sector traditionally believed to have a high rate of hidden unemployment. See M. Abaza, 'The Changing Image of Women in Rural Egypt', *Cairo Papers in Social Science* (Cairo, The American University in Cairo Press, 1987).

8 See G. Sabagh, 'Sociology', in L. Binder (ed.), *The Study of the Middle East* (New York, Wiley, 1976).

9 H. H. Ayrout, *The Egyptian Peasant* (Boston, Beacon Press, 1963).

10 See N. S Hopkins and S. Mehanna, 'Egyptian Village Studies' (Cairo,

Agricultural Development Systems Project, US AID, Unpublished
Report, 1981).

11 See E. L. Sullivan and K. Korayem, 'Women and Work in the Arab
World', *Cairo Papers in Social Science* (Cairo, The American University in
Cairo Press, 1981).

12 See N. El-Saadawi, *The Hidden Face of Eve: Women in the Arab World*
(London, Zed Press, 1980).

13 Traditionally, Iraqi rural society attributed low social prestige to
vegetable cultivation, mainly because of the degree of manual labour
involved. (See R. A. Fernea, *Sheikh and Effendi: The Changing Patterns of
Authority among the El Shabana in Southern Iraq* (Cambridge, Mass.,
Harvard University Press, 1970).) It appears that, specifically in the
central and southern parts of Iraq, where tribal norms were particularly
influential, the traditional mode of agricultural production tended to be
hierarchical: the date-palm owner followed by the cereal cultivator, both
of whom enjoyed a higher social status than the vegetable producer.
Though the Iraqi peasantry's increased contact with the market
economy, and the spiralling urban demand for fresh produce, have been
gradually eroding this negative attitude towards cash crops requiring a
relatively high labour input, this factor nonetheless continued to wield
some influence within Iraqi rural society as late as the mid-1970s, i.e. the
period when these Egyptian peasant families were resettled in Khalisah.
Hence, it is no coincidence that the bilateral accord between Iraq and
Egypt explicitly specified that the settler household would be required to
concentrate its efforts predominantly on vegetable cultivation.

14 Though, as mentioned earlier, there is a conspicuous regional variation.
Of a total of 73 settler wives, 79 per cent of all those from Lower Egypt
are illiterate, against 90 per cent of all those from Middle and Upper
Egypt. Of a total of 68 settlers, 41 per cent of all those from Lower Egypt
are illiterate, against 73 per cent of all those from Middle, and 91 per
cent of all those from Upper Egypt.

15 R. Adams aptly illustrates how patron–client relationships have
succumbed to the changing socio-economic circumstances in rural
Egypt. Whereas in former times poor peasants would tend to have one
rich patron at any one time, such ' "patron monogamy" has given way
to "patron polygamy". The much diminished resources of rural
patrons . . . mean that poor Egyptian peasant clients must now circulate
between several different patrons in order to survive.' (R. Adams,
Development and Social Change in Rural Egypt (Syracuse, Syracuse University
Press, 1986), p. 145.)

16 While this code is stipulated in the Quran, in practice there is a
perceptible difference between the two main sects in Islam. Among
Sunni Muslims, wife and daughters cannot claim all the inheritance if
there is no male heir. Rather, the husband/father's male kin receive a
share according to strictly observed regulations. Among Shi'a Muslims,
a man's inheritance remains within the nuclear family even if he has no
sons. In both sects, however, where there are sons and daughters, the
latter receive half their brothers' share.

Briefly, the Shi'a branch of Islam refers to Muslims who believe that the succession belongs to the descendants of Ali, the fourth Caliph and son-in-law of the Prophet Muhamad. Sunni Moslems believe that the succession is not restricted exclusively to the Prophet's direct descendants.

17 It remains unclear how additional housing and land was to be allocated to other sons wishing to become cultivators: within Khalisah by expanding the settlement, or elsewhere? The problem was inadvertently solved by the departure of some families. Specifically, 17 settler families were asked to leave during the first year because the Iraqi authorities deemed that they did not have sufficient agricultural experience. The Egyptian officials involved in this resettlement project claim that they included these non-cultivators (carpenter, butcher, blacksmith, grocer, etc.) in order to avoid an occupational imbalance in the new settlement. Their Iraqi counterparts are equally insistent that this was not part of the agreement, since it was planned that such services would be provided by neighbouring Iraqi villages in order to foster social contacts between them and the newcomers. Over the years, other families left of their own accord, either to take up wage employment elsewhere in Iraq, or to return to Egypt with their savings. A number of settler sons were given their own homes and land upon marriage. There are also some Egyptian peasant families who joined the settlement at a later date and under similar conditions, except that they had to pay their own travel expenses to Iraq.

18 N. Youssef, 'Cultural Ideals, Feminist Behaviour and Family Control', *Comparative Studies in Sociology and History*, 15 (1975), pp. 326–47.

19 *Ibid.*

20 Another example of how the ideal (female seclusion) accommodates reality (economic expediency), leading to a modification of traditional behavioural norms, pertains to the settler wives' marketing activities. Even the most conservative settler from Upper Egypt has begun to encourage his wife to sell the household's produce in the market-place. The reason is that if a woman is caught selling above the official price (broadcast regularly in the media), at the most the authorities would confiscate her scales which, however, she can redeem upon payment of a small fine. By contrast, men who are repeatedly caught contravening this law are liable to receive a short prison term.

21 Past experiences in a number of Arab countries also indicate that successful farmers tend to invest their profits in non-agricultural enterprises and, more significantly, their sons will almost without exception not be agriculturalists. See G. Foster, 'Community Building', in L. El-Hamamsy and J. Garrison (eds), *Human Settlements on New Lands: Their Design and Development* (Cairo, The American University in Cairo Press, 1979).

22 Of 69 settler families, 47 per cent are sending all their unmarried daughters to school, 16 per cent are educating all daughters except the eldest (whose fate it is to help her mother in the household), while in 37 per cent of the families no girls are attending school. Here again a regional variation is conspicuous. Thus, of the 14 families educating all

their daughters, 50 per cent are from Lower Egypt, 29 per cent from
Middle Egypt and 21 per cent from Upper Egypt. Of the 5 families who
are not educating the eldest daughter, only one is from Lower Egypt.
The 11 families in which none of the daughters are receiving any
education are without exception from the provinces south of Cairo.

23 Even the two settler families who claim to originate from the non-
peasant class in Egypt and to have owned over 5 feddan, believe in
female circumcision. All their daughters are continuing their education
beyond the secondary level in order to become teachers, a career deemed
the most suitable for women. Though the wives in these families have
been educated and are quite aware that this ritual is dying out among
the educated classes in urban Egypt, they hesitate to follow suit out of
fear that no respectable man would wish to marry their daughters.

24 See S. Morsy, 'Sex Roles, Power and Illness in an Egyptian Village',
American Anthropologist, 5 (1978), pp. 137–50.

25 However, M. Abaza points out that claims that the wife left by her
migrant husband in the Egyptian village has gradually been taking over
some of his responsibilities, thus adding to her status, fail to take into
consideration that the process of migration itself devalues the sphere of
activities left by men to women. For men now move into non-peasant,
monetized occupations (Abaza, 'Changing Image of Women in Rural
Egypt').

26 The different schools of Islamic thought hold different views on this
subject, but essentially milk-kinship implies that a woman who has
breast-fed a child other than her own has established a kinship bond
with this child. The latter and her own children are considered siblings
and are not permitted to marry.

27 See, for example, V. Maher, *Women and Property in Morocco: Their Changing
Relations to the Process of Social Stratification in the Middle Atlas* (Cambridge,
Cambridge University Press, 1974), and A. Rugh, *Family in Contemporary
Egypt* (Cairo, The American University in Cairo Press, 1985).

28 Few if any of the Egyptian peasant families in Khalisah were aware of
the distinction between the two main Islamic sects until their migration
to Iraq. Shi'a Muslims in Egypt are a very small minority. Egyptian
Muslims generally refer to themselves simply as Muslims, though the
more knowledgeable may add the particular legal school they adhere to:
Maliki (traditionally in Upper Egypt), Shafi' (traditionally in Lower
Egypt), or Hanafi (supported by the former Turkish rulers, whose
adherents are located mainly in northern Egypt).

Editors and Contributors

Camillia Fawzi El-Solh is of Egyptian/Irish parentage. She received her master's degree in economics/sociology from the University of Cologne, West Germany, and her PhD in sociology from Bedford College, University of London. A freelance sociologist, she has recently co-edited, together with Soraya Altorki, a volume on the sociology of knowledge – *Arab Women in the Field: Studying your own Society* (Syracuse University Press, 1988) – and is presently engaged in post-doctoral research on Arab labour migration in Britain.

Babacar Fall has been a Lecturer in History at Ecole Normale Superieure, University of Dakar, since October 1983. He holds university degrees (Masters and PhD) from Dakar.

Alula Pankhurst has a BA from Christ Church, Oxford and is currently working on his Doctoral Thesis at the University of Manchester on resettlement programmes in Ethiopia, where he has recently spent time in field work.

Shubi L. Ishemo was born in Tanzania. He studied History at Cambridge. His history doctorate, from the University of Manchester, was on the Economy and Society of the Lower Zambezi Basin in Mozambique. He is a member of the Editorial Board of the *Review of African Political Economy* and has taught African studies at several institutions. He now works with the Sheffield City Education Authority developing a Third World Curriculum for the city's new tertiary colleges.

C.M.F. Lwoga was born in Tanzania where he attained his

BA and MA at the University of Dar es Salaam before gaining
his PhD at the University of Cambridge on Labour Migration
and Rural Development in a former labour reserve in
Tanzania. He is currently a Senior Lecturer at the University
of Dar es Salaam and has published two books, *Twenden:
Kwenye Ujamaa* (Eastern Africa Publications Ltd., Dar es
Salaam), 1979 and *Uhuru Wa Banderg* (Utamaduni Publishers,
Dar es Salaam, 1985).

Marjorie Mbilinyi is an American-born Tanzanian citizen,
Professor of Education in the Institute of Development
Studies, University of Dar es Salaam and a founder member
of the Women's Research and Documentation Project. She
has written many books and articles on women's resistance
and struggles over colonial and neo-colonial gender relations,
including *Women in Tanzania* (co-authored with Ophelia
Mascarenhas, Uppsala, Scandinavian Institute of African
Studies, 1983) and *Big Slavery: The Crisis of Women's Employment
and Incomes in Tanzania* (Dar es Salaam University Press, in
press, 1989).

Mohamed Mbodj is Associate Professor (Lecturer 1978–
81), Department of History, and Director, Laboratory of
Historical Demography, University of Dakar. He obtained a
Masters degree from the University of Dakar and a PhD from
the University of Paris.

James Clyde Mitchell successively held the chair of African
Studies and Sociology at the University College of Rhodesia
and Nyasaland before becoming Professor of Urban Sociology
at the University of Manchester in 1966. From 1973–1985 he
was official Fellow of Nuffield College. He conducted fieldwork
in Southern Africa for over two decades, and has published
extensively in the fields of anthropology and sociology, as well
as currently being on the editorial board of various journals
including *Urban Anthropology, Connections* and *Social Network*.

Richard Moorsom has written extensively on Namibia since
completing an MA dissertation at Sussex University in 1973
on the country's economic history. Articles on the contract
labour system were followed by sector studies on fisheries and
agriculture in the CIIR series *A Future for Namibia*. He is
currently a research fellow at the Chr.Michelsen Institute,
Bergen, Norway.

Colin Murray teaches sociology of development at the Institute of Public Administration and Management, University of Liverpool. He has published a study of migrant labour from Lesotho, *Families Divided (1981)* and numerous articles on regional social history and the political economy of forced relocation in South Africa. A book on the Thaba'Nchu district in the Orange Free State will be published shortly.

Abebe Zegeye has studied in the US and the UK, completing his DPhil for Oxford University in 1986. He currently directs the Oxford Centre for African Studies, an independent research and teaching centre.

Tiyambe Zeleza (BA Malawi, MA London; PhD Dalhousie) is a Senior Lecturer in History at Kenyatta University. He has taught at the Universities of Malawi, and the West Indies, and was a Research Associate at the University of Nairobi. His publications include articles in scholarly journals and books. He is also the author of several books, including *Imperialism and Labour: The International Relations of the Kenyan Labour Movement* (1978); *Labour, Unionization and Women's Participation in Kenya* (1988). He is also a creative writer and has published *Night of Darkness and Other Stories* (1976); and *Smouldering Charcoal* (forthcoming).